CH01508286

SWINDON

Fifty Years Ago (More or Less).

Reminiscences, Notes, and Relics of ye —

Old Wiltshire Towne,

BY

Master William Morris,

Author of " FRANCE AND THE FRENCH" "IRELAND AND THE IRISH " IN SEARCH
AFTER OZONE AND OBLIVION " OUT AND HOME AGAIN BY WAY OF
CANADA AND THE UNITED STATES" WHAT A SUMMER'S
TRIP TOLD ME OF THE PEOPLE AND THE COUNTRY
OF THE GREAT WEST, &c. &c.

Reprinted from ye Swindon Advertiser.

Swindon :
PRINTED & PUBLISHED BY THE AUTHOR, AT THE "ADVERTISER" OFFICE,
10, VICTORIA STREET.

18 12 19 3

INTRODUCTION.

I can add but little by way of preface to what may be found stated at the end of the first paper of the circumstance under which it was written. I had then no thought of writing other papers, although it had occurred to me that the old Date and Initial Stones on some other house fronts might be made the subject of a paper in connection with Swindon at some archæological meeting. But before I could make up my mind to deal with these old stones, the Ghosts of the neighbourhood seemed to meet me with a request that I would have a word or two about them. And, what was more, they seemed to plead that unless they were very shortly taken in hand by someone, they would pass out of memory altogether, for while, up to the time when cheap newspapers and books for the people came in, they were duly kept alive and handed down from generation to generation in the oral traditions of a town or village, they were in danger of losing their record and of being altogether snuffed out by that more active life which must follow in the trail of a Free Press, and a reading and writing education, if nothing more, of even the very poorest in the land. And then they also seemed to tell me that the oral traditionary period was rapidly passing away, and that unless some of the facts of the common life of our fathers and grandfathers, as well as the tales and traditions in which they indulged, were at once set down in writing, they would pass away from men's memory, and be for ever lost. Entering into a kind of mutual compact with my interviewers, I thought it possible I might find material for three or four other papers, and I thus very innocently entered upon a work—I admit it has been a most pleasant and agreeable one—which has resulted in the production of the present volume. Each new subject has suggested others, until the one paper has found some forty or fifty companions.

I need hardly add I have studiously avoided attempting anything like a formal history of the town. There is absolutely no material for such a purpose, and I could hardly have ventured to use it had it been forthcoming, for such an undertaking would have required more thoughtful research than I could have given it, whereas the papers as they now appear have afforded me week by week, as I wrote them for the columns of the *Advertiser*, a few hours of real enjoyment, which has been again and again heightened by the assurance that what I wrote was generally acceptable to a large body of readers, many of whom have been good enough to express a wish to see my weekly scraps and fancies placed between the two covers of a book.

For the purpose of helping on or illustrating any particular subject, I have not hesitated to avail myself of the labours of those who have dealt with cognate matters, always, however, admitting the source of the extract. The accounts of the Rioting in Wilts and adjoining counties by the agricultural labourers in 1830, and the trials of the prisoners, had previously appeared in newspapers and other publications, and more particularly in a series of letters in the *Poole and Bournemouth Herald*. Instead of attempting to go over the ground taken by the writers of the letters, and being anxious to bring some of the details of these terrible times before my readers in a permanent form, I have ventured to adopt the matter in one or two of the papers almost without alteration. The sketch of the Swindon Troop of Yeomanry Cavalry was compiled from the Orderly Book of the Troop, and therefore partakes more of the character of "veritable history" than some of the other papers can pretend to, and which are based principally on what I have myself seen and heard, or have gathered in conversation with those who have known the town and neighbourhood longer than I have.

My object throughout has been to preserve and amuse, rather than to lecture and instruct; and in this I trust it may be found I have not altogether failed.

What the changes of the next half, or even the next quarter, of a century may be the most ingenious must find it difficult to satisfy his own mind about, whilst to realise the changes of the past half century must be equally difficult, except to those who have passed the greater part at least of the period in active public life, and in direct contact with the people. In the all-important matter of the education of the people, in the enjoyment of political rights, in popular amusements, and social habits, not only of the poor, but of the well-to-do classes, the change has been as great as that from the darkness of mid-night to the brilliancy of mid-day. Were it possible for us to meet in promiscuous assembly our grandfathers and grandmothers, with their uncles and aunts, all the editions of "Who's Who" and "What's What" ever published would not suffice to explain. There may never again be a period in the whole range of English history between now and the time when the New Zealander takes his view of the ruined St. Paul's, in which, in so few years, the changes will be so marked as those which belong to the last fifty years, and that being so, anything which will serve to make these changes understandable cannot, I venture to think and hope, be otherwise than acceptable.

It will be noticed that I have occasionally travelled slightly outside the Swindon parish boundary. But I have done this principally for the purpose of illustration. I might have looked to some of the neighbouring parishes for altogether new, as well as supplementary, material, and I have felt some difficulty in restraining myself from doing this. Within the last twenty-five or thirty years it has occasionally fallen to my lot to write sketches of some of the neighbouring parishes—principally on the occasion of the restoration of the parish church—for publication in my paper, and I have been urged by many kind friends to add these sketches to the present volume. This, however, I could not well do and keep it within reasonable compass. Should, however, the public favour accorded to this volume justify it, I shall be pleased to prepare a second or supplementary volume to the one for which I would now ask from those into whose hands it may fall a kindly consideration and a generous allowance for the circumstances under which it has been produced.

WILLIAM MORRIS.

"ADVERTISER" OFFICE,
10, VICTORIA STREET, SWINDON,
August, 1885.

CONTENTS.

A MASONIC RELIC, 1704.

PAGE.

The "Bull"—The Smithies—Street Nomenclature—The Architecture of the Squatters—Struggling through the Lime-wash—On the Scent—The Relic Disclosed—Land at Last—Still a Mystery—What can it Mean?—More Mystery—An old Gem with a History   1-13

GHOSTS AND GHOST LAYING.

Gallows Gate—Suspense—The Explanation—The Man whose Ghost Walked—The Ghost Obdurate—The Ghosts in the Old Passage —Serious Complications—The Ghost that defied the Clergy—A Practical Ghost—Imploring for Mercy   14-24

SOME OLD HOUSES.

Before the Printing Press—The Old Builders—The Old Manor House—The Old Trade Mark—The Old Dutch Hostelries— Bellarmines—The Drink of the Dutchman—Public-House Signs —Smuggled Goods—Royal Licences—The Trade of the Smuggler —Some other Stones — An Old Inhabitant's Tomb — Oral Tradition   25-39

FLEMISH CLOTH WORKERS.

Potters' Marks—The Productions of the Loom—Wool and Wool-Stapling—Flemish Cloth Workers—The Cloth Workers' Mark or Token—The River Avon and its Treasures—Sailors Propitiating the Gods—All the World Clothed from English Wool—Wool : England's Principal Export—The Merchants of the Staple— The Founders of Noble Families   40-51

PAGE.

BUSH HOUSES.

Ale-House or Tavern Signs—" Aspiring to the conceite of a Sign"—
The Red Lattice—The Green Lattice—The Chequers—The Cat
and Fiddle—The Bull and Gate—The Bush Inn—The Old
Fiddler—The Delight of the Rustics—Thick'en or Thuck'en . 52-63

TURNPIKE GATES.

Turnpike Trusts—How Turnpike Tolls were Let—Gatemen and
Gatewomen—Rival Gatemen—"I'll have a Pound"—Shrewd,
Hard-headed Men of Business—The Risk and Responsibilities
of Gatemen 64-71

NEWSPAPERS.

How Newspapers were sent into the Country—Mrs. Browning and
her Clock Case Reckoning—The London Newspaper Agent—
The County Newspaper—Enormous Properties—" Publicola "
and the " Dispatch"—The Taxes on Newspapers—The Starting
of the " Advertiser" 72-80

THE OLD WORKHOUSE.

The Pernicious Spirit called Gin—Pitfalls of Debauchery—Sir Robert
Walpole in Disgrace—The Old Cellar at the Workhouse—The
Sheep-stealers' Hearth and Home—Amy Ponting bidding the
Officers do their worst—The Old House in Cricklade Street—
Underground Mystery—Akerman's Tales—The Keeper and the
Poacher—The Blister on the Chest—Wiltshire Moonrakers—
Desperate Characters — Smugglers and the Excise — Royal
Proclamations 81-96

A WILTSHIRE ROYAL RESIDENCE.

Aldbourne Chase—John of Gaunt—Waylen's History of Marlborough
—King John at Marlborough—Old Miriam Brind—The Ghosts of
Impecunious Tenants—The Old House at Upper Upham—Sir
Christopher Wren—John Goddard, of Aldbourne—Old Coins
found on the Downs . . . . . , . . . 97-107

THE WILTSHIRE DOWNS AND THE THAMES VALLEY.

The Wiltshire Downs—The Valley of the Thames—The Elevation
of the Downs—How the Chalk was Formed—The Watershed
of the Thames Valley—Sun Worshippers—Remnants of the
Sacrificial Fires—The Grand Panorama of Natural Scenery—
The English Sabbath—Seeing Scenes with the Mind's Eye .108-118

THE POPULAR AMUSEMENTS OF OUR GRANDFATHERS.

Bull Baiting—William Cobbett at Swindon—The Wilts and Berks
Canal—Amusements for the Navvies—Sports in the Days of
Good Queen Bess—Bear-Baiting before the King—Ancient
Rights and Privileges—Disgusting Brutalities 119-127

PAGE.

THE POPULAR AMUSEMENTS OF OUR GRANDFATHERS.

Young Gamesters and Old Gamesters—Blood to Run One Inch—The Scouring of the White Horse—Old English Sport and Modern Recreation—Wroughton and Stratton Feasts—The Beginning of Better Things—Practising Accuracy of Aim—Wilts versus Somerset—"Aldhelm and Ethelfled"—The Renowned Robert Blackford—The Last Great Bout at Swindon—The Stocks and Pillory 128-140

IN-DOOR AMUSEMENTS—THE MUMMERS.

The Mummers' Play—The Wiltshire Mummers—The Dialogue—The Cumberland Version—The Cornish Version—Shoeing the Colt—Gloucestershire Mummers—The Popularity of the Mummers' Play 141-150

YEOMANRY CAVALRY AND NIGHT WATCHMEN.

Drying Gunpowder on the Hob—The Call to Duty—A Ludicrous Scene—Night Watchmen—A Great Discovery—His Majesty from Below—The Occasion and the Opportunity—Drawing the First Blood 151-158

THE OLD PARISH CHURCH, THE OLD MILL, AND THE MANOR.

The Architecture of the Old Church—Wiltshire Landholders—The Domesday Survey—Value of Church Property—The Old Yew Trees—The Old Church and the New—The Seignorial Mill—Church Well—The Mill of Domesday—The Dedication of the Church—Canon Jackson's History of Swindon—The Conqueror's Sponge—The Goddards at Swindon—Restoration of the Old Church 159-173

THE OLD CHURCH.

The Great Bell Period—What was believed in the Parish — The Old Church as seen by John Aubrey—The Inside View of the Old Church—The Church Choir — The Old Clerk — What a Box of Blair's Pills did—An After-Dinner Amen —The Parish Registers—"Bonny" Noad—Curious Memoranda — A Small Item—The Book of Church Goods—The Old Vicar of My Childhood—The Changes of Forty Years — The New Church on the Hill—The New Churches of St. Paul's and St. John's —Mr. Baily leaves Swindon 174-192

LIST OF PERSONS INSTITUTED TO THE RECTORY AND VICARAGE OF SWINDON, from 1302 to 1885 . .193-194

SWINDON WORTHIES.

William Pike—The "Wonders of Geology"—The "Penny Encyclopædia—The Father of Geology—A Distinguished Company—John Britton's Account of William Smith—The Wilts and Berks Canal—Artesian Wells—Dr. G. A. Mantell—Robert Sadler—The Author of "The Melancholy Man"—A Deep-thinking Man—Real Suffering and Affected Misery 195-208

PAGE.

SOME OTHER WORTHIES.

Licenses to Preach—The Squire's Judgment Seat—Mr. Stubbs, the Minister of Wroughton—The Conventicle Act—A Marlborough Bye-law—Newport Street Chapel—Mr. James Strange—The Rev. T. Mantell—The Nonconformists of the Neighbourhood—The Death of Mr. Strange—The Old Chapel in Newport Street—The Ministers of the Newport Street Chapel—Sturdy Nonconformists 209-222

TOWN AND TRADE OF SWINDON.

The Characteristics of Richard Strange—The Morning Pipe—Waiting for the Inevitable—The Marvellous Escape—The "Square"—The Stocks and Pillory—The Parish Supplying Bread—The Cost of Pauperism in 1801—Swindon Manufactories — The Leather Breeches of our Grandfathers—Documents Saved from Burning—William the Third's Poll Tax — Swindon in 1662 — Charles the First's Ship Money—A Census of 250 Years Ago .223-238

TOWN AND TRADE OF SWINDON (Continued).

Waggons and Waggoners—"Wooset-Hunting"—The "Skimming-ton"—Going to Bath for the Fashions—The Little Guard and his Big Trumpet—A Remarkable Day—The Navvies—The Wonderful After-glow as seen in the "Sands"—Mischievous Boys and the Irate Old Man—Old Town Characters—The Wonderful Bit of Garden Ground—Phlebotomy, or Blood-Letting . .239-251

TRADESMEN'S TOKENS.

Swindon Tradesmen's Tokens—Small Silver Coins: Leaden Tokens —The Prerogative for Coining and its Abuse—"Token" Orthography — Trade Companies' Tokens—Canting Heraldry—The Number of Wiltshire Tokens—Swindon in 1806 and in 1885 .252-260

BANKS AND BANKERS.

Mr. Mountford, the Bank Manager—Joint Stock Banks—More Banks —Wootton Bassett before Swindon—The Bank of England Charter—Seizing a Corpse for Debt—Mr. Strange and the Coach —The Coachman and the Fourpenny Pieces—An Explosion .261-270

OLD TOWN CHARACTERS.

War and its Results—Mellowed Sight—Nanny Kernel—The Ghoul of Mill Lane—Old Tom Marcham—Old Tom and his Wounds —The Old Crow in Peacock's Feathers—Jenny Simmonds and 'Ria Ladd—The Old Parcels Women—The Mother and Daughter—Billy Noad and Bobby Wood—The "Pitch-Plaster Business 271-283

MY SCHOOLS AND SCHOOLMASTERS.

Dame Schools—Recollections of a Convalescence—Lessons from a Sick Room—The Schoolmaster of Fifty Years Ago—The Newport Street School—Old Mr. Turvey—The Old Exciseman as Schoolmaster—Mr. George Nourse—Sad Ending to a Life's Work 284-293

PAGE.

MARKETS AND FAIRS—MARKETS.

Swindon Market in 1272—The King, Lord of Marlborough—The Swindon Charter—A Gin-and-Water Market—A " Pitched " Market Established—The Town Hall and the uses to which it was put—The Central Market Company—A Candle and Lantern Cattle Market—Up in the Morning Early—The Business of the Sale Yard 294-304

MARKETS AND FAIRS—FAIRS.

The Swindon Charter of 1627—Strutt's Sport's and Pastimes—The Origin of Wakes and Fairs—Hiring Fairs—Standing in the Market Place for Hire—Cattle and Horse Fairs—The Blind Horse Dealer—The Great Wiltshire Fairs—Courts of Pie-Powder—Lynch Law and the Pick-Pocket 305-315

THE TROUBLOUS TIMES OF 1830.

One Pauper to every Nine Inhabitants—The Poors' Rate of Sixty Years Ago—The Maintenance of Bastard Children—Surplus Labourers—What the Poor Cost Then and Now—The Wages of Fifty Years Ago—A Pound of Bread per Day—Midnight Conflagrations—Cock and Bull Stories 316-325

THE TROUBLOUS TIMES OF 1830—THE TURNING OF THE WORM.

The Inventor of the Thrashing Machine—Threatening Letters signed "Swing"—Rioting at Andover—A Melancholy Wreck—A "Warm Reception" not Bargained for—A Fatal Encounter with the Rioters—The Riot Act Read—The Effects of Machine Breaking—"The Guards" to the Rescue—A Terrible Reckoning 326-336

THE TROUBLOUS TIMES OF 1830—RETRIBUTION.

The Commission opened at Winchester—The Charges to the Grand Jury—The Personal Appearance of the Prisoners—The Charges Stated—A Verdict of "Guilty"—Several Hundred Prisoners on their Trial—Death Recorded against 95 Prisoners—130 Berkshire Prisoners on Trial 337-345

THE TROUBLOUS TIMES OF 1830—THE TRIALS OF THE WILTSHIRE PRISONERS.

The Wilts Commission Opened—A Demand for Two Shillings a Day —Sacking a Woollen Factory—330 Prisoners at Salisbury—The Dread Sentence Passed—A Scene not to be Described—A Most Painful Scene—The Terrible Cries of the Prisoners—The Parting of Prisoners and Friends—Opening of the Commission at Dorchester—More Convictions — Cooper and Cooke Executed — Lush and Withers Respited—Rents Lowered; Wages Raised .346-360

PAGE.

THE G.W R. BROUGHT THROUGH SWINDON.

The Population of Neighbouring Towns—The Great Western Rail-
way Projected—The " Hooter " and the Pheasants—Landlord
Restrictions on Enterprise — The Opening of the Railway—A
Modest Claim for Damages—The First Excursion Train .   .361-368

PIONEERS OF NONCONFORMITY.

Cennick, the North Wilts Evangelist—Cennick Visits Swindon—A
Spectacle of the Utmost Shame—Cennick Visits Stratton—
" Persecuted, but not Forsaken "—Taking a Thorn from an
Assailant's Foot—The End of the Wicked—A Prophetess whose
Disciples had Fits—Cennick's Early Youth—What Contemporary
Events say about the Matter—Mural Testimony—North Wilts
and "Sour Theology"—Jackson's Life of Wesley—The Curate
of Devizes—"The Devil's Infantry"—Conversion of the Mayor's
Son—The Old Serpent—A Drunken and Enraged Multitude—
Wanted : A Promise—Fierceness and Diabolical Malice—Wor-
ship, Thanks, and Blessing 369-390

THE WESLEYANS.

The Early Days of Wesley—George Pocock, of Bristol—A Novel
Machine—The First Chapel Built—How Methodism Established
Itself—The Wits of Wanborough—Mr. Thomas Bush, of Lam-
bourne—A Vow, and what became of it—Martyrs for Conscience
Sake—A Weakness for Making Vows—The First Preacher Ap-
pointed—No Money to Spend—The Request to Send in " My
Little Bill "—Mr. Bush's Last Will and Testament—The Cen-
tenary of Methodism—The Wesleyan Jubilee as Kept at Hodson
—Swindon and Wesleyanism both Growing—Wanted, More
Chapels 391-409

PIONEERS OF NONCONFORMITY—THE PRIMITIVE METHODISTS.

Old Chapels Discarded : New Ones Built—The Veteran of the Circuit
—The Prospect Chapel—The Establishment of the First Mission
—The Brinkworth Circuit—Services at a Public House—Hugh
Bourne Visits Swindon—More New Chapels—Opening Services
—How the Money is Got Together—The Golden System .   .410-421

THE SWINDON TROOP OF YEOMANRY CAVALRY.

The Swindon Troop Called to Purton—Wheat, £3 12s. ; and Flour,
£5 per Sack—The Muster Roll—Joining the Yeomanry to
Escape the Militia—Peace Proclaimed—The Thanks of Parlia-
ment—Withdrawal of the Government Allowance—Unusual
Activity—A Peaceful Time—Militia Riots at Devizes—The Muster
Roll for 1824—Busy Times for the Yeomanry—Royal Honours
for the Yeomanry—A Rest from Active Duty—Wootton Bassett
Peace Preservers—The Marlborough Troop 422-438

PAGE.

PARLIAMENTARY ELECTIONS.

The Parish Handy-Man—The Man in the White Hat—Mrs. Page and Her Illumination—Wiltshire with 37 M.P.'s—The Cricklade Election Case—The Cricklade Constituency in 1790 and in 1880 —The Wootton Bassett Constituency—Notorious Bribery at Cricklade—An Act to Prevent Bribery—My First Election Experiences—Refreshments for the Voters—The Nomination Day— The Wootton Bassett Election Scene—Chairing the Member— An Impertinent Questioner—Mr. Goddard Turns Tail—The Etymology of " Pot Walloper"—A Wootton Bassett Election Bill—Malmesbury and its Elections 439-458

THE SWINDON JUSTICES.

The Execution of Watkins—The Rose and Crown—The Swindon Magistrates—Old Tom Tinson—Old Tom and the Chairman— The Old Blind House—Court Houses and Police Stations— Taking Care of a Prisoner—The Swindon Quarrymen—How News about the Railway was Received—The Old Farmer who had seen a Post Chaise 459-470

SPRINGS, WELLS, AND WATER SUPPLY.

No Water below the Hill—A Band of Quicksand—The Springs Church Well—Wroughton Road Spring—Holy Well Spring —The Minor Springs—The Iron left Behind—Quicksand a Bad Foundation—The Wells and their Varying Depths—The Shrine Well of St. Anne—Holy Wells and Health Springs –The Pilgrims' Path—Chalybeate Springs 471-484

SWINDON HILL AND ITS LESSONS.

An Enthusiast with " A Find"—Looking out from Liddington Castle —The Out-look, East, South, and West—The Blowhole in the Mud—The Swindon Quarries—The Portland Sands—The First Navigators—Fossil Remains—A River Running over Swindon —Swindon's Earliest Inhabitants—Kangaroos and their Food —A Fossil Tree—The Vitality of Buried Seed——Icebergs at Swindon 485-499

SCRAPS.

Selling a Wife—Old Superstitions—Superstitious Beliefs . . 500-504

APPENDIX.

The Charter Granted by Charles I. to Thomas Goddard, Esq.—The Eastcott Enclosure Award, dated September, 1657—The Geology of the Swindon Quarries . . . .

PAGE.

PARLIAMENTARY ELECTIONS.

The Parish Handy-Man—The Man in the White Hat—Mrs. Page
and Her Illumination—Wiltshire with 37 M.P.'s—The Cricklade
Election Case—The Cricklade Constituency in 1790 and in 1880
—The Wootton Bassett Constituency—Notorious Bribery at
Cricklade—An Act to Prevent Bribery—My First Election Expe-
riences—Refreshments for the Voters—The Nomination Day—
The Wootton Bassett Election Scene—Chairing the Member—
An Impertinent Questioner—Mr. Goddard Turns Tail—The
Etymology of "Pot Walloper"—A Wootton Bassett Election
Bill—Malmesbury and its Elections 439-458

THE SWINDON JUSTICES.

The Execution of Watkins—The Rose and Crown—The Swindon
Magistrates—Old Tom Tinson—Old Tom and the Chairman—
The Old Blind House—Court Houses and Police Stations—
Taking Care of a Prisoner—The Swindon Quarrymen—How
News about the Railway was Received—The Old Farmer who
had seen a Post Chaise 459-470

SPRINGS, WELLS, AND WATER SUPPLY.

No Water below the Hill—A Band of Quicksand—The Springs
Church Well—Wroughton Road Spring—Holy Well Spring
—The Minor Springs—The Iron left Behind—Quicksand a Bad
Foundation—The Wells and their Varying Depths—The Shrine
Well of St. Anne—Holy Wells and Health Springs –The Pil-
grims' Path—Chalybeate Springs 471-484

SWINDON HILL AND ITS LESSONS.

An Enthusiast with "A Find"—Looking out from Liddington Castle
—The Out-look, East, South, and West—The Blowhole in the
Mud—The Swindon Quarries—The Portland Sands—The First
Navigators—Fossil Remains—A River Running over Swindon
—Swindon's Earliest Inhabitants—Kangaroos and their Food
—A Fossil Tree—The Vitality of Buried Seed——Icebergs at
Swindon 485-499

SCRAPS.

Selling a Wife—Old Superstitions—Superstitious Beliefs . . 500-504

APPENDIX.

The Charter Granted by Charles I. to Thomas Goddard, Esq.—The
Eastcott Enclosure Award, dated September, 1657—The Geology
of the Swindon Quarries . . . .

⚊ꓱ✳Masonic✳Relic⚌1704.⚊

MANY a "nook and cranny" in many a back
street of some old town or city is rich in
interest to the archæologist and antiquary, and therefore to the Mason.
The most fertile imagination, however,
could scarcely conceive of anything of the sort
existing in Newport street, Swindon. The street had
its characteristics, it is true, but they were not drawn
on lines of beauty, nor of art—modern, mediæval,
or ancient. It was a back street, and was generally
known to that generation of Swindonians of which
there are but a few remaining representatives as
"Bull" Street. The other streets of the town were
known as High-street, and Wood-street, and these
three, with Short-hedge, formed the four sides of the
square, or block, which constituted the town of Old
Swindon. It is not many years since there were
quite a number of very poor thatched cottages,
occupied by labouring people, in Wood-street; there
were no less than two blacksmiths' forges opening
right on to the street, as they are now occasionally to

be seen on the street of some village, and around
whose fires the plough-boys, and ox-men, of the
neighbourhood used to congregate in the evening,
after the work of the fields was done, and, in company
with the ostlers and stable-boys of the town, enjoy
their jokes and their "backey," whilst their harness
or their tools and implements of husbandry were
being repaired and put straight by the brawny smiths.
But Bull-street never rose even to the dignity of
receiving such company ; it seemed to be a street too
far back for even a smith to look at.   The street had,
of course, its public-house or inn, which was called
the " Bull ;" and the " Bull " gave the name to the
street.   To the ordinary inhabitant, or to the casual
passer-by, there was the " Bull," and there was the
street, and the two combined made " Bull-street."
How the street obtained the more dignified name of
" Newport " I cannot say.   Swindon street nomenclature is rather interesting, and, generally, may be
readily interpreted.   For instance, Wood-street was
formerly called " Windmill " street, from a wind-mill
which stood where the " King's Arms " Hotel now
stands.   It was then called " Blacksmith's " street,
from the smiths' forges to which I have referred. And
it was not without good reason that the street was so
called, for who, by the way, is there who can go back
in memory thirty or forty years, and cannot recollect
the feeling indulged in, that the town was downright
busy, and that the stroke of business it was doing was
enough to excite the envy of all the towns of the
neighbourhood, when either of the smiths, or what
was still more impressive, when both of them at the
same time, had a wheel to bond, or when they had to
encase the outer edge of the felloes of some massive
waggon wheel with curved strips of iron an inch or
more thick, by three or four broad, and either of which
operations was invariably performed in the front of

the smithy, and in the gutter of the public street? When such a piece of work was about to be performed the very look of the smith would tell of something unusual being "up;" from the early hours of the morning his forge would be all aglow, and his anvil in one constant ring, as he was engaged in cutting the iron into the required lengths from long and heavy bars, and bending, and curving, and nail holeing, the pieces to the required shape and pattern. And when this had been done, or probably before, if there was a spare hand to do it, the wheel would be trundled along from the wheelwrights and placed across the gutter in front of the smithy, resting on a bar or strut passed into the axle. And then, the smith, having heated the iron "red hot," would bring it out with his huge tongs and, laying it on the place it was to occupy on the wheel, would burn it into its bed, not unfrequently setting the wood ablaze, to the intense delight of the band of young urchins who would invariably be looking on. And then when the iron had been burnt into its bed, water from buckets and watering-pots would be poured over iron and wood to stop the burning, filling the street with clouds of smoke and steam, and the gutter with water, which would rush off in a stream sufficiently large to carry the impromptu boats and ships the boys and girls would launch thereon. And then when all this had been done, and all was ready for the fixing, the whole street would resound with the blows of hammers and sledges as the smith and his assistants, with their arms bared to the shoulder, and with their necks and breasts uncovered, would aim in rapid succession well-directed blows at huge square nails which were to fasten the iron to the wood, and would drive them home with a thud and a ring which might be heard far and near. No doubt, since these days, there has been many an important bit of business transacted in the town, but who can forget "how busy we used to be" in the old times, before the town had become so grand : when there was no Local Board of Health, no Town Surveyor to keep things in their proper place, and no Inspector of Nuisances to see that there was nothing to offend either the eye, the nose, or the ear; and when the jolly smith could take his work into the street and in the gutter, and there execute it in the' face of his neighbours and the world, none daring to make him afraid, or in any way to interfere with him. Never, indeed, was the old town so thoroughly awakened from its slumbers and its proverbial dulness as when one of the smiths had a wheel to " do." But for the last forty years the street has been simply Wood-street, which, I interpret to mean, the street leading out to the Wood Town of the Bassetts— Wootton Bassett. Short-hedge, now dignified by the name of Devizes-road, doubtless took its name from the hawthorn hedges which bounded each side of the road, and which were kept cut down "short." The "Bull," however, was a low, thatched, cottage looking building, very much like most of the other houses on the street. Indeed, if the houses on the street were not remarkable for their uniformity, it was owing to their having all been put up according to some rule of thumb, rather than on those lines of beauty and effect which formed the basis on which our old architects, builders, and masons worked, and which gave such an interesting and enduring effect to their handiwork. In a word, the architecture of the street may be described as that of the Squatters—of men who, by some means or other, became pos- sessed of a bit of land, and built themselves a house thereon with such materials as came readiest to hand, the walls being generally composed of the rough undressed stones of the locality, which were cemented together by a plentiful application of mud and lime ;

the timber used being roughly-hewn oak or elm trees, such as the neighbourhood could afford, and the covering invariably a thatch of wheaten straw. So rude indeed was the construction of many of these buildings, that a uniform line on the street was only occasionally observed; whilst it was still more rare to find the walls carried up with anything like perpendicular accuracy I recollect one case in particular, in a house in which I had some interest. The house in question was razed to the ground for the purpose of being supplanted by a more imposing edifice. The work, however, was considerably delayed in consequence of a dispute with the owner of the adjoining house, whose bedroom floor projected some three or four feet over the downstairs or ground floor of the house in question. I believe the dispute was ultimately arranged on a give-and-take principle, the owner of the one house giving up two feet of his bedroom frontage in consideration of receiving an addition of two feet to his downstair frontage. I do not say such complications as these are anyway unusual in old country towns of little or no consequence or repute, and the features to which I have referred are noticed only to show that Bull-street, Swindon, was simply without promise of any interest to the archæologist, the antiquary, or the Mason. And yet there was one house on the street which had always been a puzzle to me. Like most of the houses, both up and down, and on both sides of the way, its front was covered with the remains of many coats of lime, or, as it is locally called, white-wash, which it had received time after time, time out of mind. There was a little more uniformity in the size and form of the windows in the front of the house than in most of the other houses in the street, and it had a tiled or stone roof—thin slabs of forest marble, which must have been brought from a distance of ten or twelve

miles to the town. But, beyond this, the house was
but little or no better than the thatched or roughly-
built cottages to which I have referred. It, however,
was not singular in the superior appearance which
its tiled roof gave it, for there had evidently been
a continuous struggle on the part of the houses
at the end of the street nearest to High Street
and the Market Place, to improve in appearance,
and to march on with the times, several others
having had given them more shapely windows, as
well as tiled roofs. But it was neither the tiled
roof, nor the more shapely windows, which, for so
many years, attracted my notice, and which was such
a puzzle to me. It was this. Up between the two
up-stair windows, and about mid-way between the lin-
tel of the door and the eaves of the roof, there was,
struggling as it were through the lime-wash, certain
lines, or rather marks, which indicated a lozenge
shape or form of about two feet square, and within
these lines, under favourable circumstances, were
to be discerned many flourishes, surrounding and
supporting what appeared to be three castles—a
shield bearing arms, but whose, or what, the layers of
lime-wash, with which it was covered, rendered it
simply impossible to say. On and off for years I
tried to gain some information about this stone, which
appeared so out of place in the position in which I
found it, but no one could give me the least satisfaction regarding it. I described it to friends versed in
heraldry, and also in archæology, but all without
effect. No one could tell me anything about it, or
afford any reasonable explanation for such an imposing figure being in front of so mean a house. At
the most the house was not more than from fifteen
to sixteen feet wide, with the general ground and
bedroom floors of an ordinary cottage. At length
the house became tenantless, and fell into wreck and

ruin, and was ultimately sold by auction, being
purchased with a view to its being razed to the ground
for the purpose of making an entry into a cattle sale
yard which lies in its rear. Before this plan could be
carried out, the proprietor (the late Mr. W. Dore)
died, and his son-in-law, who succeeded to the
property, had the old place pulled down and a new
house built on its site. The builder of the new house
(Mr. J. Powell) was, at the time the work was being
carried out, the W.M. of his lodge, and well-known
as an enthusiastic Mason. As the work progressed,
I made frequent enquiries about the stone, and what
was to be done with it, and on the occasion of one of
these enquiries was gratified to find that it had been
thoroughly cleansed of the "wash" with the view to
its being inserted as near its former position as
possible in the new building. The improved view I
was now enabled to take of it confirmed me in an
opinion I had long entertained that the Arms were
those of the Freemasons, although not the same as
now in use. This, however, was stoutly opposed by
Mr. Powell, who said that in consequence of a former
suggestion of mine to this effect, he had consulted
all the available authorities on Masonry, and had
examined all the Arms he could meet with, without
finding anything like it. Considering that Mr.
Powell's position in Masonry gave him an authority
which I could not claim, I submitted, without being
satisfied, and, availing myself of the opportunity, I
took a rubbing of the stone, which was shortly afterwards inserted in the front of the re-built house, and
where it may now be seen. I then sent one of the
rubbings to such authorities on heraldry as I thought
might give me information concerning it, but all without avail. Some thought it very curious, and others
that they had seen it before, but could not tell where.
The mystery as to what it was was ultimately cleared

up in this manner :—A rubbing of the stone chanced
to be lying on the desk in Mr. Powell's office at the
time when a commercial traveller called, and he (a
Mason) at once identified it as being similar to the

Arms on a very old and curious copperplate engraving
used for the summonses of his lodge. Very shortly
afterwards I was gratified at receiving, through Mr.
Powell, a print of this old "summons" plate, with an
explanatory letter concerning its history. Having,
unfortunately, "lent" both the old summons and the
letter, they have met with the the fate of "lent"
things in general, and I am in consequence thrown
back on my recollection concerning them. I do not,
unfortunately, recollect the name of the Lodge to
which the summons belonged, and Bro. Powell having
gone to the Antipodes, I cannot fly to him for help.
It was, however, a very old Lodge, and existed long
before the present Grand Lodge, as now constituted,
existed. I think it must have died out as a Lodge,

and was afterwards resuscitated. Some long time
after its new birth, it occurred to some of the brethren
that it would be well to examine the contents of an
old oak chest, a legacy from the old Lodge. This
was done in due course, and, in the result, the old
copper-plate of, I believe, more than one hundred and
fifty years old, was once more brought to light, and
was at once pronounced to be so curious that it was
restored to its original use and purpose, and the
ordinary Lodge summonses have been ever since
printed therefrom. The engraving, which was about
twelve inches by ten, in size, was most interesting
and curious, being most elaborately covered with allegorical figures. I trust it will not be long before I
shall be fortunate enough to obtain the name of the
Lodge to which it belongs, as well as another "copy,"
which I hope to make better use of than the former
one. Of course, the special interest of the old
summons in connection with the present subject is,
that it contained the same Coat of Arms as that
engraven on the old stone in front of the old house in
Newport Street, Swindon, which dates as far back as
the year one thousand seven hundred and four.

But there was a still more subtle mystery to be
cleared up. How came the Masonic Arms to be
placed on so mean a house in the back street of an
old country town, and for what purpose could they
have been placed there, many long years anterior to
the introduction of Masonry into the town—at least
before any Lodge had been established there, or
indeed, in the county to which the town belonged?
Bro. Frederick Hastings Goldney, P.G.S., England,
G. Treasurer, P.P.S.G.W., Wilts, in his excellent
history of Freemasonry in Wilts, says:—" Though
England was not divided into provinces until 1727,
there had undoubtedly been Lodges throughout the
country in direct communication with the Grand

Lodge from a much earlier period, but there are not any records of them in this county, for the earliest Lodge minutes which have been discovered commence in 1732, whilst others commence in 1792, 1794, and 1817, and the remainder are of a still later date."

And yet the date cut on the Newport Street relic is 1704, which carries us back 28 years before the warrant for the first-known Wiltshire Lodge, and no less than 114 years before that of the first Swindon Lodge. Through the courtesy of Mr. Plummer, the present owner of the property, I have been permitted to examine all the deeds known to be extant relating to the property, in the hope of discovering to whom it belonged, A.D., 1704, but unfortunately the oldest deed in Mr. Plummer's possession bears date, March 17th, 1815, when it was conveyed from William Sevill, Chafford, in the parish of Bizley, in the county of Gloucester, to John Harding Sheppard, of Swindon. As Mr. Sheppard had up to the time of his death, in 1868, at the age of 90 years, always been known as a most ardent and enthusiastic Freemason, I was led to think I was at last on the road to discovery. In the year 1818, Mr. Sheppard, who appears at that time to have belonged to a Lodge at Devizes, applied, with Messrs. William Morse Crowdy, Robert Withers, John Wyatt, Samuel Sheppard, John Osborne, and William Gerring, to the Grand Master for a warrant of constitution for a new lodge, to be called the "Lodge of Emulation," to be held at the Goddard Arms Inn, Swindon; and which warrant was duly granted. This being only from two to three years subsequent to the purchase of the house by Mr. Sheppard, I concluded that it was purchased for its Masonic interest ; and further, that it would be found to be in some way connected with the subsequent application for a warrant to open, or possibly to re-open, a Lodge at Swindon. But these hopes were

at once dispelled when I came to the next deed of
conveyance, which I found to be made less than eight
months afterwards, viz., on the 4th November, 1815,
and which was from John Harding Sheppard to
James Tarrant, in whose family it remained until a
comparatively recent period.   A property with a
history to it so dear to a good and loyal Mason would
not have been so readily parted with.   Indeed, Mr.
Sheppard may not have even discerned the Coat of
Arms through the many coats of white-wash, and I
therefore found myself as far off as ever from anything like a satisfactory solution of the enigma: Who
put the old stone in front of the old house in Newport
Street, and for what purpose was it put there? In its
cleaned-up state, and surrounded as it now is by the
bright red bricks in the front of the new-built house
in Newport Street, it looks very white and sharp, and
is indeed a very conspicuous object to many a passer
by, who "wonders" what it can be, and what it
possibly can mean, although my experience is that
it has least of all been noticed by the Masons of
the neighbourhood, for when I have called their
attention to it individually they have invariably
declared they had never noticed it before. Among
these is a relative of the family in whose possession
the property was from the year 1815 down to within
the last few years, and who, in addition to being a
member of the Swindon Lodge has been its W.M., and
yet who assures me he had never noticed or heard
of the interesting old relic until I called his attention
to it the other day in the hope of elucidating something of its history; and it does, therefore, seem
probable that the stone was unknown even to Mr.
J. H. Sheppard, and those devoted and enthusiastic
members of the craft, who not only gave Swindon a
Lodge, but Wiltshire a Grand Lodge, and the distinction of a Province.

P.S.—As an illustration of how exhaustive a matter like this may be made, I may say I have just made an important discovery, after concluding that every available local evidence had been already exhausted. Chancing to visit the old chancel of the old parish church of Swindon, which, after having been suffered for many years to remain in a state of ruin, is now under process of restoration, I discovered affixed to the north wall a mural monumental slab representing three panels. The first, or left-hand, panel bears an inscription to the memory of Henry Pinnick, who was buried December ye 6, 1728, aged 81 years. The right-hand panel contains a similar inscription to the memory of Elinaor, the wife of Henry Pinnick, who died in the year 1727, aged 82 years ; while the middle panel contains the identical Coat of Arms which is to be seen on the old house in Newport Street. There now arises the question : Who was Henry Pinnick ?—there are no Pinnicks at Swindon now, and the name is by no means familiar here or in the neighbourhood. Was he a distinguished member of the Grand Lodge of his time ? and was he, as some special favour, allowed to adopt the arms of the craft for his own coat? And further, did he open a Lodge at Swindon in the year 1704, and distinguish the place of meeting by affixing his own and the Masons' Arms over the entrance ? But if this be so, how comes it there is no record of the circumstances ? and further, if there was a Masonic Lodge in Swindon at this early date, how came it to drop ? But, be this as it may, I am glad to add I have succeded in discovering that the old summons referred to is now in use by the St. John the Baptist Lodge, No. 39, Exeter, and through the courtesy of the present W.M. Bro. R. Jerman, I have been able to replace my lost copy, as well as to obtain the following explanatory account of the same :—

This fine old Copper Line Engraving, which is executed in good style and unique of its kind, was used by our Lodge one hundred and eighteen years ago, as shown by a circular printed from a plate of similar design, dated 1764, preserved in one of our old Minute Books and bearing the following :—

EXETER, DEC. 16, 1764.

BROTHER,
 You are Desir'd to meet the Master and Brethren at a Lodge to be held at the New Inn on Thursday next, by 11 o'Clock in the Morning, to transact Business.
 N.B.—Dinner to be on the Table at 2 o'clock.
 By order of the R.W.M.,

S. MOORE, Secretary.

If you cannot attend be pleased to signify the same by a line to your affectionate Brother,

MEDLAND } Master.

The Plate was engraved by FATHER M. SKINNER, Exon. There has been some trifling alterations made, as appears from the punching at the back, and it now bears the name of Bro. LEWIS, of Magdalen Street, Exeter, who was an Engraver, and who joined this Lodge January, 1822, from No. 91 (now No. 70, St. John's Plymouth—removed there from Exeter in 1828), and was W.M. for the year 1828.

The prefix of R.W.M. for Right W.M. was discontinued after the union of Lodges in 1813, and the No. 53 which was inserted at the foot of the Summons was the number of our Lodge prior to the closing up of Lodges in 1832, when it became 46 (now 39).

The Plate shows at the head a symbolical representation of Solomon's Temple, and at the right and left of it the Sun and Moon ; flanking the space in the centre for the Lodge Summons there are on each side three columns, each surmounted with allegorical figures—on the one side "Faith, Hope, and Charity," on the other side, "Wisdom, Strength, and Beauty." About the margin of the Summons are the Jewels of the five principal Officers in their situations as arranged in olden times ; at the foot there is a Tesselated Pavement and the Arms of the "Moderns" G Lodge before the union in 1813, without the supporters (beavers). The margin is formed of well-drawn foliage from which are suspended Working Tools with Acacia Trees below.

The Plate, which had been lost sight of for many years, has recently been discovered, and remains the same as when used in 1764, with the exception of the Summons, which has again necessarily been altered to suit our present use.

[NOTE : This paper was written to accompany a rubbing of the old stone at an exhibition of Masonic Antiquities held at Worcester in August, 1884, and I have preferred reprinting it in its original form to re-writing it, simply adding that the favour with which it was received, when published in the *Advertiser*, led to my writing the papers which now follow.]

Ghosts and Ghost Laying.

OTHER Relics, it must be admitted, are neither large in number nor striking in character. But this admission would be but a poor excuse for such as they are being left altogether unnoticed. Fortunately, there are many towns with relics which have their history strictly preserved, and not unfrequently the history has been better preserved than the relic. But in Swindon we have very few relics, and absolutely no history; and all we can therefore do is to accept thankfully what we have, and find for it the best history we can. Swindon once had a "gallows;" but we only know this through a very indirect source. The history of other towns tells us that certain powers that were, had the right of setting up a gallows, and there is very good reason to believe that one of the noble ladies who formerly "held" Swindon had a gallows here, to which evils doers were sent in a very practical manner. I have heard very old people aver that the gate at the top of the Sands, leading into the Okus Fields, was once called

Gallows Gate. From this, and from the well-defined and most authentic gallows history of some other towns, it may safely be inferred that Swindon once had a gallows, and that it stood somewhere in or near to the Okus Field. There is still extant an old map or bird's eye view of the town and neighbourhood of Banbury, and not only the site, but a rude sketch of one of these old gallows' of the period to which I refer is given—of the old town in Oxfordshire, to which we were all sent times out of number in the days of our infancy, "riding a cock horse to Banbury Cross, to see a rich lady on a white horse." Swindon, of course, at various times has had its ghosts, but they were never of a very staying character, and appeared only to disappear, and were soon forgotten. The town and neighbourhood has also had its haunted houses, and I can well recollect having had pointed out to me when a child certain houses in which it was said a "Ghost had been laid." The rule with ghosts formerly appeared to be this: Until they were "laid" they had the whole range of the house or premises in which they made their appearance, but after they had been once well and duly "laid" they were confined to a single room or part of the premises. I have a most vivid recollection of the *modus operandi* observed at the "laying of ghosts" as it was once related to me under these circumstances :—It may be fifty years ago, there or thereabouts, when on a certain Thursday there was quite a consternation in Swindon. At that time the Magistrates' weekly meeting was held in one of the rooms at the Goddard Arms, in what is now known as the Commercial-room, No. 3, and the windows of which command a full view of Wood-street and the road leading out to Wootton Bassett. Now, at that particular time the chairman of the Swindon Bench was also Vicar of Wootton Bassett, and as the rev. gentleman was as punctual in the performance of his magisterial as he was of his clerical duties, his appearance in Wood-street on his way to the Goddard Arms was almost as good an index as to the time of day as were the hands on the dial of the old church clock. But, on the particular Thursday which I so well remember, there was some unusually important magisterial business to be transacted. What it was I cannot remember, but I do know that it had created quite a sensation in the town and neighbourhood, and there was in consequence a great deal of anxiety and curiosity manifested about the meeting that day, and the whole town was anxiously awaiting the arrival of the chairman. At that very distant period of, say fifty years ago, there were no reporters to attend magistrates' and other meetings for the purpose of sending the particulars to the newspapers. Indeed, there were no newspapers to which such reports might be sent, and the only way in which particulars of cases or events of even more importance could be obtained was by "hear-say." The room at the hotel was, of course, too small to admit of the public being present at the hearing, and the only way therefore in which they could obtain particulars was by some few privileged individuals dancing attendance on the beadle, the constable, the clerk, or some other official who might chance to turn up, and extorting from him such information as he or they felt disposed to disclose, and then to hand it from one to another amidst the crowd of waiters for the good of the public. But on this particular occasion all the watching and waiting of which the town was capable failed to bring the much-expected and long-looked-for chairman, and not only minutes, quarters, and half hours, but actually hours passed by without his coming. There had been a great "craning of necks" out of the windows, and "flattening of noses" against the window panes, of the magistrates' room by those who were waiting there to begin business : a great deal of "kicking of heels" under the pent-houses at the two "corners" on the opposite side of the way, as well as much "mooning" about up and down Wood Street by those who were waiting the arrival of his reverence. But all to no purpose, for he came not. In course of time, however, an explanation of his absence came instead. He had started off for Swindon with his usual punctuality, and had made good progress on his journey, when he was intercepted, to "go and lay a ghost." If I do not give the names of persons and places it is simply because I may not unwillingly give pain to persons who may be still living. I could give names both of persons and places, but a general reference must suffice for my present purpose. I cannot, of course, vouch for the truth of the alleged facts ; I can only repeat what I was told at the time, and which tale, no doubt, had its firm believers. It was to this effect : the reverend chairman had been intercepted on his way from Wootton Bassett to Swindon to go and lay a ghost. He pleaded his magisterial duties, and the necessity of his being at Swindon. But this did not avail, it being urged in reply that the ghost had been a very troublesome one, and that it was of the utmost importance that it should be at once "laid." It was understood to be the ghost of a rather wealthy farmer who, having by ill-treatment killed one of his plough-boys, threw the body between the legs of the cart horses in the stable for the purpose of making it appear that he had been kicked and trampled upon by them whilst in the performance of his work. By this means, and aided by his position in the neighbourhood, he managed to escape prosecution for his crime. He, however, did not

C

escape punishment, for he soon began to "pine away,"
and, ultimately dying, his ghost began to " walk."
For some time efforts had been made to catch and lay
the ghost, but all without avail, in consequence of
some informality, or some imperfection, in the necessary machinery. One of the absolutely necessary
conditions was that there should be assembled a
certain number of clergy, habited in their surplices,
and holding their prayer books in their hands. A
" laying" court thus constituted having been duly
formed, and certain prayers having been read, the
ghost was duly summoned to appear, there and then,
for the purpose of having the "range of its walk"
limited to some room or place in the house, which it
had a full and perfect right to choose for itself. The
choice having been made, the ghost was duly escorted
by the assembled clergy to the room or place
selected ; all windows, chimneys, and doors were then
securely fastened and made dark by means of lath
and plaster, the last closure of course being made
with the ghost inside, and the clergy, who continued
all the while to read their prayers, outside. And with
that the matter ended, the whole domain of the ghost
ever afterwards being confined to the darkened room.
For the satisfaction of the incredulous and the
unbelieving, I may say I can refer to more than one
house in and about Swindon in which ghosts were
said to have been thus "laid," and can point to
certain blocked up windows as "proof" of the "fact."
But to return to the ghost in question. It had proved
a very obdurate ghost. On some occasions when the
clergy had met, there had not been the proper
number, or they had not all their surplices, or their
prayer-books, or something or another was found to
be wanting, and, in consequence, our ghost, standing
on its own dignity, refused to be "laid." On the
occasion in question, certain clergy had duly met, and

in answer to their prayers or incantations the ghost put in an appearance, but on discovering that the number of the clergy was wrong, he set them all at defiance, and refused positively to be laid and done for. In these circumstances it occurred to some of the company present that the reverend chairman of the Swindon Bench of Magistrates would shortly be passing along that way *en route* for Swindon, and they, in consequence, went out and intercepted him, and after much parleying they succeeded in making up the required number of the clergy! To the best of my recollection it was said they had previously twelve, and that it required thirteen to make an odd number. But this difficulty was no sooner got over than there arose another. Thursday was a day for the donning of magisterial robes rather than sacerdotal vestments, and for the study of *Burns' Justice*, rather than the Book of Common Prayer, and therefore both surplice and Prayer Book were wanting. These, however, could be obtained by going back to Wootton Bassett for them. And this having been done, the required number of clergy was made up, the ceremony was duly performed, and the ghost once and for all "laid." These various delays, however, wasted so much time that it was night before it was all over, and long before then, it is almost needless to observe, those who had been waiting for the customary administration of justice at Swindon, had ceased to wait, and had gone off to their respective homes, consoling themselves with the "reason," which I have endeavoured faithfully to set out, for there having been no magistrates' meeting at Swindon on that particular day. I may say, in conclusion, I have a very strong suspicion that many who read these lines will feel disposed to say they don't believe ghosts were ever laid in such a way. Of course I cannot object

to their unbelief, but I can say that as recently as
fifty years ago there were plenty of people who did
believe in it, and who used to look upon these ghost
layings as a matter of fact ; and I have no hesitation
in saying that the memories of many of my elder
readers will carry them back to many a similar tale
told to them in the days when they were young.
Were it not the almost special object of the present
writing to show how and why it was there was no
magistrates' meeting at Swindon on a certain Thursday many years ago, I· might give quite a number of
other *facts* in corroboration of those already stated.
There once was a pond near a church—it is filled up
now, and can only be seen, by those who never saw
it, in pictures—but I can readily bring that old pond
within the vision of my mind's eye, and. looking on
to it from the top of the steps leading to the
"dipping" place, can see along in the high wall on
the left hand side an arched indentation, resembling a
walled up doorway.   And then I can recollect having
been told that this marked the end of a passage
which ran from the pond to the cellars of a
neighbouring mansion, and which passage was in use
for certain purposes, until the time when it was
selected by certain ghosts as the place in which they
preferred to be laid. when it was closed up at
both ends and made secure against their escape.   I
also recollect most distinctly having been told that
on one occasion a very venturesome fellow, not
having the fear of the ghosts before his eyes, made a
small opening into the passage from the blocked up
door-way in the pond, just large enough for him
to peep through, and see what there was inside,
and that he there and then, saw several ghosts quietly
seated and smoking long pipes, from which circumstance it would appear they were both happy and
contented ghosts, otherwise they would no doubt

have availed themselves of the opportunity of escaping through the hole in the door-way in a cloud of blue smoke, for, as I have already pointed out, the natural propensity of a ghost always was to escape from the place where it had been laid. As a rule they never missed a chance for exercising this propensity. There used to be a well authenticated tale told in an adjoining parish, shewing how the prying propensities of the people exercised in connection with ghosts often led to serious complications. In this particular case the ghost had been laid in an old room in the family mansion, and there it had remained in peace and quietness time out of mind, until one day a prying servant thought she would have "just one peep" inside the room ; but she had no sooner managed to "just get the door ajar" than "out rushed the ghost," to the consternation and alarm, not only of the household, but of the whole village and neighbourhood. Indeed this old ghost appears to have given a great deal more trouble than any new ghost had ever been known to do. Whether it had gained strength with age, or whether it was naturally a crabbed and cantankerous ghost, I was never informed. But this is quite certain : when it did get its liberty " the pranks it played were truly awful," so that in the end there was no help for it but to again summon the clergy, and again to "lay" the ghost, which was subsequently successfully accomplished, the place of laying the second time being at the bottom of the neighbouring fish pond. Even a ghost, it would seem, may be overcome and laid low by having a sufficient quantity of cold water put on its back. I might refer to other ghosts about whom I have heard, but will only just refer to three or four others. They were not Swindon ghosts, but belonged to the neighbourhood. I introduce them because they differed

somewhat in their character from the ordinary ghost.
It belonged to a parish about nine miles distant from
Swindon, and for a long while gave no end of trouble
to those who wanted to "lay" it.   Time after time
the clergy were duly summoned and assembled for
the due performance of the interesting ceremony.
But 'twas all love's labour lost.   It not only would
not be "laid," but its pranks gradually grew more
outrageous than ever, and it continued to grow in
wickedness until it chanced that the Lord Bishop of
the Diocese had occasion to visit the neighbourhood.
It was decided by those who had "laid their heads
together" over the matter that this was the golden
opportunity, and so indeed it proved to be.   His
Grace was appealed to to lend a helping hand in the
matter, it being pointed out to him that however
much Mr. Ghost had been able to defy the common
clergy, any number of ghosts would have to
succumb if a Lord Bishop was only added.   His
Lordship, appreciating the force of the argument,
consented, the meeting was held, the ghost duly
summoned, and as duly laid.   And then there
were other ghosts beside those who walked in houses:
there were also those who wandered about in the
open.   There was the Piper's Corner ghost, on
the Coate road.   This was a much-troubled ghost,
and the tales two notorious characters of their day,
Billy Noad and Bobby Wood, used to tell about its
doings were "something awful."   It was the ghost of
some woman, who was sometimes to be "seen"
carrying her head under her arm, and at other
times carrying a child in her arms.   Then there was
in quite another direction a ghost with what may be
called accessories of a more elaborate character.
This ghost always appeared in a carriage drawn by
four milk-white horses, and attended by several
servants.   It was understood that this ghost was very

particular as to the time when it made its appearance
—twelve o'clock at night, as near as possible. Its
appearance was for a few minutes only, which were
spent in driving about the estate, its chief delight
being exhibited when the carriage came to a gate,
the servants having to dismount, and go through
the ceremony of opening the gate when closed, or
pretending to do so when found to be open. I never
heard of either of these ghosts being "clergy laid,"
and yet it is certain they have not been seen for a
very long time. It may possibly be that they have
been "laid" by some other means—by that better and
brighter intelligence of the latter half of the present
century, which has done so much in so many ways to
correct the ignorance and the superstitions of our dear
old grandmothers and grandfathers. The only other
ghost I propose introducing used to "cut its capers"
in another direction, down somewhere in the
neighbourhood of Cricklade. This was a very
practical and most outrageous ghost, and no bit of
devilry came amiss to it. Cattle were worried, property destroyed, and women and children frightened
and interfered with in the most audacious manner.
Now, there happened to be living in the neighbourhood where the chief depredations of this ghost were
carried on, a tall, very powerful, and a very resolute
yeoman, one of those men who, when they have made
up their minds to take a bull by the horns, some-
how manage, not only to take hold, but to hold on,
"I'll stand this little game no longer," one day
remarked the yeoman, as he found his cattle suffering
from a fright to which they had been subjected by the
ghost, and his property injured and destroyed through
the pranks of the mysterious midnight visitant. Like
a man of his word, as he was, Mr. Yeoman that very
night, having first armed himself with the stoutest
and toughest ash stick he could find, secreted himself

on what he rightly judged would be the track of the
ghost as it took its walks abroad.   He was right in
his conclusions and his plans, and had not long
to wait before the dreaded figure, " all in white," made
its appearance, and directly after that there resounded
on the still midnight air the reverberations of a most
tremendous whack, as the ash stick of the yeoman
fell with all the force a stout arm could give it on
the back of the ghost.   Finding that he had something very substantial under the outward and visible
signs of the ghost, to wit, the white sheet, the
yeoman continued to whack away with all his might,
until he became seriously alarmed at the consequences
which might ensue, for no sooner did he commence to
whack in downright good earnest, than the ghost
commenced to screech for mercy, and, imploring
forgiveness, promised in the most abject manner
" never to do so any more."   That ghost was the
most effectually " laid" one I have ever heard tell of.
And that's a fact.

⌐Some✲Old✲Houses.⌐

ANY years ago—very many years ago—
say, two, three, or four hundred years
ago, what is now known as the High
Street of Swindon must have presented
quite an interesting, if not picturesque,
appearance. Unfortunately, we have no written history to which we may refer for information on those
particular times, not even of those of the latter
period of, say, two hundred years. But it is simply
wonderful, when we think of it, how much we owe to
compensations. The other day my attention was
called to what appeared to be the enormous claw of
an ordinary-sized cray-fish. On taking the fish into
my hand, I found it had only one claw, the second
one having been torn off near the first joint. Here,
then, was an evidence of the law of compensation
exhibiting itself in one of the humblest forms of
life. It was by means of its claws that this simple
crustacian of our rivers and brooks moved about and
enjoyed what life it had. By accident, or some other
cause, it had lost one claw, and the law of compensation

had given it extra strength and size to the other.
It is so in the higher forms of life, when the loss of
one of the senses quickens the touch and grasp of the
other senses ; and more especially in the case of the
blind, by giving them a keener appreciation of music
and a knowledge of the laws of harmony and sound.
And it is so in the history of a nation. It is absolutely essential for the good of mankind that the
history of every race should be handed down to its
successors. To most of us this has been done
through the means of the Printing Press and the
written record. But there are thousands of instances
where this kind of evidence must be looked for in
vain. And when this is the case, we are almost certain
to find the law of compensation manifesting itself,
and giving us, to some extent at least, what we
require. Before the Printing Press, men who prepared
the history of their times for their successors worked
with greater care and precision than they do now.
They were less cosmopolitan than they are now ;
"utilitarianism" was not in their vocabulary ; they
threw themselves and their characters into everything
they did, and we are enabled to tell much about those
people who left us their old gable-roofed houses ;
who intersected the fronts of their dwellings with
string-courses ; who were particular in the formation
of their door-way jambs and lintels, their mullioned
windows, and a thousand and one other matters in
connection with their domestic architecture, but in far
more ways and matters in connection with their
glorious church architecture. The old gable-roofed
houses—which, by the way, have been gradually
disappearing for many years past—in the High-street,
Swindon, tell us of a time when the town was not
only visited, but actually taken possession of, by what
must have been a considerable body of men from the
"Low Countries," and I purpose taking these people

and dividing them into two sections, and then attempt to see what their particular object and business was in coming here. But before making this attempt, I am free to admit I have neither chapter nor verse for much which I may advance, and that the authority for a great deal of what I may write is only conjecture. As I have gone on making what enquiries I could into the matters about which I am writing, it has been brought to my recollection that when a child I had heard of a tradition among the old people that formerly there were many persons "from abroad" living in Swindon, and, I am free to admit, this recollection has assisted me very materially in my conjectures.

So far as I know, there are only four old houses in the town, and one outside of it, namely, at Westlecott, to which dates can be assigned with any positive degree of accuracy. They are the "Bell" in the High-street, the farm house at Westlecott, the offices of Messrs. Kinneir and Tombs, opposite the Market-place, the two houses now occupied by Messrs. Chapman, Bros., butchers, and Mr. Evans, corn merchant, High-street, and the old house which formerly stood in Wood-street, and was occupied by Mr. E. Smith, butcher, but which was recently pulled down for the erection of Messrs. Chandler and Sons' carpet ware-house. These five houses have, or had, not only dates exposed conspicuously on their fronts, but four of them have had, in addition, the initials of their for-mer owners and builders. I will give them priority in the order of their dates. The "Bell" comes the first. But here, as in another case, the date stone which undoubtedly was placed somewhere in front of the house, and probably over the principal entrance door, was lost long ago. The date, however, that of 1515, was preserved by being painted or cut on the sign, which, previous to the alterations of a few years ago, hung out over the footway of the street.

The second house in the order of time is the old manor house at Westlecott. In the south wall of the house there is inserted a small stone, on which is deeply cut in relief the following initials and date:

There can, I think, be no possible doubt about this stone. The Manor of Whicklescotte was bought at the Dissolution (1539) by John Goddard, of Upham, and has remained in the possession of the Goddard family from that time till now. John's immediate successor was possibly Thomas, and he, building himself a house on the estate, put his name and the date of erection to it.

The next in order of time are Messrs. Kinneir and Tombs' offices. These premises have undoubtedly undergone so many alterations that nothing of their original character remains, except a small date stone with initials which was discovered under thick coats of plaster over one of the doors at the last alteration. The stone bears the following, deeply cut in relief :—

Next come the houses occupied by Messrs. Chapman and Evans. And here again, as in the case of the "Bell," the initials and date are preserved, in the absence of the original date stone, by being cast on the heads of two of the spouts fixed on the front for the purpose of carrying off the water from the roof, as follows :—

G. H.   1631.

The only remaining date stone of which I at present know anything is one which was recently discovered, like the one at Messrs. Kinneir and Tombs', under layers of mortar and lime-wash, in the old house at the top of Wood-street. It was found in one of the corners of the front, not far from the eaves (certainly not its original position), and after being cleaned was inserted in one of the walls in the new building at the back of the premises. It reads thus:—

That there have been many other similar date stones to these lost in the various restorations and alterations, and also that there still remain many others yet to be found, and, I would venture to hope, taken better care of, there can be no doubt. These, however, which we have will serve my present purpose, and enable me, I trust, to show how they are connected with the history of our old town centuries ago, and with two separate and distinct industries : the supplying of the inner man with creature comforts, and the back of the individual with clothes and raiment.

The original builders of "The Bell" were undoubtedly from Holland, or from the Low Countries of Flanders ; people who in their day were great colonizers, and whose greed for making money by almost any conceivable means, and for the mere purpose of saving it, was proverbial. They were counted the chief manufacturers for the world of their day : they were very clanish, and they were scrupulously sensitive on religious matters, and were prepared to suffer persecution for their belief.

But why did they build and establish the "Bell," Swindon, the "Old Royal Oak," Wootton Bassett, the "Castle and Ball," Marlborough, and possibly a number of other "publics" in this part of Wiltshire ? I have already said I have but little chapter and verse authority, but nevertheless, I venture the assertion that it was as well to help them in the carrying on of a contraband trade in spirituous liquors as to meet the necessities of the ever increasing numbers of their fellow countrymen, who were constantly arriving in this neighbourhood with the view of being employed in the cloth working trade along the Stroud Valley, as well as along the banks of the Wiltshire Avon ; or, it may be, to act as intermediaries, or middle men, between the wool growers of the Wiltshire Downs and those whose business it was to manufacture the wool into cloth. But for the present I must leave the cloth working business alone, and confine myself to the more spiritual business of strong drinks. I have to connect the "Bell" with certain rude but highly characteristic pottery-ware, known as Bellarmines, and the way in which I do this must be taken *cum grano*. These curious old liquor or ale pots are referred to at length by all writers on pottery, and there has been no less than three exhibitions of specimens at meetings of the Wiltshire Archæological Society. At the first meeting of the society, in October, 1853, Mr. Cunnington exhibited one which had been found at Devizes Castle ; and at the same meeting Mr. R. Stratton exhibited two which were found at Broad Hinton. At the meeting at Swindon, in 1860, the Rev. G. A.

Goddard exhibited two which were found when digging the cellars for Clyffe Vicarage house, and I have in my possession two very fine specimens which were found near Bassett Down. It was not until 1626 that pottery of even so rude a character as these Bellarmines was made in England, in which year, on the 24th October, letters patent were granted to Thomas Rous and Abraham Cullen, who had both evidently come from the Low Countries to put into practical operation an invention which they claimed to have made for the manufacture of pots and pitchers. Chaffers, in his work, gives very full particulars of the petition to the Queen, which was presented by Rous and Cullen, for permission to make and sell in England these pots and pitchers, together with much interesting matter. Jewitt, in his *Ceramic Art*, refers more briefly to the Bellarmines, but quite sufficient for my purpose to quote. He says :—

The *Bellarmine*, or *Grey Beard*, or *Long Beard*, as it was commonly called, was a stone-ware pot of bottle form, mostly with a handle at the back and ornament on the front. The neck is narrow, and the lower part, or "belly," as it is technically called, very wide and protuberant. They were in very general use at the "ale-houses" to serve ale in to customers, and were of different sizes—the *gallonier* containing a gallon ; the *pottle pot*, two quarts ; the *pot*, a quart ; and the *little pot*, a pint. The jugs were derisively named after Cardinal Bellarmine, who died in 1621. The cardinal having, by his determined and bigoted opposition to the reformed religion, made himself obnoxious in the Low Countries, became naturally an object of derision and contempt with the Protestants, who, among other modes of showing their detestation of the man, seized on the potter's art to exhibit his short stature, his hard features, and his rotund figure, to become the jest of the ale-house and the byword of the people. Allusions to the bellarmines are very common in the productions of the English writers of the period.

Ben Jonson, in his *Gipsies Metamorphosed*, gives the following amusing version of the origin of these vessels :—"Gaze upon this brave spark struck out of Flintshire upon Justice Jug's daughter, then sheriff of the county, who, running away with a kinsman of our captain's, and her father pursuing her to the Marches, he great with justice, she great with jugling, they were both for the time turned into stone upon sight of each other here in Chester ; till at last (see the wonder !) a jug of the town ale reconciling them, the memorial of both their gravities—his in beard, and hers in belly—hath remained ever since preserved in picture upon the most stone jugs of the kingdom."

In another place he says :—

> " Whose, at the best, some round grown thing, a *jug*
> *Faced with a beard*, that fills out to the guests."

In another play, the *Ordinary*, is the following :—

> " Thou thing,
> Thy belly looks like to some strutting hill,
> O'ershadowed by thy rough beard like a wood ;
> Or like a larger jug that some men call
> A *Bellarmine*, but we a *Conscience ;*
> Whereon the lewder hand of pagan workman
> Over the proud ambitious head hath carved
> An idol large, with beard episcopal,
> Making the vessel look like tyrant Eglon."

In the curious play of *Epsom Wells*, one of the characters, while busy with ale, says, " Uds bud, my head begins to turn round ; but let's into the house. 'Tis dark. We'll have one *Bellarmine* there, and then *Bonus nocius.*"

These are but few of the illustrations that might be brought forward from the old writers, but they are sufficient to show its common use. The ale pots thus being formed with the corpulent proportions and the " hard-mouth visage" of the cardinal, became a popular and biting burlesque upon him From them, too, from the face upon the ale *mug* or ale pot, the vulgar name of " mug" for the human face is probably derived.

It is unnecessary for my present purpose to enquire by what name these quaint-looking old jugs were known previous to their being christened Bellarmines, or how long before the time of the Protestant-hunting and persecuting Cardinal they were in use in Holland and Flanders, but it was probably some considerable period. What I have to do is to suggest, if nothing more, that they were not brought to this country empty, but were made the receptacle for the conveyance of those peculiar spirituous liquors for which Holland and the Low Countries were famous, and for which no doubt the Dutch and Flemish cloth-workers who had settled down in Wilts and Gloucester had retained a special liking. I well remember once discussing with the Rev. G. A.

Goddard the question, " How is it that so many
Bellarmines or Greybeards have been found in the
immediate neighbourhood of the northern edge of
the Wiltshire Downs, and generally in a manner
which indicated that they had been placed where found
for safety and in secrecy?" The opinion of the
reverend gentleman distinctly was that when they
were placed there they were full of that particular
spirituous liquor, prepared from the juniper berries, for
which Holland and the Low Countries were both then
and now so celebrated, namely, Geneva or Hollands :
that the spirit was brought into this country in a
clandestine manner by smugglers, who, landing on the
south coast, had their depôts or stores on the most
unfrequented parts of the Wiltshire Downs, and from
thence they further removed it to places where they
could be in direct communication with those who
would become its ready consumers in the cloth working districts along the Stroud Valley, and along the
banks of the Wiltshire Avon, and, I will now venture
to add, as my own suggestion, from which such
hostelries as " The Bell," Swindon, the " Royal Oak,"
Wootton Bassett, and other old Dutch houses obtained a portion, if not the bulk, of their supply
of that particular spirit which the Dutchman, but of
course no other man, loved so well, just as a reminder
and a reminiscence of that home across the sea where
the juniper berry thrived so luxuriantly.

Here, then, we have certain things which we may
put together and see what we can make out of them
in their collective form. When I deal with the date
stones, I shall attempt to show how from one cause
and another many persons from Holland and Flanders
came into this neighbourhood with the view of
engaging in what was then a somewhat new, but
which they developed into a most important, industry.
These people had among them some of the most

D

skilled workmen of the world of that time: they
were greedy for making money, and turning everything to some utilitarian purpose. They not only
knew how to build houses, but they could build them
in the most wonderful manner, and make them most
beautiful and picturesque. Is it not, therefore,
most probable, that wherever and whenever practic-
able, they built their own houses? There was everything in the style of architecture of the old "Bell"
Inn, Swindon, to show that they built it. And then
in their own country they had a most wonderful drink
made from a berry which was indigenous there, and
which they could hardly have found in England had
they wished, or, if so, only in small quantities and
of inferior quality. In the country to which they
had come there were the ales and various decoctions
which were drunk on high days and festivals, and
possibly on some other days as well. But we may
reasonably suppose none of them came up to the
standard of that sparkling spirit which carried so rich
an aroma for both taste and smell, and which
was peculiar to their own Fatherland. It may also
even be that some of the natives wanted to taste the
marvellous liquor, and would "give anything" for an
occasional supply. And what more natural than that
there should be a corresponding desire to grant that
supply? Indeed, there exists even now a grave
suspicion in some men's minds that a taste for the
Geneva or Hollands of the Dutchman has not altogether died out in England, and it may be that so
long as ladies of high degree love and crave for their
Eau de Cologne, ladies of low estate will still indulge
in their "just a thimbleful of gin."

The nomenclature of Public House Signs is both
peculiar and interesting, but it does not come within
my present purpose. I would however suggest that
the Dutchmen having built the house afterwards

known as the " Bell," as a place of entertainment for
man and beast, took some means for exhibiting the
" only true and original " vessel in which the liquor,
for which their country was so famous, was " brought
over," as a sign that the right stuff was to be had
within ; that this peculiar vessel was afterwards called
the Bellarmine ; that in course of time, for various
reasons, it was found necessary to make contractions,
and save both words and breath, and therefore Bellarmine became Bell, which it has ever since remained.

And then as to the surreptitious storing and sale of
the liquor, and the origin of our licensing laws: the
matter is altogether too big for an occasional paper
or two; it might require volumes of space to
elucidate. There is generally, however, but a very
faint conception of the restrictions placed on the
importation of things from abroad in those days. In
the *Lansdown MSS.*, there is given a very curious
petition, addressed by a person of the name of
Simpson, directly to the Queen, Elizabeth, praying
for permission to import and sell stone drinking pots,
or Bellarmines. As I have already noticed, a somewhat similar petition to this was presented to the
Queen by Rous and Cullen. The petition, which
is very curious, is worth reproduction. It reads thus:

" The sewte of William Simpson, marchaunt.—Whereas one Garnet
Tynes, a straunger living in Acon, in the part beyond the seas, being
none of her ma[tie] subjects, doth buy uppe all the pottes made at
Culloin, called *Drinking stone pottes* and he onelie transporteth them
into this realm of England, and selleth them : It may please your ma[tie]
to graunte unto the sayd Simpson full power and onelie license to
provyde, transport, and bring into this realm the same or such like
drinking pottes ; and the sayd Simpson will put in good suretie that it
shall not be prejudiciall to anie of your ma[ties] subjects, but that he will
serve them as plentifullie, and sell them at as reasonable price as the
other hath sold them from tyme to tyme.

" Item. ' He will be bound to double her ma[tie] custome by the
year, whenever it hath been at the most.

" Item. ' He will as in him lieth, draw the making of such like

potte into some decayed town within this realm, wherebie manie a
hundred poor men may be sett a work.

"Note. 'That no Englishman doth transport any potte into this
realm, but only the said Garnet Tynes ; who also serveth all the Lowe
Countries and other places with pottes."

If there was all this trouble and difficulty in
obtaining leave and license to import and sell liquor
pots, is it not fair to suppose that the difficulty to
obtain a license to import and sell the liquor itself
would be insurmountable, and that men would
therefore prefer to introduce it in the surreptitious
manner I have indicated, namely, by landing it at
convenient points on the south coast, "running" it
on to the Wiltshire Downs, and then secreting
it at convenient spots, from whence it might be supplied to such old Dutch hostelries as the Bell, the
Royal Oak, or the Castle and Ball? At the present
time we can form but little or no conception of the
amount of "smuggling" that was carried on in this
country. As recently as forty or fifty years ago,
articles which are now in daily use by the poorest in
the land were the luxuries of the rich. I can myself
recollect men who professed to be smugglers offering
gin and tea for sale in Swindon, not openly, of course,
but on the introduction of persons who professed to
be "mutual friends," the transaction being always
carried on under the cloak of secresy. There were
Excise officers in those days, but no police, and no
doubt there was then a far more general disposition
to obtain exciseable articles in a surreptitious manner
than there would be now through the exhorbitant and
even prohibitory duties which were levied on such
articles, the price then charged for tea bought in a
regular way ranging from seven and eight to ten and
fifteen shillings per lb., the duty on tea as recently as
the days of our grandmothers being one hundred and
twenty per cent. on the cost price of the article itself.

I know a house in Swindon—it was then used as a small general shop—where orders for "smuggled" spirits and tea were regularly left   The order might not be executed for some months, but sooner or later the goods would be "left" according to order.

Some other Stones.

There are two other stones to which I may refer, although they bear no connection with those I have already noticed, and are of an altogether different character. One of them records a birth, and the other a death. The first is a curiosity in its way. At the present time the stone bearing the inscription is inserted in front of an out-house in the "Bell" yard —certainly not its original position. It was probably met with at one of the many alterations in the premises to which I have already referred, and being deemed too curious to be destroyed, was simply placed in its present position for preservation. The stone is about twenty-eight inches long by fourteen wide, and bears a well-cut inscription, as follows :—

RICHARD

FARMER

Junior, Bor^{n}

Sepr 26th

1740

ABCDE

aeiouy

The Bell Inn formerly belonged to, or was in the occupation of, a Mr. Farmer, and my suggestion is that the stone was in commemoration of, probably, the christening of a son and heir, and if so, the occasion to which it refers was long remembered by those who took part in it as being of a very exceptional and elaborate character. But what the A B C and the a e i o u y had to do with the birth of Richard Farmer I am quite at a loss even to con-- jecture. It can hardly be that he came into the world repeating the alphabet, or was at the early age of nothing endowed with the power of selecting vowels from consonants. If it was intended to act as a reminder to the youthful son and heir that the troubles of life began with A B C and a e i, the idea would seem to indicate an amount of refined cruelty which is hardly attributed to the School Boards and the administrators of our Education Acts in the present year of grace.

The other inscription records the death of John Alexander, and of Ann his wife. It is to be found on the top stone of a large tomb, about in the centre, on the north side of the old graveyard attached to the old parish church of Swindon, and reads as follows :—

IN MEMORY OF

JOHN ALEXANDER,

WHO DIED MAY 18, 1697,

AGED 117 YEARS.

ALSO ANN HIS WIFE,

WHO DIED MARCH 12, 1698,

AGED 98.

I can have no hesitation in saying this is not an original inscription. The tomb on which it is cut was probably not erected for a hundred years after the death of John Alexander. There are three other inscriptions on the tomb : one on each of the side panels, and one on the panel at the head of the tomb. The one inscription is to the memory of Francis Barnes, saddler, who died Nov. 17, 1780, aged 63 years, and to Elizabeth his wife, who died Feb. 27, 1795, aged 67 years. Another is to the memory of Henry Lubbock, saddler, who died May 10, 1816; the other inscription being to the memory of Susan Alexander, who died April 23, 1820, aged 60 years. What appears to me to be a very probable explanation of all this is: The tomb was erected by Francis Barnes to the memory of his wife, who pre-deceased him five years: that Elizabeth Barnes was the grand-daughter or great grand-daughter of John and Ann Alexander: that Susan Alexander was the daughter of Francis and Elizabeth Barnes, and the wife of Henry Lubbock: that at her death, in 1820, she being the last of her family, the opportunity was taken to add an inscription to the memory of the patriarch of the race about whom no doubt Susan had heard most wonderful tales told —Old John Alexander, who died in 1697, at the age of 117 years, and of his wife Ann, who died the following year at the good old age of 98. I should, of course, be pleased to find conclusive evidence that a former inhabitant of Swindon did actually reach the extraordinary age of 117 years, as recorded on the tomb-stone in the old churchyard, but I am bound to admit that the evidence at present appears to be based on what I may call "hear-say"—that the inscription is merely the permanent form given to an oral tradition, handed down in the family, the last of whom was Susan.

᚛Flemish᚜Cloth᚜Workers.᚛

UT what I wish more particularly to deal with, are other traders beside those engaged in keeping ale and beer houses. There are engraven in *Gell and Gandy's Pompeiana* certain inscriptions which were found upon the door-posts of certain of the excavated houses among the ruins of the city of Pompeii. Although there is a difference of opinion as to the precise construction of these inscriptions, there is no possible doubt about their giving, in addition to the name of the owner or occupier of the house, some particulars of the trade or business carried on within, or of the kind of goods manufactured there. And as these inscriptions range back to a time which may be said to be from eighteen hundred to two thousand years ago, the practice of using "signs" for business purposes is undoubtedly of great antiquity. But it was not only trades or distinct branches of manufacture which indulged in marks and signs. Many of the workmen of the middle ages were art workmen in the strictest sense of the word : they not only threw an individual character into their work, but they were careful to stamp with their mark their productions so that they might be known and valued from all others ; and thus we have the origin of " Trade Marks," a something which was a guarantee of the excellence or of the special character of the thing produced. Every potter had his mark, by the sign of which his work has ever since been known. Potters' marks on porcelain of Chinese manufacture are known to extend as far back as the year 25 of the Christian era. In Italy they are first met with in 1482, but they are not met with on the pottery of Spain, Germany, Holland, or France until a considerable later period. The names of nearly a thousand potters of the Roman period, as found stamped in relief, on coralline or samian red ware, discovered in London, is given in Roach Smith's illustrations of " Roman London." But the first date found on any pottery or porcelain of English manufacture appears to be that of 1670, and Thomas Toft is given as the name of the maker. A remarkable feature of these marks is that they are generally either the initial letters of the maker's name or some peculiar, and not unfrequently grotesque, combination of them, a date in many cases being added. One of the very earliest Italian marks consists of the date .1531. and the initials .f.x.A.R.

But what, I may be asked, has this to do with the date and initial stones found at Swindon ? Well: only this, and nothing more: The cloth workers used to do with their cloth precisely the same as the potters did with their cups and mugs, their tea cups and their saucers, but more particularly with those examples of the potter's art which were to become a thing of beauty and a joy for ever, not only in times when men and women were suffering from some attack of chinamania, but at all times to the lover of art, of form, colour, and effect. They were so proud of their work that they put their mark and seal to it. It is the custom, even now, when the production of the most beautiful fabrics is due rather to the inventive faculties of the inventor or the builder of the machine by which the article is produced than to the ability of the man who waits upon the machine, to stamp or mark certain productions of the loom either with the maker's name or to shew the locality from whence it comes. More or less all productions of the loom are marked, from the coarse hempen goods for which one outer mark per bale suffices, to the dainty velveteen which has an inner mark, "every yard," as the leading advertisers say, to prevent imitations. These marks, however, meant a great deal more three hundred years ago than they do now.

But it may again be asked : What has this to do with the date and initial stones on the houses in Swindon? It shall now be my business to answer that question. The manufacture of woollen cloth in England goes back to very ancient times. The art was probably introduced into this country by the Romans, and certain it is that at the taking of the Domesday survey by order of William the Conqueror, there were found to be a number of mills established in those very neighbourhoods of Stroud, and along the banks of the Wiltshire Avon, where it has since been carried on with such wonderful success. It is recorded that at this time, that is, about 1086, there were eight mills at Hampton, one at Honley, and five at Bisley, all in Gloucestershire. I am particular in noticing that there were five mills at Bisley, because it was at Bisley that the owner of the old house in Newport Street lived before it was purchased by the late Mr. John Harding Sheppard, and I intend making that circumstance

one of the links in the chain to show that Swindon was formerly connected with the wool trade. At Cirencester, we know, the woollen trade was carried on as early as the reign of Edward III., and further that there was established in that town a company of weavers in the reign of Henry IV., their old Hall still remaining standing as one of the antiquarian relics of that town. But the manufacture of cloth as carried on in these early days was of the most primitive character, and the article produced correspondingly rude. The master clothier of these days bought his wool in some one or other of the market towns, and, conveying it home on the backs of horses or mules, carried on the various processes needed to convert it into cloth in his own home, for with the exception of the felling all was done by hand down to the latter half of the eighteenth century, when the invention of the gig-mill and the carding engine, the jenny, and the mule, brought about the building of mills and a greater sub-division of the several processes. It does not seem at all probable that the manufacture of woollen cloth was ever carried on at Swindon, but it no doubt was a market for wool and wool combing ; and wool stapling was undoubtedly carried on here to a considerable extent, and among others by members of the Sheppard family, in the house adjoining that in the front of which one of the old date and initial stones is still to be seen. Until a comparatively recent period England was the great wool growing country of the world, and Wiltshire was one of the great wool growing counties of England. At the beginning of the present century Wiltshire had 701,000 sheep, which produced an average annual clip of 8,144 packs of 240lb. each of wool, which was far in excess of the production of any other county of equal size. Now, singular as

it may appear, from the repute which English
clothiers have so long enjoyed, the bulk of our
English wool was exported to Flanders for manufacture into cloth. At one time our trade in the
exportation of wool was of the greatest national
importance ; in fact, our commerce was almost
confined to the exportation of wool, which was the
great staple commodity of England, and upon which,
more than any other, in its raw or manufactured
state, our national wealth has been founded. The
first serious attempt made to improve the English
make of cloth was in the reign of Edward III., when
that king, in the year 1331, taking advantage of the
discontent among the merchants of Flanders, invited
them to come over and settle in this country. No
doubt many did accept this invitation, and much was
done towards utilising the consumption of English
wool in the country where it was grown. For some
two or three hundred years, however, but very little
real advancement appears to have taken place in the
manufacture of English cloth. Whether it was that
those who came over here from Flanders remained
only for a time, or that they did not keep up in
inventive and manufacturing ability with their
countrymen who remained at home, I cannot say,
but it appears certain that the very best cloth continued to be made in Flanders, and that, too, chiefly
from English grown wool, and the productions of
these Flemish cloth workers were as marvellous
as were the productions of those artist workmen in
pottery, to which I have already referred; and we
find that there gradually grew up among them the
desire to mark their productions in the same manner
as the potter, and the goldsmith, and other art workmen marked theirs. But after languishing, as it
were, for a century or two, the art of cloth working
towards the end of the sixteenth and the beginning

of the seventeenth centuries received a wonderful waking up. Flanders, Holland, and the Low Countries generally, were in a fever of excitement and turmoil. Strong religious feelings were being frequently exhibited, and religious feuds and persecutions were of common occurrence, and men like Cardinal Bellarmine became a power which men had either to submit to or to rebel against. At this time, no doubt, many of the Flemish master cloth workers voluntarily sought an asylum in this country, and they brought not only their art, but also their marks with them, and as they settled down in towns ; along the Stroud Valley and the Wiltshire Avon, and built houses for themselves, they put their marks, which sometimes consisted only of their initials and a date, but sometimes was some elaborate device, over their doors as we now see them. But they did something more than that ; they affixed to their pieces of cloth, after it had been duly measured off and rolled up ready for the market, small leaden labels, generally about the size of an English farthing, on which there were stamped in relief marks or signs, corresponding with those which they had cut in stone on their house fronts. And this was practically their "Trade mark." And this practice of those who made a superior or special kind of cloth was, no doubt, followed by those who were celebrated for a particularly fine clip of wool, and hence the origin of the date and initial stones on the old houses at Swindon. As I have pointed out, although Swindon never was a cloth manufacturing place—the absence of the necessary water course would satisfy us on that point—its position just off the Downs, from whence the best of the Wiltshire wool would come, and the facilities which existed for conveying it from hence to the Stroud Valley, would seem to point it out as possessing special advantages for a wool market. My theory, then, with regard to these Swindon stones is this: That they indicated some branch establishment of probably a Bisley cloth worker, or of a wool-stapler's business of sufficient repute to have its own independent mark.

I may here say I have been often much puzzled with these leaden tokens or marks, which I have referred to as having been affixed to bales of cloth, when they have been brought to me with the request that I would say what *coins* they were. They are necessarily very rude in manufacture, and the figures on them are often very curious. One day they chanced to form the subject of conversation with the Rev. Father Ignatius Grant, M.A., of Clifton, and on his being shewn some specimens I had in my possession, he was good enough to lend me for comparison a number of others, which he had "fished" up from the beds of the Avon and Frome rivers. I have no hesitation in accepting the reverend Father's opinion that they are "Trade Counters" of wool combers and cloth workers, and used to be affixed to the selvages of pieces of manufactured cloth as a warrant for its make or excellence. Indeed, one of these marks in my possession is an almost exact *fac-simile* of the stone on Messrs. Kinneir and Tombs' offices, whilst another has distinctly stamped on it the figure of a Bell. The Rev. Father Grant, writing to me on the subject, says in reference to his collection of these clothiers' tokens:—" Some of the larger tokens, as that which bears a figure like an anchor, were picked up in St. Wenburgh's Church, and near the altars of St. Blaize and of St. Catherine, the two patrons of clothiers, because they both suffered martyrdom, being combed to death by iron combs or spiked wheels." The reverend Father's explanation of the way in which these tokens got to the bottom of the rivers, from which they were centuries afterwards "fished," is both curious and interesting. In what we call the dark superstitious days, it was the custom with devout sailors, on entering or leaving a harbour, to propitiate their patron saints by throwing some coin or article of value into the river, the belief being that by clearing out the pocket in this manner the prospects of their becoming full again were heightened. When coins ran short, and no doubt they sometimes did run short, then, as well as now, these tokens were used instead, being probably abstracted from the bales of cloth with which the vessel was laden. These tokens have been found through the dredging machines, used in the river for the removal of the accumulated mud, and it is a remarkable fact that whenever the dredge goes a little deeper than usual, it is almost certain to bring up some coin, token, or relic of centuries ago, the deeper the dig made the more antique being the character of the article brought up. Even in the small collection of these leaden tokens which I now have in my possession, the character of the workmanship differs considerably.

But there may have been another and a special reason for the use of these date and initial stones on cloth workers' and wool sorters' premises, and it is this. As we have seen, there were no doubt men of mark and of capital, who came over to this country and settled down to trade on their own account, and there were others who were brought over simply as servants and workmen to benefit the English manufacturer, and there is no doubt but that this would not only lead to rivalry, and cause much bitterness and jealousy, and it may be that the master Flemings and others defended themselves by the use of these marks against the imitations of the English manufacturer carried on by the aid of imported servants, for it seems that these imported

workmen were not regarded with much favour by the
English parish authorities. The Rev. W. H. Jones,
in his history· of Bradford-on-Avon, gives us some
very interesting information on this point. He says,
referring to the changes which have taken place in
the leading manufacture of the town and neighbourhood, the first, in point both of time and importance,
was the introduction of a change in the manufacture
of cloth, which exercised for many years afterwards
a great influence on the trade, and consequently the
prosperity of the town. Hitherto only a coarse kind
of cloth,—a sort of drugget—had been made in
Bradford, but in 1659, Paul Methwin, the leading
clothier of the time, obtained from Holland some
"spinners," as they are termed, for the purpose of
obtaining, through them, the secrets of manufacturing the finer kinds of cloth. Before, however, the
foreigners had been long in Bradford, the parochial
officers required a bond of indemnity in the sum of
£100 to be entered into by Paul Methwin, lest they
might become chargeable to the parish. The deed
recites, that—"whereas Paul Methwin for *his own
proper gain and benefit* did fetch, or was at charge to
fetch or bring, out of Amsterdam, in Holland, into
the parish of Bradford, one Richard Jonson, *otherwise* Derricke Jonson, spinner, with Hectric, his wife,
and several small children,"—that, therefore, lest such
persons, as, it is intimated, was not unlikely, should
become a burden on the inhabitants of the parish,
the churchwardens and overseers for the time being,
thought it right to require security from Paul
Methwin in the sum above-mentioned, that he would
—"from time to time, and at all times hereafter
clearly acquit, save harmless, defend and keep, the
inhabitants of the said parish for ever free and
discharged from all manner of trouble, expense,
costs, charges, and damages whatsoever that they

may be put unto, or charged with, by the said
Richard Jonson, &c., for and towards the maintenance and breeding up of them."

It would be wrong, however, to encourage the
idea that all the Flemish cloth workers were received
in this manner, for such undoubtedly was not the case.
Matthew of Westminster, who wrote as early as the
middle of the fourteenth century (1350), while disput-
ing the absolute correctness of the assertion that " all
the world was clothed from English wool wrought in
Flanders," admits that the use of English wool by
Flemish weavers was one of the remarkable circumstances of his time.   Many years later Sir Edward
Coke declared that " wool is the worthiest and richest
commoditie of this kingdom of England ; for divide,"
says he, " our native commodities exported into tenne
parts, and that which comes from the sheepe's back
is nine parts in value of the tenne, and setteth great
numbers of people on worke ;" whilst John Aubrey,
the North Wiltshire antiquary, who, writing from
1659 to 1670, concerning the county of Wilts, says :
" If our nation in times past was the most famous for
the greatest quantity of wool in ye world, this
county had the most sheep of any other."   From
these and other similar references to wool and the
Flemish cloth workers, it will be readily seen how
much towns situate as that of Swindon were interested in the arrival of men who could manufacture
wool into cloth without the necessity of exporting the
wool to Flanders and then importing the manufactured article back into the country where the raw
material had been produced.   Successive English
rulers, even for centuries, did all that lay in their power
to encourage Flemish and other foreign cloth workers
to settle in this country, and whilst many of the
nobility entered into the trade, from the handsome
profits it brought them, there were many others who

E

amassed such fortunes through their connection with
the trade that in course of time they took their place
along with the nobles of the land.   In bringing my
notes on this particular branch of my subject to a
close, I cannot do better, for the purpose of showing
how important, as well as lucrative, this Wiltshire
wool business once was, than to quote from a very
interesting paper, by the Rev. W. H. Jones, on " The
Merchants of the Staple," published in the Wiltshire
Archæological Magazine for August, 1865, and from
whose history of Bradford-on-Avon I have already
quoted, as follows :—" Frequently have the descendants of such merchants risen to exalted positions.
Of John Halles' (a merchant of the staple, or wool-
stapler, of Salisbury) two children, his daughter,
Christian, married Sir Thomas Hungerford ; his son
William's only daughter and heir married Thomas
Wriothesly, Garter Principal King of Arms, and *his*
family (he dying without issue) became ennobled in
the person of his nephew, Thomas, Lord Wriothesly,
of Titchfield, in the County of Southampton.   Webb,
who, according to Aubrey, together with ' John Halle,'
bought up all the wool of Salisbury Plain, is still
represented by the Baronets of Odstock.   Greville
and Wenman, whom Aubrey speaks of as buying up
all the Cotswold wool, in fact as the great merchants
of Gloucestershire, are both now represented by
ennobled descendants.   One of the early members of
the Greville family is described as the ' flower of wool
merchants of all England ;' his descendant, Fulke
Greville, married the heiress of Lord Willoughby de
Brooke, and *their* son was created Lord Brooke, of
Brooke House, in the parish of Westbury, Wilts, a
title now held conjointly with that of Warwick,
by the Earl of Brooke and Warwick.   The family of
Wenman were ennobled in a subsequent age under
the same name, and in 1834 the title was revived, in

a descendant in the female line, by the creation of
Baroness Wenman, of Thame Park, in Oxfordshire.
From Stump of Malmesbury, the host on one occasion of Henry VIII., and the original grantee of the
Abbey, the preservation of which from utter ruin we
probably owe to him, descend some of our principal
nobility.   His only daughter married Sir Henry
Knyvett, and their two daughters became, the one,
Countess of Suffolk, the other Countess of Lincoln.
And Camden tells us that at the commencement of
the 17th century a clothier named 'Abbot' had three
sons, each of whom, at the same time, filled high and
honourable offices :—George Abbot was Archbishop
of Canterbury ; Robert Abbot was Bishop of Salisbury ; Sir Maurice Abbot was Lord Mayor of
London."

⌐Bush✳Houses.⌐

 FEEL no difficulty in assigning the date and initial stones, to which I have already referred, to these same Hollanders and people from Flanders and the Low Countries, to whom I attribute the building of the Bell and the other gable-roofed houses in the High Street, and which for many years past have been growing less in number, the Bell itself having been the last to be robbed of its ancient characteristics. Within the last few years it has become quite the fashion for traders and others to have their registered mark. To many persons this practice would seem to be something new. But it is nothing more than a revival, or modern adaptation, of a very ancient practice which prevailed principally among clothiers and potters. The general exhibition of "signs," setting forth the name of the person and the trade carried on, as we now see them in every town and village, is of comparatively recent date, although other means were taken for giving some distinctive character to a business and identifying it

with some particular person. The oldest, most
curious, and certainly the most conspicuous, of all
English signs are those affixed to ale or public
houses. And yet the practice, as it has more
recently existed, is of comparative modern origin, a
wisp of straw upon a pole, a birch pole, or some
growing ivy bush having been in many districts the
principal indication by which houses of entertainment
for man and beasts were known. Brand, in his
"Popular Antiquities," gives a chapter on "Ale
House or Tavern Signs," which no doubt will be very
interesting to those who are not already acquainted
with it. He says:—"Sir Thomas Browne opines
that the human faces depicted in ale-house signs, and
in coat-of-arms, are relics of paganism, these visages
originally typifying Apollo and Diana. Hudibras
asks a shrewd question on this topic, which we do not
remember to have seen solved—

> ' Tell me but what's the nat'ral cause
> Why on a sign no painter draws
> The full moon ever, but the half ?'

There is a familiar proverb that good wine needs no
bush ; nothing, that is, to indicate where it is sold.
From Good Newes and Bad Newes (1622) it would
appear that tavern-keepers anciently maintained both
a bush and a sign—

> ' I rather will take down my bush and sign
> Than live by means of riotous expence.'

Greene's Conceipt (1598) has it : 'Good wine needs
no ivie bush.' So in England's Parnassus (1600) we
find : 'I hang no ivie out to sell my wine ;' and in
Braithwaite's Strappado for the Divell (1615),
Bacchus is invoked as 'sole soveraigne of the ivy-
bush, prime founder of red-lettices,' &c. In Dekker's
Wonderful Yeare (1603) we read : 'Spied a bush at
the end of a pole (the ancient badge of a country
ale-house) ;' and similarly in Vaughan's Golden

Grove (1608): 'Like as an ivy-bush put forth at a vintrie is not the cause of the wine but a signe that wine is to bee sold there, so, likewise, if we see smoke appearing in a chimney, wee know that fire is there, albeit the smoke is not the cause of the fire.' Harris' Drunkard's Cup also supplies a quotation: 'Nay, if the house be not worth an ivie-bush, let him have his tooles about him; nutmegs, rosemary, tobacco, with other appurtenances; and he knowes how of puddle-ale to make a cup of English wine." Coles (1656) held that vintners made their garlands of box and ivy because their viridity was durable. He inclined to think, however, that ivy was preferred, 'because of the antipathy between it and the wine.' Poor Robin (1678) recites in his Perambulation from Saffron Walden to London—

> 'Some alehouses upon the road I saw,
> And some with bushes shewing they wine did draw.'

From Whimzies (1631) we gather that birch-poles were supplanted by signs in alehouses: 'He (the painter) bestowes his pencile on an aged piece of decayed canvas in a sooty alehouse, where *Mother Redcap* must be set out in her colours. Here hee and his barmy hostesse *drew* both together, but not in like nature; she in *ale*, he in *oyle;* but her commoditie goes better downe, which he means to have his full share of, when his worke is done. If she aspire to the conceite of a signe, and desire to have her birch-pole pulled downe, hee will supply her with one.' In Scotland a wisp of straw upon a pole is (or was) the indication of an alehouse. *Et unum* ale-wisp *ante me* is the expression in Dunbar's Will of Andro Kennedy, to which we have before had occasion to refer. 'In olde time,' as we read in the English Fortune-Teller (1609), 'such as solde horses were wont to put flowers or boughes upon their heads to reveale that they were vendible.' Upon the

same principle, it is presumed, an old besom (which
is but dried bush) is set at the topmast head of a
ship or boat for sale. The practice is also adverted
to in Nash's Christ's Teares over Jerusalem (1613), in
the course of his remarks upon the head-dresses
of the London ladies of his day—'Even as Angels
are painted in Church Windowes, with glorious
golden fronts, besette with Sunne-beames, so beset
they their foreheads on either side with glorious
borrowed gleamy *bushes;* which *rightly interpreted*
should signifie *beauty to sell,* since *a Bush is not else
hanged forth, but to invite men to buy.* And *in Italy,
when they sette any Beast to sale,* they *crowne his head
with Garlands, and bedeck it with gaudy blossoms, as
full as ever it may stick.'* The once familiar sign
of the Chequers seemingly was originally designed
for a kind of draughts-board, called tables, and
indicated that the game was to be played within.
From its colour and its similarity to a lattice, the
name suffered corruption into the red-lattice; by
which designation old writers frequently signify an
alehouse. Thus in Rigbie's Drunkard's Prospective
(1656)—

> ' The tap-house fits them for a jaile,
> The jaile to th' gibbet sends them without faile,
> For those that thro' a *Lattice* sang of late
> You oft find crying through an iron grate.'

The references are numerous. In Marston's Antonio
and Melida (1633), we read : 'As well-known by my
wit as *an alehouse by a Red Lattice.'* In Marmion's
Fine Companion we have: 'A watchman's widow at
the sign of the Red Lattice, in Southwark;' And
in Arden of Faversham (1592): 'His sign pulled
down, and his lattice borne away.' Again, in The
Miseries of Inforc'd Marriage (1607): ''Tis reason to
the *Red* Lattice, enemy to a sign-post;' and in Shakespeare's Henry IV. Falstaff's page is made to report

of Bardolph: 'He called me even now, my lord, through a *Red Lattice*, and I could see no part of his face from the window.' It is curious to observe that the Romans were familiar with the sign of the Chequers. It may be seen on the houses in exhumed Pompeii. On that of Hercules, for instance, at the corner of the Strada Fullonica, they are painted lozenge-wise, red, white, and yellow; and similar decorations are still to be seen on various other houses of that ancient city. Though the original meaning of the word is lost, the application of the designation to an alehouse survived to a recent period in Holborn, the sign being converted into *The Green Lettuce ;* and in the last will and testament of Laurence Lucifer, the old Batchiler of Limbo, contained in the Black Booke (1604), occurs this passage: 'Watched sometimes ten houres together in an alehouse, ever and anon peeping forth, and sampling thy nose with the *Red Lattice.*' The Gentleman's Magazine for June, 1793, has a communication to the effect that in the reign of Philip and Mary the Earl of Arundel acquired the right to license publichouses, and that, part of the armorial bearing of that noble family being a chequered board, publicans exhibited that as part of their signs, to shew that they were licensed; and in September, 1794, the same medium has an explanation that it represented the coat-of-arms of the Earls of Warenne and Surrey who bore checqui or and azure, and in the reign of Edward IV. enjoyed the privilege of licensing alehouses. But we should not omit the more plausible explanation that in the Middle Ages all matters of revenue were arranged by merchants, accountants, and judges on tables called exchequers, from their resemblance to chess-boards. The suspension of a chequered board indicated the office of a moneychanger, and the sign subsequently came to denote

an inn or house of entertainment, from the circumstance probably of the inn-keeper also pursuing the
trade of money-changer, as seaport towns still testify.
We have already seen that the chequers formed only
part of the sign. These were invariably painted on
the door-post (an example of this practice may still
be seen at the Swiss Cottage, Chelsea); and that
circumstance lends some color to the theory that
those who painted up the additional sign combined
with their trade the profession of money-changers,
and announced that fact by adopting the sign of the
Chequers. Chaucer's Merry Pilgrims, let us add, put
up in Canterbury at the sign of the Checker of
the Hope (*i.e.*, the Chequers on the Hoop); and the
inn is still pointed out in that city at the corner of
High Street and Mercery Lane. In the Corporation
Reports it is frequently mentioned under the title of
'The Chequer.' Its immediate vicinity to the cathedral of course rendered it specially appropriate for the
reception of the devout troop. Gayton on Don Quix-
ote, however, has a passage pointing to the derivation
of the sign from the circumstance of draughts and
backgammon being played in the houses to which it
was affixed. The host, he represents, taught his
bullies to drink *more Romano* (that is, according to
the number of letters in the errant lady's name);
which was a far more ingenious policy for drawing
guests to his house and keeping them there 'than our
duller ways of billiards, kettle pins, noddy boards,
tables, truncks, shovelboards, fox and geese, or the
like.' Flecknoe (1665), writing of 'your fanatick
Reformers,' observes: 'As for the SIGNS, they have
pretty well begun their Reformation already, changing the Sign of the Saluation of *the Angel and our
Lady* into the Souldier and Citizen, and the *Katherine
Wheel* into the Cat and Wheel; so as there only
wants their making the *Dragon* to kill *St. George*,

and the *Devil*, to tweak *St. Dunstan* by the nose, to make the Reformation compleat. Such ridiculous work they make of the Reformation, and so zealous are they against all Mirth and Jollity, as they would pluck down the Sign of the *Cat and Fiddle* too, if it durst but play so loud as they might hear it.' In Poor Robin's Perambulation (1678) the following lines occur—

> ' Going still nearer London I did come,
> In little space of time to Newington.
> Now as I past along I cast my Eye on
> The Signs of the *Cock and Pie*, and Bull and Lion.'

The British Apollo (1710) has—

> ' I'm amaz'd at the Signs
>   As I pass through the town :
> To see the odd mixture,
>   *A Magpye* and *Crown*,
> The *Whale* and the *Crow*,
>   The *Razor* and *Hen*,
> The *Leg* and sev'n *Stars*,
>   The *Bible* and *Swan*,
> The *Ax* and the *Bottle*,
>   The *Tun* and the *Lute*,
> The *Eagle* and *Child*,
>   The *Shovel* and *Boot*.'

The Compleat Vintner (1720) recites—

> ' Without there hangs a noble Sign,
> Where golden Grapes in Image shine—
> To crown the Bush, a little punch—
> Gut Bacchus dangling of a Bunch,
> Sits loftily enthron'd upon
> What's called (in Miniature) a Tun.'
>
> *   *   *   *   *
>
> ' If in Moorfields a Lady stroles,
> Among the *Globes* and *Golden Balls*,
> Where'er they hang, she may be certain
> Of knowing what shall be her Fortune ;
> Her Husband's too, I dare to say,
> But that she better knows than they,
> The pregnant Madam, drawn aside
> By promise to be made a Bride,
> If near her time, and in distress
> For some obscure convenient place,
> Let her but take the pains to waddle

About, till she observes *a Cradle*,
With the foot hanging tow'rds the door,
And there she may be made secure
From all the parish plagues and terrors,
That wait on poor weak Woman's errors ;
But if the head hangs tow'rds the House,
As very oft we find it does,   .
Avant, for she's a cautious Bawd,
Whose Bus'ness only lies abroad.'

The sign of the Bull and Gate exhibits an odd
combination of images.   It is a corruption of Boulogne
Gates, which Henry VIII. ordered to be removed
thence, and transported to Hardes, in Kent. Boulogne
Mouth, or the entry to the harbour of Boulogne, which
became a popular sign after the capture of that place
in 1544, was similarly converted within a century into
Bull and Mouth ; the sign being represented by a
black bull whose capacious mouth still arrests the
attention of sightseers in the neighbourhood of St.
Martin's-le-Grand.   So also the popular humorous
tradition, that the three blue balls now generally
indicating pawn-broker's shops mean that it is two to
one against the articles pledged ever being redeemed,
requires to be corrected by the statement that they
were the arms of the Medicis, a branch of which
family (together with many other Lombard houses)
settled in London at an early period, fixing their
quarters in the street which was called after them,
Lombard Street."

The hanging out of a "Bush" over the door as
indicating a house where beer was sold has been continued down to within the last thirty or forty years in
Swindon, and there now exists in the parish of
Chiseldon a licensed public house known by the name
of the "Bush Inn."   The practice, however, it must
be observed, was confined to a few days only in course
of the year, namely, on the annual feast, and certain
fair days.   So far as I can learn, there was neither
leave nor license required for these Bush Houses.

There was, however, I believe, a limit in the charge to be made for the beer which was sold. In no case was it to exceed three half-pence per quart, or six-pence per gallon! If I recollect aright, the licensing laws of those times precluded no person from selling at any time or place beer at a price not exceeding three half-pence per quart, providing it was not consumed on the premises where sold. The beer so sold at this price was probably purer than much of that which has been sold in later times, for it was generally understood not to be worth doctoring—it was simply the third, or possibly the fourth, running of the mash-tub. The product, however, could have been but a poor sample of that "nut brown ale" for which our forefathers were so famous, and in the brewing of which they were such adepts. From what I have said, I think it will be clear that the inducement to hang out a bush on the feast or fair day was not exactly that of being able to sell beer at three half-pence per quart, or that the attraction for visitors was exclusively that of imbibing third or fourth washings. I have referred to the Bush public house on the Marlborough road : so far as I know, the house since it has been fully licensed has been conducted in the most orderly manner. But there can be no doubt that formerly the hanging out of a bush was accepted as a sign that it was a rendezvous for disorderly as well as other characters. At Swindon there would be but four excuses in course of the year for hanging out the bushes, but when Chiseldon feast and the Swindon and Marlborough fairs were all combined to supply excuses at this particular house, the appearance of the bush was of so common an occurrence that the licensing magistrates of the division ultimately determined to duly license the premises, and thus give them some control over it, as well as enabling them to suppress a scandal which was somewhat notorious.

I recollect as many as five or six of these "Bush Houses" being open in different parts of Swindon on a fair day, and generally they seemed to enjoy a moderate amount of patronage, especially from those who wanted a little more rough and ready freedom than was to be enjoyed in the regularly licensed beer or public-house, for in these bush houses the attraction appeared to be rather the opportunity to indulge in a little fiddling or dancing than the drinking of beer ; or possibly the attraction may rather have been the combination of pleasures which these houses afforded. So far as I can learn, there was no legal supervision exercised over these houses, as there was over the licensed houses, and it was quite a common occurrence for fiddling and dancing to be carried on in them from early morning until late night, although it is simply impossible to conceive how they managed to find room for indulgence in such diversions, for the bush house was invariably some small cottage in which there was not room enough to "swing a cat." When the weather permitted, no doubt the yard and garden, and the whole premises, were devoted to the necessities of the occasion, and the inconveniences which had to be encountered in this as in many other matters no doubt gave an extra relish to the whole proceedings.

I have referred to the fiddler. Now, in these days the fiddler was quite an institution, and especially on these occasions. In these days there were no bands of music as there are now. The poorer classes but seldom practised instrumental music, and when there happened to be a musical family they were heard of far and wide. The piano was but rarely seen in even tradesmen's houses, the fiddle, the bass-viol, the trombone, the clarionet, the bugle, and the fife being the musical instruments most in vogue, and the players on these usually gravitated to the church or chapel choir, where they helped the services,

and not unfrequently drowned the voices of both
parson and clerk. Practically, the fiddle was the only
poor man's instrument, and the fiddler the only
musician who could truly wind him up to concert
pitch. At about the time to which I now more particularly refer — forty or forty-five years ago—the
principal musician for Swindon and the neighbourhood—that is, for the fair and feast days and the
country dance which was then indulged in by the
rustics—was a man who lived at Upper Stratton.
Early on the morning of the feast or fair day this man
would repair to one of the numerous Bush Houses,
where he would fiddle away the whole day through,
and sometimes far into the night. He was always
accompanied by his man or woman of business, whose
duty it was to collect the pence, generally, I believe,
a penny per dance per person. The fiddler would sit
out of the way in some corner whilst his secretary or
business agent would go round with his or her cap or
box and collect the pence, and when a stipulated
number of pence had been collected in this way the
secretary would turn Master of the Ceremonies,
arrange the dancers in proper order, and then, the
signal having been given, the fiddler "struck up," and
the dancers danced out their "pennoths" amid a scene
which may be easier imagined than described, and not
unfrequently amidst the wildest excitement. The
fiddler to whom I particularly refer—I knew him well
—was a man of two tunes and three words only. He
only knew two tunes: at all events he only played
two, and he was always ready to accommodate the
dancers by playing either the one or the other. The
way in which he proceeded to ascertain their wishes
on the point was this: scraping a few notes on his
fiddle, he would pause and say, "thick'en," and then
scraping a few notes of a different character—that is,
of his second tune—he would again pause and say,

"thuck'en." The votes of the dancers were then taken by acclamation on "thick'en" and "thuck'en," and then the dance began in right down good earnest. That fiddler was known to many persons as "Thick'en" or Thuck'en."

> "Thick'en" and " Thuck'en" were the only tunes he played ;
> "Thick'en" *or* " Thuck'en" were the only words he said.

There was positively no more comical sight to be seen in the whole fair than this old man, stuck up in a corner, with his eyes shut, his mouth screwed up, his head bent down over his fiddle, his arms in frantic agitation, but the lower parts of his body as immovable as a post, as he rasped away at his old fiddle, with a mob of half-demented men and women dancing away like mad to his music.

I have often, when listening to the charming music provided at the New Swindon concerts, contrasted the privileges enjoyed by the working classes of to-day, and compared them with those enjoyed by their predecessors of forty years ago, when their great delight was to dance at a Bush House or public on beer at ·three-halfpence per quart to the tune of

"THICK'EN OR THUCK'EN."

⟶Turnpike⁂Gates.⟵

TURNPIKE gates have now been for some years things of the past. When they were in existence they gave rise to a very extraordinary meeting of remarkable men and women once a year at least, namely, at the annual letting, of which due notice wa$s always given by advertisement. The tolls leviable at these gates were a very valuable consideration in very many instances, although the amount of the toll was not great. Generally, the amount leviable was regulated by the Act of Parliament which created the Trust: that is, the management under which the turnpike road was placed for the joint purposes of seeing that the wants of the general public were duly cared for, and the interest earned paid to the bond-holders, with whose capital the roads had been made and maintained. The roads belonging to a Trust did not often exceed, in this part of the country, more than 30 or 40 miles in length, whilst some of them were not more than six, eight, or ten miles long. Each Trust was under a body of Commissioners,

elected by the bondholders from among the principal
residents of the neighbourhood, and their clerk, who
attended to all financial matters, and a surveyor, who
saw to the keeping of the roads in proper order.   On
each turnpike gate-house there was affixed one or
more notice boards, on which there were painted in
large and legible characters certain extracts from
Acts of Parliament, with tables of the tolls leviable
on all kinds of carriages, horses, cattle, sheep, &c.,
using the road and passing through the gate.   And
by these tables both the renter of the tolls and the
public using the roads with horses, carriages, &c.,
were bound.   It was customary to levy one toll only
on any particular Trust, however many gates there
might be.   For instance, you might drive from Swindon to Chippenham for one toll, although five or six
turnpike gates would have to be passed through on
the journey.   At the gate where the toll was paid a
ticket would be given which would clear all the other
gates on that Trust.   But a person could not drive a
mile outside of the town of Swindon on either of the
four main roads without having to pay a toll at one of
four gates, simply because the four roads belonged to
four separate Trusts.   A person riding or driving
from Wroughton to Stratton would have to pay toll at
two gates, as would also a person going from Coate
to Shaw.   But he might go from Swindon to Chippenham, or to Marlborough, or even to Burford, in
Oxfordshire, for one toll only.   I notice this in particular to show that it was no easy matter to get at
the bottom of either turnpike toll finance or turnpike
geography.   The matter required a great deal of cool
calculation, keen observation, and not a little special
and peculiar information.   Indeed, the "characters"
which used to be assembled at a turnpike toll letting
were well worth taking stock of, and always repaid
the attentive observer of their doings for any reason-

F

able time spent on them. The Commissioners always
did their own "letting," and as Swindon was the central or chief town on several Trusts, and as the letting
of several trusts was usually arranged for on one
and the same day, the letting generally drew together
in the town, as I have said, a large number of men
and women of the most positively distinctive character. I have seen at these lettings what I may call
quite an organised system of "war to the knife"
carried on, sometimes by the "bidders" among themselves, and sometimes by the bidders in a body
against the Commissioners. Except on some rare or
special occasion, the tolls were started by the Commissioners at an upset amount, which was declared in
the advertisement. When this sum, which was usually
the amount at which the tolls were let at the last
previous letting, was considered by the would-be
bidders to be too high, and they could agree among
themselves to act in unison, they would, as with one
voice, badger, bully, and browbeat the Commissioners
for an hour at a time in their efforts to get a lower
sum to start from. It was but seldom, however, they
succeeded in this, and I have known instances where
the Commissioners have been forced to withdraw the
lot, and either to keep it in their own hands for a
year, or to call a second auction later on. But I have
known another kind of result to happen. After all
the vowing and protesting that anyone who took the
gate at such a sum would be ruined, I have known an
outsider timidly make a bid of an advance, when, like
a flash of lightning, the scene was changed, and those
who had been vowing with all their might would
tumble over each other in their anxiety to bid against
the interloper: the lot being ultimately "knocked
down" at an advance of ten, twenty, or even fifty per
cent. on the upstart price. I have known of a run
like this being made, with, of course, a corresponding

effect on the price, when one of the fraternity has broken loose from the party, and has bid up to take a gate over the head of, say, the person who had been the lessee for the past year, and who desired to keep it on.

But to understand the thing aright, and to enjoy the fun when it comes off, it is necessary we should begin at the beginning : and to do this we must watch the arrival of the bidders some hours before the time announced for auction. As they assemble, we shall find them to be about as determined looking and thorough going a lot, both of men and women, as we have ever clapped eyes on. As a rule, they look weather beaten and strong featured. If either of them happens to have a round face and bullet shaped head, the eyes are sure to twinkle, and to look as though they had seen a thing or two in their time, and could look through a mile-stone quite as far as the best pair of eyes that man or woman was ever blest with ; whilst for the lips, they are fimly set, and by no means superfluous in material. As they assemble, they start off in knots or parties, and talk earnestly together. And then there are conferences between representatives from each party, and there may be a general conference, or there may be an adjournment to some inn for a liquoring-up, and then more splitting up into parties, and more conferences, the conversation being always carried on in an under-tone, so that no outsider may hear what is going on. It was, no doubt, owing to the success, or want of it, at these preliminary conferences that the gatemen were enabled to carry, or failed to carry, their points, and make their own terms at the letting which was about to take place. Now all these men had what were understood to be their own districts, to which they were expected to confine themselves. Occa-sionaly, no doubt, this rule was broken. when the whole fraternity would combine to punish the trespasser after a manner that was generally successful. I recollect on one occasion that there was quite a number of strangers from the neighbourhood of Reading and Windsor at one of the Swindon lettings, and they ran every lot that was offered. They did not, to the best of my recollection, take a single gate, but they made those who did take them pay for them most dearly, the aggregate amount of the lettings being some hundreds of pounds in advance of what they were the year before. This action was understood to be in retaliation for a visit paid to their district by a well-known gateman from the Swindon district.

We will now enter the room in which the letting is to take place, which would be at either the Goddard Arms or the Town Hall, and here we find two or three, or more, Commissioners, with the clerk and surveyor, seated at a table, on which there stands, amidst books and papers, a large sand minute glass. As the company enter the room the leaders begin to chaff the Commissioners, and it may be the clerk and surveyor, at whose expense they try to get up a little amusement by preferring complaints, asking questions, or indulging in remarks of a facetious character. But this is soon over, and business is commenced by the chairman putting up the first lot, and announcing the sum beyond which they are prepared to receive biddings. This almost invariably led to a great deal of badinage, and efforts to get the amount reduced, on the ground that it was double what the " Geat" was worth. As a rule the Commissioners remained obdurate, and proceeded to put their seal to their declaration that they would not reduce the figure by turning the sand glass and allowing the sand to run. When this was once done the ball was fairly opened, and there was no going back—the gate put up would be either let or not let, so far as that day's proceedings were concerned. This setting the glass running always produced a remarkable and striking effect on the company. It would be known beforehand if the present holder intended taking the gate on—this would have been settled at the preliminary conferences, to which I have referred—and if so, he would be allowed to bid, or if there happened to be some new comer in the field he would bid, and his doing so would be received as a signal for an outburst of passion or merriment, or both combined, by the company, and then the biddings would go on fast and furious. If, however, there was no intention to bid, the badinage with the Commissioners would be continued until the last grain of sand in the glass had run down, and the whole of the proceedings, so far as the letting of the lot for that day was concerned, was settled. But we will suppose that there is to be a competition for the lot, and that the present holder is desirous of retaining it. He makes his intention known by making some such remark as " I'll have a pound." And saying this he advances to the table and deposits on it, with the clerk, one month's rent, estimated by the sum at which the gate was put up. When it is intended that this person shall have the gate for another year, the game of merriment is continued at its height, and every effort is made to divert the attention of the Commissioners, as well as of the company, from the glass until the sand has fairly run down, when the matter is settled, and the bidder declared to be the purchaser of the tolls for the year. But when there is to be competition, the " I'll have a pound" is followed by " I'll have another," sometimes in quick succession, so that the bidding is increased several pounds in the course of the running of the sand, or may be the " I'll have another" is purposely

kept back until the last grain is on the eve of dropping. And then the game of merriment is resumed,
the glass is again turned, and this is repeated again
and again so long as there is a bid and a deposit
from any new blood, until there has been a clear run
of the glass after the last bid was made.

As I have said, these gate-men were shrewd,
hard-headed men of business who were up to a thing
or two, and who knew what's what as well as most
men. And generally they were very successful men,
and many of them made handsome fortunes. When
they once took a gate they were loth to give it up.
They generally took a number of gates, and were
thus enabled to compensate themselves for those
which did not pay, it being often deemed preferable to
keep out a stranger at a loss than to allow the secrets,
which there were more or less to every gate, being
known. The responsibilities of a turnpike-gate
lessee in a large way were necessarily very great, and
they had to depend greatly on the honesty of their
servants to whom they entrusted the duty of collecting the tolls, and generally, I believe, had to render
an account of their takings once a week. A considerable amount of capital was also required for the
business, for it was the invariable practice of the
Commissioners to request monthly payments in
advance for the whole period of the letting. I think
it but fair to a class of people who have now passed
away—the gate-keepers having charge of the gates—
to say that I do not recollect even a single charge of
embezzlement, or an abuse of the trust reposed
in them by their employers, being preferred against
any one of them in the Swindon division.

I have alluded to women as well as men being
present at these lettings: These would be women
who were employed by the lessees to live in the gate-
houses, collect the tolls, and who, day and night, the

year through, would have to be ready to the call of
" Gate."   Many of the men present would also be
similarly engaged, and therefore would have a strong
personal interest in the proceedings, for should an
outsider take the gate there was every probability of
their not only losing their employment, but of having
also to give up house and home.   It was always clear
to see that they regarded the proceedings with the
liveliest interest, and the way in which they showed
this helped greatly to give character to the scene.
And yet their occupation was a most trying one, and
in many person's estimation a most undesirable one,
for having to be ready to the call of " gate" both day
and night, there was but little rest for them.   Indeed,
in these days travelling on turnpike roads often led to
a great deal of manœuvring.   When long out and
home journeys had to be made, and there was the
possibility of accomplishing them within the twenty-
four hours, the start would be made shortly after
midnight, or so long after only as would admit of the
last gate on the return journey being passed before
the following midnight, for the tolls ran from midnight to midnight.   To save a toll often necessitated
a great deal of both early and late travelling with
horses and cattle.   All this, however, has now passed
away, and turnpike gates with their keepers, and
turnpike gate lessees, have become, in most parts of
the country, at least, things of the past.

·≋✱Newspapers✱≋·

Y connection with newspapers commenced at a very early date in my little history, long before School Board inspectors were employed to see that children of tender age were engaged in making a given number of school attendances. And it arose in this way: At that time—that is to say, forty or fifty years ago—there was a widow woman living in Red Lion Court, Fleet Street, London, who carried on a newspaper business. I think she must have originally belonged to the neighbourhood of Swindon, for she had friends and acquaintances here and hereabouts, and this enabled her to absorb, as it were, the newspaper trade of our district. I do not say she was the only newspaper agent who did business at Swindon and the neighbourhood, but at the time of which I write I knew no other. She was not the only person who sent newspapers here, for I have heard of a daily paper coming into the town with such regularity as the times would admit of, the conveyance being by coach or carrier, and these were, as a rule, obtained

second hand from some coffee shop in London. I
may say the first daily newspaper I ever indulged in
was obtained in this way: I well recollect following
the whole of the debate on the Repeal of the Corn
Laws in 1846 in the *Times*, which I used to receive
per post, posted in London the day after publication,
for ten-pence per week, the price if posted on the
evening of the day of publication usually being one
shilling and three-pence per week. So far as I ever
heard the lady in Red Lion Court confined her trade
to weekly newspapers, and I believe I am correct in
saying that if she did not do all the trade in the
town and district, she did the major part of it.
Indeed, her connection extended to Aldbourne,
Wootton Bassett, Purton, Cricklade, Highworth,
Wroughton, and other places around. Her system of
business was to receive orders at her London address ;
to supply the papers through the post, and to send
down her accounts for the same to her agent for
collection every quarter. Now, it is these accounts
which, above everything else, I so well recollect. At
this time the postage of a letter from London to
Swindon cost ten-pence. There was, so far as I can
recollect, no stipulation as to the weight of a letter,
but it was imperative that it should consist of one
sheet of paper only. I think the lady's customers
within the district I have mentioned ranged from
about forty-five to fifty. To have sent a separate bill
for each customer would have meant forty-five or fifty
tenpences. This, of course, was out of the question.
But the only way in which the matter could be got
over was by writing out all the bills on one sheet of
paper. For this purpose a large sheet of post paper
was used. The whole width of the paper folded in
two was used for the bill, but it was only from half an
inch to about an inch in depth, a line being ruled
between each bill as a guide for the agent, by the aid

of a knife or scissors, to cut the one from the other, so that the accounts, when they were finally ready for delivery, were literally a lot of long and narrow strips of paper, like pieces of ribbon, the only room for writing a receipt being on the back. Had a receipt stamp been required then as now, there would have been positively no room for one on most of the accounts. The agent for the collection of these accounts fifty years ago was Mr. Reuben Horsell, who carried on business as a slater and plasterer. But he, giving it up, the agency was offered to my father, and it, in consequence, fell to my duty to cut up the accounts and deliver when convenient. There was one of these accounts which always afforded me an immense amount of amusement. It was for a newspaper taken in at the Bull, in Newport-street, which was then kept by a Mr. Browning. But I only recollect Mrs. Browning. She was quite a model landlady—very prim, very precise, and somewhat fantastical. She had certain views and opinions of her own on things in general, and claimed to possess an uncommon share of high breeding, which she occasionally exhibited in rather high talk, an invariable instruction of hers to her customers, when serving them with ale or liquors, being to the effect that "if they desired to have their cups or glasses replenished would they please to agitate the communicator." But it was her way of keeping her newspaper account, and my having to check the bill with her, that amused me most. She was in the habit of keeping her newspaper, as well as sundry other accounts, in chalk, on the inside of the door of the clock case. Her system was confined to the use of dates, with a few hieroglyphics, one of which stood for "newspaper." It not unfrequently happened, however, that both dates and hieroglyphics got sadly mixed up, and on such occasions the help of an almanack was called for, and while the old lady tried to make out " which was which," I had to stand by, with almanack in hand, to see whether the date corresponded with the day on which the paper was due. Sometimes the quarter's delivery was pronounced to be all right, but on other occasions two or three, or even more, were pronounced to be short, and when this happened to be the case, the corrections in the bill and the explanations demanded and given were of the most elaborate and intricate character. It generally, however, ended in the old lady paying the amount demanded, for the tenpenny postage entirely precluded correspondence with the principal in Red Lion Court. Indeed, I think I am correct in saying that the correspondence was confined to one letter each way per quarter, the names of persons desirous of becoming subscribers, or of discontinuing to be subscribers, being always reserved for the quarterly letter. As I have said, this was my first introduction to newspaper life, but humble as it was, it had its comical phases, and on many occasions, and under quite a variety of circumstances, have I looked back on those incidents of my early experiences with interest as well as with amusement.

I have often tried to realise some idea of the number of newspapers circulated within the week in Swindon, and, say, an area of eight or nine miles around, fifty years ago, and I think I am quite safe in putting the number at something under one hundred. At the present time the number circulated in the same district cannot be less than from fifteen to twenty thousand weekly, and possibly more, if we include London as well as provincial papers.

It is simply impossible for those who have not had ample opportunities for examining old newspapers, of fifty or a hundred years ago, to imagine what they were like, or of the kind of news they gave. I have by me a prospectus of a paper started at Salisbury, in the year 1715. As it affords an admirable illustration of what newspapers were like at this time, I give it in its entirety, as follows :—

"The *Salisbury Postman, or Pacquet of Intelligence* from France, Spaine, Portugal, &c., Saturday, September 27th, 1715. No. 1.

"*** This paper contains an abstract of the most material occurrences of the whole week, foreign and domestick, and will be continued every post, provided a sufficient number will subscribe for its encouragement.

" If two hundred subscribe, it shall be delivered to any private or publick-house in town every Monday, Thursday, and Saturday morning by eight of the clock during the winter season, and by six in the summer, for three half-pence each.

" Any person in the countrie may order it by the post-coach, carriers, or market people, to whom they shall be carefully delivered.

" It shall be always printed in a sheet and a half, and on as good paper ; but this, containing the whole week's news, can't be afforded under twopence.

" NOTE.—For encouragement of all those that may have occasion to enter advertisements, this paper will be made publick in every market town, forty miles distant from this city, and several will be sent as far as Exeter.

" Besides the news, we perform all other matters belonging to our art and mystery, whether in Latin, Greek, Hebrew, algebra, mathematicks, &c.

" Printed by Samuel Farley, at his office, adjoyning to Mr. Robert Silcock's, on the ditch in Sarum, anno 1715."

This voluminous title occupied two pages out of the two sheets of small folio of which this first number of the paper was composed. Part of the intelligence appears to be taken from the London papers, but one portion is declared to be "all from the written letter." An ingenious correspondent of one of the London magazines has made the following calculation of the income of a paper of this description : "The entire income of the paper, to meet every expense, including its delivery to subscribers—no trifling matter, we may infer, in the then imperfect state of the post-office deliveries, and which must have rendered special messengers indispensable to its circulation—the entire income amounted to no more than twenty-five shillings each number, or three pounds fifteen shillings per week."

How insignificant a figure must the provincial press have made in those days, taking it at this estimate! How humble must have been its workers —how cramped its means of gaining or of giving information!

What a remarkable contrast is there between the hopes and aspirations of Mr. Samuel Farley, when launching his great venture in 1715, and the experiences of some of his successors in a journalistic career in the present day. I have just taken up, incidentally, current copies of two of our best known daily newspapers, the *Telegraph* and the *Standard*. Taking the advertisements in one of the papers, and computing them at the very moderate average of ninepence per line, I find they would bring in at least £500 per day, or over £150,000 per annum. I have taken the circulation of the other at the number it claims to have, and, reckoned at one penny per copy, it would bring in £1000 per day, or £300,000 per annum ; or a total for advertisements and papers of something approaching half-a-million of pounds sterling every year. This, of course, does not represent the sum actually received by any one person or proprietary : it simply represents the gross amount paid for advertisements and papers by the public on account of papers like the *Telegraph* and *Standard*. The amount paid on account of the *New York Herald* must be considerably in excess of anything paid on account of any English newspaper.

There is yet one other of my early experiences in connection with newspapers which I must relate. At the time of which I write—fifty years ago—the *Weekly Dispatch* was the popular Radical paper. It was the property of a well-known London alderman, in whose establishment there lived the well-known

poetess, Eliza Cook : on the staff of the paper were
some of the cleverest and most racy writers of the
day, a barrister of the name of Williams, but who
wrote above the signature of *Publicola* being one of
the leading contributors.   The price of the paper was
sixpence.   And this is how six of the tradesmen of
Swindon managed to get their *Dispatch*.   It was
dated, as now, on the Sunday.   But it must have
been printed as early as the Friday, for it usually
arrived at our house by the Sunday morning's post.
As it did not begin the peripatetic work for which it
was destined until the following (Monday) morning
we always managed to have the first reading of it.
Indeed, I believe, it was part of the contract that my
father should have the use of the paper until mid-day
Monday as a recompense for the trouble he was put
to with the paper through the week, for the paper
belonged to no person in particular, but rather to a
company of six persons, who each paid their penny
per day for the privilege of having it to read.   I well
recollect that it fell very early to my lot to see that
each of the Swindon tradesmen had their *Dispatch*
on the right day the week through, and I also well
recollect that the paper was finally disposed of to old
Mr. Lawrence, who kept an ironmonger's shop at the
corner of High and Wood Streets, where Mr. Limmex
now carries on the business, when it was a week and
a day old, for an additional sum of one penny, which
generally fell to my lot for my trouble.   The old
gentleman, who was an inveterate newspaper reader,
after reading every available line that was left, would
use it up in his shop as waste paper in which to wrap
up " pennoths o' nails" and " apoths o' tin tacks."
And in this way our *Dispatch* was finally despatched.

At the time of which I write, every newspaper
printed paid a duty of fourpence to the Government.
And this continued down to the year 1836, when the

amount was reduced to one penny. This, however, was not the only tax a newspaper had to bear at that time. The paper on which it was printed paid an Excise duty, which rather exceeded the actual cost or value of the paper itself ; this duty being, on writing paper, 25 per cent. ; on printing paper, from 50 to 60 per cent. ; and on coarse paper from 70 to 200 per cent. But there was yet another tax, which appeared the most monstrous of all. On every advertisement published in a newspaper, and for every insertion of such advertisement, there was a tax of one shilling and sixpence, which the newspaper had to pay whether it got paid for the advertisement or not. In 1836 the duty on paper was reduced to three-halfpence per lb., on all papers alike ; the newspaper stamp was reduced to one penny ; and the tax on advertisements was repealed. And this naturally gave a great impetus to the publication of newspapers, although they necessarily continued high in price in consequence of the compulsory stamp which had to be affixed to every copy printed. In January, 1854, my attention was called to an action brought by the Excise authorities against Messrs. Bradbury and Evans, the printers and publishers of Charles Dickens' *Household Words.* In their publication they had given certain paragraphs which the authorities at Somerset House decided to be *news*, and therefore in contravention of the newspaper law, which provided that " news" could not appear in an unstamped periodical published at intervals of less than twenty-eight days without bringing the paper under the Newspaper Act, and making it a newspaper liable to the compulsory stamp. The result of this action was to settle the law, and make it clear that a newspaper published at intervals of twenty-eight days was not a newspaper in the eye of the law, whereas a newspaper published at a less interval than twenty-eight days was a news-

paper to all intents and purposes. Within a few days
after I was made aware of this decision I determined
on publishing a monthly newspaper, devoted to the
news of Swindon and the neighbouring towns and
villages, and in due course the first number of the
Swindon Advertiser, a small sheet, 20 inches by 14,
saw the light. It was the first penny newspaper devoted to news published in Great Britain, although it
was followed in the course of a few weeks, and in one
instance by a few days only, by others, many of them,
however, enjoying only a brief existence. For the
next year and a half the *Advertiser* continued to be
published monthly, when the absurd law making a
distinction between "news" published at intervals of
twenty-seven and twenty-eight days being abolished,
it was at once published as a weekly newspaper; and
as such it has continued down to the present day, and
I am still privileged to publish in its columns these
Relics, Notes, and Reminiscences of an old Wiltshire
town, and which, I am pleased to find, are being received with so much favour by my readers. In the
year 1861 the paper duty was totally repealed, and
the Newspaper Press of England was thereby made
absolutely free for all good and righteous purposes.

⏤The*Old*Workhouse.⏤

⏤∘◆∘⏤

PREVIOUS to about the year 1864 there was on the Wroughton Road, and at the point where the road to the Quarries turns off, and where Sanford and Springfield Villas now stand, an old brick building, known as the "Workhouse." It was no doubt originally intended as a Poor-house for the parish of Swindon, but when I first recollect it, it was let out in tenements. I refer to this place for the purpose of showing its undoubted connection with the clandestine trafficing in gin, or Hollands, to which I have already referred. As is well known, Sir Robert Walpole made himself one of the most unpopular Ministers of his time by legislating on gin. The following extract from the " Pictorial History of England " may possibly be interesting for other reasons beside that for which I make it. It is in reference to the proceedings in Parliament in the year 1743 :—" Walpole, in 1731, at the passing of the Gin Act, had foretold that it would encourage fraud and increase drunkenness. When those severe duties

G

were imposed, they were intended to check the drinking to excess of what Smollett styles 'the pernicious spirit called gin, which before was sold so cheap that the lowest class of the people could afford to indulge themselves in one continued state of intoxication, to the destruction of all morals, industry, and order.' This historian, who witnessed the horrors he describes, continues—' Such a shameful degree of profligacy prevailed that the retailers of this poisonous compound set up painted boards in public, inviting people to be drunk for the small expense of one penny ; assuring them they might be dead drunk for twopence, and have straw for nothing. They accordingly provided cellars and places strewed with straw, to which they conveyed those wretches who were overwhelmed with intoxication. In these dismal caverns they lay until they had recovered some use of their faculties, and then they had recourse to the same mischievous potion ; thus consuming their health and ruining their families, in hideous receptacles of the most filthy vice, resounding with riot, execration, and blasphemy. Such beastly practices too plainly denoted a total want of all police and civil regulation, and would have reflected disgrace upon the most barbarous community. In order to restrain this evil, which was become intolerable, the legislature enacted that law which we have already mentioned. But the populace soon broke through all restraint. Though no license was obtained, and no duty paid, the liquor continued to be sold in all corners of the streets ; informers were intimidated by the threats of the people ; and the justices of the peace, either from indolence or corruption, neglected to put the law in execution. The new ministers foresaw that a great revenue would accrue to the crown from a repeal of this act ; and this measure they thought they might the more decently take as the law had proved

ineffectual; for it appeared that the consumption of
gin had considerably increased every year since those
heavy duties were imposed. They, therefore, pretended that, should the price of the liquor be
moderately raised, and the licenses granted at twenty
shillings each to the retailers, the lowest class of
people would be debarred the use of it to excess;
their morals would in consequence be mended; and a
considerable sum of money might be raised for the
support of war, by mortgaging the revenue arising
from the duty and the licenses. Upon these principles
the new bill was framed, proposing, in addition to the
twenty shilling licenses, that a small duty per gallon
should be laid on the spirits at the still head. It
passed through the House of Commons with the
utmost precipitation, and almost without the formality
of a debate. But in the Lords it encountered a
vigorous resistance, being denounced as a license to
the people to poison themselves,—as 'a bait spread
over the pitfalls of debauchery,'—as an attempt to
raise the revenue at the expense of the health and
morals of the people. Chesterfield, who was becoming
more and more eloquent by being left out of place,
prophesied that, if the bill passed, it would depopulate
and absolutely ruin these kingdoms. Lord Hervey,
the former lord privy seal, spoke against it, and proposed that eminent physicians should be summoned
to the bar of the Lords to prove the fatal effects of
gin drinking; and Lord Gower, the new privy seal,
voted for it. 'These two noblemen,' says Smollett,
' had exchanged principles: the first was hardened
into a sturdy patriot; the other suppled into an
obsequious courtier.' The whole bench of bishops
voted with the opposition, yet the bill was carried by
a great majority. When the question was put for
committing the bill, and the bishops were joining in
his division, Chesterfield said, 'I am in doubt whether

I have not got on the other side of the question ; for
I have not had the honour to divide with so many
lawn sleeves for several years."

Now, when this old Workhouse was pulled down,
quite a variety of relics of other days were found
about in the walls, one of which I was fortunate
enough to secure. It was a remarkably well-executed
medal in condemnation of Sir Robert Walpole. It
was in bronze, and about the size of a crown piece.
On the obverse there was an inscription within a
circle, which reads thus :—

"THE BRITISH GLORY REVIVD BY ADM. L.
VERNON COM. BROWN."

Inside the inscription there were two figures in full
naval costume, and with the right hand of the one
clasped in the left of the other, there being above the
clasped hands a royal crown, and below a ship.
These were intended, no doubt, to represent Admiral
Lord Vernon and Commander Brown, and as a compliment to them, their loyalty being depicted by the
crown, and their calling by the ship. The reverse,
however, was a reverse in more senses than one. In
the centre there was a figure of Sir Robert Walpole,
in full court dress, with a rope round his neck, by
which he was being led into the open jaws of a mon-
ster, evidently intended to represent a place the poet
Dante writes about, by a gentleman who, when represented in full dress and in the usual orthodox fashion,
appears with cloven feet, a long forked tail, horns
to his head, and a five-grained fork in his right hand.
That there might be no possible mistake about what
was meant by all this, from the mouth of his Majesty
there was a lable on which was the inscription, "make
room for Sir Robert," and below, under the platform
on which Sir Robert and his companion were standing, was given the cause of Sir Robert's much

offending in the words "No Excise." That this medal, which fell into my possession a century and a quarter afterwards, once belonged to those who felt all that was thereon expressed, I can have no possible doubt, and for this reason : There had always been a general opinion or feeling among the oldest inhabitants that the old workhouse had been the scene of many a strange adventure, and that it had been the rendezvous of people whose lives and occupations were of a somewhat lawless character. Time after time efforts were made by such local authorities as a town like Swindon then possessed, to be "down upon" the evil doers who were supposed to make this place their home. But although it was felt that these suspicions were not without foundation, success does not appear to have rewarded the efforts of those who worked so steadily for a discovery. But, as I have said, the time at length came for the old building to be pulled down to make room for the pair of villas which now occupy the site, and then the discovery, which had been so long sought for, was made. I have it on the authority of Mr. Barrett that when the excavations were being made for the foundations of the new buildings a brick-built and arched cellar was discoverd, the entry to which was obtained by the removal of a large stone, which did duty as part of the floor on the basement story of the old house. On the removal of this stone, a kind of well was disclosed, which led into the cellar, which had been strongly and carefully built. By keeping some kind of mat, or carpet, or piece of furniture, over the entrance to this cellar, its existence was never even suspected by those who were not in the secret, although so many persons, it is said, felt so certain "there was something somewhere." There can be, I think, no doubt but that this cellar was originally built for the storing away of Hollands, or gin, and it is easy, therefore, to arrive at the con-

clusion that the building was, at the time when Sir
Robert Walpole was in such disgrace, with a certain
class of people, through his legislation on gin, in the
possession of those who felt warmly on the matter,
and who no doubt prided themselves on the possession
of those medals which were struck in his honour, and
one of which I have in my collection, having been
found at the demolition of the same old Workhouse.

But later than what I may call the gin period,
this old cellar was no doubt used for the secreting of
another kind of goods.   Formerly, Swindon and the
neighbourhood enjoyed an unenviable notoriety from
the frequency with which sheep-stealing was carried
on, and it is well known that the old Workhouse was
more than once or twice searched for stolen mutton,
but always, I believe, without success, the old cellar
no doubt being used as a receptacle for its safety.
On one of these occasions, so I have been told, the
officers of justice were not only on the trail of the
sheepstealers, but very close on their heels.   Indeed,
they entered the room where there was part of the
stolen carcass ; and yet they saw it not, for it chanced
to be in a bucket, which the woman of the house, or
rather tenement—for the old workhouse was at this
time let out to no less than from eighteen to twenty
families—converted into a seat for herself as the
officers entered the room.   It has been declared that
with the greatest *sang froid* imaginable the woman
seated herself on the bucket, thereby covering up the
mutton, and from that dignified position invited the
most thorough examination of *her* house for mutton
or anything else they pleased.   The mutton, which of
course was not discovered by the officers, was no
doubt, on their leaving, removed to some other place
of security, and possibly found its way into the old
vaulted cellar, which was reached by a well, which
was entered by the removal of a portion of the floor.

I have often thought of old Amy Ponting seated on her bucket, and in indignant terms bidding the officers of justice to perfect their desecration of her hearth and home by well searching every nook and cranny thereof, and have then thought that Patience sitting on a monument smiling at Grief, or Wellington or Napoleon giving orders for the disposition of their armies on the eve of battle, as the only fitting companion pictures.

I have also the authority of Mr. Thomas Barrett for the statement that there formerly existed beneath a cottage at Chisledon a well-built secret cellar, which agreed in every respect with the one at the old workhouse, and which was approached in a similar manner —by a well in the floor.   And no doubt there are others of which I have not heard.   In the temporary Museum at Swindon, in connection with the seventh general meeting of the Wilts Archæological Society, there were exhibited by the Rev. E. Meyrick, Vicar of Chisledon, five somewhat similar medals to the one I have described.   They were struck in honour of Admiral Vernon, and the capture of Porto Bello, and were found in an old cottage at Chisledon.

There are other cellars in Swindon, to which reference might be made, which are undoubtedly of an extraordinary character, and altogether out of all proportion to the houses with which they are connected. As they are, however, strictly private property, I do not feel justified in referring to them in detail, except to say that there are at least three which are most elaborately and expensively built of brick, and exhibiting first rate workmanship and ability both in design and construction.   What they may have been originally intended for I can only conjecture, although it is quite certain it had no connection with their present or recent use.   I may say that in the construction of the three cellars to which I more particularly allude, more material was used, and more constructive ability displayed, than is to be found in many of our modern houses. To one of these three cellars some public notice may be permitted perhaps on the ground that it was some years ago adopted as "Bonded stores," under the direct control of the Excise officers of the district. The old house in Cricklade-street, which was formerly known as "The Hall," but which is now let out in offices, and among others those in connection with the County Court, is one of the most interesting specimens of domestic architecture we have in the town. Until recent years it was in use as a private residence, the oldest occupier about whom I can hear anything being a Mr. Harding, to whose memory a tablet, with the following inscription, may be seen in the chancel of the old parish church :—

M.   S.

HANNÆ TUBB, Viduæ JOANNIS TUBB nuper
De Goosey in Comitatu Berceriæ, Armigeri :
Et MARIÆ reoum et Filiæ et Hæredis,
Uxoris ROBERTI HARDING de Swindon
Generosi
Eadem spe instructæ
Eodem tumulo sepulta,
Summum naturæ diem
(Vitæ quippe æternæ natalitium,)
Ambæ expectant, exoptant.

HANNA }   obijt   { die Novbris. 29 }
MARIA }   { die Januarij 1 }

Anno Salutis { 1756 } Ætatis { 72
              { 1759 }   { 46

Hoc posito Monumento.
ROBERTUS HARDING obiit Die Novembris 23°.
Anno Salutis 1770°. Ætatis 49°.

Which may be read in English, as follows :—This monument has been erected to the sacred memory of Hanna Tubb, widow of John Tubb, formerly of Goosey, in the County of Berkshire, Armiger, and of Mary, their daughter and heiress, the wife of

Robert Harding, of Swindon, gentleman. Instructed in the same hope, Buried in the same tomb, Both looking forward to, and ardently desiring, the last day of Nature, inasmuch as they are born of eternal life. Hanna died November 29th, in the year of our Lord, 1756, aged 72 ; Mary died January 1st, in the year of our Lord 1759, aged 46 ; Robert Harding died the 23rd November, in the year of our Lord, 1770, aged 49.

Such cellars, however, as those in connection with this house could hardly have been required for the ordinary purposes of such a house, or by such an occu-, pant. Indeed, I think it probable that they were in existence long anterior to the building of the present house, which I am disposed to put at from one hundred and fifty to two hundred years ago, and possibly by the above mentioned Mr. Harding or his predecessor in the ownership of the property, who may have been a Tubb. Beyond what I am told by this monumental inscription, I can learn nothing about any of the Harding family.

For as long as I can recollect anything, I can recollect certain tales about the cellars under the old house, and about there being passages running from them to different parts of the town. But, unfortunately, I have failed to get even a hint as to the purpose for which they were originally built, except, indeed, that when I have suggested that they might have been used for smuggling purposes, the suggestion has almost invariably awakened a memory or recollection of a similar idea indulged in by others years ago. I believe, however, I am quite correct in saying that at any time previous to the commencement of the present century the whole of the inhabitants of Swindon might have found a hiding place in them, leaving room for others after they had taken up their places.

There can be, I think, but one explanation
offered about these cellars, and it is that they were
constructed and used for the purpose of storing and
secreting smuggled goods. Of course, it may be
answered that such places could not have been built in
the dark, nor could they have been used without such
local authorities as then existed knowing something
about them. To such an objection I can only answer
that as we go back into the eighteenth century we get
back into the very heart of the time when superstition
was very rife among the people, and when ghosts and
hobgoblins were most religiously believed in. I think
there can be no doubt but that nine-tenths of the
ghost stories which used to affright people so much
were invented for a purpose. The old Workhouse
used to be haunted ; the old house in Cricklade-street
used to be haunted, as well in the attics as in the
cellars. There is, I think, quite a variety of evidence
to show that Swindon and the neighbourhood was once
the very home and stronghold of a band of smugglers
such as scarcely any other part of the country
possessed. As is well known, formerly the country
people were remarkable for their simplicity. And
in the north of Wiltshire—about the neighbourhood of
Swindon in particular—they were called "Moonrakers." The late Mr. John Akerman, in his "Wiltshire Tales," gives us the origin of this term, as follows :

"Piple zay as how they gied th' neam o' *moonrakers*
to we Wiltshire vauk, bekase a passel o' stupid bodies
one night tried to rake the shadow o' th' moon out o'
th' bruk, and tuk 't vor a thin cheese. But that's th'
wrong ind o' th' story. The chaps az was doin' o' this
was smugglers, and they was a vishing up zome kegs
o' sperrits, and only purtended to rake out a cheese !
Zo th' exciseman az axed 'em th' questin had his grin
at 'em ; but they had a good laugh at he, when 'em
got whoame th' stuff !"

But this is by no means the only evidence that the Wiltshiremen of other days, as well as some now living, were up to a thing or two, and were not in the habit of losing their wits when they wanted to exercise them the most. Here is another example :—

"Tom Ockle met th' exziseman one night as a was goin' from Ziszeter wi' a basket o' zmuggled baccur. The exziseman wanted to zee what Tom had got in the basket. 'There's nothin' but pegs' innerds there,' zays Tom.—'That may be,' zays t'other : 'but I must zee anyhow.'—'Well, well,' zays Tom, 'if I puts a haaf-crown in thee mouth, I dare zay thee'lt not be able to speak.'—'No, to be zhure not,' zays the exziseman, lettin' gwo th' basket, 'and if th' puts one auver each eye, I zhant zee no mwore nor a 'oont.''

And this is another, still from the same source :—

"When I was a young man I had a dog, a precious 'cute un a was, too! A'd catch a hare like a greyhound. I've cot a score o' rubbuts wi' hin in one night. By and by zomebody zays to the kippur, thuck William's got a dog as plays th' devil with ael th' game. Zo th' kippur comes up to m' one day, and zays, zays he, 'Maester Little, thuck dog o' yourn's a bad un; a gwos huntin', I'm twold.'—'Lar bless 'e!' zays I ; 'a wou'dn't harm a mouse, that a wou'dn't.'—'Dwon't b'lieve it !' zays he. 'Come along wi' I by thuck copse yonder.'—Zo as us walked alang, up jumps a hare and away a scampers. 'Hollo! hollo!' zays I to the dog, but a slunk behind m' *di*rectly, wi' 's tail between 's legs.—'Ha!' zays th' kippur, 'I b'lieves 'e now, Little. Them as zays your dog hunts be liars, that's zartin. I'll be cussed if I dwon't thenk a's vrightened o' th' game, that I do!' an' zo a walked away, and wished m' good marnin'.'—'Zo, ho! thought I : 'you be 'nation 'cute, you be, Maester Kippur. If instead o' '*hollo !*' I'd a cried '*coom hedder !*' a'd a run a'ter thuck hare like mad !'

There is, however, yet another authority, whom I cannot refrain from quoting, for he covers the whole of the ground on which I have been touching. The Rev. A. C. Smith, in an interesting paper read before the members of the Wiltshire Archæological Society at Swindon, September 16th, 1873, "On certain Wiltshire Traditions, Charms, and Superstitions," says :—
"I will give the following case, which occurred within my own personal knowledge, within the limits of the borough of Devizes. A labourer, being confined to his bed with a rather sharp attack of pleurisy, was visited by the parish doctor, who, together with other remedies, said he would send a blister, which should be at once applied to the patient's chest. On the following day, when the medical gentleman visited his patient, he was met at the door by the sick man's wife, who with great glee, expressed her admiration at the effects of the blister, which had done wonders; and said that her husband was in consequence much the better. The doctor, of course, expressed his satisfaction, but when he came to examine the sick man, he was surprised to find no trace of a blister, and on enquiring how that was, the wife with great readiness explained, 'You see, Sir, he had'nt got no chest, but he's got a good-sized box in the corner, and we clapp'd en on that:' and there, sure enough, on a deal box, was the blister which had worked such a magic cure, to the no small merriment of the doctor. After this authentic anecdote, I fancy I shall hear remarks of a disparaging character as regards the shrewdness of the Wiltshire labourer; and I dare say the word 'Moonraker' may be mentioned, without much reverence for the term : and I should like to say a few words here on this epithet, as applied to Wiltshiremen, because it is (I believe) very greatly misunderstood. Everybody in the county, indeed, knows the generally received origin of the name, how

the labourers of a certain parish in this county were surprised on a moonlight night, as they were raking in a pond ; and when in answer to the enquiry what they were searching for, they answered that they were trying to get the moon out of the pond, which they took for a good North Wiltshire cheese, they were ridiculed in no measured terms, and were thought the most simple and credulous of dullards. But the laugh was not altogether against them, neither were our Wiltshire 'Moonrakers' so simple as they seemed: for when their questioners had gone off in a merry mood at their simplicity, these shrewed (if not very honest) men raked out of the pond many a keg of smuggled spirits, which had been hidden there ; for that was in reality their occupation on that moonlit night. And if the trade of the smuggler seems to any somewhat an unlikely one to be pursued in this inland county, so far removed from the coast, it will probably surprise them to be told that there are certain retired villages in the heart of the downs of North Wiltshire, and not very far distant from Swindon, whose whole population, some seventy years ago, was employed in little else ; and who, in connection with others on Salisbury Plain, and others again on the Dorset or Hampshire coast, carried cargoes of contraband goods by the little-frequented ridgeways or trackways, or paths little known to, and seldom used by, any but themselves, which ran along the edge of the downs ; and so handed them on to the very middle of England, doubtless dispersing some of them on the way, and driving a very lucrative business. The trade of the smuggler, it must be remembered, was by many in those days not thought very dishonest, and there was a dash and peril attending it which in great part concealed its ugly character ; but when these same villages of smugglers became also villages of sheep-stealers, and

the two trades were carried on by the same gang,
they not only verified the old Wiltshire saying :—

"Salisbury Plain, Salisbury Plain,
Never without a thief, or twain."

but these lawless occupations were a severe tax upon
their neighbours, and so, in process of time, they were
denounced by all honest men, followed up and put
down with a high hand, and while a few of the ringleaders were sent to the gallows, considerable
numbers of them were transported for life ; and I am
old enough to remember in one of those villages
being struck with the extraordinary number of
widows, until it was explained to me that they were
only so called by courtesy, their husbands having (as
it was euphoniously described) 'gone abroad ;' though
it might have been added, ' at their country's expense,'
and ' to Botany Bay ;' and ' for the term of their
natural lives.' "

The following extract from a publication known
as " The Highwaymen of Wiltshire," will best
illustrate the formidable and desperate character of
the smuggling fraternity, as recently as a century
ago :—" The state of the country in 1779 was most
lawless and desperate ; the destruction of fleets and
armies abroad paralysed the merchants ; Government
lotteries at home were destroying the taste for steady
industry ; and the National Debt was increasing in a
fearful ratio ; while domestic treachery, keeping the
country in constant dread of seeing the arsenals in
flames, added to the general dismay. It was on the
charge of a burglary committed in the house of a
Mrs. Lowe, of Calne, that the miscreant, a Scotchman
(better known as " Jack the painter "), was captured at
Odiham, who afterwards suffered for setting fire to the
rope-yards of Portsmouth. In the district of Cran-
bourne Chase, through which runs the boundary line
between Wilts and Dorset, fierce conflicts were period-

ically taking place between large parties of smugglers and soldiery. Thus, for instance, on Friday, 19th March, 1779, a prolonged contest was maintained at Hook Woorl, near Farnham, in Dorset, between fifty smugglers on the one side and a party of Dragoons on the other, which ended in the discomfiture of the soldiers, who lost all their horses and arms, and were dreadfully beaten. Of the smugglers, two or three were slain, and many wounded with sword cuts. The contraband goods for which this battle was fought were carried by no less than twenty pack horses. The smugglers could, however, in case of emergency, muster a still larger number. On the 9th of January, 1783, Mr. Critchell, the Ringwood Exciseman, having notice of a large depôt of goods at Burley, in the New Forest, repaired to the spot with his men and made the necessary seizure. At this moment a body of eighty smugglers made their appearance, all mounted on horseback, and charged the affrighted Revenue officers, who fled precipately towards Ringwood. Mr. Critchell was the only one of the party who fell into their hands, and him they half killed. Another case occurred within the limits of the Borough of Devizes, during the same year—1783. A seizure of 600 lb. of tea having been made at the house of a person named Sheppard at the village of Cheriton, was conveyed to the house of the Supervisor at Devizes, and Sheppard was by the Justices fined in the penalty of £150, which was paid the same day. In the evening the quiet of the town was disturbed by the entrance of a body of armed smugglers, who, confident in their strength, brought out the whole of the forfeited goods and carried them off in triumph. A warning of the intended rescue had been made to the Superviser, but discrediting the information, he neglected to adopt any precautionary measures. A similar occurrence took place at Hindon in South

Wilts, and also at Corsham, on the premises of a supervisor named Robert Mann, occasioning at length two proclamations from the Home Office, as for instance,

" WHITEHALL, 17 Feb. 1784. Whereas it has been humbly represented to the King that in the months of September and December last, divers gangs of armed men assembled in the night-time, at the towns of Hindon and Devizes in the Co. of Wilts, and by force and violence took away from certain houses in the said towns a large quantity of tea which had been seized by the officers of Excise and deposited in the said houses ; discharging their firearms against all who opposed them, to the great terror of the inhabitants :—His Majesty, for the better discovering and bringing to justice the persons concerned in the daring outrages above mentioned, is hereby pleased to promise his most gracious pardon to any one of them who shall discover his accomplice or accomplices therein, so that he or they may be apprehended and convicted thereof.

"SYDNEY."

" And as a further encouragement, the Commissioners of Excise do hereby promise a reward of one hundred pounds to any person or persons making such discovery, to be paid by their Secretary, on conviction of any one or more of the offenders.

"J. FISHER, Sec."

⟶A∗Wiltshire∗Royal∗Residence.⟵

 MAY add as a postcript to the preceding paper, as well as to a previous one on " The Bell," and the use to which the old Belarmines were put by smugglers of Hollands, or Geneva gin, that the other day I paid my first visit to the old mansion at Upper Upham, which, through the courtesy of the present occupant, Mr. Frampton, I was permitted to examine. All who know anything of our local and county history know that this old place has been an object of great interest to the archæologist and antiquarian. John Aubrey makes no mention of the place in his " Wiltshire Collections," although the Rev. Canon Jackson, in his " Notes on Aubrey," makes several references to it, but, unfortunately, only incidently. John Britton, however, refers to it in connection with Aldbourne, in which parish it is situate, as having been anciently a place of more importance than it is at present. In support of this I may add there are at the present time to be seen in many of the cottages remnants of looms and other evidences that weaving and other

H

manufactures were carried on to a considerable extent, principally, I believe, of fustian, in the village. It was also celebrated, far and wide, for its Bell Foundry. It does not, however, come within my present purpose to refer at any length to the old town and trade of Aldbourne, and after remarking that the place never recovered from a great fire, which happened in 1760, and which destroyed seventy-two houses, doing damage to the extent of £20,000, I must content myself by saying that Aldbourne gave the name to a royal chase, and tradition reports that King John occasionally resided at a hunting seat near the town, part of which is said to have been converted into the house known as Upper Upham. The fullest notice I have been able to meet with respecting this house is in a paper by the late Mr. F. A. Carrington, of Ogbourne, published in the "Wilts Archæological Magazine." vol. II., page 128-9, where he says : " I was informed by the late Rev. J. Seagram that Aldbourne Chase was a favourite hunting ground of John of Gaunt, who lived at a very curious old mansion at Upper Upham (now the residence of Mr. Frampton), and also occupied a house which stood on a site of the Court-house, situate near Aldbourne church-yard, because there is no well at Upper Upham, and no water except rain water. Mr. Seagram also said that the Chase consisted of about 5,000 acres, and that there was a common of nearly 1,000 acres more, and I was told by the late Mr. Church, of Hillwood, who died in the year 1852, at a very advanced age, that he recollected Aldbourne Chase before the enclosure in 1805, when a great part of it was covered with brambles, gorse, and thorne bushes, which grew up as high as a man's shoulders ; so that persons with waggons, on horseback, and on foot, could only go along the drives that were cut through this Wiltshire specimen of a jungle." In a subsequent paper by Mr. Carrington, published in the same volume, he says :—"To the statement that John of Gaunt lived at the ancient house at Upper Upham, it ought to be added that it is very doubtful whether any part of the present house existed in the time of John of Gaunt. If it did, the house was evidently *modernized* to a great extent by the Goddard family in the reign of Queen Elizabeth, or rather ealier. On the front of the house, in raised letters, there are the initials

T : G :   A : G :

and below there is engraved in gilt letters surrounded by a border line

I was informed by Sir Thomas Phillips, Bart., that the initials T G and A G are those of Thomas Goddard, of Upham, who bought the Swindon property in 1562 ; and of Anne, sister of Sir George Giffard, his wife : the initials R G and E G being those of Richard Goddard (son of Thomas), and Elizabeth, daughter of Thomas Waldron, of Aldbourne, his wife : the will of this Richard Goddard being dated in 1614."

It would seem from this that there is nothing more than tradition for it that Upper Upham was ever a royal hunting seat. And it must be further noticed that the tradition, as handed down by John Britton and the Rev. J. Seagram, does not exactly tally, the former referring to the place as being the hunting seat of King John, who reigned from 1189 to 1199, and the latter to John of Gaunt, who died 1398. Of course, it may be that both King John and John of Gaunt made use of Upper Upham as a hunting seat.   And this would seem to be very probable.   King John's connection with Marlborough, the almost adjoining parish, is well authenticated. Mr. Waylen, in his " History of Marlborough," says : —" John's connection with Marlborough is still further testified by the fact that he selected it as the scene of his marriage with the heiress of the Earl of Gloucester, which took place in conformity with Richard's wishes, and in all probability with the sanction of his presence, 29th August, 1189.   John appears to have been attached to the spot as a place of occasional residence : and as Richard deemed it necessary before going abroad to shut his brother out of London and Windsor, and to remove all inducement to interfere with the government, he prudently loaded him with favour, and provided for his amusement. From the days of the Romans, Wiltshire had been the centre of a district especially selected for the villas of the wealthy, and though violence had swept many of these memorials from the soil, its manors were still the envy of the lords, and its forests the resort of the monarchs.   From this time the documents among the Tower records associating the name of John with Marlborough are extremely numerous. We gather from them that the Castle was constituted by him, when he became king, the depository of a large portion of his treasury and other personalities. The burgesses also shared in his bounty. He remitted to the men of Marlborough ' all dues owing from them to himself at the time he was Earl of Mortagne, and granted them various charters.   A tradition survives, and has often been repeated, that certain members of his family were christened at the font of the neighbouring church of Preshute.   The more probable supposition is, that the christening took place in the chapel of St. Nicholas, within the Castle, and that on the dismantling of the fortess in after years the

antique font of St. Nicholas was transferred to the
church of that parish in which the larger portion of
the Castle grounds lay."

Here, then we have King John in "occasional
residence" within a few miles of Upper Upham, and
what therefore more probable than the tradition
alluded to by John Britton, "that King John occasionally resided at a hunting seat near Marlborough"
—that is, within the royal Chase of Aldbourne at
Upper Upham. There is this advantage with this
supposition : it leaves it quite open to those who are
disposed to do so to show that John of Gaunt used
the same house for the same purpose from a hundred
and fifty to two hundred years afterwards, although I
admit I am not prepared to do this. And that
brings me in the natural order of events to what is a
simple impossibility, and that is to show that John,
who died 1199, or John of Gaunt, who died in 1398,
ever lived in a house which was not built until 1599,
which is the undoubted date of the present old house
at Upper Upham. Mr. Frampton believes, and, I
venture to think, rightly, that the existing is the
second—it may possibly be the third—house that has
stood there or thereabouts, the existing one having
been built some two hundred years after the time of
John of Gaunt, a fact which is attested both by the
style of the house, its architecture, and the date
which is engraved on the front. But what I wish
more particularly to show is this : that some hundred
years ago there were, in addition to the present
house, the ruins of a still older one in an adjoining
enclosure. And this is how I prove it. Mr. Frampton went to live at Upper Upham over thirty years
ago, and at that time an old lady of the name of
Miriam Brind, who was ninety years of age, and who
had lived there all her time, was living in a cottage
close by. It was, Mr. Frampton told me, his delight

when he first knew this old lady to listen to her tales about the place when she was a child. As she sat at her spinning wheel she would spin tales as well as wool, and in particular would tell of how the smugglers used the cellars in the old ruins for putting away their spirits, which they used to bring there in bladders. When Mr. Frampton told me this I could not help thinking how thoroughly it corroborated what I had ventured to advance as a theory in my paper on " The Bell." Even now the population, for a considerable distance around, can barely average one person to the square mile, and a hundred years ago it must have been far less than this. And then, as we have seen, the whole district was covered with gorse and brush wood, so that there was one immense cover in which those who had an object in keeping out of sight might secrete themselves. With a few confederates on the spot, or in the immediate neighbourhood, and helped by the ingenious and very common device of circulating reports to the effect that the place was haunted, and that spirits walked there, it was no doubt an easy matter to secrete in the old cellars any quantity of contraband goods, and to elude the vigilance of the local authorities, however active and persevering they might be. There can, I think, be no doubt but that it was a very common practice formerly to put about reports that houses or places were haunted for no other purpose than that of screening some rascality which was carried on there. It has been related to me by several persons, in consequence of their having read my paper on " Ghosts and Ghost Laying," and who appeared to be thoroughly acquainted with the circumstance, that many years ago there was a case in point in the parish of Swindon. The facts are these : The tenant of a lone farm house, being unable to pay his rent, and being in daily dread of his landlord making a seizure of his goods, at length hit upon the expedient of circulating a report that the place was haunted, and that occasionally the most fearful noises were to be heard in the night time. At length the landlord, disregarding these reports, put a man in possession. But he did not stay out the first night, for no sooner had darkness set in than the noises, as they had been described, began all over the house. The man bolted. The landlord put in a second man. He also bolted. And thus the game went on until positively no man could be found to summon up courage enough to go into possession, and, as a consequence, the poor impecunious tenant was left alone in his glory—that is, with his ghosts. In course of time the secret oozed out, and it became generally known that the noises which had created so much alarm were produced principally by chains of iron which were used and acted upon in quite a variety of ways, sometimes by being let fall, and at other times by being drawn along the floor or ground, and in other ways. It was a long time, however, before the credulous ceased to believe that the house was haunted, and it is certain that the ingenious tenant succeeded in getting time to pay his rent through the inability of his landlord to get anyone to go into possession, if nothing more.

If these notes were not confined to the old town of Swindon, I might have something to say about the old house at Upper Upham and its remarkable and interesting surroundings. I might be tempted to say in regard to the old house that it is a fine specimen of an old Elizabethian mansion, full of points on which to hang a tale. I might tell how you come suddenly upon the old house, and find that the principal front, which faces due south, is approached by a court-yard or enclosed garden ; how the entrance porch and the large mullioned windows at once strike

you as giving character to the place. I might then
enter the house and tell you how it consisted of three
principal apartments : first, the common room, which
was entered from the porch, and which extended the
full length of the house—the daïs for the lord and his
family and friends being at the west end, and the place
below the salt, for the dependants and retainers, at the
east end ; how there was a handsome carved wood
gallery projecting out from the north wall of this lower
room, which was made to serve quite a variety of
purposes, and among others that of a stage or platform
for the minstrels, mummers, or jesters, whose business
it was to entertain the company below ; as well as a
connecting link with the grand staircase, which lay to
the north of the common room, and which led to the
grand banqueting room which was over, and corresponded in size with the common room below, another
entrance to the stair-case being through a passage
leading from the north-east corner of the common
room, which passage served also as an entrance into
the kitchen. And I might then go on to point out
how the sleeping apartments formed a third storey,
up above the banqueting hall, and how in and about
these apartments, up under the old roof, there are still
extant certain secret chambers or hiding holes, in
which you might play hide-and-seek to your heart's
content, or so long as your patience and provisions
lasted. And then I might return to the front of the
old house, and invite you to take particular notice of
the entrance porch, which bears marks or traces of
having been designed or built by some other hands
than those which built and planned the other portions
of the front. And I might ask you to consider the
suggestion that this porch was designed by no less
eminent an architect than Sir Christopher Wren.
Sir Christopher could, of course, have had nothing
whatever to do with designing the front, or even of the

original porch. But what I would suggest is this: that on the occasion of some visit to Upper Upham the great architect, finding fault possibly with the porch as it then stood, designed certain alterations, which were subsequently carried out. If I should be tempted to attempt all this it would, of course, be my duty to admit the fact that I have only the old porch itself to show that Sir Christopher Wren was ever at Upper Upham. There is, however, the authority of that eminent antiquary, Sir Thomas Phillips, for it, that the Rev. Oliver Brunsell, Vicar of Wroughton from 1614 to 1641, married Elizabeth, daughter of Elizabeth Martyn, of Upham, and that their son Henry married a sister of Sir Christopher Wren. Now, my suggestion would be, that is, if I was not precluded from writing about the old house at Upper Upham, that through this circumstance Sir Christopher visited Upham, possibly in course of his more active career, or, what is more probable, in his later life, when, "through the effects of the ignorance and malice of his many enemies," he was deprived of his post as Surveyor-General at the age of eighty-six, and was driven " to betake himself to a country life." And then again, but for the same standing reason, I might go on to ask, "Why should Sir Christopher Wren alter the porch at Upper Upham?" And then I might attempt to answer it in some such way as this : Because the original porch was out of character : it probably had been removed bodily from the old house of King John, or John of Gaunt, as the case might be, from the ruins of the old hunting lodge, about which tradition tells us, and which stood a short distance from the present house. That the ruins from this old house were utilised for the building of the existing house there can, I think, be no doubt. The Royal Arms over the fire-place in the north-east corner of the common room were, no doubt, brought

from the ruins of the old house and placed where they
are now to be seen. And then again, the quoin stones
in the walls were formerly used for quite another purpose, for they are not only carefully dressed, but have
been artistically designed, and bear beautifully executed carvings. A number of these stones had
evidently formed parts of shafts, pillars, and philasters,
in a house of greater pretensions even than the existing one.

This, then, is what I would suggest as the probable history of Upper Upham, and the interesting
old mansion there, and it will be allowed that
the suggestion has the advantage of admitting the
possibility of all the things we have heard about
the place:—That there was a mansion or hunting seat
which belonged to either King John or John of
Gaunt, and possibly to both; that this house fell into
ruins; that in 1541 John Goddard, of Aldbourne,
acquired the lands at Upper Upham, on which the
ruins were, along with lands in Wanborough, Wicles-
cote, and Wroughton, which lands had previously
belonged to Lacock Abbey, through a grant from the
Crown; and that John Goddard's successor to the
property, Richard Goddard, built the present house,
not far from where the old royal hunting seat had
stood, and using therefor in the building such stones
and material as was available from the ruins; and that
probably, some thirty years afterwards, the entrance
porch, not satisfying the critical eye of Sir Christopher
Wren, was altered as it now stands in accordance with
his designs. I am unable to say how long the property remained in the Goddard family after 1599, but
I believe I am correct in saying it was repurchased
some years ago by the present representative of the
family, Mr. A. L. Goddard.

I may add that relics of former inhabitants of the
neighbourhood are frequently found on the Downs.

Mr. W. H. Avenell, of Draycott Foliatt, very recently brought me a small silver coin which was picked up by a labourer on the Downs not far from Upper Upham. It proved to be a groat of Edward III. (Father of John of Gaunt). On the obverse, surrounding the effigy of the king, is the legend, "Edward, D.G., Rex Angl. z France. D. Hyb." The reverse has the plain cross extending to the edge of the coin, with the three pellets in the angles, the motto being, "Posui Deum ajutorem meum," slightly abbreviated ; in an inner circle is "London civitas." No doubt this coin once belonged to the exchequer of John of Gaunt, and was probably received by him direct from his father's mint. It is, however, by no means a rare occurrence to find old coins on the Downs about here, including Ancient British and Roman. I have been fortunate enough to obtain both gold and silver Ancient British coins found within a mile or so of Upper Upham. I mention the one in the possession of Mr. Avenell in some detail as it bears directly on the matter on which I am writing.

The * Wiltshire * Downs * and * the Thames * Valley

UT what am I to do now that I am up on the breezy, health-giving Downs at Upper Upham? It has taken me many years to get up here: and now that I have had my say about the old Royal Hunting Seat and its traditions, must I hasten down again to the Swindon low-lands? It can hardly be. The temptation to say something about the neighbourhood in which the old house stands is too great to be resisted, and I cannot help making an attempt to point out how the country hereabouts is at an elevation of something approaching a thousand feet above sea level. The water-shed of the *Thames* Valley is the greatest in England, and includes the drainage of no less than 4,613 square miles of country. Upper Upham is situate on the highest point on the south-west boundary line of this vast area. A little to the west there commences two other water-sheds, and at the south and south-east, two others. But they are all of comparative small area to the one which lies out north and north-east of Upper Upham. And it is to

this circumstance that I should attempt to attribute
the very remarkable conformation of the surface of
the ground for some miles around this particular spot
on the north-west point of the Wiltshire chalk downs.
But to enable me to do this it would be necessary to
ask my readers to go with me back to those times when
the whole of the Wiltshire chalk downs were at the
bottom of the sea, instead of being, as now, so many
hundreds of feet above the sea. I might find it a
terrible task to carry some of my readers back such a
distance; but I should have to do it before I could
make much headway. And then, just after there had
been some terrible convulsion in the earth — not
necessarily in England, or even in Europe—but when,
and through the agency of which, the crust of the
earth had been forced out into the form of mountains,
raising the beds of oceans and of seas high and dry
above the waters, and lowering and depressing hitherto
dry lands on to which the waters were afterwards to
flow, and causing them to become in their turn beds
of oceans and of seas. And then, as this grand
transformation scene was progressing, and spots of
dry land began to be seen on some of the highest
points, I should ask my readers to take up their
position with me at, say, Upper Upham, and there
watch the action of the mighty waters as they swept
along in their course from the south, and then swerved
round to the east and north-east along the valley of
the *Thames* and out into the German Ocean ; I should
ask them to notice that the waters were so powerful,
and travelled with such a fearful rush, that they swept
away in their course the soft chalk and the friable
greensand, and carried it all away towards the east,
until the Purbeck and the Portland at Swindon and at
Bourton, and then the coral reefs at Blunsdon and at
Highworth, and then Coxwell and Faringdon, and
then the distant Cotswolds, had all in their turn been

disclosed and had become dry land—little islands in
that great sea of waters which swept away all the
layers of rock and of earth which had overlain the
Kimmeridge and the Oxford clays, and which waters
rushed on in their mighty course from off the great
table lands of the Wiltshire chalk downs, cutting as
they went those gorges along the northern edge of the
downs which are now so marked at Wroughton, at
Chisledon, and Bishopstone, and many other places.
And then, still watching these rushing seas as they
travelled eastward, I should ask them to notice how
the sea began to subside, and then to pass off
altogether out of sight, until there was nothing left
but the valley they had cut and then left—the valley
of the *Thames*, with its river and its many tributary
streams only remaining. And then, having seen all
this, I should ask my readers to turn their faces
southward, and there notice how the surface of the
earth had been cut up into hill and valley, until for
miles around there had been left scarcely an acre of
ground with a smooth and level surface. At some
points the lands had been left far stretched out in hill
and dale, running along in one undulating course as
far as the eye could reach, whilst at other places it was
left in hills and pit-holes of the most picturesque form
and character. And then, going a little to the west, I
should ask them to stand on the bold promontory,
beneath and around, rather than off, which the waters
had rushed, leaving bold escarpments which were to
remain as the northern boundaries of the great Wiltshire table lands for all time to come. Carrying the
eye still westward by south, attention would be called
to the chalk bluffs at Bassett Down, Bynoll, and at
Cliffe, about which latter point there had been a
divergence of the waters as they rushed off from the
Downs, one portion going west and forming the valley
of the *Avon*, and the other portion going east and

forming the valley of the *Thames*. But all this, as I have said, is on the presumption that, in writing about some of the characteristic features of an old Wiltshire town, it was competent for me to write about things that have been quite as plainly written in the great Book of Nature, but which goes back to times and things which existed, and were done, before towns or men were, but only the great Creator, and the materials out of which He formed worlds and made our own fair earth what it is for our use.

And then, having attempted all this, I might pause and ask how these vast chalk hills and downs were formed, and of what they were composed. But I could only ask this to find the certain answer that they were all formed under some deep ocean. There is now no possible doubt in the minds of geologists that our Wiltshire Chalk Downs, which now stand at from 500 to 1,000 feet above sea level (the highest point being at Inkpen Beacon, in Berks, where it is 1,011 feet, the elevation of Upper Upham being probably only a few feet less), were formed under the waters of a deep sea in a very similar manner to that formation which is now going on across the bed of the Atlantic Ocean by means of the Gulf Stream, and which, in the very far future, it may be, may come out as a long strip of land connecting South America with the northern regions. It is a well ascertained fact that the waters of this Gulf stream are highly charged with minute particles of earthy and other matter, which are gradually released and sink to the bottom of the ocean as the waters rush along their course for thousands of miles, from the burning regions of the south towards the ice-bound regions of the north. The vast range of Wiltshire Chalk Downs were formed in a precisely similar manner, for a microscopical analysis of chalk proves it to be composed almost entirely of minute shells of a low class of

animals known as *foraminifera*. Countless millions
of these tiny creatures still inhabit our oceans, and as
they die their shells sink to the ocean-floor, forming,
by their incessant rain, great thicknesses of whitish
mud, like that in which many miles of our Atlantic
cables are laid, and which, if hardened and compressed,
would form a rock undistinguishable from the chalk
which underlies our Wiltshire Downs. In the neighbourhood of Upper Upham the beds of chalk which
have been thus formed measure no less than eight
hundred feet through. When the process of formation
of these chalk beds had been going on for possibly
millions of years, there would appear to have been a
cessation of the deposit taking place for a sufficient
period of time to allow of the bed of the ocean to
harden, and to become covered with sponges, mixed
with a variety of marine plants and animals. There
would be subsequent deposits of chalk - forming
material, which would be largely charged with silica,
and also iron, for both of which these sponges, plants,
and animals would show a great affinity, and ultimately
absorb, and thereby become converted into those flints
which are found in the upper chalk. From indications
which are to be seen in many a chalk quarry and railway cutting, it would seem that there were several
distinct cessations of the chalky deposit, and for
sufficiently long periods to allow of the ocean bed to
be completely covered with sponges, animals, and
plants, as they are now to be seen in those remarkable
bands of dark coloured flints which form so striking
an object in the masses of white chalk in so many
places, whilst at other times the growth of the sponge
and the plant and the deposit appears to have gone
on simultaneously. Always, however, the sponge and
the plant, by absorbing the silica and the iron which
was in the water, have become what we know as flints,
while the minute shells of the *foraminifera* have gone

to form what we know as chalk. With, then, only a
slight knowledge of the lessons geology teaches us,
what wonderful thoughts a ramble on our Wiltshire
Downs give rise to, and how much better qualified are
we to find real pleasure and instruction in the simplest
and meanest of objects than are others when they
stand in the presence of the grandest creations of
nature or of art. When the disruption in the earth's
crust took place which caused the waters which had
covered the Wiltshire Chalk Downs to rush off in the
direction of the Thames valley in a north-eastern direction, its effect was felt most at the north-west corner
of Wiltshire, about in the neighbourhood of Malmesbury; for at this point some of the lower strata, or older
formed rocks, are found broken through, and to some
extent tilted up from their original horizontal position,
so that we have geological formations or rock strata
coming right on to the surface many hundreds of feet
higher than they would have been had no rupture
taken place; and this upheaval no doubt forced backwards and upwards that portion of the great chalk
range lying to the south-east, and which forms the
north-west corner of North Wiltshire. And it is to
this circumstance that we may attribute the fact that
it is from this point in the North Wiltshire Downs
that so many watersheds take their rise, or, rather,
that this point forms the boundary to so many water-
sheds, and which run practically north, east, west, and
south. As I have already noticed, the watershed of
the *Thames* valley takes the surface drainage of 4,613
square miles of land; the *Avon* watershed takes 673
miles; the *Test*, 477 miles; the *Itchin*, 232; the
Lymington, 91; the *Stour*, 459, and the *Severn* water-
shed 4,350 miles. But what is more particularly
interesting is the fact that all these several watersheds
are given their directions, or parting lines, by the
upheaval of the rock formations near Malmesbury,

I

which had the effect of crushing back and giving
their present elevation to the Chalk Downs of Wiltshire.

It is, indeed, a fair and glorious earth on which we
live : as full of wonders as it is of lessons. And there
are but few occasions when it may be seen to greater
advantage, either as regards its beauty or its interest,
than that which is afforded by a walk of a few miles
along the northern edge of the Wiltshire Downs. If
a lover of natural scenery—which often presents the
most glorious sight a man can lay his eyes on—and
one who has also a keen perception and relish for the
simple and the true, should commence a walk along
the edge of the Downs, beginning, let us say, at the
bold chalk promontory at Broad Town, where the
land-slip started some years ago, and which is still
going on, causing quite an upheaval of the land in
the meadows below by the lateral weight and
pressure of the mass of earth which is sliding away
from the side of the cliff, and leaving it white and
perpendicular, until it has become a striking object
for miles around, he will find much to interest him
before he has proceeded many yards in an eastern
direction. There is no written record for it, but the
assertion may with confidence be made that this was a
selected and favourite spot with those early inhabitants
of Britain who worshipped the sun and offered up
sacrifices of burnt offerings. It was their practice to
come to the edge of this table-land, which overlooks
the beautiful valley below, and which commands one
of the most perfect and enchanting views of the
setting sun as it sinks to its rest in the west that could
be afforded by any spot in the whole country, and
there build up their fires and offer up their sacrifices,
and worship their God with all the earnestness of their
natures. How do I know this it may be asked. Well,
I know it in this way : The land-slip to which I have

referred commences right at the top of the extreme
edge of the Downs, and in some places has taken a
portion of the edge away.   And when this has been
done there have been disclosed, a slight distance below
the surface, black lines or layers, which, on being
examined, have proved to be charcoal, embers of
wood, and ashes.   If you trace these layers inwards
you find they form circles, such as would be occasioned
by the burning of large fires.   And then again, if you
search about among the charcoal and the ashes you
will find the charred bones of sheep and deer and
other animals in great abundance.   I have collected
in the course of an hour quite a large basketful of
relics and remains like these which have lain buried
for many centuries just under the surface, and which
have been exposed to view as they lay *in situ* in the
edge of the chalk cliff by the slipping away of the
land down into the vale below.   I need only mention
Avebury and Stonehenge to arouse feelings and
thoughts which carry us back to other people and
other forms of worship and of sacrifice.   Both these
great historic places without histories are to be reached
in comparatively a few miles on foot, but which are
instinctively visited in an instant in thought as we
look on the sight which is presented to us in the land-
slip at Broad Town.   And then, as we proceed on our
journey eastward, we reach some of those remarkable
gorges, to which I have already referred, and which
were undoubtedly cut out from the solid chalk hills
by the rushing waters which covered the whole of the
Wiltshire Downs as they were drained off into the
Thames Valley, passing off into the German Ocean.
And then there comes in sight, on our right, the old
British road, along which probably the most ancient
traders England ever had travelled to and fro between
London and Wales and Cornwall with their tin,
copper, and other merchandise.   And then, as we go

on, there lies to our right and in our front those remarkable memorials of those warlike people who constructed Barbury, Liddington, and Uffington Castles. And then at Bishopstone there are the remarkable "lynches," or natural terraces, rising one above another with remarkable regularity, cut out in the side of the steep chalk hill. And then there is Wayland Smith's cave, made memorable by Sir Walter Scott, and a whole host of other objects of interest, which are simply fascinating to all intelligent and devoted observers. And then again, there is the ever-memorable White Horse Hill, with which the history of Alfred the Great is so inseparably connected, and which Tom Hughes has made so memorable. But if we reverse our journey, and turn our backs on these things which tell us more particularly of the past, and of long extinct peoples and races, and cast our eyes and our thoughts northward, we shall find that there lies between the two points, marked by Uffington Castle on the east and Liddington Castle on the west, a panorama of natural scenery which can scarcely be surpassed both for extent, variety, and effect in any part of England. At some points the view is somewhat contracted by the narrowing of the valley by some rising ground or picturesque hills on the opposite side, whilst at others it extends as far as the eye can reach, and the objects in the view pass off in misty indistinctness. At some points some village nestling amidst clusters of tall trees, between which the spire or tower of some grand old church is playing hide and seek, forms the boundary line on the horizon, but at other points the view extends into several counties, and embraces many churches, villages, and towns. At every point and everywhere, as the country stretches out from the foot of the chalk range, the land is of the richest ; vegetation is most luxuriant ; and everywhere there is that beauty which is perfectly

indescribable, but which when once seen and realised
remains imprinted on the mind and memory—a joy
and a blessing for ever. I have seen what are counted
some of the grandest natural scenes in the world. But
it has not been the actual seeing of these sights with
my two eyes that has at the moment of seeing struck
me the most ; but it has been rather those mental
sights of the selfsame scene which have been reproduced a thousand times before the mind's eye that
have charmed me the most, and have served to sink
the deepest into my very nature. And so it has been
with the views as seen from these Wiltshire Downs.
Back behind, everything was bleak, barren, and
rugged : In front, everything was exquisitely beautiful.
It has seemed to me as though I were standing on the
border line between two worlds when I have looked
behind and then in front. But if it was death on the
one side it had only been placed there that the life on
the other side might be made more glorious and worth
the living for—a recompense for all. And this grand
panorama is continued for many miles. As the crow
flies the distance from Uffington Castle to Liddington
Castle is not more than eleven or twelve miles, with an
additional four or five miles on to Barbury Castle. But
you may spend many days, and even a whole season, on
the journey, and every step you take discover some fresh
enchantment. There has never been but one thing to
which I could compare the view from off these Downs
and that is the sanctity of the English Sabbath,
when all is hushed and still, and you can feel the
very breath of the Almighty around you everywhere,
when all is so quiet, so grand, so calm. I mean the
sanctity of the English Sabbath of years ago, before
noisy brawlers and disturbers of the peace had taken
possession of our streets on that day, and made their
profession of religion a thing of noise and rant, and a
nuisance to all peaceably disposed men.

My experience of the great natural sights of the world tells me that we only thoroughly realise them in the after-views we get of them : when they come before the mind's eye with the imagination set at rest. When we approach these great sights—the Falls of Niagara for instance—for the first time, if we possess anything of that sensitive nature which brings us into sympathy with nature in all her works, small as well as great, and in all that God has made, we are already overweighted and weakened by the excitement which others have created in us. I can never forget that the grandest realisation I have ever had of Niagara was when I was some miles away from that place. It was in the night after the day when I had spent some hours gazing in sheer bewilderment and confusion of thought and mind—dazed as it were—on those mighty falls, that walking along a solitary road, and alone, in intense darkness, with nothing but the stars in the heavens overhead, and a few fire-flies as they sported about on the bushes, that I fully realised the sight I had that day seen. Gradually, as I walked along, and with the roar of the mighty cataract filling as it seemed the whole world, and shaking to its foundations the whole earth, bit by bit that mighty sight was realised by my mind's eye, and I saw it plainer then than I had seen it in the day time when standing in front of it. And more or less it always is so with natural scenery. I have seen that beautiful panorama of the Thames Valley and the Vale of White Horse, as seen from the Wiltshire Downs scores of times when far away from it. Some time or another I must write about things I have seen with my eyes shut. But not until I have exhausted all my notes and reminiscences of the old Wiltshire town, to which I must now return. At the present time I am only a trespasser, as it were, on the Downs, but I could not help saying what I had to say about them.

≈·The Popular Amusements of our·≈ —Grandfathers—

IFTY years ago the inhabitants of a town like Swindon were thrown very much on their own resources for such amusements as they were able to enjoy. In those days the Mop, the Feast, or the Fair was a something to be looked forward to, and when they came they excited quite a lively interest. Between these events there were a few other amusements. But they were only occasional, and consisted most generally of a dog-fight, bull-baiting, a bout at wrestling or single stick, or a visit from some company of strolling players. I have no personal recollection of bull-baiting as carried on in the present Market Square, at Swindon, but I have often conversed with an old friend, now some years deceased, who had been a witness of the "entertainment" many times, and from a circumstance which has been related to me I am enabled to fix the last bull-baiting at Swindon somewhere about the years 1810 or 1812. On this occasion a butcher's lad at Cricklade obtained permission from his master to take his dog to a bull

bait at Swindon. He went to Swindon, but returned without his dog. As usual, there was a large crowd assembled to witness the sports, which then took place in the Market Square. In the centre of the Square a large oaken post was let into the socket or square frame of timber, which was firmly embedded in the ground, and which was always ready to be uncovered to receive the post. [I well recollect, many years ago, when the first drainage works were being carried out in Swindon, seeing this frame dug up through the course of the drain from Dammas Lane into the High Street, passing by it, and to being then told by some of the elder workmen the purposes for which it had been used.] Around this post there ran a loose iron ring, to which there was fastened an iron chain, which, being fastened to the bull, kept the infuriated animal within the bounds of a limited circle when being worried by the dogs which were set on it. It was quite common to witness at these sports most shocking scenes of brutality, and on the occasion to which I now more particularly refer there were several instances of this. But from what I have been able to learn respecting it, it was chiefly remembered in consequence of the butcher boy's dog from Cricklade proving an unusually *good* one. Having been set at the bull in proper form, it got tossed several times, till at length the bull, thrusting one of its horns into its side, literally disembowelled it. When in this state its master offered to bet a guinea that the dog, if again set at the bull, would even yet attack it. The bet was accepted, and the dog, having been again set at the bull, succeeded in seizing it by the nose, to which it held on until it died, thereby giving the only proof it was capable of giving that it was a dog of the right sort by holding on till death. From what I have heard of this particular exhibition, it was the good qualities displayed by this dog, and not the horrid brutality of the whole business, that caused it to be remembered and afterwards referred to.

It having occurred to me that there might be still living among our "oldest inhabitants" some who had been actual eye-witnesses to these "sports," I resolved on making enquiries, and was soon rewarded for my trouble by a conversation with Henry Jones, now in his 84th year, and who tells me he saw the bull-baiting in the Square to which I more particularly refer, and further, that to give additional *eclat* to the occasion, before the baiting commenced he has seen the bull decorated with ribbons and led by ropes round the town with a man of the name of William Mills riding on its back. From what Mr. Jones tells me there was quite a revival of the sport in consequence of the making of the Wilts and Berks Canal bringing large numbers of persons into the town and making trade unusually brisk. It is but very seldom we hear anything about the Wilts and Berks Canal now, but fifty years ago it was very different. It was not only the greatest public work that had ever been undertaken in this part of the country, but the revolution it was to effect, and the impetus it was to give to trade, was simply marvellous. Of course, it has nothing to do with my present subject, but I cannot resist quoting, *inter alia*, a passage from a letter by William Cobbett, written in October, 1826, and published in his " Rural Rides," in which he says :—

"Just before we got to Swindon, we crossed a canal at a place where there is a wharf and a coal-yard, and close by these a gentleman's house, with coach-house, stables, walled-in garden, paddock *orné*, and the rest of those things, which, altogether, make up *a villa*, surpassing the second and approaching towards the first-class. Seeing a man in the coal-yard, I asked to what gentleman the house belonged : ' To the *head un* o' the canal,' said he. And, when, upon further enquiry of him, I found that it was the villa of the chief manager, I could not help congratulating the proprietors of this aquatic concern ; for, though I did not ask the name of the canal, I could readily suppose that the profits must be prodigious, when the residence of the manager would imply no disparagement of dignity if occupied by a Secretary of State for the Home, or even for the Foreign, Department. I mean an *English* Secretary of State ; for, as to an *American* one, his salary would be wholly inadequate to a residence in a mansion like this."

Now, if the canal superintendent's house produced such an impression as this on a stranger passing casually through the town, we may readily understand that the cutting of the Canal, and the building of such a house, were events in the history of the place which produced something more than a passing sensation. The works in connection with this Canal were specially important in the neighbourhood of Swindon. The high level of the place involved serious engineering difficulties, and called for a very great expenditure of both capital and labour. On the north, east, and west, series of " locks" were required to carry the Canal down from the highest point between London, Bristol, and Gloucester, whilst on the south there had to be constructed the " Reservoir," extending over sixty acres of land, in which to store a supply of water for filling up the Canal at Swindon, and compensating it for the loss sustained through the "locks," at each opening of which a certain quantity of water was drawn off or lost. A work like this of course necessitated the employment of large bodies of "navvies," and from what I have been told it would seem that the population of Swindon and the neighbourhood was doubled for a time in consequence of this large amount of imported labour. There was then, no doubt, quite as much anxiety

exhibited by the inhabitants as there would be now
to meet the wants and wishes of the visitors. Amusements would be got up for them then as well as now,
and there would be a general interest manifested in
their welfare, especially so long as they had any
money to spare, not of course for the purpose of getting it from them, but only to help them to take care
of it, and see that it was not lost. We know how
such things are done now, and it is undoubtedly a
pleasing feature of our own times that no sooner is
there a large gathering of working men in any particular locality for the carrying out of some special
work than there are found those who are ready and
willing to make some sacrifices for the moral and
social comforts of those who are thus congregated.
And it is specially worthy of remark that in the recent
construction of a railway in our neighbourhood arrangements were made by the contractors and others
to provide innocent amusements and recreation in
the long winter evenings for the navvies on the works,
as well as for giving them, while at their work, the
opportunity of refreshing themselves with such drinks
as tea and coffee, instead of leaving them to the one
drink—beer. It was so fifty or sixty years ago.
There was the same readiness to provide amusement
for the visitors then as now. The only difference is
in the character of the article provided. At such
times and under such circumstances men are likely to
bring out that which accords best with their own
natures. When the Canal was being made in the
early part of the present century, the chief amusements indulged in by the gentry was scandal and
tittle-tattle at places of fashionable resort, like Bath,
and cock and dog fighting, and bull-baiting, by
all classes alike in our rural districts. And the
shopkeepers and inhabitants of Swindon, therefore,
knew of no higher compliment they could pay to the

navvies who had come among them to make the Canal than by re-introducing for their amusement the sport of bull-baiting.

Strutt, in his "Sports and Pastimes of the English People," first published in 1801, says :—

"Bull and bear-baiting is not encouraged by persons of rank and opulence in the present day ; and when practised, which rarely happens, it is attended only by the lowest and most despicable part of the people ; which plainly indicates a general refinement of manners and prevalency of humanity among the moderns ; on the contrary, this barbarous pastime was highly relished by the nobility in former ages, and countenanced by persons of the most exalted rank, without exception even of the fair sex. Erasmus, who visited England in the reign of Henry VIII., says, there were 'many heards of bears maintained in this country for the purpose of baiting.' When Queen Mary visited her sister the Princess Elizabeth during her confinement at Hatfield-house, the next morning, after mass, a grand exhibition of bear-baiting was made for their amusement, with which, it is said, 'their highnesses were right well content.' Queen Elizabeth, on the 25th of May, 1559, soon after her accession to the throne, gave a splendid dinner to the French ambassadors, who afterwards were entertained with the baiting of bulls and bears, and the queen herself stood with the ambassadors looking on the pastime till six at night. The day following, the same ambassadors went by water to Paris Garden, where they saw another baiting of bulls and of bears ; and again, twenty-seven years posterior, Queen Elizabeth received the Danish ambassador at Greenwich, treating him with the sight of a bear and bull-baiting, 'tempered,' says Holinshed, 'with other merry disports ;' and, for the diversion of the populace, there was a horse with an ape upon his back ; which highly pleased them, so that they expressed 'their inward-conceived joy and delight with shrill shouts and variety of gestures.'"

Brand, in his "Popular Antiquities," supplies quite an abundance of information concerning these old English sports. But perhaps the most interesting and amusing item is to be found in Gilpin's "Life of Cranmer," inasmuch as it serves to show that what we call the "Reformation" in England was at one time in danger of being wrecked through a baited bear stepping into a boat on the *Thames* in its desperate efforts to escape from its brutal tormentors. The sentence reads as follows :—

"Bear-baiting, brutal as it was, was by no means an amusement of the lower people only. An odd incident furnishes us with proof of this. An important controversial Manuscript was sent by Archbishop Cranmer across the Thames. The person entrusted bade his Waterman keep off from the tumult occasioned by baiting a bear on the river, *before the King;* he rowed, however, too near, and the persecuted animal overset the boat by trying to board it. The Manuscript, lost in the confusion, floated away, and fell into the hands of a priest, who, by being told that it belonged to a Privy Counseller, was terrified from making use of it, which might have been fatal to the Head of the Reformed party."

But the connection of both the Church and the Crown with these sports was of by no means an exceptional character in these days. Indeed, the honour of patronising sports of the most brutal and degrading character appears to have been pretty equally divided between Church and State. I have already referred to John of Gaunt and his connection with the neighbourhood of Swindon. It is worthy of note that this same John of Gaunt was the special patron of a company of minstrels belonging to the Manor of Tutbury, in the county of Stafford, and who enjoyed certain peculiar privileges granted to them by a high dignitary of the Church, the Prior of Tutbury. Some of the particulars connected with these rights are interesting. In the Charter it is required of the minstrels to perform their respective services upon the day of the assumption of our Lady (the 15th of August), at the steward's court, held for the honour of Tutbury, according to ancient custom. They had also, it seems, a privilege, exclusive of the charter, to claim that day a bull from the prior of Tutbury. In the seventeenth century these services were performed the day after the assumption; and the bull was given by the Duke of Devonshire, as the prior's representative. The historian of Staffordshire informs us that a dinner was provided for the minstrels upon this occasion, which being finished, they went anciently to the abbey gate, but of late years to "a little barn by the town side, in expectance of the bull to be turned forth to them." The animal provided for this purpose had its horns sawn off, his ears cropped, his tail cut short, his body smeared over with soap, and his nose blown full of beaten pepper, in order to make him as mad as it was possible for him to be. Whence, "after solemn proclamation first being made by the steward, that all manner of persons should give way to the bull, and not come near him by forty feet, nor by any means to hinder the minstrels, but to his or their own safeties, everyone at his peril; he was then put forth, to be caught by the minstrels, and none other, within the county of Stafford, between the time of his being turned out to them and the setting of the sun, on the same day; which, if they cannot do, but the bull escapes from them untaken, and gets over the river into Derbyshire, he continues to be lord Devonshire's property: on the other hand, if the minstrels can take him and hold so long as to cut off but some small matter of hair, and bring the same to the market cross, in token that they have taken him, the bull is brought to the bailiff's house in Tutbury, and there collared and roped, and so conveyed to the bull-ring in the High-street, where he is baited with dogs ; the first course allotted to the king, the second for the honour of the town, and the third for the king of the minstrels ; this done the minstrels claim the beast, and may sell, or kill and divide him amongst them according to their pleasure."

There would seem to be but one redeeming feature in connection with these disgusting practices, and this horrid brutality to dumb animals, and it is to be found in the fact that in the game of backsword, and wrestling, and some other sports, those who took their parts in bull-baiting did not hesitate to inflict somewhat similar brutalities on themselves, and on each other. But I must reserve any detailed reference to these other sports of our grandfather's for another paper.

Backsword, Bull-Baiting, and other Olde Englishe Sports.

WRESTLING and Single-stick, or Back-sword playing, has been carried on down to a much more recent date; and as recently as forty years ago there were men living in and around Swindon who enjoyed the repute of being among the best Backsword players in England. The last great " Bout at Backsword " in Swindon was given in about the year 1840 or 1841, by two brothers, James and Thomas Edwards, as well in commemoration of the opening of the Great Western Railway to Swindon as in celebration of some victory they had won through a law-suit, and by which they came into possession of the fields through which Regent-street and Bridge-street now run. The whole of the land between the Primitive Methodist and the Baptist Chapels, with all the side streets on the left-hand side towards the railway, belonged to them, and, as I have said, they celebrated their coming into possession of it by giving a grand backsword bout, themselves offering such prizes for competition as brought together some of

the most renowned players in the country ; the sport,
as it was called, being continued for two days.   The
stage, which was about seven feet high and fourteen
or fifteen long, by ten or twelve feet wide, was erected
alongside what was then the green road, at about
where the Rifleman's Arms now stands in Regent
Street, and on this stage there were witnessed scenes
which it is impossible to forget.   There were two
classes of backsword players, who were denominated
Young Gamesters and Old Gamesters, and there were
also two styles of playing, the rough and the smooth;
and they differed quite as much in their character as
did the styles of wrestling : deliberate kicking of each
other's shins being pemitted in one style, while kicking was strictly prohibited in the other.   At the
sports to which I more particularly refer, both styles
of backsword were played ; but it was the rough
style I more particularly recollect.   The practice and
mode of proceeding was this : The players, having
been called up from the crowd of spectators, would
take their places on the platform.   They were then
given a piece of linen tape of a certain length, the
ends of which were sewn together.   And this tape
they would place around their left thigh, and also
around the thumb of the left hand, which had the
effect of preventing the wearer raising his left forearm
otherwise than in a horizontal position, and just about
on a level with the top of his head.   Each player
would then make his selection of the ash stick, which
was of a certain length—from three to four feet—and
one end of which was covered with a small basket as
a protection for the hand of the player.   And this
having been done, the combatants would shake hands
and then proceed to "show their science."   The
object of each player was of course to protect his
own head from the assaults of his opponent's stick,
and whilst doing this to manage to strike the head of

K

the other player in a manner to cause the "blood
to run one inch." It was customary, I believe, for
these backsword players to go into training for weeks
at a time before a great bout was coming off, and to
adopt all the arts and practices they knew of to so
train their heads to bear any number of knocks
before showing blood. Directly the blood ran the
player from whose head it came was out of the game,
the conquerors in each bout being afterwards pitted
against each other, "playing off the ties," as it was
called, until there was only one sound head—that is,
one from which blood had not run an inch—left, and
to the owner of that head the prize would be
awarded. The fact of winning a prize had the effect
of altogether altering the standing of a player—that
is, if he was a "Young Gamester" he at once became
an "Old Gamester," and was suffered to play as such
only. It used to be the pride, I believe, of some of
the most celebrated players, that they could use
the stick so gently and so artistically that they could
draw blood without the person from whose head it
came really feeling that he had been struck. Others,
however, played after a very different manner, and
they would commence their play by belabouring their
opponent about the arms and body in the most
ferocious manner. And I recollect that this was particularly the case at the New Swindon sports. The
left arm and side and thigh of one of the players was
so cut and bruised that it had the appearance of raw
meat, and although the man himself kept on, and
always came up to time, the spectators became so
alarmed at his terrible condition and lacerated appearance that some attempt was made to get him to leave
the stage and insist that a medical man should be
requested to attend him, one of the noisiest of those
who made the latter request being a gentleman who
had come over from Highworth to see the sport, and

at whose expense a regular laugh was raised on the allegation that he had also come to look out for a job, when his identity was made known, and when he was forced to admit being himself a medical man, but one "who never acted until sent for." The last great bout at backsword in our neighbourhood was that given in celebration of the scouring of the White Horse, at Uffington, and which has been immortalised by Tom Hughes, on the 17th and 18th of September, 1857. On this occasion the sports drew together many thousands of persons from the adjoining counties, competitors for the prizes (which in the aggregate amounted to a very large sum), coming from Cornwall in the west, and from Cumberland in the north. But as the proceedings on this occasion have been already fully described by a far abler pen than mine, I will not further refer to them. I cannot, however, resist adding that although men in a very fair social position occasionally became noted as backsword players, the generality of them went from bad to worse, and not unfrequently died as paupers in the Union Workhouse. Several of these men within the past few years have died at Stratton, and one of the inmates at the present time was quite a noted player. Very frequently, however, they were not spared to live to an old age, the injuries inflicted on them often having a fatal termination, but delayed only for a time. Shrivenham was one of the places noted for its backsword players, and I have been told that on one occasion a player in that village continued to play after one of his eyes had been cut out and lay on his cheek, and slices of flesh had been cut off his arms. Of course, such an one would receive much encouragement from the spectators as being a "good plucky fellow," and the flow of pence into his basket at the close of each bout would be most liberal. It was one of the recognised features of this backsword playing that at the end of a bout the combatants were privileged to ask their admirers and friends for money, which they did by reversing the stick, and taking hold of the small end, collect what money they could in the basket at the other end. I believe the amount which a favourite player would thus collect was oftentimes very considerable. In villages like Stratton and Wroughton, backsword play continued to be the main attraction at the annual feast for years after the great display at the White Horse Hill; but, happily, the practice has now altogether died out. The brutal scenes I witnessed on these and similar occasions, more particularly at the village feasts in the neighbourhood, where backswording was the principal amusement, made me resolve to do all that lay in my power to bring such sports into disrepute, and to establish in their stead others of a less objectionable character.

In the *Advertiser* for Monday, August 4th, 1856, I wrote as follows :—

"OLD ENGLISH SPORTS AND MODERN RECREATIONS.

"At Wroughton, a week or two since, at Stratton, to-day, and at various other villages in the neighbourhood at other times in the course of this season of the year, Englishmen knock about each other's heads with ashen staves for gain ! the *fortunate* fellow who can crack his opponents skull and make the blood run *one inch* receiving two shillings and six-pence—*and some beer :* the *unfortunate* fellow, with his head cracked, and the blood running one inch, receiving the lesser sum of one shilling, and some beer. Who'd have thought skulls and blood had been so cheap in eighteen fifty-six ! Englishmen look on, clap their hands, cry bravo, exhibit various other demonstrations of joy and pleasure, and call the degrading, debasing, exhibition ' *Fine Old English*

Sport.' What we saw at Wroughton the other day
may be seen at Stratton to-day, and at the other
skull-cracking villages in the course of the season. A
stage, some ten or twelve feet square, by three feet
high, is erected in the immediate neighbourhood of
the public house. At the appointed hour for the
commencement of the *sport* the landlord makes his
appearance on the stage, graciously smiles on the
gaping crowd below, appoints an umpire, retires, and
sends up some beer,—such sport as that about to
follow could not go on without beer. The umpire
takes his place on the stage, arranges the ashen
staves, holds up the pot of beer, takes a draught from
it, motions to his friends that it is remarkably nice,
invites them up to taste it, and compete for the prizes
he has to offer. Two men accept the invitation, and
then the sport commences. In the struggles that
afterwards took place we saw one man with his right
arm so lacerated and swollen that it became nearly
double its natural size, and the blood running from
the wounds left a track on the ground as the man
walked about. Another man, upon receiving a terrific
blow across the head, fell prostrate on the stage, and
it was some minutes before the men who picked him
up knew whether he was dead or alive. Upwards of
an hour after we saw that man reeling about like one
drunk, and his hair was matted and his face smeared
with blood from the wound in his head. This is
merely a sample of what took place at Wroughton,
and is taking place to-day at Stratton. We ask, can
nothing be done to put an end to this ' Fine Old
English Sport'? Any attempt to suppress the ' Feast-
day' would be unavailing : it is the only day set apart
as a holiday in the course of the year. Young and
old, for generations past, have looked forward to the
day as an holiday, and spite of all efforts to wean
them from it they will continue to do so. We turn

now to a more attractive picture. At New Swindon a collection has been made by the inhabitants and the workmen in the Factory, for the purpose of securing the attendance of a band of music in the cricket-field one evening in the week so long as the weather will permit. The consequence is that the inhabitants of New Swindon repair to the cricket-field every Thursday evening, and there, some by promenading and listening to the strains of the very excellent band of music, others by engaging in some of the numerous games of cricket, quoits, and other such like games, pass a pleasant and interesting evening. Could not something of the kind be got up by the inhabitants of Wroughton and Stratton? We do not mean on every Thursday night as at New Swindon : that would be expecting too much, but they can open a very excellent opposition shop to the givers of prizes to competitors in Old English Sports on the next Feast-day,—if they will only set about it. It may take years to reason the people out of their holiday, but a short time will suffice to work that day into one for rational and innocent amusement."

And yet, as I have pointed out, there were those who could play the skull-cracking game of backsword with such gentleness and skill that a scratch with the end of the stick, or a slight abrasion of the skin, was all the damage done, and was sufficient to enable the umpire to decide the "bout" or award the prize. I have heard of a family living at Purton—a father and several sons—who were all noted players, and distinguished wherever they went for their gentle play. They practised the game on what may be called scientific principles. In connection with their dwelling there was a fruit orchard, and their practice was to drive the point of a nail (such as is used by slaters and plasterers) slightly into the bark of one of the trees, and at from five to six feet from the ground. They would then take their position at varying distances in front of the tree, and while practising all the movements necessary to guard their own heads, would strike at the head of the nail, until they would succeed in driving it home by blows with the point of their sticks, without damage to the tree; and in this way they became as celebrated for the accuracy of their aim in breaking an opponent's head with their stick, as some of the old coachmen were for their ability to kill a fly on a *leader's* ear with their whip.

Since the original publication of this paper, I have been favoured with several communications concerning the "sport," and I have gratefully to acknowledge the information by Mr. C. A. Wheeler, that there was still in existence a placard announcing the last backsword entertainment given in the Square, Swindon; and I am further indebted to Mr. Blackford, of the Grapes Inn, New Swindon, for permission to copy the same. [See page 139.]

I have also to acknowledge the kindness of W. F. Parsons, Esq., Alderman and ex-Mayor of Wootton Bassett, in sending me the following :—

BACKSWORDING.

The following paragraph relating to the match at backswording or single-stick at Salisbury, in August, 1783, at the time of the races, is copied from a Salisbury paper of that date :—"The sports began on Wednesday morning at 11 o'clock, continuing till two, when the stage was cleared. The gamesters were nine Somersetshire men—six from the country and three from London—against the Wiltshire players. Our countrymen surely testified their respect for their visitors this day, for not a Somersetshire man lost a

head, whilst twelve heads were broke on the Wiltshire
side. The prize was won by Jupe, who broke three
heads. Harris also broke three heads, apparently
without losing his own, but on his dismounting from
the stage some blood was discovered on his eye-brow,
and on examination was found to be broke. This, he
protested was done by a shilling (thrown to him as a
reward for his good play). However, the spectators
adjudging otherwise, he was not allowed any claim to
the prize. Jupe came from London, and was on the
Somerset side, but he is a native of Mere, in this
county.—Thursday : The visitors now mounted the
stage, flushed with success, and our brave, though unsuccessful countrymen, nothing daunted, entered the
lists with equal spirits and good humour. The
spectators beheld for three hours most excellent play.
Would that we could say that our brethren were
fortunate as deserving, but the battle is not always to
the strong ; those who obtained the wreath yesterday
obtained it also to-day, breaking eight heads to one.
The prizes were won by Stevens, Barnet, and Cooke.
This day Dowling, a Wiltshire gamester, broke the
head of Jupe, who won the prize on Wednesday.
Blackford, the Swindon butcher, played a bout with
Stevens, but both retired unsubdued.—Friday : The
gamesters mounted the stage, and continued to show
great dexterity and excellent play. Five heads were
gained this day by the Somersetshire men, and one
by the Wiltshire, Blackford breaking the head of
Jupe, who submitted to Dowling on Thursday. The
prizes were equally divided. We are sorry to hear
that Wilkins, a noted left-hand player, was brought
from London to pit against Blackford, the Swindon
player. When the last bout was played the little
Swindon butcher got upon the stage and addressed
himself to the Somersetshire players, as follows :—
'Gentlemen, I have not much ability, as a gamester,

to boast of, and less money to lose; yet I will stake twenty guineas on my own prowess against any Somersetshire player that will enter the lists with me, but, gentlemen, we must have no padding, none of those large·wool-packs on our arms. I wonder you do not wear a helmet, or an iron pot, on your heads. Let us depend on our own skill, and let him (as usual) who breaks two heads out of three be entitled to the prize, and let this day month decide the contest.' A murmur of applause ran through the assembly, but the challenge was not accepted. When some disagreement happened, and Stevens, a Somersetshire gamester, was assailed by some rude people in the crowd, Blackford instantly jumped from the stage and defended his antagonist."

Extract from a metrical story intituled "Aldhelm and Ethelfled," by the late Jeremy Jepson Ripley, Esq. (brother of the late T. H. Ripley, Vicar of Wootton Bassett), dedicated to the Earl of Clarendon, London, 1818. The date of the story is supposed to be subsequent to the year 1349, when Richard, Duke of York, succeeded the Duke of Bedford as Regent of the Kingdom. The scene is laid at Bradenstoke, or Clack, as it is now called :—

" Forth from their homes which bine and brake
Had perfumed for the hamlet wake,
To lead and grace the moonlight game
Fond youth and conscious maiden came—
The aged to admire apart—
The triumphs of their country's art,
Such as their wives were wont to prize
And future sons will solemnize.
These in a swift and simple round
Pursued the tabor's merry sound ;
These placed the loftiest vats turn'd o'er,
And lightened of their generous store ;
Thereupon transverse perches closed
The level planks a stage composed ;
The bonnets there aloof were hurled,
A challenge to the rustic world

The gage each stout appellant gave,
Accepted by a foe as brave.
There, too, a bonnet hung on high,
The aim for village rivalry ;
The umpires there of skill and force,
Once matchless in the rural course,
More temperate then and timely wise,
Stood to award another's prize.
By them the handkerchief was wound
The champion's nether thigh around ;
By them the ground-ash sapling peeled,
And fitted with an osier shield.
To guard his right, his weaker hand
Was fettered by the silken band.
'Twas theirs the onset to deride,
And watch th' essay on either's side ;
The arm fix'd motionless and high,
Before the front the level eye,
Th' half-open lip—the wrist's swift play,
And each descending weapon's sway,
Impelled now here, now there withstood,
'Till one or other blow drew blood.

As an illustration showing the repute in which single-stick players were held in their day and generation when they were the pets of the country squire, and were anything but discarded by the country parson, Mr. Parsons sends me the following anecdote concerning a Robert Blackford, of Swindon, probably the Salisbury hero, or at least his son : " I have heard my mother relate," writes Mr. Parsons, "an anecdote of him, which is worth preserving : He came to Wootton Fields to buy some fat calves of her father, and whilst there a tramp came to ask for relief. He was insolent on being refused, and Blackford threatened him if he did not take himself off. He, however, was not afraid of Blackford, and they had a tremendous pugilistic encounter in the Cowleaze, just in front of the house. The contest was long and doubtful, but my grandfather happening to cry out, 'Well done, Blackford!' the tramp at once gave up, saying that he little thought he was fighting a man of such repute."

WILTS.

Backsword Playing.

On FRIDAY and SATURDAY, the 23rd and 24th of
Sept., 1808,

THE FOLLOWING PRIZES WILL BE GIVEN
TO BE PLAYED FOR AT BACKSWORD,
IN THE
SQUARE, AT SWINDON.

FIRST DAY.
A PRIZE OF FIFTEEN GUINEAS.

For old Gamesters, the best Man to have 12 Guineas and the Second-best
3 Guineas.—Also a PRIZE of FOUR GUINEAS for Young Gamesters
that never won a Prize above 10s. 6d.   Value, the best Man to have 3
Guineas and the Second-best 1 Guinea.

SECOND DAY.
A PRIZE OF TEN GUINEAS

For old Gamesters, the best Man to have 8 Guineas and the Second-best 2
Guineas.—Also a PRIZE of THREE GUINEAS for Young Gamesters,
the best Man to have 2 Guineas and the Second-best 1 Guinea.—And as
a further Encouragement to good Gamesters, 2 Shillings will be given to
every Man who breaks a Head until the Tyers are called, and 1 shilling to
every Man who shall have his Head broken.

Every Man who breaks a Head, the Blood to run one Inch, and saves his
own, to be considered a Tyer, but no Person to quit the Stage as a Tyer
until the Umpires shall have determined *as such*, by having fairly broken
his Opponent's Head *and saved his own*.

No head to be allowed previous to the calling of the Tyers unless actually
broken,

The Players on mounting the Stage to give in their names to the Umpires
and declare on which *side* they play.

The Tyers to play *out in sides* as they shall gain the Tye and be called by
the Umpires, and any Tyer not appearing when called for to forfeit his
Head to the Tyer on the opposite Side with whom he ought to play.

On Account of the Shortness of the Days the Gamesters to mount the
Stage each Day precisely at Ten o'Clock and play till One (when an adjournment will take place), to mount the Stage again precisely at Two, and play
till Five, when the Tyers will be called ; and as an inducement to Gamesters
to be early in their Attendance Seven Shillings will be given to the first two
old Gamesters and Five Shillings to the first two young Gamesters that
shall mount the Stage and contend for the Prizes each Morning at the appointed Time.

Proper and *Impartial* Umpires will be appointed, by whom all Disputes
are to be determined.—No Person will be allowed to be on the Stage during
the Play but the Parties playing and the Umpires, and *no Pads or sham
Play* will be allowed.

Harold, Printer, Marlborough.

I have heard old inhabitants speak of the Square being used for other purposes beside backswording and bull-baiting. It was, for instance, also used for punishments of the minor sort, the stocks and pillory being erected there. I think it quite possible there may be still extant some record of the last use of the pillory, for from the social position of the offender, who was a medical man of the town, it must have created some little sensation at the time. I, however, have been unable to obtain any particulars of either the offence or the offender, although I have heard that a medical man of the name of Thompson, on being charged with a most disgusting offence, suddenly left the town, and was never afterwards heard of. The stocks were removed from the Square to the high bank just below the lodging house, and nearly opposite the present church in Cricklade Street, where I well recollect them. The stocks and pillory must have afforded rare fun at the time when they were in common use, and their exhibitions must have come in as most enjoyable interludes between the periods devoted to bull-baiting and single-stick, and the various fairs.

In-Door ✳ Amusements.
⁓The ✳ Mummers.⁓

IN addition to the out-door sports, there were the in-door amusements, and most notable of all among these were the Mummers, which, forty or fifty years ago, were to be met with in every town and village in North Wilts during the winter months, up to Christmas Eve. These Mummers, who used to go about from house to house, and more particularly to the public-houses, during the winter evenings, performing a rude kind of play founded on the legend of St. George and the Dragon, consisted of six or eight men, who used to wear various kinds of disguises, and who during the season would throw the money they got for their performances into a common fund, which they would distribute at the close of the season *pro ratio* among themselves. Sometimes the company would aspire to nothing more than a recitation set down for each character, but occasionally there would be found a company numbering some ten or twelve persons, including a fiddler, a comic singer, and a dancer, and then the performance would be of

a more elaborate character, and the services of the
company could only be obtained by a previous
engagement, for their "rounds" were so formed as to
include a visit to all the principal residences and farm
houses in the neighbourhood.   The words of the play
performed by these Mummers were partly traditional,
and partly local, and were handed down by word of
mouth from generation to generation.   The plot
of the Mummers' play, as I recollect it, was very simple, and quite orthodox.   It opened with a general
challenge to any knight in Christendom to come forth
and dispute some point which was elaborately set
forth.   The challenge having been accepted, a deadly
conflict with swords followed.   Fabulous sums of
money and everlasting fame were then offered to anyone who should restore the dead knight to life again,
which had the effect of bringing forth some wonderful doctor who had a magic pill, one of which being
thrust into the mouth of the prostrate body restored
animation and the *statu in quo ante*, which consum-
mation was duly celebrated by singing, dancing, and
what other forms of rejoicing the company was
capable of.   As my father was at this time the only
bookseller in business in Swindon, I well recollect that
every year, just before winter set in, there would be
no end of applications for "Mummer's books."   But
these we could never supply, for the simple reason
that they were not in existence ; and there was therefore no help for it but for those who would play the
Mummer's part to get some old Mummer to repeat
the words of the several parts over and over again
until the learner had got them by heart.   Of course,
this mode of transmission from the old 'un to the
young 'un had its disadvantages.   But it had its
advantages also, for it admitted of such addition to
the dialogue as wit, or fancy, or the circumstances of
the times dictated.   I have never known of but one

attempt to reduce the Mummer's play to writing with a view of publication, and that was undertaken many years ago by the late F. A. Carrington, Esq., of Ogbourne, who published the result of his labours in the "Wiltshire Magazine," Part 2., 1854, as follows :—

The verses repeated by the Mummers of the different places are all founded on the same origin, but as they are committed to writing they vary in a trifling degree, and have in some instances considerable interpolations.

About fifteen years ago, one of my friends applied to different sets of Mummers, and wrote down their verses from dictation. The interpolations were, of course, not the same with different sets of Mummers, but the original verses were so—indeed, some of the interpolations had reference to Napoleon and the French War which ended in 1814, and were easily separated from the original text. The characters in the Drama as performed in Wiltshire are :—

1. OLD FATHER CHRISTMAS,
2. MINCE PIE.
3. A TURKISH (evidently a Saracen) KNIGHT,
4. ST. GEORGE,
5. An ITALIAN DOCTOR,
6. A character called LITTLE JACK ;

and the verses they repeat, divested of modern extraneous matter, were as follows :—

Enter OLD FATHER CHRISTMAS *with a long beard* :

Oh! here come I, old Father Christmas, welcome or welcome not,
 I hope old Father Christmas will never be forgot.
   Make room! room! I say!
   That I may lead Mince Pie this way.
   Walk in, Mince Pie, and act thy part,
   And show the gentles thy valiant heart.

Enter MINCE PIE.

Room! room! you gallant souls, give me room to
  rhyme,
I'll show you some festivity this Christmas time.
  Enter a TURKISH KNIGHT, *with a wooden sword.*
  I am a valiant Turkish Knight,
  And dare with any man to fight ;
  Bring me the man that bids me stand,
  Who says he'll cut me down with audacious hand,
  I'll cut him and hew him as small as a fly,
  And send him to Satan to make mince pie.
  Enter ST. GEORGE *with a wooden sword.*
Oh! in come I, St George, the man of courage bold,
With my sword and buckler I've won three crowns of
  gold ;
I fought the fiery dragon and brought him to the
  slaughter ;
I won a beauteous Queen—a King of Egypt's
  daughter :
If thy mind is high, my mind is bold,
If thy blood is hot, I will make it cold.
[ST. GEORGE AND THE TURKISH KNIGHT *fight—
  the latter falls.*]
Turkish Knight   Oh ! St. George spare my life !
Father Christmas   Is no Doctor to be found
  To cure this man who's bleeding
  on the ground.
Enter the DOCTOR.
  Yes! an Italian Doctor is to be found
To cure the Knight who's bleeding on the ground :
  I cure the sick of ev'ry pain
  And raise the dead to life again.
Father Christmas.   Doctor, what is thy fee ?
The Doctor.   Ten pounds is my fee,
  But fifteen I must take of thee
  Before I set this gallant free.
Father Christmas.   Work thy will, doctor.

The Doctor.   I have a little bottle by my side
　　　　　　The fame of which spreads far and
　　　　　　　wide,
　　　　　　I drop a drop on this poor man's nose.
[*The* DOCTOR *touches the* TURKISH KNIGHT'S *nose,
and he instantly springs on his feet quite recovered.*]
Enter LITTLE JACK, *a Dwarf, with several dolls
strapped on his back.*
　　　Oh ! in come I, little saucy Jack,
　　　With all my family at my back.
　　　Christmas comes but once a year,
　　　And when it comes it brings good cheer ;
　　　Roast beef, plum pudding, and mince pie,
　　　Who likes that better than you and I ?
　　　Christmas ale makes us dance and sing ;
　　　Money in purse is a very fine thing.
　　　　　　Ladies and gentlemen give us what you
　　　　　　please.

The acting of this Drama, more or less modified,
is not confined to Wiltshire, as the Right Hon.
Davies Gilbert, M.P., mentions it in the county of
Cornwall, and Mr. Hone, at Whitehaven, in the
county of Cumberland ; indeed, it will be seen from
the extracts given hereafter, that the play is the
same, though in these versions of it some of the
characters are omitted.

Mr. Davies Gilbert, in his Work on Ancient
Christmas Carols, published in 1823 (preface p. 4),
says—" Two of the sports most used in Cornwall
were, the one, a metrical play exhibiting the successful prowess of *St. George* exerted against a
Mohammedan adversary ; the other, a less dignified
representation of some transactions at a market or
fair.

[*In the first,* ST. GEORGE *enters accoutred in complete
armour and exclaims—*

　　" Here come I, St. George,

L

The valiant champion bold,
And with my sword and spear
I've won three crowns of gold.
I slew the Dragon *he*,
And brought him to the slaughter ;
By which I gained fair Sabra.

The PAGAN *enters.*

"Here come I the Turkish knight,
Come from the Turkish land to fight

.   .   .   .   .

.   .   .   .   bold
And if your blood is hot
I will soon make it cold."

[*They fight: the* TURKISH KNIGHT *falls ; and rising
on one knee—*

"Oh pardon me St. George!
Oh pardon me I crave!
Oh give me but my life
And I will be thy slave ! "

[SAINT GEORGE *however again strikes him down ; but
immediately relenting, calls out—*

"Is there no doctor to be found
To cure a deep and deadly wound ? "

[*A* DOCTOR *enters, declaring that he has a small
phial filled with the juice of some particular plant,
capable of recalling any one to life ; he tries, however,
and fails, when* ST. GEORGE *kills him, enraged by his
want of success. Soon after this, the* TURKISH
KNIGHT *appears perfectly well, and having been fully
convinced of his errors by the strength of* ST. GEORGE'S
arm, he becomes a Christian, and the scene closes.]

The Fair, or Market, usually followed as a farce.
" Several persons arranged on benches were supposed
to sell corn, and one applying to each seller in his
turn, enquired the price, using a set form of words to
be answered in a corresponding manner. If any error
were committed, a grave personage was introduced,

with much ceremony, grotesquely attired, and provided with a large stick, who, after stipulating for
some ludicrous reward, such as a gallon of moonlight,
proceeded to shoe the untamed colt, by striking the
persons in error on the sole of the foot." This is the
whole of the account given by Mr. D. Gilbert of these
Cornish Dramas.

Mr. Hone, in his Every Day Book (vol. 2, p. 1646),
under the date of Christmas Day, gives extracts from
a Mumming acted at Whitehaven. The title page of
it is "Alexander and the King of Egypt, as it is acted
by the Mummers every Christmas :—Whitehaven :
printed by T. Wilson, King Street ;" (eight pages,
8vo.). It appears also from Baker's Biographia
Dramatica (Tit : Alexander), that this Drama was
printed in 4to. at Newcastle, in 1788. The characters
are :—

    THE KING OF EGYPT.
    PRINCE GEORGE, *his son.*
    ALEXANDER.
    A DOCTOR.
    AND ACTORS, *who were to be a sort of Chorus.*
The Actors say at the beginning *(inter alia)*—
"Room ! room ! brave gallants, give us room to sport,
  For in this room we wish for to resort ;
  Resort and to repeat our merry rhyme,
  For remember, good sirs, this is Christmas time."
    Prince George says :—
" I am Prince George, a champion brave and bold,
For with my spear I've won three crowns of gold :
'Twas I that brought the Dragon to the slaughter,
And I that gained the Egyptian monarch's daughter."
    And Alexander says *(inter alia)*—
" 'Tis I that will hash thee, and slash thee, as small as
    flies,
And send thee to Satan to make mince pies."
[PRINCE GEORGE *and* ALEXANDER *fight, and* PRINCE

GEORGE *falls.*]
The King of Egypt says—
  "Is there never a doctor to be found,
  That can cure my son of his deadly wound ?"
The Doctor says—
  "Yes, there is a Doctor to be found
  That can cure your son of his deadly wound."

All the other verses are quite different from those of the Wiltshire Mumming, but the most identical phrases in these appear to show that both must have had one common origin.

In the Penny Magazine (vol. vi. p. 339), published in 1837, by Mr. Charles Knight, to whom we are greatly indebted for the preservation of much Antiquarian lore, the verses of the Mumming are given; but in that version of them the character of the *Saracen King* does not occur, and it is *Mince Pie* who fights with, and is vanquished by, *St. George;* but the drama is in substance identically the same as that enacted in Wiltshire.

Sir Walter Scott (in the notes to 6th Canto of Marmion), gives the characters in one of the Masques of Ben Jonson for the Court and their Costumes. The characters are Christmas and his ten children; one of whom is Mince Pie, but the other characters are wholly unlike those in the Mummings which I have referred to.

At Christmas, 1853, a party of Mummers performed at Painswick in Gloucester; the interlocutors were—*Father Christmas; A Turkish Knight; A Doctor* and his *Man;* and *Beelzebub.* The following is a specimen of their verses :—
    Enter OLD FATHER CHRISTMAS.
  " In come I, old Father Christmas,
    Welcome, or Welcome not,
    Old Father Christmas must not be forgot."
      Enter TURKISH KNIGHT.

"In come I, a Turkish knight,
I came from a Turkish land to fight,
And fight I will till I am slain,
For my blood is good in ev'ry vein."

[FATHER CHRISTMAS *and the* TURKISH KNIGHT
fight ; the latter falls.]

Father Christmas, "Five pound, ten pound, fifteen
pound,
If there's a doctor to be found
To raise this dead man from the
ground."

[*The* DOCTOR *is introduced after some laudatory
verses from his man, and performs the cure.*]

BEELZEBUB *then enters and says—*

"In come I, old Beelzebub,
On my back I carry a lump,
In my hand an empty can,
And don't you think I'm a jolly old man."

This is evidently the same character who is called
Little Jack, in the Mummings at some other places,
and affords a clue to the explanation of who *Little
Jack* originally was.

Although neither of the versions given by Mr.
Carrington corresponds with the one that was
generally in use in the neighbourhood of Swindon,
they all serve to show the intellectual character of the
entertainments indulged in by our forefathers in country districts as recently as the last generation. Rude,
however, as the entertainments were, they were very
popular, and when the Mummers could manage to
include in their party a fiddler and a singer, their
takings for the season were occasionally very considerable.

⇜Yeomanry✳Cavalry✳and✳Night⇝ Watchmen.

———◦◆◦———

THE Right Honourable E. P. Bouverie, speaking at the New Swindon Mechanics' Institute, on November 20th, 1882, on the occasion of the distribution of prizes to students in the Science and Art Classes, said :—" He could remember when there was no New Swindon, when there was not a house or cottage in that part : nothing but the decaying old town of Swindon, which there seemed no reason why it should continue to exist. His earliest recollections of Swindon dated back rather more than 50 years ago, and those of the younger generation would hardly believe it, but at that time he was once driving through the town with his father, the late Earl of Radnor, when they found the inhabitants of Swindon had been in a state of dreadful alarm for some days, for they thought they were going to be attacked by a large mob of their own countrymen, who had risen in the country for the purpose of destroying agricultural machinery, believing these machines were going to take the bread out of their mouths. . . . . .

He did not know whether any of them recollected old Mr. Goddard—he did not mean his friend "Ammy" up at the Lawn, whom they all knew—he was a very absent, silent, odd man.   He was going to tell them an anecdote about him, which was characteristic.   At that time he (Mr. Bouverie) was a young man ; his father, who was a rather prominent man in the county of Wilts, happened to be travelling through Swindon, and found the whole town in a dreadful state of alarm, thinking they were going to be sacked by an English mob.   His father thought it was his duty to go and see Mr. Goddard, who was the resident squire, and to lay their heads together to satisfy themselves as to what could be done.   He saw Mr. Goddard at his house, and they were seated in a room were there was a large fire.   Pointing to something which was on the fireplace, his father asked, 'What is that you have there ?'   'Oh!' he replied, 'that is a canister of gunpowder that has been sent me, and I have put it there to dry.'   His father told him that if he remained any longer in conversation with him he must remove the gunpowder, for if they were not in danger of being destroyed by the mob, they would be blown up in a few minutes by the gunpowder."

It must have been in connection with this same Mr. Goddard that I have heard another tale told in connection with the doings of these same troublous times.   Mr. Goddard, as is well known, was Captain of the Swindon Troop of Yeomanry, and on this particular occasion to which I am about to refer, he and his troop, by some means or another, over-stepped the boundary line of their own county.   How this came about I am unable to say.   It may be that the fame of this famous troop had spread far and near ; or it may have been that the Gloucestershire Hussars were engaged in another direction, and, therefore,

could not come. But this is certain : a summons
suddenly came to the Captain of the Swindon Troop
to proceed at once to Fairford, where the labourers
were out and threatening a wholesale destruction of
life and property. Ever ready to the call of duty,
Captain Goddard was not only soon in his saddle, but
he had also gathered around him such of his Yeomen
bold as were within call, and with them he went off to
Fairford as fast as their horses could carry them and
military etiquette admit of. They must have presented all the appearance of a motley crew, this troop
of Yeomanry Cavalry, as they journeyed from Swindon to Fairford. There probably was not one out of
the whole lot who was fully and properly equipped as
a soldier bold. Some lacked hats, some coats, some
breeches—that is, of the proper cut for military men
when out on duty. Such a turn out in the present
day, when appearances count for so much, would no
doubt excite as much derision and contempt as does
the appearance of General Bombastes and his gallant
nondescript army excite laughter when they make
their appearance on some mimic stage. But there
always has been, as there always will be, a mighty
difference between the time for action and the time
for play—the time for fighting and the time for review
and parade. This was the time for action, and, if
needs be, for fighting, and therefore neither Captain
Goddard nor his men had spent much time over their
toilets, or in getting themselves up, on this memorable
occasion. As I have said, they had one and all
answered promptly to the call "to arms," and had
proceeded with all haste to the scene of danger, and
where it was understood "death or glory" awaited
them. In due course "The Military" reached the
Market Place, Fairford, where sure enough the rioters
had already assembled, armed with such implements
of warfare as they had been able to improvise. Some

had old scythes, others hooks, others prongs, and
others such things as they had been able to lay their
hands on, and which as a rule they had fastened by
some means or other to the ends of sticks or poles, so
that they might stand the longest possible distance
off while giving the enemy a cut or a poke.   As the
military rode up and began to form in battle array
the scene as presented on both sides was of the most
ludicrous gravity.   Up till now " heads up" and "eyes
straight" had been the order of the day.   But now!
Well!   To say the least of it, troubled hearts began
to feel a qualm ; firmly-set teeth degenerated into
wide-open and insipid mouths.   Tame and meek-
looking eyes, which had only been looking " forward"
—aye, forward—began to look down noses, out of
which there had been rushing the hot breath of
defiance, and, generally, they one and all began to
feel an especial interest in their legs and feet.   Even
the gallant Captain Goddard had now an opportunity
for taking stock of himself and looking himself over.
It was in course of one of these examinations, and
when casting his eyes down on his toes—I have never
heard it insinuated that he was looking down to see
what it was oozing out from his toes—he made the
grand discovery that in his hasty toilet he had
neglected to button up one of his gaiters.   The discovery was the happiest that could possibly have been
made, as the result proved, for no sooner was it made
than Captain Goddard, accosting a man who appeared
to be the leader of the rioters, and who had been
certainly the most demonstrative of the whole lot,
shouted out, " Hi, there : you fellow, there : Put down
that thing and come and button up my gaiter, will
you ? "   The fellow did as he was bid.   He threw
down on the ground his terrible implement of warfare,
and at once approached the Captain : the Captain
cocked out his leg, and the gaiter was there and then

duly buttoned. There was no fighting that day, although there was won a great victory. The rioters shortly afterwards returned to their homes, and Capt. Goddard and his gallant yeomen had a quiet ride back to Swindon. And what is more, I never heard of the services of the Wiltshire or any other Yeomanry Cavalry being required either at Fairford or its neighbourhood ever afterwards.

But the Fairford episode was by no means the only one arising out of the troublous times of five-and-fifty years ago. Not only were the Yeomanry Cavalry constantly kept as it were in the saddle—or, perhaps it would be more correct to say, kept ready to mount the saddle—but special night watchmen were appointed to patrol the neighbourhood, and especially the vicinity of corn ricks, throughout the long winter nights. I have no doubt there are many persons still living who took an active part in these midnight perambulations. I, however, can only recollect hearing tales told of the most notable events and of the appearances presented by these men when on duty. Nor can I say how many of these special constables it was deemed necessary to appoint for Swindon, but there were probably six or ten, who were divided into three or four parties, each of which had a special district assigned to it. I, however, remember tales told, and laughs raised, at their expense, for their appearance was very grotesque. First of all, a very warm great coat, in which the whole person might be completely enveloped, was necessary, for slow and stealthy movements were considered absolutely essential to the success of the enterprise in which they were engaged. They were described to the children as men with large cravats round their necks, which also enveloped the lower half of their faces, and with slouching hats which covered the other half, there being room between the two for the nose and eyes

only to appear. In their girdles they carried a huge
rattle, in the one hand they carried a stout staff, and
in the other a dark lantern. In the pockets of their
coats, which were usually described as being very
much bulged out, they carried sundry bottles and
flasks containing just a little drop of something to
keep out the cold. And this was the equipment of
the night watch of Swindon five-and-fifty years ago.
I never heard of their running away from, or after,
any of the incendiaries who were so terrifying the
neighbourhood, and who in some places were causing
so serious a destruction of property, and creating so
much fear and alarm. Indeed, I believe it was never
clearly ascertained that there were any of these
dreaded incendiaries actually in or around Swindon,
although it was once rumoured that a most important
discovery had been made, and that in the course of a
very few days something of a very important character
might be expected to turn up. In those days the old
barn in Okus Field would be surrounded in the autumn
months by many ricks of wheat, barley, beans, hay,
and other farm produce, and the place was in consequence a special object of interest to the Swindon
Night Watchmen. And it was in connection with
this particular barton that the discovery to which I
have alluded referred. It was understood that something had been seen and footsteps heard somewhere
about the ricks. But what it was no one for some
time could clearly make out. It was understood,
however, that the circumstances connected with this
place were becoming so suspicious that very shortly
something or another was sure to happen, and further,
that the Watchmen, whose duty it was to take Okus
Barn, never took it without first taking a blunderbuss
with them. At length it was understood that "the
something" had really happened. And great was the
anxiety to know all about it. According to the best

of my recollection the explanation ran thus:—The
"something" had a very mysterious way of moving
about. Sometimes the fall of its footsteps fell most
distinctly on the ear of the listener, whilst at other
times there was perfect silence. On some few occasions there had been seen what appeared to be a
reflected shadow of a pair of long ears or horns, and
on one occasion it was suggested that there came on
the perview the forked end of a long tail. Here, then,
there were no less than three separate and distinct
hints for surmises, and it is but fair to say they were
readily seized hold of and turned to good account.
For a time even the dreaded incendiaries were forgotten in favour of the one idea that the visitor to the
rick-yard in the Okus Field was none other than His
Majesty from down below. And in favour of this
hypothesis the mysterious footfalls, the horns, and the
forked tail were adduced as proofs. As I have already
said, at length some of the more venturesome of the
Night Watchmen, having armed themselves with a
blunderbuss, which they loaded nearly up to the
muzzle, proceeded to lay in wait for the mysterious
visitant to the ricks. At length patience and perseverance met with their reward, for on the eventful night
there was to be seen the pair of horns projecting from
behind the side of one of the ricks. "Bang" went the
blunderbuss. backwards went the two Night Watchmen who had fired it off, for through the heavy charge
which had been placed in it, the rebound was so great
that it sent them both sprawling backwards, whilst
Mat Tuck's, the sweep's, old donkey, which, it appeared, had a special penchant for visiting these ricks
for feeding rather than for incendiary purposes, and
which had received some of the "pepper," set up a cry
of "He-haw! He-haw!" sufficiently loud to be heard
afar off, as it proceeded to execute a skedaddle and to
seek other pastures.

But these were not the only incidents of these
eventful days.   There was one occasion on which the
Yeomanry Cavalry not only drew swords, but one of
them actually drew blood.   The news having reached
Swindon on the over-night that things were nearing a
crisis up on the hills beyond Liddington, and that the
labourers were gathering together and vowing vengeance, the Yeomanry Cavalry were out early on the
following morning.   After assembling in the Market
Place, the Swindon Troop was marched off towards
the scene of the expected disturbance, and the hill
leading into the village of Liddington was duly
reached without anything of note happening either to
the troop or any other body.   Those who know the
spot will recollect that Liddington Hill is bounded on
either hand by rather high banks, on which there are
growing stout hawthorn hedges.   Now, it so happened
that just as the Yeomanry neared the foot of the hill
several labouring men, who it afterwards appeared did
not belong to the disaffected party, and who were not
in any way implicated in their doings, chanced to
turn round the abrupt corner at the top of the hill,
and began to descend the same before noticing what
was approaching them from below.   When, however,
they saw what was to be seen, they were overtaken by
fear and knew not what to do.   To turn round and
run back was out of the question, for they would most
certainly be overtaken, and so they began to clamber
up the sides of the banks and make their escape
through the hedges.   One unfortunate fellow, however, either through getting entangled in the bushes,
or not being quick enough in his movements, presented
his starn end right in front of the Cavalry as they
marched by.   The occasion and the opportunity was
too much for one of the non-commissioned officers of
the troop.   Whether he took the position of the man
to be intended as an act of defiance, of contempt, or

a declaration of war, was never satisfactorily explained, but certain it is that, drawing his sword, he immortalised both himself and the troop to which he belonged by drawing the first and only blood a member of the troop had ever been know to draw, by means of a cut which went right down to the bone of the unfortunate man's buttock.

The*Old*Parish*Church,*The*Old Mill,*and*The*Manor.

 KNOW of nothing in which there has been so complete a change within my recollection as there has been in our old parish churches. With the theology of the business I have nothing whatever to do, and whether the change is desirable or otherwise I will not attempt to say. My simple duty will be to note and record facts as they have been seen by the mortal eye, rather than as they are seen by the schoolman, the cleric, and the controversialist. I know not that I dare venture even to refer to the change in desponding tones in face of the fact that in connection with old church matters nothing is of more common occurrence than to find the Bishop of the Diocese congratulating himself and his clergy on the fact that there are but very few churches under his charge in which the most radical changes have not already taken place. If there is any one thing more than another I would have this paper not be, it is that it should not be theological or conceived in a party or controversial spirit. And yet I cannot help saying,

with a certain amount of regret, I do not know where
in our neighbourhood I can turn and witness one of
the characteristic church services in our rural districts
of thirty or forty years ago ; where I might witness
one of those living active scenes in the flesh which
Wilkie and Hogarth transferred so vividly to canvas.
Fifty years ago, the parish church of Swindon was
the plainest and most insignificant ecclesiastical building in the whole neighbourhood.   With one very
trifling exception, it positively had no architectural
feature about it, and that one exception was a low
Norman column, with cap, around which there ran the
well-known dog-tooth moulding, indicative of the
period of about the middle of the thirteenth century
workmanship.   This pillar was between two arches
situate about the middle of the north chancel wall,
the chancel, it would appear, in the early history of the
church, being open to a chapel which occupied the
north-east corner next to it.   With the exception of this one solitary relic, there was not, so far as
I have been able to learn, another feature in the
whole church which calls for notice.   All the rest may
be placed under the general category of " Churchwarden's architecture."   With the exception of the
statement that "internally the parish church of
Swindon presented a neat appearance," I can find nothing relating to it in any of the notices of Swindon
in the ordinary guide books or gazetteers.   Why was
this ?   Let us try if we can see.   Swindon never
troubled any of our older historians and antiquaries ;
Camden makes no mention whatever of the place,
and Cox, in his " Magna Britannia," only mentions it
to say : " Swindon is so inconsiderable a place that
our histories take no notice of it."   At the taking of
the Domesday survey it appears to have belonged to
no person in particular—that is, as a whole.   There
were, indeed, no less than five persons among whom

the Swindon lands were divided—a most unusual circumstance, there being ordinarily only one land-holder in a parish. Not that a whole parish sufficed for a landholder in those days ; for not a few of them held many parishes, and were even then probably hungry for more. At this time there were only sixty-eight landholders in the whole of Wiltshire, and yet no less than five of them held land in Swindon. But the tale is not even told with these five : there was a sixth, but he was returned only as a "claimant," as a would-be " Sir Roger." How the claimant fared with his claim I know not, nor do I know what particular lands he claimed, or by what means he sought to establish his rights. This I think, however, may be taken as granted : That if he got his discharge on a ticket-of-leave he was not suffered to stump the country with impunity, and, by bringing the most odious charges against the constituted authorities of the land, allowed to keep up one of the most mon-strous crazes that have ever been invented to turn men's heads. The records of the lands and their holders in Swindon in the Domesday survey shew, as usual, that the first and foremost holder was a bishop. The several entries, which are very curious, read as follows :—

" The same bishop (of Baieux) holds Svindune, and Wadardus under him. Leuiet held it T.R.E. when it was assessed at 5 hides. One of these is in demesne, where is 1 ploughland and 4 servants. Five villagers and 2 borderers occupy 2 ploughlands. Here is a mill of the value of 4 shillings, 30 acres of meadow, and the same quantity of pasture. It was valued at 40 shillings ; now at 4 pounds."

" Alured (Alured de Merleberg) himself holds 1 hide and a half in Svindone. He are 6 oxgangs. It is worth 12 shillings."

" Ulurics (a Thane who held by military service

M

under the King) holds 1 hide and a yardland in
Svindone.   Here is half a ploughland.   It is worth
7 shillings."

"Ulward, prebendary of the King, holds 2 hides
in Svindone.   Here are 6 oxgangs.   They are worth
15 shillings."

"Odinus, the chamberlain, holds Svindone.   Tor-
bertus held it T.R.E., and it was assessed at 12 hides.
Here are 6 ploughlands.   Two of them are in demesne
with 2 servants.   And 6 villagers and 8 borderers
occupy 3 ploughlands.   The mill pays 4 shillings.
Here are 30 acres of meadow, and 20 acres of pasture.   It was valued at 60 shillings ; now at 100.
Milo holds 2 hides of this manor, and he has a
ploughland.   Odinus claims them."

There is one other extract, which I may give
here, from another well-known official document or
register concerning the Church, its value, income,
properties, &c., viz., from the *Liber Regis*, ordered to
be taken by Henry VIII., the instructions for which
were as follows:—

"Instructions devised by the Kyng's Hignes by
the advise of his counsail for knowlaige to be hadd of
the hole true and just yerly values of all the possessions, mannors, londys, tenements, hereditamentys,
and proffits, as well as spirituall as temporall, apper-
teynyng to any manner of dignitie, monastrie, priorie,
priorie churche, collegyatt, churche conventuall,
personage, vicarige, chauntrie, ffree chapell, or other
dignitie, office, or promocion, spirituall, within this
realme, Walys, Calice, Berwyk, and marches of the
same, as well in placys exempt as not exempt ;
whiche his pleasure ys, that suche as shall have
charche by his commission to survey the same, shall
effectually with all uprightness and dexteritie followe
and ensue ; as they will answere unto his Majestie at
their perrell."

Clear Yearly Value   Yearly Tenths

£17 0 0   SWINDON   V.   (Holy   Rood).   £1   14   0

100 0 0   Archidiac. 12s. 3d. Prox.

4s 3d. The KING. The
Priory of Southwyk, in
Hampshire, olim Propr. Val.
in decim. gran. fœn. lan.
agn. in minut. decim., &c.

I understand that the present income of the
Vicar of Swindon by no means compares with this
entry : that it is not more than one-half what it
should be according to its value as entered in the
King's books. But Swindon is by no means the only
church in the neighbourhood in which the revenue has
been palpably diverted into some other channel. I
may just notice, in illustration of this, a few of the
entries in the King's books. Liddiard Millicent is
returned at the annual value of £17 4s 4½d. ;
Wroughton, at £31 4s. 4½d. ; Hinton Parva, at
£13 6s. 8d.; Cricklade St. Sampson, at £18 11s. 10½d.;
Castle Eaton, at £19; Liddiard Tregoze, at £10 5s. 5d.;
Liddington, at £14 ; Purton, at £22 17s. 6d. ; Rodbourne Cheney, at £17 ; and Wanborough, £21
10s. 7½d. I must leave the clergymen of the
respective parishes to say in what degree their present
incomes, compared with each other, agree with the
value of their livings in the time of Henry VIII.

As it was not intended by the Domesday survey
to take stock of, or in any way interfere with, the
property of the Church—that was left for a later time,
and for the survey from which I have just quoted, and
which is known as the " *Liber Regis del Thesaurus
Rerum Ecclesiasticarum*" — we can gain no information from this source as to whether any provision
had been made at this time for the performance of
divine worship in either Over Swindon, Nether Swindon, Even Swindon, or West Swindon, and there is
not even the old yew standing, as there is in many
of the surrounding parishes, to mark the spot where

the clergy and people would occasionally assemble
for that purpose before the erection of a permanent
building like that of a church or chapel. At Purton,
Wroughton, and some other parishes in the neighbourhood, there are still standing in the churchyards
magnificent specimens of these old yew trees, but so
far as I can learn, there is not even oral tradition that
they ever existed at Swindon, although I have heard
some mention of their standing in the churchyard, in
some old document belonging to the church.

[Since the original publication of this paper,
I have obtained, principally from the Rev. H. G.
Baily, the late Vicar of Swindon, some interesting
particulars respecting the Yew Trees. They were
undoubtedly a different kind of yew to those planted
on a spot selected for the assemblage of priest and
people for religious service. They were of a straighter
and quicker growth, and designed for another purpose, *i.e.*, for supplying the inhabitants with material
for the making of their bows for the practice of
archery, as well as sticks and staves of various kinds
for use in their various games and sports. Just below
Lower Town, on the Marlborough Road, there is a
field known as "The Butts," which, no doubt, originally belonged to, and was used by, the inhabitants for
the practice of archery, for which it was most admirably situate, and the carrying on of their many
diversions. And then these yew trees were planted
in the old churchyard for ornamental as well as for
useful purposes. How many there were there is no
record to tell. But this is certain : Before the building of the tower, at the western end of the nave,
there had been planted, and were growing, four fine,
tall, and straight yew trees, which formed, as it were,
a natural evergreen tower to the old church, and also
acted as a screen to shut out of sight the mean
proportions of the body of the church, as it was

approached from the town, as well as adding to the
picturesque effect when viewed from the churchyard.
Indeed, from the high knoll on which these trees grew
they must have presented a most picturesque appearance.   The original plan of the church, I think, was
simply a chancel, nave, and two aisles, with a western
entrance porch.   It was around this porch that the
four yew trees were planted, and at exactly equal distances apart, so that they formed a perfect square.
Originally planted to serve the purposes of ornament
or decoration, they appear to have grown into tall and
noble trees, and were ultimately converted into a very
utilitarian use.   Possibly there may have been a great
respect entertained for their ancient and noble appearance, and when it was found that they stood in the
way of the new tower which it was proposed to add to
the old church, there may have been heard many a
pathetic lament, as well as a pouring forth in spirit, at
least, and in the sentiment of the afterwards memorable words of the song—

> Woodman, spare that tree,
>   Touch not a single bough,
> In youth it sheltered me,
>   And I'll protect it now.

Or it may have been simply that in those ancient
days the people of Swindon were only very utilitarian
in their views, and seeing how the old trees might be
made to save a penny and serve a purpose, allowed
them to stand.   Be this, however, as it may, the trees
were not cut down, nor were they allowed to stand in
the way of the proposed new tower.   What was done
was this : their tops were cut off at a given height,
their trunks were squared up as they stood growing in
the ground, and then the walls of the tower were built
just outside, but close up to them.   In the completed
tower, each corner or angle in the inside would
be occupied by the squared-up trunk of one of the

old yew trees. Cross beams were then placed on the tops of these corner posts, and on them the bed of the bell chamber was laid. And there these trees stood, serving this very purpose, down to the time when the bells were removed to the tower of the new church, and when the old tower was pulled down and the material of which it had been composed carted away.]

In resuming my notes on the Old Church, I may say the probabilities are that there was no religious building here at the time of the Domesday survey, nor, indeed, until something like a century afterwards, when the pillar and its cap to which I have referred was erected as part of a small chapel oratory. But, be this as it may, at this early date—at some time prior to the year 1080, there was in Swindon a mill. The fact is referred to twice in Domesday, and both accounts agree in describing it to be of the then considerable value of four shillings. Considered in connection with some recent legal proceedings taken by the inhabitants of Swindon to maintain their rights to certain public roads, this evidence of the existence of a mill in Swindon upwards of eight hundred years ago is both interesting and important, for there can be no reasonable doubt but that the very roads which have been in dispute led to and from this very mill. Nor can there be any reasonable doubt as to the exact situation of this mill. It could not, indeed, have been in any other situation than in the bottom, where the old mill of thirty or forty years ago stood, and where the water from what was known as Church Pond was available for its use. May we not go farther and say that eight hundred years ago this mill constituted, to all intents and purposes, Swindon ? Just above the mill, and until its source was tampered with a few years since, there was a very considerable spring of pure water. To preserve this water and make it available for the use of the inhabitants and their cattle was no doubt the anxious care of the earliest inhabitants of Swindon. The water, right at the fountain head, was in sufficient volume to at once form a considerable stream, *and to turn a mill*, and hence they put their mill there, renewing the structure, which was doubtless of a very rude character, as occasion required, the last renewal being when a former lord of the manor granted a lease to a Mr. Kemble of a building which was finally razed to the ground at the termination of that lease, some twenty-five or thirty years ago.

John Britton, in his " Beauties of Wiltshire," thus refers to the pond and mill :—" Near the church-yard is a large pond, supplied by a spring called Church Well, distinguished not only for the purity of its waters, but for the quantity it supplies. Connected with this is *Swindon Mill*, remarkable for the largeness of its water-wheel, and for its proximity to the spring head. The water is conveyed through pipes to the overshot wheel (the periphery of which is about 100 feet), and falling into buckets, or troughs, gives it a slow, but regular rotatory motion. Though apparently slow in its revolutions, its operation on the interior machinery is as effective, and almost as rapid, as other river mills." It used to be said, I recollect, that this was the largest overshot wheel in England, and no doubt a wheel standing over thirty feet high was calculated to produce this impression. But, if I am not mistaken, this wheel was not the only remarkable feature in connection with the motive power of the Mill. I have a distinct recollection of being told that the machinery of the Mill could be put in motion independent of the wheel, the motion being obtained by the pressure of a column of water, contained in a hollow perpendicular shaft, at the bottom end of which there were two arms, having a small orifice in each, and out of these the water rushed with sufficient force to turn the column on its pivots,

and with it the machinery of the Mill.   The same
principle, I believe, was applied by some of the early
makers of rotary steam engines.   Britton adds : " At
the northern extremity of the town is another spring,
called Holy Well, which supplies the neighbouring
inhabitants with an ample supply of pure water."
This character for " pure water" has long since been
lost.   But I only allude to it here for the purpose
of recording the fact that within living memory this
Holy Well, as well as the row of fine elm trees,
which run from the well nearly to the canal, were on
the waste by the side of the road, and were not
enclosed as private property as now.   But I must
reserve particulars concerning this for some future
paper.

But to return once again to the Mill of Domesday.   As time went on, both the mill and its surroundings gradually grew in interest and importance.
It would be the one centre around which the business
of the place would be done, and no doubt at certain
seasons there would be a considerable gathering of
persons coming to the mill.   And these gatherings, it
may be, in time, necessitated the attendance of a
priest, and then the erection of probably an oratory,
the immediately adjoining knoll being selected for the
purpose.   And then, as time still further went on,
and the people multiplied, and began to establish
laws and customs for their government and the maintenance of order and discipline, they would require a
pond in which to duck their shrews and termagants.
To meet this want, no doubt what became to be
known as Church Pond was formed.   And then
again, as the people became more strict in their
religious observances, and placed themselves more
thoroughly under the direction of their Priests, and
more desirous of observing the fasts, feasts, and festivals of the Church, they would require their fish

ponds and their regular supplies of fish for Lent and other fasting days. Then, again, the bountiful spring of water would come to their aid, and they were enabled, at the smallest possible expenditure of labour, to construct quite a series of ponds on what was no doubt the waste surrounding the old mill. And yet, notwithstanding all these provisions, there are no evidences whatever of there ever having been anything like such a church or religious building as those which undoubtedly existed generally in the neighbouring parishes. Why was this? I have already proposed that we should try if we could see. In answer to this there is but one proposition I can make, and it is this: That through the Swindon lands being divided between so many persons, all of whom held considerable estates elsewhere, there was really no one person in particular who had a sufficient interest in the place to make that provision for the spiritual wants of the inhabitants which we find in all the surrounding places. But, be this as it may, whether the church was large or small, the only thing certain about it is that it was originally dedicated to the Holy Rood, and, for some reason which does not appear, it was afterwards—and some time prior to 1302—rededicated to St. Mary. Undoubtedly, the fullest account ever written of Swindon is that which is to be found in a paper by the Rev. Canon Jackson, and read by him at the meeting of the Wilts Archæological Society, at Swindon, in August, 1860, and in which we read as follows :—

"Many years before the Conquest the land belonged to the Saxon Crown of Wessex, and had been by charter granted to a Saxon Thane or Nobleman, and so became what was called Thane-land, free from certain burdens. About the time of Edward the Confessor, A.D. 1050, that Saxon nobleman, whose name was the Earl William, had given it back to the Crown

in exchange for some other lands in the Isle of Wight.
Consequently, at the Conquest it was again in the
hands of the Crown.   At the time of the great survey
called Domesday Book, about A.D. 1084, the lands
called Swindon had been divided among five proprietors, two larger and three smaller ones.   The
largest was a person of whom nothing more appears
than that his name was Odin, and that he had filled
the office of Chamberlain to William.   The next
largest landlord was the Bishop of Bayeux, a foreign
prelate.   Of the smaller proprietors, one was Alured
of Marlborough, a small owner here, but of comfortable dimensions elsewhere.   The two remaining ones
were Uluric, and Ulward, who, as he is called the
' King's Prebendary,' was probably not badly off in
the world.   All these five estates are registered in the
Great Survey under one and the same name of Swindon.   Besides these there is Wicklescote, now called
Weslecot.   At Wicklescote, in after times, we find
successively the names of these owners—Bluet, Bohun
(his holding there being under the Manor of Wootton
Bassett), Everard, the Darells of Littlecote, and the
Lords Lovell, who had a vast property in this neighbourhood.   By a Katharine Lovell, certain lands at
Wicklescote were given to the Nuns of Lacock Abbey,
and at the Dissolution of Monasteries those particular
lands were bought by Mr. Goddard, then of Upham.
The five properties, all called Swindon in Domesday,
are afterwards variously called Haute, High or Over-
Swindon, Nether-Swindon, Even-Swindon, and West-
Swindon.   They passed into different hands ; and
among other owners were, in Edward I, Philip Avenel,
holding   under the Abbess of Wilton, Robert de
Pontl'arge, holding under the Crown, the Bassetts, the
Despensers, the Abbey of Malmesbury, the Monastery
of Ivychurch, near Sarum ; and, at a later period, the
families of Everard, Alworth, and Vilett, the last

named being now represented by Mrs. Rolleston.
Some of the lands that belonged to Monasteries were
purchased in 1541 by Sir Thomas Bridges, ancestor
of the Dukes of Chandos, and some at Even-Swindon
by the Wenman family, With more access to documents, and an acquaintance with localities, a thing
essential to accuracy in these matters, all this might
be developed ; but for the present we can only dwell
upon the descent of the principal manor and lordship
of Swindon. The Bishop of Bayeux, already mentioned as holding, by the gift of the Conqueror, one
of the larger estates, was Odo, half-brother to King
William : created Earl of Kent. The best description
of him is from his own seal, an extremely rare and
very curious one. On one side he appears as an Earl
mounted on his war-horse, at full speed, clad in armour,
and holding a sword in his right hand. This is one
moiety of him. On the reverse is the other : a Bishop,
in full *pontificalibus*, bestowing the benediction. He
was one of the prime instigators to the invasion, and
performed the part of a military chaplain : celebrated
mass before the whole army the night before the
battle of Hastings, and sang their requiems after it.
Historians speak of him as a cruel, luxurious, over-
bearing man : and as the principal agent employed by
William in dividing the prey—the lands of the defeated English. In this department he washed them
all so clean that he obtained the name of 'The Con-
querer's Sponge.' This Earl Bishop did not forget
himself. His possessions were immense elsewhere :
in Wiltshire he had only the small matter of the
Manors of Swindon, Tidworth, Ditchampton, and
Wadhill. The Conqueror had an odd habit of throwing. away his sponges when they had served their purpose long enough : and so, on a suitable, pretext he
threw Bishop Odo, not exactly away, but into prison,
and deprived him of all his estates. The next time

that the lordship is mentioned is not until the reign of
Henry III., when, among others, it was again bestowed
by the Crown upon a French nobleman, who also
again happened to be the King's half-brother, William
de Valence, created in England Earl of Pembroke, of
Goderich Castle.   He was one of the foreign leeches
who sucked the blood of this country, and whose con-
tinued importation roused to resistance the native
Barons of that reign.   He had a son, Aylmer de
Valence, who succeeded him, and died in 1323. Upon
his death, without children, it was held by his widow,
Mary, Countess of Pembroke, foundress of a College
at Cambridge, at first called the College of Mary de
Valence, but now Pembroke Hall.   At her death,
Swindon passed to her late husband's niece, Elizabeth
Comyn, who brought it in marriage to Richard, second
Baron Talbot, of Goderich Castle; and in 1473 it
belonged to his descendant, John, Earl of Shrewsbury.
About, I believe, the year 1560, it was purchased by
Thomas Goddard, Esq., of Upham, ancestor of the
present owner.   This was just 300 years ago; but
there is a family deed which mentions Goddard of
High Swindon in 1404.   The Rectory and Advowson
belonged at a remote period to the Augustine Priory
of Saint Mary, of Southwick, near Winchester.   In
the year 1323 that Priory obtained licence to impro-
priate it ; i.e., to apply the great tithes to their own
use, converting the resident officiating minister into a
Vicar ; but the endowment does not seem to have been
settled (unless there is some error in the dates) until
1359.   At the dissolution of Southwick Priory, the
Rectory and certain woods *super rectoriam*, were
purchased by Mr. Stephens, then of Burderop, whose
family, in 1602, sold it and the advowson, to Nicholas
Vilett and heirs, now represented by Mrs. Rolleston ;
but the nomination to this vicarage in some way
passed to the Crown.   The Monks of Wallingford

used to have a small pension from the tithes. In the list of Vicars are three peculiar names : Milo King, Aristotle Webbe, and Narcissus Marsh."

What the church was like in appearance when Milo, Aristotle, and Narcissus preached therein there is absolutely nothing to show. I think, however, it must have been of a somewhat rude and unpretentious character. It would appear, however, that about one hundred and fifty years ago it had fallen into such a ruinous condition that a general restoration was decided on, and the way in which this was effected may be best explained by an entry in the Charity Commissioners' report, dated January, 1833, and which reads as follows :—" It appears from an entry in a parish book, that in the year 1748 divers lands were sold by the churchwardens to Ambrose Goddard, Esq., William Kemble, Lawrence Boxwell, and Thomas Purton, for sums of £238, £220, and £29, making together £487. It is not known what estates were sold, but it is believed in the parish that these sales took place for the purpose of rebuilding part of the body of the church." The building thus restored continued to serve the purposes of a parish church down to the year 1851, when, it having again fallen so hopelessly out of condition, and there being really nothing worth restoring, the present parish church, which was erected from designs by the celebrated architect Sir Gilbert Scott, was built and substituted in its place.

Having thus traced the old church down from its earliest existence to within living memory, I will now endeavour to look at it as I saw it just previous to its demolition.

⌐The◦Old◦Church⌐

REVIOUS to its partial demolition in 1851 (the chancel and nave arches only are now standing), the old parish church differed but slightly in its general appointments from the generality of country churches. Its form was that of the Latin cross, but inverted, the foot lying to the east instead of to the west. This was occasioned by the limbs or arms of the cross being formed by the north and south porches, and not by transepts. Internally, there was a nave with north and south aisles with chancel, and at the west end there was a stunted-looking square, and somewhat rough-built, tower, in which there was a peal of five bells. Perhaps I had better ring these bells at once, and have done with them. They were, like the church itself, comparatively new. It is generally found that church bells not only bear the names of those who cast them, but also a date, and not unfrequently an inscription, some of which are very quaint. The most popular inscription appears to have been " Hope well," for it is to be found in

most peals.   The names of donors, and also of church
officers, are frequently recorded by inscriptions on
bells.   On a bell in Aldbourne Church there is this
inscription :

> " The gift of Jos. Pezzi and Wm. Gwynn.
> " Music and singing we like so well,
> " And for that reason we gave this bell."

At Devizes one of the bells bears this inscription :—

> " I am the first, although but small."
> " I will be heard above you all."

And on another Devizes bell there is this :—

> " On Earth bells do ring,
> " In Heaven angels sing : HALILUIAH."

And quite a number of bells bear this :—

> " Come when I call
> " To serve God all."

There are but very few church bells in Wilts of
a date anterior to 1600.   There is one at Coombe
Bassett dated 1586.   But there are hundreds ranging
from 1600 to 1650, which appears to have been the
great bell period in Wilts.   Cliffe Pypard has a bell
dated 1604 ; Devizes two bells dated 1610 ; Chiseldon one dated 1610, with the inscription, " Hope
well," and another dated 1617, with the inscription,
" Be merciful ;" Wanborough, a bell dated 1662 ;
Wootton Bassett has two dated 1663 ; Liddington
one, dated 1664 ; and Broad Hinton no less than four
dated 1664.   It would seem pretty clear that the bell
founders of the period rang the changes pretty successfully on the people of the last mentioned four
parishes.   Getting an order to put in a new bell at
Wanborough they worked the Liddingtonians up to
new bells pitch for the next year, increasing their
success at Wootton Bassett, where they put in two
new bells, and then completing their triumph at Broad
Hinton, where they put in no less than four new
bells.   But they do not appear to have aroused the
Swindonians, for the whole five bells in the old church

at the time of its demolition, in 1851, bear the date
1741, with inscriptions as follows :—

1.   '' Peace and good neighbourhood.''
2.   '' Prosperity to the parish.''
3.   '' Prosperity to the Church of England.''
4.   '' Wm. Nicolls, Vicar.''
5.   '' Richard Wayt and Wm. Lawrence, churchwardens.''

A sixth bell, by C. and G. Mears, of London, was
added to the peal in 1851, when the new church was
erected, and the bells were removed there, and a
seventh and eight by Llewellyn and James, of Bristol,
in 1883.

I have heard it said it was just about this time—
that is, about one hundred and fifty years ago—that
the tower to the old church was built, and that it was
for the purpose of paying for this tower, rather than
for rebuilding the body of the church, that the charity
lands were sold. But if fifty years ago the Charity
Commissioners had no better evidence to guide them
than what was " believed in the parish" in connection
with matters of serious importance, I can hardly hope
to be in a position to give positive evidence about
anything. Of this, however, I feel quite certain :
For some purpose or other, and probably about
1750, there was a wholesale destruction of parish
documents. Every scrap of evidence which would
protect the rights of the inhabitants mysteriously disappeared, and from that time downwards great
changes have doubtless taken place, and right after
right, which the inhabitants had previously enjoyed,
has been lost. John Aubrey visited the church in
1672, and he says of it :—" In the church is nothing
observable left in the windows, except in the first, on
the south side of the chancell, viz., the coate of Clare.
On a tombe, about a foote higher than the pavement,
on the north side of the aisle, belonging to . .
Goddard Esq., there is this cross [a Cross of Calvary
—that is, a Latin cross mounted on three steps, said

to represent the three graces of Faith, Hope, and Charity].   In the same aisle, beneath his picture, was buried, aged 25, in 1641, Thomas Goddard, Esq., husband of Jane, daughter to Edmund Fettiplace, Knight. . . . .   Somebody is buried by, I suppose his wife, but the inscription is not legible."

After describing the Coat-of-Arms . . . impaled with Grubbe, of Potterne, sinister ; and also of Stephens, of Burthrop [Burderop] on an old and nearly worn out stone in the chancel, Aubrey proceeds to say :   " Near this lye buried two children of William Levet, Esq.   They were buried 1667."   [Aubrey here gives what he calls the coate of Levet ; but Canon Jackson, in his " Notes," says the arms are not those usually assigned to Levet, and adds : As a Swindon name, Levet occurs in the Domesday Survey].

Aubrey next notices an inscription under the altar, thus :—" Here lieth the body of Thomas Vilett, Gent.   He departed this life the 6th day of November, 1667."   On both sides lye buried his two wives.   At the upper end of the church, this inscription :—" Christus, qui mortuus est ut per mortem suam superans mortem triumpharet, a mortuis ad vivos exsuscitabit.   Buried the 5th of June, An. Dom. 1610, the body of Elenor Huchens, the wife of Thomas Huchens, of Ricaston : shee to this parish twenty pound gave to the relief of the Poore, the use for ever.   James Lord, and Henry Cus, her husbands, twenty pounds each of them gave to the Poore of this Parish, the use for ever."

This in the chancel :—" Hic jacet Henricus Alworth" in hâc viciniâ natus, Qui adolescentiam in Scholâ Wintoniensi, juventutem in Academiâ Oxoniensi, senectutem in patriâ Wiltoniensi, feliciter consecravit, ubique castè, sobriè, piè, sibi parcus, suis, beneficus, egenis effusus, ab omnibus desideratus Obijt XVI die Augusti 1669, Ætatis suæ 75."

N

With this exception, so far as I have been able to
learn, there are no notes or memoranda extant concerning the old church, or from which any particulars
concerning it could be obtained.

As seen just previous to its demolition, the body
of the old church presented that mixed appearance
of box pews, of all heights and sizes, and which
differed just as much one from the other as did the
houses in the town, which was the characteristic
feature of the country parish church of fifty years ago.
There were four rows of these box pews : two up the
nave and one in each aisle. And there was a gallery
over the north and south aisles for the accommodation
of the parishioners, and another in a recess in the
tower at the west end for the accommodation of the
organist and the choir. At the junction of the nave
with the chancel there was the customary double or
two-storied pulpit, the top one for the sermon, and the
one below for the lessons, and with occasionally a
third one for the clerk. It is these old rural church
characteristics which we have so completely lost, and
to which I have already referred : The parson and his
clerk in their places high up above the congregation
in their respective places, the parson in his black
academical gown, and the clerk in the "Sunday best"
of an English citizen ; the organ and the choir,
placed still higher up in the recess over the
western entrance, with the occupants of the family
pews, which covered the whole floor of the church, as
well as filled the side galleries, devoutly performing
their part in the service, or heartily joining in the
singing of the Old Hundredth. In many of the
village churches the choir consisted of men like the
village schoolmaster, the village smith, carpenter, and
not unfrequently the village boniface, with other
inhabitants who had a taste for music, and a few of
the village school children. And such choirs as these

were always seen at their best when there was no
organ to "assist" in the music; when the music consisted of what could be got out of a bass-viol, a violin,
a flute, a clarionet, sometimes a trumpet, and such
voices as could be got together, and who were always
as ready to do a psalm as they were a roystering
mummer song, or one of Dibden's popular and
patriotic ditties. To watch a choir composed of such
as these was to witness a sight never to be forgotten.
The finest choir of this kind I ever saw was at Cliffe
Pypard, where, in addition to the instruments I have
mentioned, there was a double-bass, the choirmaster
being the village boniface, a tall, fine, and imposing-
looking man, who, as he sat in the front row in the
western gallery, with a few dexterous scrapes with his
bow, would bring out at the proper moment the rich
deep tones from his instrument, looking for all the
world like a man who had been born for the post he was
filling; who entertained no mean idea of the importance of that post, and who was determined that it
should lose nothing at his hands, or through him. In
some places where "instrumentalists" were not available for the services, a barrel organ, from which there
might be turned off by the turning of a handle some
half-dozen tunes (invariably including "The Old
Hundredth," a "Long Meter," a "Short Meter," and
a "Peculiar") was brought into use. In other places
a step beyond this even was taken, and the choir was
supported by an organ with keys and bellows, as well
as some three or four instrumentalists. This was the
case at Swindon. The organ stood in the middle of
the little western gallery, leaving a space on either side
where the vocalists and instrumentalists took their
places, taking their cue from the clerk, who, as was
not unfrequently the case when provision was not
made for him in the second pulpit under the parson,
took his seat in the singing gallery. I well recollect

that the poor old clerk had anything but a comfortable
time of it with the boys of the period. He belonged
to a race of parish clerks which had existed for
generations. He was a martyr to the gout, and the
boys knowing that he could not run after them, very
often took advantage of him. I, however, was a bit
of a favourite with him, and no doubt had I then entertained any idea of preserving notes about the old
town, I could have obtained from him much information which would now be both interesting and
valuable. It happened in this way : His duties were
of a very miscellaneous character, and far exceeded
those of his successors. In addition to his part in the
services, he had to see to the chiming of the bells, and
keeping order in the singing gallery. And then, as I
have said, he was a martyr to the gout. On a particular Sunday his troubles were greater than usual—
were more than he could bear with that equanimity
which became a person in his position in the church.
Those who usually helped him in the "chimes" kept
at a respectful distance from him, and the consequence
was he had to do three of the bells himself. Happening to go into the belfry, I saw him seated on his stool
as usual, up in a corner on the right hand side. He
had a bell rope twisted round each arm, one of his feet
being at the same time inserted in a loop tied in a
third rope. The picture of misery presented by the
poor old man as thus seen was simply perfect, and
enough to soften the hardest heart. The near
proximity of his stout walking stick, however, had
the effect of silently repelling all assistance even from
those who were willing to render it. Knowing that
the old man's favourite was Blair's pills, and that he
had been trying without avail for some time to obtain
a box, I at once made up to him and told him my
father had got in a stock from London on the previous
afternoon, and that if he wished I would fetch him a

box. The effect was magical; the old man's contracted and distorted muscles at once let go their
hold; the furrows in his face made lines of pleasure
rather than of pain, and as I ran off home for the old
man's pills the old bells in the old church seemed to
ring all the merrier, and I feel quite certain that the
poor old clerk's "Amen" at the service which shortly
after followed was all the heartier through his having
in his pocket that box of Blair's gout and rheumatic
pills which I had fetched for him.

I have heard an anecdote concerning the old
clerk and his official duties, which may be worth
repeating. It was formerly the custom for the parish
clerk of Swindon to dine on the Sunday with the
servants at the Lawn. This custom had become a
right by prescription, and was enjoyed for many
generations, the servants' Sunday dinner at the Lawn
being invariably roast beef and plum pudding. On a
particular Sunday Old Bonny, for that was the name
by which the old clerk—whose name really was Noad
—was known, had taken his roast beef and plum
pudding at the Lawn as usual, and, it may be, just "a
glass" to keep it down. But as I was not there to see,
I cannot, of course, speak positively as to the latter
item. This, however, is veritable history. He had
long acquired the habit of prefacing his "Amen" by
a peculiar clearing of his throat, which in effect par-
took very much of a cross between a suppressed sneeze
and a short cough, after which preliminary he would
proceed to pitch a very high and long Au-u-u-u, and
then suddenly changing his voice to a deep and sonor-
ous bass, would bring out "MEN" with remarkable
emphasis and telling effect. On the Sunday to which
I have referred, Old Bonny had taken his seat as usual
in front of the singing gallery, the afternoon service
had proceeded after the most approved and orthodox
fashion, and the Vicar had got a good way on with

his sermon, when, to the consternation and alarm of those who were sitting near, the old clerk, evidently waking up from a nap, began to clear his throat for his "Amen," and before they could give him a "nudge," there resounded throughout the church the well-known Au-men, the "Au" coming as it were down from the ceiling and the "men" up from the vaults below, and at, of course, the one identical moment in the whole sermon when it was least wanted.

I have referred to the old Clerk being known as "Bonny" Noad. Fifty years ago "nick-names" were more common than they are now. But the prefix of "Bonny" as applied to Noad was not regarded as being used offensively. There were at least three or four distinct "Noad" families in Swindon, and it was really necessary to distinguish them from each other. One family I recollect were known as "Cooper" Noad's, the trade or business of a cooper having been carried on by them for generations. The old Clerk belonged to the family of the "Bonny" Noads. I am indebted to Mr. C. A. Wheeler for the following origin of the term : It chanced one day when a former member of the old clerk's family was out walking that the King or some leading member of the Royal Family drove along the road in a small pony carriage. Taking fright at some passing object one of the ponies became restive, and was on the eve of making a bolt, when Mr. Noad, seizing hold of its head, succeeded in pacifying it, and probably thereby prevented an accident, for which he was rewarded by the driver exclaiming "That's bonny," and from that time forth "Bonny" was used as a prefix to Noad by the members of that particular family.

I have referred to the destruction or loss of parish documents in Swindon. There is a circumstance in connection with the old clerk which bears indirectly

on this matter. When the old church was demolished
and the new one built it was sought to obtain a more
suitable residence for the Vicar, and in furtherance of
this idea the old vicarage on the Planks was offered
for sale by auction. To effect a sale it was, of course,
necessary to give a title, but none whatever could be
found in deed, document, or writing, the best that
could be offered by the vendors being an affidavit
made by the old clerk, in which his knowledge of the
premises and its occupation by the Vicars of Swindon
was duly set forth and verified on oath.

The Registers of Baptisms, Marriages, and
Burials for the parish of Swindon, which fortunately
have been preserved out of the general destruction,
commence with the year 1640, and it is just about
this time that dates on old tombs in the church and
churchyard also commence. In the oldest of the
Registers, on what appears to have been a stray or
loose leaf afterwards affixed to the cover, there are
the dates of 1608 and 1609, but there is nothing to
show that they are at all connected with the ordinary
contents of the book. The Registers, therefore, may
be fairly taken to commence with the year 1640, when
the first ordinary entry was made. These Registers
naturally form the best possible guide to the names
of the inhabitants of the parish two hundred and fifty
years ago, and in going over these names it is interesting to note the changes which have taken place.
There are, of course, many names which have altogether passed away and have been forgotten, while
there are others which not only appear very frequently,
but are continued down to within living memory, and
even to our own time. And this is particularly the
case with the name of Noad, but what is more remarkable, with Noad *alias* Bonny Noad, and, what is
even more remarkable, with Noad *alias* Bonny, Parish
Clerk. In the first Register, and among the earliest

of the entries, there is to be seen the following
among the burials :—" Roger Noad, *alias* Bonny,
parish clerk, December 24th, 1685." Whether there
was a previous Bonny Noad to this one who was
parish clerk there is no evidence to show, although
there is an abundance to prove that from this early
date down to about five-and-thirty years ago, when
the old clerk died, Swindon was never without a
Bonny Noad for its parish clerk. Indeed, the office
was always regarded as being hereditary in the family,
and it was therefore not without good reason that the
evidence of the old man was tendered in proof of the
title when the old vicarage was put up for sale by
auction.

Unfortunately there are but few entries in these
old Registers which call for remark. In a number of
instances there is the customary record of the period,
that the person was buried in linen in accordance with
the requirements of the law. And there is one entry
showing that this was not done, and the law broken.
It reads as follows :—" Thomas Vilett, gent., buried
contrary to ye Act ye forfeiture was paid. July
21st, 1685." Another entry reads thus :—" Lucretia
Knapp, a stranger, who dyed coming down from
London in a waggon, Sept. 21, 1708." The most remarkable entry, however, reads thus :—"The Rev.
Mr. John Neate, late vicar of this parish, who was
twice made happy by being born and married to
a kind and loving wife on two Thursdays in two leap-
years ; was much more made so by exchanging this
life for a far better on Thursday, the 25th day of
February, in this present leap-year, 1719, and was
buried by the Rev. Mr. Green, of Chiseldon, in the
chancel of the church of Swindon on Saturday the 27th.

Another remarkable entry in the Swindon
Registers of Births, Deaths, and Marriages appears
on an otherwise blank page at the end of the book,

where there are several blank or unused parchment leaves, and which reads as follows :—

"Patience Ody performed penance 2d April, 1786.
" WILLIAM JONES, Curate."

The brevity of this record is tantalising, for the question naturally arises : For what offence did the lady perform penance ? And to such a question there is absolutely nothing to supply, or even to suggest, an answer. The punishment could hardly have been for an offence against public morality, for there is an abundance of evidence to show that the public morals at this time were sufficiently lax to make breaches fashionable, rather than exceptional, and calling for such a punishment. And then, why should William Jones, Curate, verify the fact that penance had been performed ? Was the offence against the church, and, if so, was the punishment inflicted *in* the church ? But I can only suggest questions, without being in any way able to answer them. At this time (1786) the Rev. Thomas Smith was Vicar of Swindon, and presided at the vestry for auditing the church accounts on July 24th in that year. If the vicar could give his personal attention to such duties why should it have been left to his curate to enter Patience Ody's record ? In the audited accounts of the Overseers of Swindon for 1786 there are two or three items which are worth notice, such for instance as the following :—

	£	s.	d.
" To Moneys recd. of the late Overseers for Work, Bastards, &c.	70	14	7
Recd. by 7 Rates	192	8	5
Recd. by 2 Rates	85	7	3

The accounts of the Churchwardens for this same year are exceptionally brief. I have examined them in the hope of finding items for "a sheet" and "a candle," but have not succeeded. This, however was not because trifles were not accounted for in these

days, for in the accounts about this time there is to be
seen this interesting entry :—

> "To ½doz buttons for surplice   ... £0 0 1½"

There is another item in these churchwarden's
accounts which reads very curious in the present day.
It was, however, a common and regular charge a
hundred years ago in many parishes. It is that of a
payment to the "Dog Whipper," who was duly appointed at the annual vestry, and whose salary for very
many years appears to have been six shillings per
annum. Ultimately, however, an additional office,
that of " Shutter of the church doors on Sunday," was
added to that of " Dog Whipper," the salary remaining
at six shillings. Whether it was that the money was
not enough to sustain the dignity of the joint offices,
or that the dogs got better behaved and the doors
more tractable, and shut of their own accord, I cannot
say ; but by some means or other the additional duties
appear to have been fatal to the office of " Dog
Whipper," for he directly after disappears from the
accounts, never to reappear.

I well recollect that there was always a general
impression that the old church, as seen from the inside,
had a very neat appearance. To the best of my recollection this was the description given of it in some
gazetteer, and the inhabitants adopted it. And neat,
no doubt, it was. The roof both of the chancel and
the nave was circular or waggon-roof shape, lath and
plaster covering every particle of frame work, and both
roof, walls, and pillars being made scrupulously white
with lime wash. There were one or two very fine
memorial monuments affixed to the side walls, and
also between the arches—one to the memory of Mrs.
Millicent Neate (daughter of the Rev. John Neate,
formerly vicar of the parish of Swindon, whose death,
as recorded in the parish register, I have just re-

ferred to), who died July 9, 1764, aged 72 years, being really a work of art, and exhibiting a remarkable combination of coloured marbles. The Communion plate in use at the Swindon parish church was, I believe, a gift of Mrs. Millicent Neate, to whose memory this monument was erected. It may be here mentioned in connection with the church plate that in an entry in "The Book of Church Goods in Wilts," seized by the Crown under a Commission, dated March 3rd, 1553, there appears the following entry :—

Swyndon. deliuered to Robt. heathe and to
    George Carleys j cupp or chalis by Inden-
    ture of xij ovnc di iiij bells   .   .
In plate to the Kings vse   .   .   .   .   lvij ovnc

In these old village churches the services were always of the simplest and plainest character. Disputes between Church people were seldom, if ever, heard of. There was then but one division, and that was between those who went to church and those who went to chapel. As a rule, Parson and People pulled along together, and bickerings, controversies, and heart-burnings were but seldom or never heard of. The parson was then *The Person* of his parish in no figurative sense. There are but very few parishes in the country where, in the comparatively short period of forty or fifty years, there has been so great an alteration in Church matters and Church accommodation as there has been in Swindon. It hardly comes within the purpose of this present series of papers to notice the new churches of Swindon, and the changes to which I have referred. And yet it is quite within the range of probability that hereafter some slight sketch, which may serve as a connecting link in the history of the church as it was in, shall I say 1850, and the church that is to be in 1900, may not be without interest. I will, however, be very brief, and will scrupulously make no remark in a partisan spirit.

The first Vicar of Swindon of whom I have any recollection was a venerable looking old gentleman with a studious and intelligent face. He was rather under middle height, and of a very spare figure. He always wore a tall beaver hat, which dropped decidedly on the poll. His head was well placed in a large and deep coat collar (belonging to a pigeon-tail coat), inside which there was a still deeper and larger white linen collar. When abroad he always wore a long cloth cloak, which reached from his slightly rounded shoulders to his heels, and which cloak was fastened in front under the chin by a large hook. On his feet he always wore a pair of large slippers over his boots. His wife was a tall and rather burly woman, who wore spectacles on her nose and pattens on her feet, and who carried a good substantial gingham umbrella. As a child I had quite an affectionate interest in the old Vicar. There was, I recollect very well, an eclipse of the sun on a Sunday. For days, if not weeks, before it came off there had been a great deal of talk and speculation about that eclipse. The almanacs all said that it was to be "total," and Old Moore predicted something very terrible as likely to happen in connection therewith, which was understood in some way to mean that if the eclipse proved to be so total that not even just a little bit of the sun should be seen, there was to be there and then an end of the world ; but if there should be just this little bit left visible, then the only inconvenience would be a temporary darkness, which passed, things mundane would return to their normal condition. Reports like these served to invest this particular eclipse with a great deal of special interest, and something like a universal preparation was made to watch it through its various phases, scores of buckets of water being conveniently placed where the sun would strike them,

and hundreds of pieces of glass being smoked, through
which the sun might be seen. It may have been a
year, or two, or more, after the time of the eclipse,
that a parcel of books was received at my father's
shop to be sent off to be bound. When overhauling
them, as I usually did all such books, I chanced to see
in the *Mechanics' Magazine* a very interesting article
by the Vicar of Swindon on this very eclipse, explaining its characteristic features. The astronomers of
the day had evidently been waiting for and watching
this eclipse for some special feature which it was to
exhibit. And then they contributed to such scientific
papers as there were their observations, and, as I have
said, there came into my hands the books in which the
observations of the Vicar of Swindon were given to
the world. To me there was something simply fascinating in the fact that whilst the inhabitants of
Swindon were watching the eclipse through pieces of
smoked glass or in a bucket of water, and watching,
as it were, in sheer ignorance, there was one in their
midst who had seen it all through a telescope, and
who could then write and explain all about it as he
had done. The poor old vicar became from that
moment a most learned and wonderful man in my
estimation. I afterwards learned that he was a
botanist as well as an astronomer, and was generally
regarded as a person of more than ordinary attain-
ments, and who delighted in scientific and other
studies.

Coming to Swindon in the year 1843, the Rev.
H. G. Baily, the present vicar found the parish in the
first throes of that great change which was to overtake
it in its history. The old parish church, as I have
described it, soon became too small for the accommodation of the rapidly increasing population, and after
some years of indomitable perseverance and unceasing
labour, Mr. Baily succeeded in erecting the present

handsome church, built from the plans of Sir Gilbert
Scott, and which was opened for divine worship as the
parish church by the Right Rev. Dr. Ollivant, Bishop
of Llandaff (acting for the diocesan), November 7th,
1851; and in this new structure what are known as the
Low, or Evangelical, principles of the Church of
England have been continually and consistently
preached. That is, the services at this new church are
conducted on precisely the same lines as were the
services in the Old Parish Church for generations : a
surpliced choir has never been introduced, processions
are unknown, altar lights have never been used, and
the preacher preaches in the orthodox black gown.
The debt incurred in building the new church was not
finally cleared off until the early part of the present
year, 1884, having taken over thirty years to liquidate.

Previous to this, however, the parish had been
divided for ecclesiastical purposes, and St. Mark's
district formed, and a church built by, and at the expense of, the Great Western Railway Company, the
architect being Sir Gilbert Scott. I mention it here
merely as a matter of history, which it may be convenient to have recorded for future reference if 'necessary, that the attempt to conduct the services at this
church on those High Church principles which were
just then coming into vogue led to long and persistent
opposition and disturbances. Meetings were held,
letters written, protests made, correspondence published, and appeals made to the public as well as to the
bishop, until for months there was but little talked
about or thought of beside the Ritualistic practices
carried on at St. Mark's, the end of it all being that a
clergyman, who was otherwise much esteemed, and
was personally much liked, was driven to resign the
incumbency and seek elsewhere a field for his labours,
the result being that for some years the observances
did not differ very materially from those practised at

the mother church in the old town. It would seem, however, that the determination to conduct the service according to the High Church or Ritualistic standard had never been abandoned, and constantly it has been found that from time to time, and as opportunity offered, fresh additions have been made, two candles on the altar have been increased to four, and so on, just as the efforts to "educate" the people up to these changes have been successful or otherwise. Two other church districts have been formed and new churches built, one dedicated to St. Paul and the other to St. John, while mission and parish rooms have also been opened, with mothers' meetings and special services for men and special services for women. At one of these churches, that of St. Paul's, the services are highly Ritualistic. On special occasions the altar is ablaze with candles; there are processions with banners, and the chanting of processional hymns; members of the congregation bow their heads and cross themselves, and those in office bend the knee as they pass the altar. I do not mention this for the purpose of either praising or condemning, but simply to record the fact and to draw a contrast in the services as conducted now and when they were held in the old parish church down by the mill. If the services of the "Churches" of Swindon should go on "advancing" as they have for the past thirty years, it is simply impossible to conjecture what point they may reach. At the present time (the beginning of 1885) there would seem to be but one solitary link connecting the services of to-day, as performed in the " Churches of the Establishment," with those which were performed in the old parish church of fifty years ago, and that link is supplied by the services at the Mother, or Christ, Church: the services at all the other churches no doubt supply links, at least in name, but in different degrees, and which would seem to aim at connection with some church of the future rather than with the old reformed protestant Church of England.

[Since the original publication of this paper, the Rev. H. G. Baily, who for the long period of close upon forty years had been Vicar of Swindon, has accepted, on the presentation of Lord Bolinbroke, the Rectory of Lydiard Tregoze.   At the last services which the reverend gentleman performed in the church he had been instrumental in building, and in which he had so long ministered to a large and ever-increasing congregation, the attendances were so great that standing room for many hundreds of persons desirous of attending could not be obtained, and on the following Wednesday evening a public meeting was held in the Corn Exchange, which was most numerously attended, when Mr. W. A. Barns, on behalf of the donors, presented the reverend gentleman with a handsome clock, vases *en suite*, and a purse of £50. The clock and vases having cost £30.   The vacancy occasioned by the removal of the Rev. H. G. Baily has since been supplied by the appointment of the Rev. H. Armstrong Hall, of Holy Trinity Church, Bristol, on the presentation of the Lord Chancellor.]

LIST OF PERSONS INSTITUTED TO THE VICARAGE OF SWINDON SINCE A.D. 1302.

As printed in Sir Thomas Phillips's "WILTS INSTITUTIONS."

	Date.	Patron.	Rector or Vicar.
Rectory of St. Mary Swindon.	1302	R. Prior of St. Mary of Southwick, Diocese of Winchester.	Richard de Haghemaz.
Rectory do. Vicaragedo.	1319	Prior of Southwyk	Nicholas de Haghemaz, on res. of R. de H.
	1361	"	Richard de Taillour
	"		John de Wotton
V. Hye Swyndon.	1381	The King	John Brok
"	1388	Abbot St. Mary, Southwick	Richard Suggeworth by exch. with John Brok
V. Swyndon	1390	Prior St. Mary, Southwick	Richard Suggeworth
	1440	"	John Stocbrygg
	1481	Philip, Prior of S. Mary.	William Camell, on death of J. Stocbrygg
	1486	Prior of St. Mary.	William Brown, on res. of Wm. Camell
	1527	"	John Unthanke on death of Wm. Brown
	1560	Thomas Stephans, Gent.	Aristoteles Webb on death of J. Unthanke
"	1575	Thomas Stephens, of Burderop., Esq.	William Wattes on death of A. Webb
"	1579	Thomas Stevens, Esq.	Richard Powell

Date		Patron	Vicar
V. Swyndon	1580	Thos. Stevens, Esq.	Thomas Painter
"	"	"	John Bestpich, on death of Thos. Painter
"	1584	"	Milo Kendal, on res. of J. Bestpich
"	1623	Thos. White, of Thornhill	William Gallimore, on res. of M. Kendal
"	1634	The King	William Gallimore, on his own resignation
"	1662	"	Narcissus Marshe
"	1663	"	Henry Thompson, on res. of N. Marshe
"	1703	The Queen	John Neate, on death of H. Thompson
"	1719	The King	Gilbert Cowper, on death of J. Neate
"	1728	"	John Broadway, on res. of G. Cowper
"	1737	"	William Nichols, on death of J. Broadway
"	"	"	William Nichols, on his own resignation
"	1758	"	Thomas Smyth, on death of W. Nichols
"	1790	"	Edmund Goodenough, on death of T. Smyth
"	1809	"	*Matthew Surtees, on death of E. G.
"	1823	"	James Grooby
"	1847	The Queen	H. G. Baily, on res. of J. Grooby
"	1885	"	H. Armstrong Hall, on res. of H. G. Baily

* Sir Thomas Phillps's list ends with the institution of the Rev. Matthew Surtees, who, I think, must have been a Pluralist and a non-resident, for I can find no trace whatever of him in any Swindon record. Between 1809 and 1823 the Registers are signed by a Mr. Gray and a Mr. Jones respectively, and both of whom sign as "Curate." The latter person, who was a Welshman, is still remembered by some of the older inhabitants as Taffy Jones. None of them, however, are prepared to regard him as having been anything less than Vicar of Swindon, and their obstinacy on this point occasioned me no little difficulty in filling up the blank between 1809 and 1823, but which I am now enabled to do with absolute certainty through the courtesy of the Registrars of the Bishop's Court at Salisbury, Messrs. Macdonald and Malden.

—Swindon＊Worthies—

HAVE already explained how I came to
have something like a venerable regard
for the good old vicar of my childhood
days. There was another man for whom
I had an equally profound respect, and
who was first brought to my notice from a circumstance somewhat similar to that which first directed
my attention to the old gentleman who could see
an eclipse through a telescope and then write and
explain all about it. But this second worthy of mine
was a man in a very different position in life—a
natural genius rather than a scholar : one of nature's
rough and unpolished gems rather than an educated
and refined gentleman. I have also stated that my
father carried on the business of a bookseller in the
town. Now, it so happened that almost as soon as I
could write and put a few things together I was put
to write out the monthly orders for books, to be
forwarded to the London agent. Sometimes I had to
take the names of books down from *viva voce* instructions from persons who wished to be supplied ; whilst

at other times I had to file or otherwise preserve the
scraps of paper on which orders were received until
the time should arrive for the order to be sent off.
And in this way I first came to know and notice
William Pike, the boots, waiter, and handy-man at
the "Goddard Arms." There was just such another
man at the other hotel—the "Bell"—that is, so far as
their ordinary occupations were concerned, although in
their ages there was a great difference.   If there was
any difference in them in any other respect the boots,
waiter, and handy-man at the "Bell" was the more
important of the two, for, in addition to those duties
which I have enumerated, he was the postman who
every day delivered the letters in Swindon town and
parish, and I can well recollect what an important
personage he was in the town on the day when the
postage on a letter from Swindon to London was
reduced from tenpence to fourpence, and how he was
welcomed at every house as he went about explaining
all about the revolution that had taken place—how
the charge would shortly be still further reduced to a
penny ; and then as to how his opinion on the change
was sought for and attentively listened to.   At this
time the Post Office for Swindon was at the "Bell'
Hotel ; a very small portion of a very small bar-
room on the right hand of the side entrance was set
apart for the mails, which the barmaid and the boots,
waiter, and handy-man attended to when they could
conveniently do so, and the ordinary duties of the
house were not interfered with thereby.   But the man
at the "Bell" I only remember as "Old Job," whereas
I remember the man at the "Goddard Arms" as the
person through whom I first heard of the science of
geology, and of the wonderful revelations it has to
make to those who devote themselves to its study.   I
first knew William Pike through his making enquiries
about books and their prices, and amongst other

books my father obtained for him were Dr. Mantell's "Wonders of Geology," and the same author's "Medals of Creation." When these books came down they produced a most extraordinary impression on my youthful mind. I had never seen anything like them before, and the illustrations in them were more wonderful than anything I had ever seen in picture books. As well as I could, I literally devoured these books, and I need hardly say they helped to open up a new idea of life and of existence to me. As well as I dared try, I was in the habit of "looking through" such of the books obtained for customers as took my fancy, and in these particular books I was especially interested. But I became still more interested in the man who could buy and possess such books. Pike was my senior only some eight or ten years, but this was, of course, sufficient to make all the difference between a little boy and a young man between us ; but what made a greater difference than that of age in my eyes was his being the first person I had met with who had a conception of that life which revels in the study of books, of the sciences, of nature, and of art. One half the young men of the town at this time, of the same age as William Pike, and enjoying about the same advantages, would have been unable to read a book, or even to write their names. The time of which I am now writing was the time when the *Penny Cyclopædia*, the *Penny Magazine*, the *Saturday Magazine*, and other similar publications, supported by men like Lord Brougham, and published by Charles Knight, the Society for the Diffusion of Useful Knowledge, and others, were becoming to be among the most popular of the day, and were attaining an enormous sale. It was my good fortune just at this time to be brought into contact with a few working men, one here and there, who were always ready to make some personal sacrifice to obtain these pub-

lications, and nothing gave me greater satisfaction
than the opportunity to have a chat with them. There
was an old man, a mason, living at Wroughton,
another working as a quarryman at Highworth, and
another working in the garden at Blunsdon House,
who took in the *Penny Cyclopædia*, which came out in
quarterly volumes at seven shillings and sixpence each,
and nothing ever afforded me greater pleasure than
the opportunity to take these men their volumes as
they came out. I used to tie the volumes in a handkerchief, and, slinging them on my back, make my
way to the homes of these men, feeling quite proud of
the work, and also that I was taking them a precious
treasure. But I was very selfish in all this : I always
anticipated the opportunity of paying myself for my
labour in a conversation with men who read and
cared for such books. William Pike became quite a
hero in my eyes, and I could not rest satisfied until I
had ascertained the why and the wherefore of his
spending his money on books like those I have mentioned, and the result of it all was that I found he was
a geologist, and was well known to many of the leading scientific men of the day.` On several occasions I
got him to show me his specimens, which were
collected principally from the local stone quarries and
clay pits. It was a great favour to be allowed to see
these specimens, for they were stowed away in cup-
boards, boxes, and drawers, and to get them out
involved no small amount of trouble. Many years
afterwards I found that William Pike was in the habit
of collecting them for sale, buying from the workmen
and selling them to the collectors, who always accepted
him as an authority on the geology of the neighbourhood ; and there are, I believe, specimens collected by
him occupying posts of honour in the British Museum.
What led William Pike to become a geologist I can
only conjecture. I have, however, little or no doubt

he received his first lessons from the "Father of Geology" himself, Dr. William Smith. William Smith, who was born at Churchill, in Oxfordshire, in 1769, and who died in 1839, was the first man who reduced geology to a science, and who was enabled to read in the different formations, and in the fossil remains found in them, the history of the world, and to trace the development of animal life from its rudest form up to its most perfect development. And William Smith must have known Swindon well, and probably was a frequent guest at the "Goddard Arms" Hotel. In his joint capacity as engineer and geologist, he was consulted by the promoters of the Wilts and Berks Canal Company, and there was no place along the whole course of the canal where the advice and assistance of such a man was so much required as at Swindon. At Rushey Platt the engineering difficulties were very great, in consequence of the canal being carried through what was little better than a moving bog at that time. Mr. McIlquham, one of the engineers engaged on the work, was not only a frequent visitor to the "Goddard Arms," but he married one of the daughters of the landlord of that well-known hostelry, and I think it may be stated with every confidence that Mr. Smith also "put up" there : and as William Pike's father was waiter at the hotel before him, there is no doubt that as a boy William Pike was known to William Smith, and from him he imbibed his knowledge of, and love for, geology.

John Britton, in his "Autobiography," makes the following reference to William Smith :—" At the latter end of the last century, and the beginning of the present, the truly romantic and rustic parish of Farleigh Hungerford, near Bath, was honoured with and distinguished by a group of men of science who, though comparatively obscure and of humble habits and pursuits, have become eminent in the scientific

annals of the country.   The Rev. Benjamin Richardson was settled in the rectory of this parish in 1796,
and in the following year I had the good fortune of
being introduced to, and afterwards meeting, him
at his parsonage, with the Rev. Joseph Townsend, of
Pewsey ; William Smith, who was employed as
engineer to the Somerset Coal Canal, and who subsequently was honoured with the title of L.L.D. ;
William Cunnington, of Heytesbury ; the Rev. John
Skinner, of Camerton ; and Edward Eryer, M.D.,
editor of a memoir and of the literary works of
James Barry, R.A., and professor of painting to the
Royal Academy.   Later in life Colonel Houlton
came into possession of the Farleigh estate, and
expended much money on his mansion there, and on
improvements in the parish.   In such company, and
at such a place, on different occasions, my time was
most delectably spent.   Every succeeding day was
excitingly occupied in examinations, readings, discus-
sions with my new friends on their new speculations,
and varied novelties in fossilology, stratification, &c.,
whilst I occasionally visited some of the ancient
buildings of the neighbourhood.   The ruins of the
once spacious and formidable castle, with its chapel
and monuments ; the village church ; the remains of
Hinton Abbey, with the early Anglo-Norman church
at Lullington, were to my mind and eyes objects of
curiosity and interest.   Though I had not previously
read or heard much on extraneous fossils, every
specimen exhibited, and every comment made by my
learned friends were new sources of pleasure to my
latent fancy, and afterwards induced me to explore
many quarries, heaps of stone, and new diggings
among rocks and soils with avidity.   Though the
learned divines secured great deference and respect, I
remember that they listened attentively, and with
polite courtesy, to the opinions and novel accounts

which were brought forward by the other parties. The
surveyor, however, seemed the main-spring or moving
power, in the newly-formed machine, as he was enabled
to communicate new discoveries, or fresh matter, at
every successive meeting of the parties.   The very interesting brief 'Memoirs of William Smith, L.L.D.,
by his nephew and pupil, John Phillips, F.R.S., F.G.S.,
&c., 8vo., 1844,' furnish a lucid account and exemplifi-
cation of his travels over different parts of the island ;
of his keen examination of the prominent and even
minute features of the different strata, and of such
configurations of extraneous fossils as belonged to
each varied specimen and its locality   Hence
originated the new science of geology, and to Mr.
Smith is it indebted for its parentage and first nurture.
In the volume referred to are portraits of that gentleman, of Mr. Richardson, of Mr. Townsend, and of
Francis, Duke of Bedford, forming interesting representations of the heads of persons whose zeal and
talents were exemplarily employed in a new science
which has proved so valuable and important to the
country.   In the portrait of Dr. Smith is recognised
the plain, simple, unsophisticated, thinking man,
whose amiability of heart and calm deliberative in-
tellect rendered him the founder of a new science. He
was aged 69 when the portrait was drawn by Fourau.
In the year 1839 he had made arrangements to join
the Scientific Association at Birmingham, and stopped
at Northampton, at the house of Mr. and Miss Baker,
whose first studies in topography and antiquities commenced with their accompanying me to many places
and objects in their native county, when I visited it
for the Beauties of England, and for the Architectural
Antiquities. Illness arrested the progress of the good
and estimable doctor, and terminated his worldly
career in a few days."
   In constructing the Wilts and Berks Canal, the

great difficulty was in devising means for keeping up
the supply of water to the high level which branched
out on every side from Swindon, and which would be
lowered every time a boat passed through one of the
locks.   To keep up the supply a very large body of
water would have to be kept in reserve at some high
level, and William Smith was consulted as to how this
could best be accomplished.   His first plan was to
obtain the necessary supply of water by means of an
artesian well to be sunk in the Kimmeridge clay at
New Swindon, and under his directions a well was sunk
a short distance east of the Wootton Bassett road,
near to the canal, and between it and what is now
known as Westcott-place.   The well was sunk to the
depth of several hundred feet, and to a certain extent
the anticipations of Mr Smith were realised, for, a
water-bearing strata having been struck, the water
rapidly filled the well to within a few feet from the
top.   This was disappointing, as it had been hoped
that the water would flow over the top, as in the case
of the other artesian wells, and, by being conveyed
into the canal, would keep up the supply to the
necessary level.   In the hope that the supply in the
well would be constant—the presumption being that
the supply was inexhaustible, only requiring more
force to eject it—it was decided to erect steam-pump-
ing machinery at what is now known as the old canal
house.   A powerful steam-power pump was erected
but on being put to work it was found that the supply
of water was so limited as to be altogether insufficient
for the purpose required, it being possible to pump the
well dry ; and when this had been done a considerable
time elapsed before it would fill up again.   It was
after these unsatisfactory results had been arrived at
that it was resolved to construct the Coate Reservoir,
and obtain the necessary supply of water from that
source.   Many years afterwards an artesian well was

sunk by the Great Western Railway Company about
two miles distant from the one sunk by Mr Smith, in
a north-east direction, with somewhat better success,
and at the present time the same company are prosecuting extensive works in sinking another well mid-way
between the two wells, but with what success time alone
can tell.   What I wish, however, to point out is this :
that the matter of the supply of water for the canal
must have brought Mr. Smith frequently to Swindon ;
that he no doubt, " put up" at the "Goddard Arms,"
and that it was through him that William Pike, my
Swindon Worthy, imbibed a liking for geology : that
it was through him that the lad who occupied the
humble position of boots and waiter at a country hotel
became a no mean proficient in the science and study
of geology.   William Pike subsequently gave up his
situation at the "Goddard Arms," which position had
been held by his father before him, and opened a public
house on his own account.   This, I believe, was an
unfortunate move on his part, and he died at Swindon
very shortly afterwards, in the year 1847, at the early
aged of 29 years.

But if I am not altogether wrong in my conclusions, there was another man who rose to much
greater eminence as a geologist than even William
Smith, and who got his first lessons in the science at
Swindon.   I mean no less a person than the author of
the "Wonders of Geology and Medals of Creation."
One of the former ministers of the Independent
Chapel in Newport-street was a Rev. George Mantell,
who died February 6th, 1832.   I have no recollection
of this gentleman, but I do recollect that, through
noticing a marble tablet erected to his memory in the
old chapel, I was led to make some enquiries about
him, and was told that in addition to his being minister
he used to have a few pupils, and that among them
was the celebrated geologist, Gideon Algernon Man-

tell, L.L.D., F.R.S., and member of many English and foreign societies. I regret being unable to refer to this matter with any degree of authority, but it seems quite probable that although Dr. Mantell was born at Lewes, in Sussex, he was sent to his uncle (for such I understood the relationship to be) at Swindon for his education. And then, what more natural than that, having the genius and ability in him which won for him a world-wide reputation, he should have been attracted by the wonders which the Swindon Quarries at that time in particular were disclosing. John Aubrey, referring to these Quarries, remarks :— " Swindon is famous for the Quarrie, which is neer the towne, of that excellent paveing stone, which is not inferior to the Purbec Grubbes, but whiter, and will take a little polish ; they send for it to London ; it is a white stone ; it was not discovered till about thirty years agon ; and I am now writing in 1672 ; yet it lies not above four or five foot deep." The Quarries, however, were never better known or in more active operation than about the commencement of the present century. The whole of the space on the western brow of the hill towards Westlecott was excavated about this time, the stone being principally used for bridges and other buildings belonging to the canal, and I have heard that the fossils obtained at this time, and from this part of the Quarries, were particularly abundant and interesting. What more probable, then, that a school-boy, like young Mantell, should become fascinated by what he saw here, and should have laid the foundation for those studies which afterwards made him the master of a science, as well as an authority throughout the civilized world ?

I would, if I could, add to the number of my Swindon Worthies, but, unfortunately, I do not know where to look for them. Of course, I mean " worthies" in the estimation of the world: men and women who have either won or deserved renown in art, science, or literature. No doubt Swindon possesses, and always has possessed, its fair share of worthy people in the ordinary sense. But in the sense in which I have put it, the number is very few. John Britton, in his "Autobiography," mentions a Swindon worthy, one Robert Sadler, who was born at Swindon in 1754, his father being a glover and breeches-maker. Mr. Britton waxes rather enthusiastic over the virtues of Robert Sadler as the author of a number of publications in prose and verse, including three novels and three poems. I, however, have failed to trace any connection of the name with Swindon, nor have I ever heard of Mr. Sadler's productions, except through Mr. Britton. Sadler, it appears, remembered Britton in his will, and left him a legacy of £100. This possibly may have quickened Britton's enthusiasm for Sadler, and have induced him to tell us what he has about him. John Britton's sketch of his friend Sadler, however, is not without its interest, as shewing the kind of life men of literary tastes had to lead in those not very long past days, when both books and newspapers were scarce and dear, and they were left almost exclusively to their own resources :

"Sadler was a man of singular person, manners, and abilities : the first was natural, but disfigured by costume ; the second arose from the station and connection wherein he was placed ; and the third, like the first, was formed by nature, and developed by associations and self-culture. Had the same mind been well instructed and disciplined in early life, it might have become eminent in art, in literature, or in science; for it manifested, on many occasions, the rudiments and principles, as well as the union, of philosophy and poetry, whilst the disposition was philanthropic and generous. Unfortunately, he seems to have been a victim to circumstances and connections. He was

born at Swindon, a town near the northern boundary
of Wiltshire, in 1754, but soon removed to, and
settled at, Malmesbury. His father was a glover and
breeches-maker, and being one of the Moravians—a
sect of religionists then in its infancy—young Sadler
was initiated into their opinions and doctrines, and
also into the elements of school-learning, by their
minister. Of this peculiar sect he has detailed many
curious particulars in the novel of 'Wanley Penson,
or the Melancholy Man.' Mr. Sadler, after marrying
in 1775, settled in Chippenham as a draper, but from
bad health, and an ardent love of reading, was not
calculated to manage and attend to the trifling details
of a retail shop. His wife soon died, and in 1779 he
wedded another, with whom he lived in harmony and
unity for more than half a century. When we have
read many of his hearty, generous letters, and the
sentiments inculcated in his "Wanley Penson," we
feel surprised at the contrasted theories and practices
of the man and the author; for my friend often
exhibited singularities, bordering on eccentricities, in
dress, habits, and manners. Like most sedentary,
studious persons, his whole frame was morbid, and
the animal·secretions being irregular, the muscles re-
laxed, and, the nervous system deranged, his physical
powers were always weak and languid. In person he
was tall, thin, and apparently in a state of consumption. The face narrow and pale, the cheeks were
collapsed, and his general physiognomy was that of
an abstracted and melancholy, but highly intellectual,
man. It was generally said that the imaginary
'Wanley Penson' was drawn from, and exhibited the
leading characteristics of, Robert Sadler; and these,
as exemplified in the now obsolete but interesting
novel, were calculated to win the affections of all who
best knew the one, and had read the other. His
countenance very much resembled that of the amiable

and highly intellectual Dr. Priestley, and from the memoirs and letters of the latter, I should infer that there were striking similarities of mental faculties in the two. He is thus described by a mutual friend, who was familiar with him for nearly half a century:—'His countenance was that of a deep-thinking man ; his manners were mild and bland, as usually shown in the tones of his voice, and in the remarks and sentiments he expressed. His conversation displayed varied and extensive knowledge, conveyed, generally, in appropriate, often terse and eloquent, language, with an earnestness and impressiveness indicative of conviction and sincerity.' With such qualifications and attributes, it is not surprising that his company, advice, and opinions were much coveted and courted by intimate and familiar friends. With one or more of these he passed many hours in his shop, the usual scene of converse and consultation ; for he rarely invited them into his simple, humble parlour. I have spent many hours thus in his company, but was never invited to dine or partake of refreshment with him until the very latter end of his life, and after he had converted the shop into a sitting-room. In one of his letters to me, dated 1802, he says, ' It is a misfortune, my friend, for a man to be supposed to possess talents, for (like property) if once the supposition takes place, he is sure not only to be heavily taxed, but surcharged beyond his real amount. Hence I am scarcely ever alone, have but little time for reading or writing, or any species of personal amusement. My visitors are not merely private friends, but persons of the town, many unknown to or by me ; and others, from villages in the neighbourhood, who, in difficulties or troubles of any kind, and often imaginary, break in upon me, take up my time, and sometimes try my philosophy and equanimity. I have often made wills, marriage settle-

ments, contracts, indentures, and agreements ; even
written love-letters, and other confidential epistles,
communicating good and bad news to relations and
friends. Indeed, I have been solicited to "tell the
fortunes" of some sighing maidens ; and even to
discover thieves, murderers, highwaymen, &c. On
one occasion I was nominated, and required to act as
"Overseer of the Poor" of this large parish, which
proved a heart-rending, distressing occupation. Real
suffering and affected misery were constantly preferring claims and petitions for relief.' Besides the
novel already referred to, Mr. Sadler published three
small poems, on local persons and events, under the
titles of ' The Discarded Spinster, or a Plea for the
Poor' ; allusive to the time and effects of introducing
machinery into the manufacture of cloth. The others
were, ' True Patriotism, an Apostrophe inspired by
the public Loss of Sir James Tilney Long, Bart.,
M.P. for Wilts' ;—' An Elegy on the Death of an
esteemed friend, Wm. Colbourne, Esq.' Amongst
manuscripts in his possession at the time of his
decease, and which he bequeathed to John Lewis, of
Malmesbury, a nephew, with legacies to pay for their
revisal, printing, &c., were two novels, ' The Pupil of
Experience,' and ' The Proselyte of Principle,' which
I have reason to believe possessed considerable merit,
and therefore calculated to be popular. The party to
whom they were given is dead, and the present state
and even existence of the manuscripts are alike
unknown ; both probably are lost to the public, as
much other valuable property has been, by that dis-
reputable den, the Court of Chancery."

⁓Some*other*Worthies⁓

————◦♦◦————

E must be always ready to admit that whatever eminence England has attained to as a nation, or whatever glory her people may have won, it is due to the indomitable perseverance of her people, and their determination, whenever they believe in a thing, to believe in it with all their might and main. It was the possession of this great English characteristic which enabled our forefathers as well to win victories as to suffer martyrdom, if needs be, in a cause which they believed to be just and right. And it was in this respect that many of our old Nonconformists proved themselves to be real Britons. In the various notices which I have from time to time published in connection with the Nonconformist cause in Swindon, I have shewn, at least by inference, how much we owe to the perseverance, and the indomitable courage of men who were loyal first to their own consciences, and their determination to worship their God, and to perform their acts of devotion, after their own fashion, at all cost. There have been some of these men in Swindon, and the object of the present paper will be to bring one or two of them prominently before my readers. Before doing this, however, I would very briefly adduce an illustration shewing what a difference of opinion with the constituted authorities really meant a century or two ago, the laws under which pains and penalties were enforced having been allowed to remain on our statute books to within a comparatively recent period. Indeed, it is only a few years since a "local preacher" living in the neighbourhood of Cricklade shewed me his "license," duly signed by two Justices of the Peace, authorising him to preach, and freeing him from the penalties which would otherwise attach to him should he dare to assemble and address a congregation consisting of more than five persons. Unfortunately, in consequence of the entire absence of all documents, even those of record, I am unable to give particulars of the granting of these Licenses to Preach by the Swindon magistrates. I am, however, enabled to repeat an anecdote related to me by the late Henry Calley, Esq., of Burderop, in connection with a former owner of Burderop—the late Tom Calley, Esq. Mr. Calley, it appears, was exceedingly sensitive about being regarded as the Justice for Chiseldon. He, of course, attended the meetings of the Bench at Swindon, but, notwithstanding this, he looked upon it as his absolute right to settle all disputes, and dispose of all cases, arising within his parish of Chiseldon, and his ire was never more thoroughly aroused than when he chanced to find any of his parishioners going to Swindon for justice. Another peculiarity of this worthy justice was: His justice seat was invariably his front door step! Those who required justice at his hands had to assemble in front of Burderop House during the time the squire was having his breakfast, and then, at the close of the repast, he would sally forth, and, placing himself in the open door-way, would proceed to hear and adjudicate. One day, being at Swindon for the purpose of administering justice with his brother magistrates, Mr. Calley chanced to cast his eyes around the crowd of persons who had gathered together in the justices' room at the "Goddard Arms," and there discovered one of his parishioners of the name of Romans, and whom he at once addressed in anything but gentle tones, and in the most peremptory manner, by enquiring what he wanted there? "If you please, your worship, I want a license to preach," timidly replied old Romans. "A license to preach—a license to preach!" exclaimed the squire, boiling over with rage, and resorting to the common vernacular of the time and locality, the better to throw feeling into his words—"I'll gie thee a license to preach! I'll kick thy d——d old —— for thee if thee doosn't get on back to thy work and *finish chopping up that wood I set thee at this morning.*"

I recollect old Romans very well as a Local Preacher among the Wesleyan Methodists. He was an uneducated man, and possibly could do little more than just manage to read and write. After working the week through as a labourer in the fields, he would spend his Sundays among his fellows in the villages around, doing his very best to impress them with the importance of a religious life, and to spread among them the doctrine and practices of the party to which he belonged. The poor old man was but seldom "planned" to preach at Swindon, his range of language being deemed hardly sufficient for that congregation, but wherever he was sent he went readily, and, in his own rude and uncultured manner, told all he knew to all who would listen to him.

The most notable case of persecution for conscience sake, in the immediate neighbourhood of

Swindon, I have been able to meet with is recorded thus by the Rev. Canon Jackson, in his "Notes on Aubrey":—"In 1658, 10th August, Mr. Stubbs, 'Minister of Wroughton,' was reprimanded by William Blissett, chairman of the Commissioners for ejecting 'scandalous ministers.' His offence was that of brawling and quarreling with his neighbours, scoffing and reviling professors of godliness." There is no record of what became of this scandalous (!) minister; but in Waylen's "History of Marlborough" there are particulars of how it fared with quite a number of those who were made victims of the notorious Act of Uniformity, as it was called—of that Act of Parliament which was designed to make all men uniform in their allegiance to the Church and State. And among others I may quote the case of a clergyman who came into the neighbourhood of Swindon, deprived of all his preferments, but not of his religious faith, for it not only illustrates what was too often the fate of men who were prepared to suffer for conscience sake during the latter half of the sixteenth century in particular, but will serve to bring us on down to, and understand the position and characters of, men to whom I shall presently refer as being the founders of the Nonconformist churches in Swindon.

James Burwood, of Pembroke College, Oxford, being turned out of the lectureship of St. Petrocks, at Dartmouth, became a farmer, and rented an estate at Batson, near Marlborough. He preached in his own house to great numbers who flocked to hear him from the adjacent parts ; and when the house would not contain them, he made use of his orchard. He was constantly annoyed by a noted informer named Beer or Bear, who, for his good service in disturbing conventicles, had been advanced to the degree of justice of the peace. This man, being aided by the parson of the parish, [John Wilde, vicar of Ramsbury?] also a justice, with a crew of informers at their heels, watched every opportunity for confiscation or annoyance. The Conventicle Act forbade the private meeting for worship where there were five persons present besides the household. As Mr. Burwood had (first and last) seventeen children, he must always have had a congregation, and when the Act was put into more stringent exercise in 1670, it is probable that he took care to limit his auditors to the prescribed number, for the justice hesitated not to disturb the little community by walking into it with his train of followers. In September, 1670, a troop of informers beset the farmhouse, but their scrutiny could detect no more than four persons besides the family; but the door being opened in consequence of the house dog having set upon a girl outside, the young woman, greatly affrighted, rushed in, and the dog with her. There was now the illegal number of five in the house. The justice, therefore, entering, with the informers at his heels, proceeded forthwith to levy a fine of £20 on Mr. Burwood for preaching, £20 more for his house, and five shillings a piece for all the rest. The reactionary spirit of the times was a guarantee for every enormity. His persecutors would unhang his doors, rifle his house, strike the locks off his barn-doors, and put others on, and scatter his family among their neighbours. All this he endured for five years, and then removed to Hicksdown, about a mile from Begbury, where he took another farm. But he was not yet beyond the reach of his old enemies, and in the course of seven years decided on going back to Dartmouth, where, after various ups and downs, he closed his labours, 1693, aged sixty-six.

This is a fair and by no means overdrawn picture of the way in which the Fathers of our Religious Freedom enjoyed their liberty, and of the way in which men were made to conform to those religious observances which the party in power declared to be orthodox. And then the way in which all the Jacks-in-office played their parts, from those who held the highest offices in the State down to the parish con-stable, is equally instructive. In illustration of this, I may again quote from Waylen the following bye-law, made by the Mayor and Corporation of Marlborough against Nonconformity in their borough, which reads as follows :—" An order for conformity to the Church government [abridged]. Whereas, now of late some of the magistrates, or of the common council of this borough, have permitted their wives, children, or servants, to absent themselves from the public service of Almighty God, in the public congregation in the several churches within this borough, on the Lord's Day, commonly called Sunday, and to resort to un-lawful conventicles, contrary to the law and the established government of the Church of England, to the great discouragement of the ministers of both parishes, the evil example of others, and the encour-agement of faction and disloyalty. It is now therefore ordered and decreed by the mayor and major part of the common council, that if any of the council, burgesses, or freemen allow their wives, children, or servants, willingly and obstinately to absent them-selves from the churches, or resort to conventicles or unlawful assemblies, they shall be incapable of exer-cising the office of mayor, justice of the peace, or to be of the council, or to bear or execute any office of trust within the borough, until such time as they shall conform themselves and their families unto the estab-lished government of the church, according to the laws and statutes of this kingdom. Dated 6 Aug., 1678."

It may seem a long jump from 1678 to 1800, and yet the whole intervening period is little better than one long dark day and night, with barely a ray of

light or a scrap of life in it—a time of wars abroad
and of profligacy and corruption at home.   The only
wonder really is that anything like an earnest religious
feeling was not crushed out of existence.   For
generation after generation men continued to live
passably under laws which could not exist now for a
single day.   What provision there was in Swindon, if
indeed any at all existed, for public worship, except
that afforded by the parish church, up to the end of
the last century, I am unable to say.   In this respect
Swindon appears to have been far behind even the
surrounding villages, for under date of January 26th I
find in the *Evangelical Magazine* for May, 1804, the
following notice of the opening of the old Independent
Chapel (now pulled down) in Newport-street:—"A
neat and commodious chapel was opened at Swindon.
The following ministers conducted the services of the
day:—Mr. Thresher, of Abingdon, preached in the
morning; Mr. Holmes, of Faringdon, in the afternoon;
and Mr. Elliott, of Devizes, in the evening.   Messrs.
Wase, Bagnel, Clift, Best, Muston, and Watts severally
engaged in prayer.—Swindon is a populous and
genteel town, situated in the centre of several villages,
where the gospel has long been preached with success.
A respectable family, which attended at Stratton (one
of the nearest of them) thinking it would be a benefit
to the town, as well as an accommodation to themselves, built a chapel for public worship; and completely repaired an adjoining house, principally at their
own expense.—The chapel was thronged; many went
away for want of room, and the services were solemn
and impressive.   One spirit pervaded all the ministers,
—that of zeal for God, compassion for souls, and the
warmest attachment for their King and Country!
The friends of the gospel will be pleased to hear that
Mr. Mantell statedly preaches at this place; and
that the people, in great numbers, attend his ministry."

Under the date of September 3rd, I find in the November, 1806, number of the same magazine the following :—" A new chapel (45 by 20) was opened at Wanbro, Wilts. Mr. Garrett, of Lavington, preached in the morning, from Luke xv., 2 ; Mr. Holmes, of Wantage, in the afternoon, from Matthew xiii., 43 ; and Mr. Elliott, of Devizes, in the evening, from Acts viii., 8th. The congregation, consisting of about 400 persons, had been gathered by the labours of Mr. Mantell, of Swindon, in the two preceding summers, by preaching in the open air. The ground for erecting this place was given by Mr. J. Strange, of Bishopsgate Street ; and who, in conjunction with his brothers and the friends of the gospel in Swindon and its vicinity, furnished the means for its erection."

And in the October, 1827, number there is a memoir of the late James Strange, Esq., of Swindon, Wilts, as follows :—" Mr. James Strange was the third son of the truly pious and highly esteemed Mr. Thos. Strange. He was accustomed, from his youth, to attend with his excellent father on the ministry of the Gospel, under the Rev. Messrs. Davis, of Thorncot, Biddulph, of Wanborough, and the students of the late Countess of Huntingdon, who used to make itinerant excursions in preaching the Gospel among the inhabitants in the benighted district of North Wilts. Mr. Thomas Strange lived under the influence of redeeming grace, and his heart and house were open to receive and entertain the ministers of Christ without respect to name or party. At what time, or by what means, the subject of this memoir became decidedly serious, is uncertain. It is probable this blessed change was effected by the gracious answer which the Lord granted to his fervent prayers in a season of sickness, from which the physician gave no hopes of recovery. From that period, which is nearly thirty years since, he manifested his attachment to the doctrines of sovereign and efficacious grace, in the salvation of redeemed sinners. He professed his decided regard for liberty of conscience in religious matters, and evinced his compassionate concern to promote the best interests of perishing sinners in the place of his nativity and its vicinity. Hence, in union with his three benevolent brothers, a neat chapel was erected in Swindon, with a dwelling-house appropriated for the use of the minister. The Rev. George Mantell, late pastor of the Independent Congregation at the Upper Meeting House, Westbury, Wilts, being at that time moveable, was earnestly solicited by these generous brothers to enter into this field of labour. The new chapel was opened in the beginning of 1804. The novelty of this event; the power of the word preached by some eminent ministers; and the happiness experienced by the professors of the Gospel, who sanctioned the meeting with their presence; were an occasion of long and grateful remembrance. Mr. Strange made a bold and noble stand to support this infant cause, through much opposition; and valiantly co-operated with his minister, while he published the Gospel in the neighbouring towns and villages. Large congregations used to attend the preaching of the Gospel in the streets; and on the approach of the winter and rainy season, it was necessary to erect places for the accommodation of the minister and people. Mr. Strange's influence and generous example contributed much on these occasions. Hence places of worship were built at Wroughton, Wanborough, and Moredon. The ground on which the chapel is erected at Wanborough was given by John Strange, Esq., of London; that on which the chapel is now built at Moredon was the gift of Mr. Edwards, uncle to the Messrs. Strange. Mr. Strange felt a lively interest in the formation and prosperity of those societies whose benevolent object is the advancement of the Redeemer's kingdom in the world. The Sabbath Schools at Wanborough, Moredon, Lidding-ton, and Purton, and the Sabbath and Evening School at Swindon, had, in Mr. Strange, an able and generous benefactor. Mr. Strange successfully employed his natural vivacity and fluency of speech in reproving sin, and putting to silence the ignorance of foolish men. He was eminently endowed with the gift of prayer, which he fervently exercised, to the edification of his family, the comfort of his brethren at prayer-meetings, and the benefit of the villagers, among whom he was in the habit of reading evangelical sermons. He was an example worthy of imitation in the strict attention which he paid to the worship of God in his family, and the regularity with which they attended on the ordinances of public worship. He sedulously brought up his children in the fear of the Lord, fervently praying that they might be a seed to serve God on earth, and reign with Him in Heaven. Mr. Strange was blessed with a family of ten children, who, for their mutual love to each other, their filial affection to their parents, and amiable manners, are justly esteemed among the circle of their acquaintances. Mr. Strange was a firm believer in the doctrines of salvation, gloriously reigning through righteousness to eternal life, by Jesus Christ our Lord. He lived under their influence, and was supported by their efficacy, through a great variety of mental and bodily afflictions. In the last closing scene of life, he eminently experienced the faithfulness of God to his promises. The anxiety for a beloved daughter labouring under a wasteful disorder, of which she died a few months after his own decease, the pains and langour of his own affliction, and a conscious feeling of his sinful infirmities, combining together, threatened the speedy dissolution of his frame. Amidst these accumulating evils he stood upon a solid rock; he felt an inward and gracious power, which strengthened him, and bore him above all sublunary things. The cheering promises of the Gospel, and the visits and fervent prayers of his minister, were remarkably blessed to his soul. About this time he observed to one of the family, ' I am now come to that period of my existence which I have long anticipated. I have done with the world, and the things of the world ; and am anxiously waiting to be borne by angels into the presence of my dearest Saviour.' He found much delight in the repetition of some appropriate hymns from the collection of Dobell and Dr. Watts, and received great consolation from the delightful meditations of Mr. Mason. That on Hebrews vii, 25, which was read to him by a beloved child, was so singularly blessed to his soul, that he chose the text for his funeral sermon. When apparently dying, and incapable of articulation, he was observed to be in the exercise of mental prayer. He suddenly rose up in the bed, and addressed his dear children and nephews, who were stationed around him, in a most suitable, eloquent, and impressive manner, exhorting them ' to set loose to earthly things, and to give all diligence to make their calling and their election sure ; to seek the kingdom of heaven and its righteousness, while youth and health were with them ; and not to defer it until sickness and old age overtook them, and totally incapacitated them for business of such eternal importance.' He then sunk again into a doze or stupor, from which he scarcely revived, until a few hours of his decease, when, with a composed countenance, he surveyed his agonized family stationed around his dying bed, and articulated, ' I shall soon be there' ; then turning his eyes upward with sweet composure, he exclaimed, ' My dear Saviour !' and immediately fell asleep in Jesus. Mr. Strange died on the 2nd of February, 1826, in the sixty-fourth year of his age; and on the 9th his remains were interred in the family vault in the chapel. His minister officiated, and gave an oration at the interment; and on the Lord's Day following he improved the mournful event in a subject from the text selected by the deceased, to a very crowded and attentive congregation, which evinced the respect so justly due to our departed friend. On Lord's Day, February 26, Mr. Cannon, the Missionary at Wanbro', preached a funeral sermon on the occasion, at Wanbro' Chapel, from Matthew xxv, 21, to an attentive congregation, who properly estimated the good offices of their late patron and benefactor. In the useful life and happy death of our departed friend, we have an illustrious example of Divine Grace—an encouragement for steady confidence in the faithful promises of our covenant God—and an animating excitement to zealous activity in the cause of Christ. May his bereaved family, church, and acquaintance, have grace so to follow his example, that, through faith and patience, they may, with him, inherit the promise!

"G. M."

The initials G.M. at the end of this memoir are no doubt those of the Rev. George Mantell, the schoolmaster, as I attempted to show, of the celebrated Gideon Algernon Mantell. Mr. Thos. Barrett tells me he well recollects Mr. Mantell, and his having as many as sixteen or eighteen pupils at a time. Mr. Mantell himself died in February, 1832. There were, prior to its destruction, several marble monuments to the memory of members of the Strange family, as well as one to the Rev. George Mantell, in the old chapel in Newport Street; but they have been so defaced or destroyed by time and neglect that the following is the only one I have been able to decipher, and which I would hope to still further preserve in memory of one of those sturdy predecessors of ours, who, through believing what they did, believed with all their might and main, and did more for securing for us that liberty of conscience, and that right to worship God after our own intent, far more than we think or are prepared to give them credit for :—

IN MEMORY OF
MARTHA
THE WIFE OF THE REV. GEORGE MANTELL,
WHO DIED
ON THE 8TH OF SEPTEMBER, 1821,
AGED 70 YEARS.

ALSO OF THE
REV. GEORGE MANTELL,
WHO DIED
ON THE 6TH OF FEBRUARY, 1832,
AGED 75 YEARS.

AND OF BETTY, SECOND WIFE
OF THE REV. GEORGE MANTELL,
WHO DIED
ON THE 14TH JUNE, 1840,
AGED 78 YEARS.

During the time of Mr. Mantell's pastorate, Newport-street Chapel was, no doubt, a place of considerable repute among the Independents, and its pulpit was occasionally occupied by some of the leading ministers connected with that body, and among others by the Rev. W. Jay, of Bath, the Rev. Richard Elliott, of Devizes, and others. In addition to the families I have already mentioned, the chapel was attended by a number of others living in the neighbourhood ; and I have heard of Newport-street presenting quite an animated appearance on many occasions when it was known that some well-known minister was to conduct the services. Even down to a comparatively recent period the members of several

Nonconformist families living in the neighbourhood were in the habit of regularly attending the services at the Newport-street Chapel; but fifty or sixty years ago, on a Sunday morning, but more particularly when some noted preacher was announced to occupy the pulpit, from ten to twenty conveyances, principally "tilted" carts, such as were used by the old carriers, were occasionally to be seen in the street, bringing in persons to the chapel from even long distances. The persecutions and disqualifications of those days seemed only to make the sturdy Nonconformists of that period more determined to surmount the obstacles which were intended to rob them of that liberty of conscience which they prized so much.

⸺Town✲and✲Trade✲of✲Swindon⸺

MEMBERS of the Strange family, who I have already shown were the founders of the cause of Nonconformity in Swindon, were at the same time the leading traders of the place. Forty years ago the late Thomas Strange carried on the principal drapery business in the town and neighbourhood: the business being very extensive. His uncle Richard at the same time carried on the business of a grocer, and he was perhaps the best known of the whole of the Strange family. It was both his custom and delight to sit on a chair in his shop and talk and joke with everyone who came in. In himself he made quite a jolly-looking and interesting little picture. He had a round, happy-looking face: he always wore his hat— the hat characteristic of the period—a rather low-crowned, broad-brimmed beaver hat, that would last a man for years, worn somewhat in his poll, and resting on his coat collar. His coat was pigeon-tailed in cut and his breeches and gaiters drab in colour. I never saw him without his good stout walking stick, which he would always keep in a perpendicular position in front of him and between his rather widely spread-out feet, and the top of which he would use as a resting-place for his hands. He was immensely fond of a chat, a joke, and a laugh; and when anything tickled his fancy, or became the motive power for a laugh, you could watch its whole operation. The effect would be first seen on the hands, which would be pressed with greater firmness on each other and on the top of the stick; a tremulous motion would then be seen gradually working up the bowed arms, until it reached the shoulders, which would then begin to work as though they were acting as a pump on the liver; the jolly old face would broaden into a grin, and the whole frame become convulsed in the throes of ecstatic delight, and present a picture of supreme merriment, the old hat which crowned the edifice occasionally requiring a little fresh setting up to prevent its toppling off. His shop was the most frequented and best known in the town, and it was a common occurrence to see the old gentleman the centre of a laughing crowd of, in particular, old women and of children, who would be always ready to run on an errand to Strange's as an excuse for stopping and having a chat and a laugh. I do not, of course, wish it to be understood that Mr. Strange did nothing else beside sitting in his shop joking with the old women and playing with the children. I have described him as I recollect him as a child of from four to five years of age. One house only intervened between Mr. Strange's shop and my father's house. I must, therefore, have had daily opportunities for seeing him, whereas, had a few more houses intervened, it is probable I might never have noticed him. Mr. Thomas Barrett, who knew the old gentleman many years before I did, while agreeing with me as to his general afternoon habits, says he had quite another habit for the morning. His favourite place was still on the stool or chair at the end, but in front, of the counter, a little to the right of the entrance door, from which place he could not only see everyone who entered the shop, but also all who passed up or down the street. And here he would sit for an hour or more every morning, smoking his "backey" or morning pipe, which was invariably a long clay, or "churchwarden," as they were called, and it was in this position that he would receive his friends and business men, and transact the greater part of his business, which was of an extensive and important character, a large tallow chandlery and candle manufactory being attached to it at that time. The old gentleman died on February 12th, 1832, aged 77 years, and was buried in the family vault under the old chapel in Newport-street, but some time in the year 1884 his remains were removed, with others of the family, to a new vault in the cemetery. The old man had a notorious shopman named Dickey Wood, who had a still more notorious companion named Billy Noad; but I must leave this precious pair to be dealt with along with some other Swindon "characters" I have known.

From a hundred to a hundred and fifty years ago the town of Swindon must have presented a very primitive appearance. , At that time what is now known as the "Goddard Arms" Hotel was a building of a much more rural and less pretentious character. It was a low thatched building, with a post and swinging sign hanging in a frame, in front, and was then known as "The Crown." Brock-hill was then much steeper and far less accessible than now, whilst the boundary to the road leading towards Cricklade and High-worth was on the eastern side of the Church-well and the row of magnificent elm trees leading down to the wharf, instead of on the western side as now. The

Q

enclosure of this well and of these old trees, and their conversion into private property, is only one of several encroachments on public rights which old people still living can tell of. The easing or lowering of Brockhill appears to have been quite an undertaking at the time it was executed, and there was quite a battle between "vested interests" and the parochial authorities over it. Even for some time within the present century the entrance and exit to Swindon by the Cricklade road was most difficult and dangerous. The old road appears to have been carried right over the brow of the hill, which reached its highest elevation just about where the footway entrance to the church now is. Indeed, the "pitching" in front of Anderson's Almshouses, as now seen, pretty correctly gives us the original elevation of the road, which is now some seven or eight feet lower. The elevated ground on both sides of the road shows pretty accurately the original level of the road, which must have been positively dangerous even for foot passengers, while for conveyances heavily laden it is difficult to understand how they could be got either up or down. The difficulty, it appears, gave a little employment and profit to one or two persons who kept horses always ready for a "hitch-on" and a "consideration," to help a carriage, coach, or waggon over the brow; and that circumstance, it may be, was deemed a sufficient excuse for allowing it to remain. The fearful accident (?) which must always have seemed inevitable, however, at length took place, and steps were then taken to lower the hill and leave it pretty much as we now see it. The accident was to one of the coaches—I think it must have been the Oxford coach. The drag or skid had been applied as usual at the brow of the hill, but just as the descent had been commenced the skid gave way, with the result that the whole lot was sent with fearful rapidity down the hill. Before, however, it reached the bottom the front wheels gave way, and the coach, which was heavily laden at the time, pitching forward, performed a complete somersault, killing in its fall one of the passengers, a Mr. Myers, of Faringdon, and some of the horses, other passengers being seriously, although not fatally, injured. This fearful piece of business appears to have forced the people of Swindon to see the necessity of doing something to the hill. But, as I have said, they were at once met by the cry of vested interests and private rights. Mr. Harding, who lived in the old house now occupied as County Court and other offices, complained that any alteration of the level of the road would interfere with his convenience in getting his carriage into and out of his yard, and therefore strenuously opposed any alteration being made. How the opposition was got over I cannot say, although several old inhabitants tell me they well recollect the accident and the subsequent levelling of the road. I have only heard of one other accident to the Swindon coaches, and this one I have always heard referred to in terms of high commendation for the brilliant display of coachmanship it brought out. The coach had just been started to make the descent of Blunsdon hill when the skid gave way, and the coach was forced with fearful velocity down the steep incline. The coachman, happily, was equal to the occasion. He at once saw that his only chance was in making his horses step out faster even than the coach was going, and with this view he lashed them into a gallop, and thus kept them in front, and well out of the way of the coach. Had the horses lagged for an instant, or swerved for only a few inches, the result must have been the destruction of both passengers, horses, and coach. The old coachman, however, won everlasting renown as a " whip " by landing the whole concern at the bottom of the hill with nobody any the worse except from fright. I have more than once been considerably amused listening to a person who happened to be one of the passengers as he attempted to relate the circumstances, but who invariably failed to finish his tale through the excitement into which the relation and recollection of the event would throw him.

And then the Square: I can myself recollect it when it presented a very different appearance to what it does now. On the south side, where the Town Hall now stands, there were some roughly-built stone stables, in which the London stage waggon horses were kept, with a long room or tallot over, in which cheese and other like produce was stored until it was convenient to load it in the waggons for transit to London. On the opposite, or north side, where the corn stores were afterwards built, there were a couple of small stone-built cottages, the fronts of which were occasionally brightened up with a coat of limewash. These cottages were distinguished from most of the other cottages in the town, inasmuch as they were covered with stone tiles, one-half at least of the houses in Wood-street at this time having only thatched, *i.e.*, straw, roofs. My father lived in one of the houses in the Square, and the other was in the occupation of a Mr. Goold, who, being the manager of the Savings Bank, held his offices there. It was on the mantleshelf over the fire-place in the office that I first saw a plaster bust—it was that of Shakespeare. Goold was a builder, marble mason, and sculptor, and, no doubt, had the bust there as an emblem of his trade. There is only one other thing I can recollect in connection with this office, and it is this : Something had gone wrong about the bank, and the poor people who had their savings there were in terrible alarm about their safety, and for some time there was a great deal of weeping, wailing, and gnashing of teeth in consequence. I cannot say if any actual loss was sustained by anyone by the collapse, but I believe it had the effect of putting the bank on a better foundation, and the making of many of the clergy and gentry of the town and neighbourhood, who constituted themselves managers and trustees, responsible for the proper management of the concern.

As recently as the beginning of the present century, there must have been very few tradesmen indeed in Swindon. There was not even a butcher in the whole town. Once a week a man of the name of Tidd, living in Dammas-lane, used to wheel some portable shambles into the Square, and there he kept shop, supplying such of the inhabitants as required it with fresh meat. An old friend of mine, Mr. John Weeks, who died in 1860, at the great age of 92 years, used to tell me of a small circular market or penthouse in the centre of the Market-place, under which people used to assemble to do their marketing. From the description he gave of it, I think it must have been not unlike a huge umbrella, the nearest thing like it I have ever met with being the old butter market standing in the Market-place, Witney, within the last two or three years. The stocks and pillory used to find shelter under this rude and ancient building, which was ultimately razed to the ground by the assistance of a team of stout horses and some strong chains. It may seem strange that such a place was found sufficient for the marketing of a town like Swindon ; but when we recollect that in the year 1801 the weekly wage of an able-bodied labourer was not more than sufficient to buy from twelve to fifteen pounds' weight of bread, it will be readily understood that there was very little marketing to be done. I hope to treat on this matter fully in another paper, but I would just mention here that in March, 1801, the average price of wheat was *seven pounds eleven shillings and twopence per quarter*, or FIVE times the average at the present time (December, 1884). With wages at from six to seven shillings per week, and bread àt from one shilling and sixpence to two shillings per four pound loaf, there was but little room left for any tradesman beside the baker. Indeed, it is questionable if the baker had much to do, for it would seem that the duty of providing food to eat devolved mainly on the parish officers acting on behalf of the ratepayers. And this was undoubtedly the case at Swindon at the period about which I am writing (1801), as the following page from the parish accounts will show, and which I take from a book which I have been permitted to inspect since this article was originally published :—

At a Vestry held at the Parish Church of Swindon, the 14th day of April, 1801, pursuant to notice given for that purpose, Joseph Ellison. Overseer of the Poor of the Parish aforesaid, audited his accounts for the preceding year, as follows :—

	£	s.	d.
Cash received of the late Overseers	164	9	4½
To ditto recd. for sundries as appears by book	40	14	9¾
Recd. by Rate at 4/- in the Pound	927	16	5½
Do. by Do. at 3/- Do.	693	18	9
	1826	19	4¾
By allowances crav'd uncollected as appears by the same book	0	9	9
	1817	10	4¾
Cash Recd. for Bread, Flour, &c.	23	9	10¼
	1840	19	2¼
By Cash disbursed as appears by the same book	1826	6	11
	14	12	3½

Left in the Bake House 7 sacks Pease ; Between 3 and four Bags Barley flour.

The above accounts were audited and allowed by us

RICHARD FARMER
JNO. RANDELL.

16 April, 1801, passed and allowed by us (having been first verified on oath).

E. GOODENOUGH
T. G. VILETT.

From this account, which I prefer to give with its errors rather than alter, it would appear from the item for cash received for bread, &c., that the parish officers undertook to supply others beside actual paupers with food at, possibly, less than cost. At this time the population of the parish may be put at 1,200, so that the cost of the Poor for that year was equal to a rate of something over thirty shillings per head of the population, whereas at the present time (1885) the cost of the Swindon Poor, reckoned in the same way, does not exceed three shillings and threepence per head of the population.

How the working classes managed to pay for their food, as well as their rates, out of the wages that were paid at this time it is simply impossible to imagine. From accounts of payments entered in the same accounts I find a mason being paid four shillings and sixpence for three days' work, and a labourer two shillings and eightpence for four days' work, wheeling sand. Another labourer, who, no doubt, was employed on a more responsible job, was paid three shillings for four days' work.

I well recollect on one occasion, I think it must have been in the year 1839, when what were counted quite respectable tradesmen in Swindon tried the experiment of mixing barley-meal with their wheaten flour (many families making their own bread at that time), in the hope of making the loaf go farther, and of reducing the weekly flour bill. The experiment, however, was only tried to be given up, for the barley proved indigestible, and occasioned illness through heart-burn. I need hardly add that such businesses as that of a chemist and druggist and of a printer have been introduced into the town within the memory of persons still living.

John Britton describes his friend Robert Sadler as being the son of a glover and breeches-maker living at Swindon. This is not the only or the oldest reference I have been able to meet with to what may be called some "special" business or manufacture as carried on in Swindon. In a document relating to the poll tax in the reign of William III., for the parish of Swindon, reference is made to one William Webb, a tobacco cutter or manufacturer, which I believe is the oldest known reference to any manufactory carried on in Swindon. From the circumstance that Webb is described as a tobacco cutter, it seems probable that that was his principal, if not only, calling at this time. I think, however, that it must afterwards have been merged with a grocery business, also carried on by Webb, and subsequently discontinued altogether. It will be seen from the list of "Swindon Tokens," which I shall deal with in my next paper, that William Webb had his halfpenny in 1669, on which there were two pipes crossed. The glove and breeches-making, as carried on by Sadler and his predecessors in Swindon, must I think, have been a much more important business for the town than was that for the manufacture of tobacco. Even to within the last five and twenty years the dressing of leather and the manufacture of gloves was carried on somewhat extensively in Swindon by the members of a family of the name of Lawrence, whose ancestors must have been people of good standing in the town a couple of centuries or more ago. It may be but a small matter, but with the exception of candle making and tobacco cutting this leather goods trade of glove and breeches-making are the only manufactures I can trace as having been carried on at Swindon, and of these the leather goods trade must have been by far the most important, many hands being employed in it. The gloves made were those known as "hedgers' and ditchers'" gloves, such as labourers use when handling thorns and briars when

cutting hedges and cleaning out ditches ; while the
breeches were all of a kind that never wore out, and
were occasionally bequeathed from father to son, and
which, provided there was no insurmountable difficulty about "size," were well calculated to last
throughout one, two, three, or even more generations.
They were usually made of the best picked buck-skin
leather, generally for the squire or well-to-do person,
who, after some years use, would make a present of
them to some dependent. I recollect a pair of these
old breeches in particular. They were worn by a
little old man of the name of Buy, who had himself
worn them thirty or forty years, and it was understood that as regards age, they were quite old before
they came into his possession. The last glove and
breeches maker to any extent in Swindon was a
George Lawrence, a well-known inhabitant some
twenty or thirty years ago, a man of very good
property. The sewing of the gloves was always, I
believe, "put out"—that is, women took the cut-out
article to their own homes and added certain specified
work to it, very similar to the practice now observed
at the factory at New Swindon, until it was fit
for the market or for sale. Unfortunately I am
unable to say how the breeches were made, but the
turning out of a few pairs must have been quite
an event. I cannot, of course, vouch for the exact
age of these old leather breeches, which may have
been a year or two more or less; all I know for
certain about them is : they were wonderful breeches
—just such wonderful things as the old leather bottles
of our grandfathers, and about which they used to
sing, and which, when no longer fit for the storing
liquor in, were nailed up in some conspicuous place
among the household goods as a depository—

> ———to put odd trifles in,
> Ink, and soap, and candle ends.

Indeed, the leather breeches of the period of which I write may be described as being historical breeches, on which you may hang a legend or a romance.

Having referred to an old document of the time of William III., in which the names of Webb and Lawrence first appear in connection with Swindon, I may add that this document, with a number of others, was exhibited at the Twentieth General Meeting of the Wilts Archæological Society, held at Swindon in September, 1873, and which was referred to by Mr. Cunnington, as follows :—

"Mr. Cunnington said that he had before him five very interesting and almost unique documents, which had been presented to the Library by Mr. Richard Mullings, of Cirencester. Mr. Mullings had told him that many years ago he had saved these documents literally from burning. They were assessments upon parishes in the neighbourhood of Swindon, in the reign of William the Third, and contained a list of a large proportion of the inhabitants of that period. The papers had been bound by Sir Thomas Phillips, whose writing was on the covers. Mr. Mullings had carefully analysed these documents, and had prepared a short but very interesting paper upon them. 'The documents, to which the attention of the Society is invited, consist of assessments made for the parish of Swindon, and several other surrounding ones in the time of King William the Third, under the Acts for levying a poll tax on births, marriages, and burials, and on bachelors. The papers were saved by me literally from burning, very many years ago. Most of the assessments have the signatures of Justices of the Peace of the district and the assessors certifying their accuracy. They were deemed interesting, curious, and instructive, by my late friend, the profound antiquary, Sir Thomas Phillips, Bart., of Thirlestaine House, Cheltenham, by whose care they were stitched

and put in what he called ' Middle-hill binding'—such
as you now see them in.   It may be proper to preface
the consideration of the documents with a few remarks
on the taxes they relate to.   The poll tax of William
the Third's time differed from the mediæval tax of
that name with which our English histories have made
us familiar.   They were alike in their object of reaching all classes, but the historic poll tax was a certain
charge, generally 1s. a-head on persons of all conditions and estates above fifteen years of age (mere
beggars only excepted).   The poll tax of William the
Third, on the other hand, was upon a scale of degrees ;
such as were worth £50 paid 4s. a year ; those worth
£300 and reputed gentlemen £4; tradesmen and shopkeepers £2.   Persons chargeable with finding a horse
for the Militia to pay after the rate of £4 per horse.
A person keeping a coach and horses, a peer of the
realm, a clergyman of £80 preferment, and an attorney
each paid alike £4.   Non-jurors in every case had to pay
double.   This, the last instance of poll tax, produced
over two and a half millions, which was far short of
what would have been raised if it had been rigorously
exacted.   But it was an obnoxious impost.   Under
the Act of 1695, granting duties on births, marriages,
burials, and on bachelors, the tax was upon a property.
Thus a scale : For persons possessed of fifty pounds
per annum or £600 personal estate, the burial fee was
£1 4s, and so on.   The parish paid tax on the burial
of paupers, but neither their marriage nor the birth of
their children were liable to duty.   As to the bachelor's
tax, it was upon those of twenty-five years and upon
such widowers as had no children.   It was an annual
tax according to degrees.   Thus a bachelor duke
paid £12, his eldest son £7 11s., his younger sons
£6 5s. ; an esquire paid £1 6s., his sons 6s. ; a gentleman and his sons 6s. each.   Persons of £50 per
annum or £600 personal estate, 6s., their sons 3s. 6d.

The lowest degree was persons not otherwise charged,
who paid 1s.   The exceptions were Fellows of the
Universities and almsmen.   It is said that these taxes
were carelessly collected, but they produced in William
the Third's reign £275,517.   These assessments on
burials, &c., if they had been continued, would have
helped to a knowledge of the state of population.
There was also the property tax or rate.   These were
expedients to levy a revenue to meet in part the
extraordinary outlay required to carry on the war
with France.   In the assessment of Swindon to the
aid of 4s. in the £, in 1662, the list of contributors is
headed with the name of Thomas Goddard, Esq., for
all his lands, £80 19s., of three gentlemen of the name
of Vilett, one at £8 13s., another at £23 9s., and
another at £12 5s., and Henry Thomson, the vicar, is
assessed at £7—and so on, in all £132 for lands.
The list ends with 'John Robins for his Quar," which
is set down at nothing.   This list may, therefore, be
taken as a census of the proprietors of the land and
houses.   Besides this a list of persons possessed of
money or goods is given; they had to pay 24s. in the
hundred on the value.   The list also contains twenty-
one other names, all assessed at very small sums,
amounting altogether to £12 2s. 3d.   The land, &c.,
assessment amounted to £446.   The assessors were
Charles Vilett and Charles Hughes; the collectors,
Boxwell and Garrard.   In order to assess the duties
on burials, &c., the assessors seem to have written out
the names of all the housekeepers, their wives, children, apprentices, and other inmates, and put columns
opposite to their names for entries of births, &c.   The
families are kept distinct.   It is therefore a census
and a genealogical register.   Thus it gives—Thomas
Goddard, Esq., Mary, his wife, Richard, his son, Ann,
his daughter; John Gilbert, gentleman, Susan, his
wife, Elizabeth, his daughter, Henry Pinckney, ap-

prentice. After the trades others are mentioned, John
Holloway, translator (whatever that means), William
Webb, tobacco cutter, and so on. In some cases property is mentioned—Stephen Lawrence, £600 personal estate ; Charles Hughes, £50 per annum. The
names of covenant servants and of persons receiving
weekly allowances are given at the end. The census
for Swindon parish shows the population in 1697 to
have been 808 ' "

I am glad to think that I also saved some of
these old documents from the burning, as Mr.
Mullings puts it, for many years ago there came into
my possession—I, in fact, begged to have them, as
they were about to be destroyed—a bundle of old
parish documents. Unfortunately, however, one of
them only refers to Swindon, and that of as recent a
date as 1805.

Through the courtesy of H. N. Goddard, Esq., of
Cliffe Pypard, who has been good enough to send me
the original levy for Ship Money in the Kingsbridge
Hundred, I am enabled to give the list of the inhabitants of the parish of Swindon at a date anterior to
that given by Mr. Mullings, viz., in 1635. The amount
of the levy for the Hundred was—

Ship Money ...	...	...	...	...	£384	0 0
Coate and Conduct Money ...		...	...	137	0 0

Towards this the following Parishes and Tythings
contributed, as follows :—Wanborough, £39 ; Liddington, £25 ; Chiseldon, £39 10s. 0d.; Swindon,
£25 10s. 0d.; Overtown, Salthrop, Westlecot, Elcombe
(four Tythings), £39 0s. 4d.; Ufcott, £4 10s. 11d.;
Hilmarton, £32 ; Tottenham Wood, £7 4s.; Cleeve
Peyer, Thornhill, Broadtowne, £22 ; Lyneham, Tottenham, Clacke, Woodloeshaye, £26 ; Lyddyard Tregoze and Midghall, £47 ; Wootton Bassett, £47 ;
Binknoll, £12. Possibly there was a second levy for
the following year (1636) for the balance, or it may

be that there were a sufficient number of village
Hampdens in the Kingsbridge Hundred to render
the collection of the obnoxious impost not only
difficult, but impossible.   The chief interest in the
document, however, at the present time is through its
furnishing us with what is practically a census of the
Hundred two hundred and fifty years ago.   The names
of the Swindon owners and occupiers, with the sums
each one was called upon to pay, were as follows :—

	£	s.	d.
Thomas Goddard, Esq.	5	0	0
Mr. Edward Martin, of Upham	0	3	4
Mr. Henry Martin	1	0	0
Thomas Violett ..	1	15	0
Robert Turbey, sen.	2	0	0
Lawrence Stirhall	1	0	0
Mr. John Stirhall	1	0	0
Elizabeth Stirhall, widdow	0	10	0
Arthur Violett ..	0	15	0
Willi: Lawrence ..	0	15	0
Mr. Willi: Gallimour ..	0	10	0
Thos: Heath, sen.	0	13	4
John Huse	0	13	4
Thomas Edney ..	0	13	4
Henry Farmer, sen.	0	10	0
Willi: Dier	0	10	0
Willi: Ewen	0	6	8
Roger Ewen	0	3	4
Thos: Chandler ..	0	10	0
Jo: Looker	0	6	8
James Looker, jun.	0	6	8
Tho: Looker	0	5	0
Mr. Totten	0	3	4
Henry Skilling ..	0	5	0
John Barnard	0	5	0
Anthonie Stroots	0	5	0
Richard Martin ..	0	4	0
John Holloway	0	5	0
Jo: Ewen, sen. ..	0	5	0
Robert Turbey, jun.	0	5	0
Roger Harris	0	5	0
Thomas Heathe, jun.	0	3	4
John Allworth att Alder	0	5	0
Jo: Heathe, sen.	0	2	6
Jo: Heathe, jun.	0	2	6
Willi: Heath, colthworker	0	1	0
Jo: Ewen, jun. ..	0	3	4

	£	s.	d.
Richard Turbey ..	0	3	4
John Corlis	0	2	6
Willi: Smith	0	3	4
Jo: Stirhall	0	1	0
Widdow Restirey	0	3	4
Tho: Wilde	0	1	6
Jo: Flure	0	2	0
Samuel Lanne	0	3	4
Edward Fewtrill	0	3	4
Thomas Stirhall ..	0	2	0
Tho: Ewen	0	1	0
Nicholas Holloway	0	2	0
Milos Holloway	0	2	0
Milos Wilde	0	2	0
Richard Hopkins	0	2	0
Alexander Cattle	0	2	6
Amos Wilkins ..	0	1	0
Willi: Avenill	0	1	0
Robert Carpenter	0	2	0
Samuell Strong ..	0	1	0
Ambrose Taylor ..	0	1	0
Jo: Rudle, sen. ..	0	1	0
Richard Wylde ..	0	1	0
Samuell Haggard	0	1	0
Edward Thrushe	0	1	0
Willi: Flure	0	1	0
Noahe Webb, of Draycot	0	3	0
Richard Webb, sen., of Draycot	0	0	9
Daniel Porbins, of Werdy ..	0	0	9
Richard Phillips, of Wanborouhe..	0	2	6
John Webb, of Wanboroughe	0	2	6
Jeffery Bayly, of Whroughton	0	3	4
Jo: Horney	0	3	4
	£25	10	0

⟶Town⁕and⁕Trade⁕of⁕Swindon⟵
⁘CONTINUED⁘

---◦◆◦---

REVIOUS to the opening of the Great Western Railway, Swindon was quite an isolated little town. It had been, it is true, for many years connected with Bristol, Gloucester, and London by means of the Wilts and Berks Canal; but I never recollect the canal being used to any extent except for coal. And even as regards coal I have heard old inhabitants say that for many years an old man of the name of Heath, who kept a couple of donkeys and a small cart, could manage to deliver all the coal in the town that was required from the Wharf. The bulk of the carrying trade was done by what were known as stage waggons and carts, and by these passengers as well as goods were conveyed both to London, Bristol, and other places. The largest and most important concern was, of course, the stage waggon, to which I have already referred as starting from the Square. It used to be quite an imposing sight to see this huge covered waggon, drawn by six or eight horses, arrive or depart; and there was probably a no more important person-

age in the whole parish than the waggoner when seen
in his clean white Saxon frock, with its elaborate
needlework decorations front and back, and who, with
his long whip and his "whoa" or his "come hedder,"
would lead his horses just where he wanted them to
go. The out and home London journey would be
performed once a week, the load on the "up" journey
consisting of dead meat, packed in huge wicker
hampers, cheese, butter, and other farm and dairy
produce, which had been collected from the farms
around Swindon during the week, and on the "down"
journey the load would consist of merchandise for the
various tradesmen. The route the waggon would take
would be by way of Hungerford, where the Great
Western road, both for waggons and coaches, would
be struck, and from thence on to Newbury. The only
other waggon I can recollect was a much smaller, and
an altogether inferior affair, sometimes drawn by two,
and never by more than three horses. It belonged to
a Robert Jefferies, of Wootton Bassett, and its proper
route was to and from Bristol and Wootton Bassett,
with what may be called a feeding or supplementary
journey every Saturday from Wootton Bassett to
Swindon. This waggon used to be started very early
in the morning for Bristol from Wootton Bassett, and
I have known persons leave Swindon over night for
Wootton Bassett, where they would sleep, in order to
be in time to journey to Bristol by the waggon. In
addition to the waggons there were carriers' carts to
Cirencester, Faringdon, Newbury, Marlborough,
Devizes, and Bath. All these carts made what are in
America called "connections" with other carts which
went to still more distant towns, so that even in those
days Swindon had pretty direct communication with
all parts of the country, although it very often took a
considerable period of time, and involved much trouble
and no small amount of risk, to make it. In the list

of towns to which the carriers' carts went I have mentioned Cirencester first for the reason that my first ride
in any public conveyance was in the cart from Cirencester to Swindon, on the occasion of my parents
removing from the former to take up their abode in
the latter town. I also have a reason for putting
Bath last in the list, for it was in connection with the
proprietor of the Bath cart that I recollect the circulation of a very grave scandal, which afforded the men
and boys of the period an opportunity for reviving a
very old Wiltshire custom, known as "Wooset-
hunting," and to which I must refer. Mr. F. A.
Carrington, from whom I have already quoted in
regard to the Mummers, includes "The Wooset"
among the ancient Wiltshire customs, and says in
respect of it that :—

"In the villages near Marlborough this is a mock
procession got up by the village lads, when conjugal
infidelity is imputed to any of their neighbours. At a
little before dusk, a blowing of sheeps' horns and a
sounding of cracked sheep bells may be heard about
the village, and soon afterwards the procession is
formed. I saw two of these Woosets: one in the year
1835, at Burbage, the other about five years after at
Ogbourn St. George. The procession was in each
instance headed by what is called 'a rough band,'
which, in the latter instance, was numerous. Some
beat old frying-pans, others shook up old kettles with
stones in them ; some blew sheeps' horns, others rang
cracked sheep bells, and one of the performers was
trying to extort music from a superannuated fish
kettle, by beating its bottom with a marrow bone.
Four more carried turnips on long sticks, each turnip
being hollowed out very thin, and the features of a
face cut thinner still on it, and a lighted candle put in
the inside. These were followed by a person bearing
a cross of wood of slight make, and seven feet high ;

R

on the arms of which was placed a chemise, and on
the head of it a horse's skull, to the sides of which
were fixed a pair of deer's horns, as if they grew there;
and to the lower part of the horse's skull the under
jaw bones were so affixed that, by pulling a string,
the jaws knocked together as if the skull was champ-
ing the bit; and this was done to make a snapping
noise during pauses in the music.   This procession is
repeated on three nights following, when it goes past
the houses of the supposed guilty parties; it is then
discontinued for three nights; resumed for three
nights—discontinued for another three nights, and then
resumed again for three other nights, and then it
concludes.   This is a different procession from that
called the 'Skimmington,' which takes place when a
woman beats her husband.   When I was quite a boy
I saw a Skimmington in Gloucestershire; the principal group in the procession being a stuffed figure of
a man placed on horseback, behind whom rode a man
in woman's clothes, who, as the procession went on,
kept beating the stuffed figure about the head with a
wooden ladle.   The Wiltshire people call the Wooset
procession a 'ooset,' as they never pronounce w before
o, calling wood 'ood,' and the like."

I recollect several exhibitions or entertainments
of this character in my younger days, before Sir
Robert Peel gave the country his "New Policeman."
And I also well recollect that there was a general
belief that the offence not only justified, but the law
sanctioned, the proceedings, if the rule of observing a
three-nights' interval between the exhibitions—that
is, three nights on and three nights off—was strictly
adhered to.   But the instance which I most particularly recollect was that which arose in this way :—
A certain Swindon tradesman had a wife, who by
some of her neighbours was "counted" rather "fast."
It so happened that she became a somewhat frequent

traveller by the carrier's cart to Bath.   As time went
on, and the visits of the lady to Bath became even
more frequent, remarks began to be made.   These,
however, were for a time silenced by the explanation
that her business, that of a milliner and dress-maker,
necessitated these visits in order that she might give
the ladies of Swindon the advantage of the very
latest fashions, both in body dresses and head gear.
In course of time, however, it was generally understood that pretty good evidence was forthcoming that
the real object of her visits to Bath was that she
might the better enjoy the society of the proprietor of
the Bath carrier's cart, who was also its driver.   And
on this discovery being made it was duly celebrated
in the usual orthodox Wiltshire fashion.   I have
known the Wooset attempted on other occasions, but
never so thoroughly as on this one.

In addition to the stage waggon and the carrier's
cart, there were the stage coaches.   And of these
there were three.   There was a coach which left the
"Bell" three times a week, early in the morning, and
which reached London in the afternoon of the same
day, returning to Swindon on the afternoon of the
next day.   There was a second coach which passed
through Swindon every day on its journey from
Oxford to Bath : it would go down one day and back
the next.   And then there was a third coach which
passed through the town on its journey from Southampton to Cheltenham, going down one day and back
the next.   And these were, I believe, all the conveyances we had either for passengers or goods (I mean
regular established conveyances, for there were occasionally "opposition" concerns introduced, but which
were soon taken off again) up to the time when the
Great Western Railway was opened as far down as
Steventon, when several of the fine and well-appointed
four-horse coaches were taken off the Great Western

coach road, which ran through Devizes and Marlborough, and were run through Swindon to make a
connection with the railway at Steventon. I remember this was just about the busiest time I have ever
known in Swindon. Every coach would be crowded
to its utmost capacity, both with passengers and
parcels ; the horses would be some of the finest that
could be obtained ; they would always be driven at
their full speed ; whilst the little top-booted and big-
hatted guard, with a brass trumpet, generally longer
than himself, would herald the arrival and departure
of the splendid turn-out over which he and the driver
presided, in the loudest and shrillest notes which he
and his trumpet were capable of sounding. And then,
while all this was going on, day after day, and nearly
all day long, there was another sight scarcely less
striking every evening, but more particularly every
Saturday afternoon, and that was the troop of navvies
as they poured into the town after their work. These
men earned hitherto unheard-of wages, which they
spent freely—especially in beer ; they were employed
in very large numbers, the deep cuttings at Marston,
and between Swindon and Wootton Bassett, as well as
the long stretch of embankment between Swindon and
Purton, necessitating the employment of an unusual
number of men for a lengthened period. Their work
was very often of a most dangerous character: they
were paid for the risk as well as the work, and they
appeared to try to drown all thought of both by freely
spending all the money they could obtain. Accidents
of a fatal character were frequently happening among
these men, and there is one row, if not more, of
navvies' graves, extending right across from side to
side of the eastern boundary end of the old churchyard.

There was one picture formed by these men
which made such an impression on my youthful mind

that I have carried it about with me ever since, and I have reproduced it before my mind's eye hundreds of times, and under the most opposite of circumstances. The day had been remarkable for certain peculiar and very singular atmospheric changes. It must have been just one of those days which are said to be met with in countries which are subject to earthquakes. The sky : sometimes bright, then overcast. The air : sometimes light and enjoyable, then heavy and oppressive. The light : sometimes brilliant, then overpowered, as it were, by some invisible hand, which shut it out from view, leaving only some dead and dull reflection behind, and then coming and going in fits and starts as though it had St. Vitus's or some other dance. It had been one of those days which appear to be made up of a conglomeration of uncertainties and surprises ; when you would, as sometimes when putting one foot before the other in the act of walking, hesitate in doubt as to the safety of the step, and then find you had made it in a glow of light, which, however, had only a momentary existence, and which as it vanished left the doubt all the stronger. But, as the evening began to set in, these fitful changes settled down into a grand and mysterious after-glow, which seemed to suffuse the whole Western heavens, and to fill up space with a something which you could touch and feel, and which formed a kind of halo, or a rainbow garniture to all objects, both animate and inanimate, intervening between the eyes of the spectator and the place out beyond, where the sun was sinking down to his rest. At this time there were neither trees or buildings in the Sands beyond Eastcott-lane, so that standing at the top of Wood-street, or in Bath-road, the Western heavens lay out before you, as it were, at the end of an avenue, a circumstance which on this particular occasion seemed to concentrate the effects of the scene, and to make it more remarkable. It was

just after the after-glow to which I have been referring
had set in that the navvies began to pour into the town
by way of the Sands, in gangs of tens or twenties, or
more, or less. At any time, or under any circumstance,
the appearance of these men was most remarkable,
and even picturesque. It may have been that coming
as they did almost suddenly upon the neighbourhood
as a distinct and peculiar race of men, their appearance produced an impression which was scarcely
maintained afterwards, or which would have been possible under other circumstances. I can well recollect
that when they were first seen in the neighbourhood
of Swindon they appeared like a race of giants. As
a rule, they were tall, robust, and most powerful. On
their feet they wore enormous laced-up boots, which
came half-way up their legs, and which appeared
to be a good load for an ordinary man to carry.
They invariably wore very thick white duck trousers,
the legs of which were rolled or tied up to close
under the knee, displaying their enormous calves
encased in coarse knitted stockings. Their only other
principal garment was a kind of coat and waistcoat
combined, the front of which consisted of some very
loud coloured and large pattern fancy cloth, with
many rows of large glittering buttons, the back being
of heavy white duck. This garment would be without
sleeves, and worn sufficiently long to cover the hips.
Around the neck would be twisted very lightly a large
loud coloured and big pattern kerchief, and on the
head some slouching billycock or cap. There was
one other garment inseparable from a navvy's outfit,
and that was his white home-spun slop, which served
quite a variety of purposes. On ordinary occasions it
was worn slung across the back, one sleeve being
brought over the right shoulder and the other one
under the left arm, and then tied in front. When
moving about the country, or in marching order, this

slop would be utilised as a sack, in which would be
stowed away all the owner's worldly goods and
chattels, and which he would strap to his back by
tying the two sleeves. As I used to see them coming
into the town in gangs, they would invariably have
their shirt sleeves rolled up over the elbows, their
neckerchiefs and shirts would be open at the throat so
as to allow their necks and breasts to be exposed,
and not unfrequently they wore beards of all shapes
and colours ; the colour of their arms, faces, necks, and
breasts, however, through constant exposure to the
sun, rain, and all weathers, being invariably that of a
dirty brick red. As I have said, on the evening of
the day of the memorable after-glow, I stood in the
Sands and watched these men trooping into the town
at the close of their day's work. As I was not half
their height, from my point of view their heads and
shoulders were thrown, as it were, right against the
heavens, which formed a background to the most
weird-looking picture I had ever beheld—a mysterious
appearance I shall never forget. They appeared to
be passing through some palpable material of something, which, as it was forced aside for their passage,
was formed into a variety of layers, through which the
light from the back penetrated, and which, when seen
from the front where I stood, gave the appearance to
each individual or group as though they were surrounded by a many-coloured halo or rainbow. The
sight was a most peculiar one, and one which I have
never forgotten. You may see a somewhat similar
result produced when you enter a darkened room into
which a strong stream of sunlight is struggling through
some hole or crevice in the shutters, and painting with
all the colours of the rainbow the floating atoms of
dust as they dance and gambol in the sun stream.
The only difference was this : the navvies as they
trooped along disturbed the myriads of atoms with

which the air was charged, and sent them flying in
layers of clouds, as it were, around their heads and
bodies, where the after-glow took hold of them, and
played on them, and gave them life, light, and colour.

At this time, a third at least of the houses in
Wood Street had thatched roofs ; there were no buildings whatever on the left-hand side of the road leading
out towards Wootton Bassett beyond where Mr.
Chandler's shop now stands ; there were only some
half-dozen buildings in what is now known as Devizes
Road. On the left-hand side of the road, where the
Post Office now stands, from opposite Little London
to nearly opposite Eastcott Lane, there was a belt of
fir trees. I recollect those fir trees very well. They
bounded a field occupied by a Mr. Burt, a solicitor in
partnership with Mr. Bradford—Bradford and Burt it
was then. One morning, as the old gentleman was on
his way to his office, he spied me with other boys "up"
one of these trees. He did not attempt to get at us,
for to have done that he would have had to clamber up
a stone wall five or six feet high, but he made a call at
our shop, where he managed to put my mother in such
a fright that she did not recover from it for some time.
He began by asking her if she wanted a situation for
her son. To this my mother replied that when I was
a little older she would be pleased, &c., &c., and for
some time an apparently innocent conversation was
carried on about me and my prospects in life, which,
however, was brought to an abrupt termination by the
old gentleman expressing his determination to find me
a berth on the tread-wheel at Devizes. It was not
very long after this that I heard of the old gentleman
again through my mother. He was anxious to get
someone to read to him, and consulted my mother
about my doing so. Before, however, anything was
decided, he died ; and never having forgiven him for
his threat to send me to Devizes, I seized the occasion

to perpetrate the first, and I think only, bit of doggerel I have been guilty of. I wrote on the wall close by his grave :—

> Near this spot old Burt lies buried ;
> Quickly from this earth he was hurried.
> Where, oh where, is he now ?
> Say, oh say, ye who know ;
> Up above, or down below—
> Who's now got him—poor old Joe.

It is, however, always refreshing to look back on these Old Town charactèrs of the slow and sure generation. It would be difficult now to find men to correspond with Parsons Jones or Grooby, Lawyer Burt, or Doctors John and Joseph Gay ; men who had not only the entire confidence of their clients and personal friends, but of the whole community in which they lived. I have heard it said that the late John Gay was entrusted with the keeping of everybody's secrets. And I can well believe that such was the case. There was generally something so sterling in the characters and lives of men like these, who, through a long series of years, had grown into the confidence of the people, that their influence was simply irresistible. In the faster and more furious times in which we live, there seems scarcely time or opportunity for such men in real life : we are constantly, however, meeting with them in pictures. The artists in *Punch* and other similar publications are for ever reproducing these men in their ideal representations of JOHN BULL : The round, jolly-looking, and close-shaven face ; the rather low-crowned broad-brimmed hat, the pigeon-tailed or cut-away coat, the loud-pattern waistcoat ; the huge watch-chain and bunch of keys and seals ; and the drab cloth breeches and gaiters : Men of the " Thee" and "Thou" period and school, who were as blunt and unaffected as they were honest. No doubt these men lacked much of the cleverness and science of many of their successors :

they could neither draw men into law-suits for the purpose of fleecing them, nor could they kill or cure on scientific principles so adroitly as some of those who have followed them. But they managed, nevertheless, to get on in the world, and to perform their part in it, and who, when their turn came, could go down to the grave sincerely mourned and respected.

There is an anecdote in connection with one of those whose names I have mentioned which I must relate. The house pulled down for the erection of the County of Gloucester Bank premises in the High Street was formerly in the occupation of Mr. Joseph Gay. At the back of the premises there is a large and somewhat long garden, stretching down towards the great field, and in which Mr. Stone, who was gardener and handy-man at the Bank, took great pride and interest. After having been at the Bank for several years as manager, and having noticed that a particular spot in the garden did not receive the usual dressing of manure like the other parts, Mr. Wearing called Stone's attention to the circumstance, and remarked that it also would require manure, when a conversation, which may be thus epitomised, took place between master and man :—

Stone: That patch won't want no manure for a long time yet.

Mr. Wearing: Why not? It has not had any since I have been here.

Stone: Oh! no. And it don't want any now; and it won't want any for a long time.

Mr. Wearing: But, why not?

Stone: Why, can't you see how rich it is? [Suiting his action to his words, Stone here sent his spade into the earth and turned up a spitfull.] It be the richest bit of land in the whole garden.

Mr. Wearing: How do you account for that. Is there anything peculiar in the soil?

Stone : Why don't you see, sir, this used to be Mr. Joseph Gay's bleeding ground, when he had his surgery here. He used to have one day a week for bleeding, and people who wanted to be bled had to attend at a regular time, like they do now when they want their children vaccinated. And when they were all ready in the surgery, Mr. Gay used to bring them out on to this bit of land, and after they had got in a row or in a circle, and had got their arms ready, he would bleed them, and let the blood run on the ground, and that's what makes it so rich !

It will be recollected that at one time phlebotomy, or blood letting, was accepted by a large number of people as the one remedy for all the ills flesh is heir to. The late Lord Radnor was a staunch believer in this remedy. It mattered but little what the ailment was, the remedy was to be found in a little blood-letting. I have heard it said that Mr. Joseph Gay never thought of leaving his surgery without a lancet in one pocket and a box of camomile pills in the other. Subsequent to this period there was another, which I well remember when it was said that the price of brandy was raised several shillings a gallon through a craze that brandy and salt had been discovered and accepted as the universal cure-all.

The motto of a celebrated doctor of his time ran as follows :—

> " I phisics 'em, I bleeds 'em, I sweats 'em,
> And then, if they *will* die, I let's 'em.

Doctors may be, and no doubt are, far cleverer now than they were then, both in physicing, bleeding, and sweating, as well as in the penning of their mottoes. They don't think aloud as Dr. Lettsom did.

⌐Tradesmen's⁎Tokens⌐

 MONG the oldest trade records of the town, and certainly by no means the least interesting, must undoubtedly be placed the Tradesmen's Tokens of the Commonwealth period—those small, very thin, and somewhat rude coins which are occasionally dug up in gardens or found in some old wall of an old house, into which they may have fallen through some crack or crevice. These tokens, which always bear the initials or name, or both, of some tradesman, were always of small value, generally that of a farthing, but occasionally, although very rare, that of a halfpenny, while there were none above that sum, although afterwards both halfpenny and penny tokens became very common, many of them being struck from expensive and well-executed dies. In some places the Overseers of the Poor used to pay their paupers in money, or rather "Tokens," specially struck for their use, having, no doubt, arrangements with certain tradesmen that "their money" was to be accepted at its full nominal value, and exchangeable,

when supplying their Poor with food or other necessaries.   In Swindon there were eight Tokens altogether, two of the value of a halfpenny, and six of
the value of one farthing each.   I give a list of these
with their inscriptions :—

> O.   WILLIAM . HEATH=W . E.   ...   .   ¼
> R.   IN . SWINDON=W . E.
>
> O.   HENRY . MUNDAY . CHANDLER=The Grocers' and
>   Tallow chandlers' Arms.   ...   .   ½
> R.   HIS . HALF . PENY . IN . SWINDON=H . M. 1669.
>
> O.   HENERY . RESTAL.=Two tobacco-pipes crossed.   ¼
> R.   IN . SWINDON . 1656=Three sugar-loaves.
>
> O.   HENERY . RESTALL=Two pipes crossed.   ...   ¼
> R.   IN . SWINDON . 1664=Two pipes crossed.
>
> O.   JOHN . SMITH=The Bakers' Arms. ...   ...   ¼
> R.   IN . SWINDON . 1664=I . C . S.
>
> O.   WILLIAM . WEBB=Two crossed pipes.   ...   ½
> R.   OF . SWINDON . 1669=HIS . HALF . PENY . W . W.
>
> O.   AMOS . WILKINS . IN=The Grocers' Arms....   ¼
> R.   SWINDON . IN . WILKSHER=A . W.
>
> O.   AMOS . WILKINS . AT=The Mercers' Arms.   ¼
> R.   SWINDON . IN . WILTS=A . M . W.

The contractions used are, " O." for the Obverse
side of the Token, "R." for the Reverse ; the mark =
signifies that what follows it is in the field, or central
part of the Token ; ½, and ¼, signify Halfpenny, and
Farthing, showing the value of the piece.

I have specimens of most of the farthings, but
have no recollection of having ever seen one of the
halfpennies.   There were 192 of these Tokens issued
by the tradesmen of Wiltshire, all of them being of a
special character, and altogether distinct from those
which were put into circulation at a subsequent period.
These Tokens are generally regarded as being very
curious by those who possess them, and as but very
little appears to be understood about their history, and
the circumstances under which they were produced,
the following extract from an exhaustive work on the

subject by W. Boyne, F.S.A., may not be without interest:—"The small coinage of England from the earliest times was of silver; transactions requiring money of inferior value were carried on by means of black mail, turneys, Abbey-pieces, crockards, dotkins, staldings, and other base foreign currency, as well as by English leaden Tokens, all of which were illegal, and against the circulation of which many severe laws were enacted by our earlier kings. Silver money was coined as low in value as the penny, three-farthings, halfpenny, and farthing; all these were in common use, but from their small size and weight—the silver halfpenny of Elizabeth weighing only four grains— they were extremely inconvenient and were easily lost. Small change of a more useful size and weight was required, even though it must consist of a baser metal. In the reign of Elizabeth, pattern-pieces were struck, and a proclamation drawn up, legalizing the circulation of copper money; but owing to the difficulties the Queen had experienced in restoring the standard of silver money, which had been much debased during the extravagant reign of Henry VIII., her aversion to a base currency was so great, that the project was abandoned without trial. Pennies and halfpennies of small size, however, were issued in 1601 and 1602 for circulation in Ireland, and authority was granted by Elizabeth to the Mayor and Corporation of the city of Bristol to issue a Corporation farthing Token. The need for small change being urgent, leaden Tokens, generally of mean workmanship, continued to be issued by tradesmen until 1613, the eleventh year of the reign of James I., who then delegated his preroga- tive of striking copper money to John, Baron Haring- ton, for a money consideration; the patent, however, was granted for farthings only. On the accession of Charles I. to the throne, in 1625, the patent for the coinage of farthings was renewed. The privilege was

grossly abused by the patentees, who issued them in
unreasonable quantities, and of a merely nominal
intrinsic value, the coins weighing only six grains
each. They encouraged the circulation by giving
twenty-one shillings in farthings for twenty shillings in
silver; by this means many unprincipled persons were
induced to purchase them, and would force five, ten,
and even twenty shillings' worth of them at a time on
all with whom they had dealings. In a short time, not
only the city of London, but the whole kingdom, and
especially the counties adjacent to the metropolis—
Kent, Essex, Suffolk, and Norfolk—were so burdened
with them, that in many places scarcely any silver or
gold coin was left, the currency consisting entirely of
farthing Tokens. The issue of this patent was one
of the many arbitrary acts of the first two Stuart
Kings, which tended to destroy the attachment of the
people to the Royal Family. It is remarkable that
among nearly 9,500 Tokens, the name of Charles is
found on only forty-four. The numerous families
named Smith, who issued above one hundred Tokens,
have not a single Charles amongst them. James, being
a Scripture name, has been more fortunate, though it
is not so common as might have been expected. The
accumulation of the patent farthings in the hands of
small tradesmen, caused the latter so great a loss, from
the refusal of the patentees to rechange them, that in
1644, in consequence of the public clamour, they were
suppressed by the House of Commons, which ordered
that they should be rechanged from money raised on
the patentees' estates. Apparently an authorized
currency was then intended, as two pattern farthings
were struck, one of which is dated 1644; the design
however was never carried out, men's minds being
then too much occupied with the Civil War between
the King and the Parliament. The death of the King
put an end to the exclusive prerogative of coining

copper and brass; Tokens immediately began to be
issued, and were circulated without authority, and, as
stated on some of them, for 'necessary change.' As
they were received again by the issuer when presented,
they were far preferable to the patent farthings. The
earliest date on Tokens is 1648. (A few were probably
struck previous to the King's death.) During the
whole period of the Commonwealth no copper money
was coined by the Government, except a few farthings,
which are very rare, and were probably only patterns
for an intended coinage. Silver money continued to
be issued of the value of twopence, one penny, and
halfpenny. That the Government of the Commonwealth was as unpopular as that which it had over-
thrown is evident from the Tokens, which were
undoubtedly an index of public opinion; whilst after
the Restoration the Royal Arms, the King's Head,
and other insignia of Royalty, are exceedingly common. The spelling of words in the inscriptions is
most irregular, owing partly to the unsettled state of
English orthography at that period, and partly to the
ignorance of those who struck the coins.—Thus, 'on,'
is often spelled ONE; 'HENNERE' for Henry; 'ST.
EEDS' for St. Neot's; 'OLFA-TREE' for olive-tree;
'HORSES SHOW' for horse-shoe; &c. [On a Wootton
Bassett farthing the name appears thus, 'Wheten
Basett.'] The coining of the Tokens seems to have
been performed by the issuers themselves. In the
'Gentleman's Magazine,' vol. xxvii., page 499, there is
an account of the discovery of a Token-press and
dies, found at Chesterfield. For the convenience of
rechanging the numerous varieties of Tokens, tradesmen kept boxes with several divisions, into which
those of the various tradesmen and corporations were
sorted, and when a sufficient number were collected,
they were returned to the issuers, to be exchanged for
silver. The devices on Tokens are very numerous,

and may be classed under twelve divisions :—I. The arms of the Incorporated Trade Companies of the city of London. These were generally adopted by persons of the same trade throughout the country. The colours of the arms are not shown on the Tokens, and parts of the bearings are often omitted, with other inaccuracies. In addition to the Trade Companies, numerous individual tradesmen issued them, as a Coal-man, Comfit-maker, Pipe-maker, &c.; as well as Bailiffs, Churchwardens, Lords of the Manor, Mayors, Members of Parliament, Overseers of the Poor, one Rector and one Esquire.—II. The Arms of Cities, Towns, Abbeys, the Nobility, and private families.—III. Merchant's marks. In early times, when few persons could read, these curious marks must have been very useful, to enable work-people and others to distinguish bales of merchandise by the particular mark stamped on them. They appear to have been in use from the twelfth century. Common devices of this kind are, a cross, the figure 4, a heart, a circle, and the initials of the issuer. Many merchant families adopted for armorial bearings their trade-marks in a shield. They are partially used by shipping merchants at the present day.—IV. Taverns and Shop Signs. The earliest Tokens having been issued by publicans, they have, on that account, been frequently called Tavern Tokens. The usual device is the sign of the Inn. The oldest were often of a religious character, as the Holy Lamb, the Salutation of the Virgin (which had degenerated at that period into two men saluting each other), the cross keys, &c.—V. Articles of Dress sold by the issuers, as hats, caps, neck-whisks, piccadillies, leggings, &c.—VI. Implements of Trade, Agriculture, and War ; as hammers, croppers' shears, teazle-brushes, scissors, windmill, swords, &c.—VII. Animals; as oxen, antelopes, cranes, peacocks, lobsters, &c.— VIII. Articles of domestic use ; as black-jacks, tan-

S

kards, gridirons, cleavers, tennis bat and ball, &c.—
IX. Heraldic signs ; as the phœnix, griffin, portcullis,
Catherine-wheel, three legs of man, &c.—X. Conveyances ; as coaches, waggons and packhorses, fish-
ing boats.—XI. Views of public edifices ; as churches,
castles, bridges. These are mostly unlike the structures
represented.—XII. Punning devices on the issuer's
name, after the manner of *canting* heraldry.   As
examples, there are Bush (a thornbush), Cox (two
cocks), Harbottle (a bottle on a hare), Samson (Samson
standing), Yate (a gate, still pronounced *yate* in the
North), &c.   The earliest dates are 1648, 1649, and
1650 ; but Tokens of these years are scarce. After
1650, until 1660, they are more plentiful, and nearly
the whole of them are farthings : halfpennies are few
in number, and there are no pennies.   Those of a date
subsequent to the Restoration of Charles II. are the
most abundant ; halfpennies are very common among
them, and there is a good number of pennies.   The
years 1665, 1666, 1667, 1668, and 1669 are the most
prolific, in particular 1666 (the year of the great fire
of London) ; whilst in 1670, 1671, and 1672 they again
became scarce : of the latter year there are very few.
The Tokens were in circulation exactly a quarter of a
century ; they originated with a public necessity, but
in the end became a nuisance ; they were issued by
nearly every tradesman as a kind of advertisement,
and being payable only at the shop of the issuer, they
were very inconvenient.   The Government had for
some time intended the circulation of Royal copper
money, as we have pattern-pieces of halfpennies and
farthings of the year 1665 ; but it was not until the
year 1672 that the farthings of Charles II., of a
similar size to those of the present day, were ready
for circulation.   Tradesmen's tokens were then put
down by a stringent Proclamation, dated 16th August,
1672.   A few attempts were made to continue them,

but the threat of Government proceedings against the
offenders effectually suppressed them, and we hear no
more of them in England. In Ireland the latest
circulation was in 1679. On the Tokens the initial of
the surname is usually placed over those of the
Christian names of the husband and wife : though
sometimes the wife's initial is at the top, sometimes
the three initials are in a line, the middle one being
the surname, and at other times the surname is at the
bottom."

The number of separate Tokens issued was
naturally in accordance with the importance of the
town at the time for trading purposes, and we therefore find that Salisbury had no less than 39 Tokens,
Marlborough and Devizes 14 each, Malmesbury 13,
Chippenham 10, Highworth 9, and Wootton Bassett 2.
At Purton there were also two tradesmen who issued
their Tokens, and it will doubtless be within the
recollection of many of my older readers that as
recently as twenty or twenty-five years ago there
was issued at Purton, Wootton Bassett, and Cricklade
what was known as the Lamb Farthing. It was
issued by a draper and grocer of the name of Lamb,
who carried on business at these places, and who
adopted the figure of a lamb for the reverse of his
farthing. For some other places only one Token was
issued, and among them the following :—Bishopstone,
Downton, Great Bedwyn, Hilmarton, Lacock, Luger-
shall, Steeple Ashton, and Stratton St. Margaret.
It is somewhat remarkable that no less than three
places in the county of Wilts which were so poor,
from a trading point of view, as to be worth only
a solitary farthing, were counted of sufficient importance to rank as independent boroughs, sending their
own representatives to the House of Commons.
Comparing the list of names of Swindon tradesmen,
who issued their own Tokens, with those of persons

who were assessed for Duties on profits arising from lands, tenememts, hereditaments for the year ending 5th April, 1806, in the parish of Swindon, I can find only the name of Heath remaining. But in this document I find the names of John and Richard Strange, both of whom occupied their own premises, and who, no doubt, had succeeded to the businesses of those who had previously issued their own tokens. It may be interesting to note that at this time (1806) the total assessable value of lands, tenements, and hereditaments in the parish of Swindon amounted to £5,293, and which was either owned or occupied by one hundred and ten persons. At the present time (1885) the gross annual assessable value of the lands, tenements, and hereditaments in the parish of Swindon is of the aggregate amount of £112,515, the number of houses in the parish on the 2nd December, 1884, being 4,250.

—Banks and Bankers—

EXT in the order of time, if not in importance, to the Token must be taken the
issuing of Bank-notes by local Bankers.
Mr. William Brush, who is now in his
ninetieth year, tells me he can recollect
when the nearest Bank was at Marlborough, and that
any Swindon tradesman who required the assistance
of a banker had to go to Marlborough or Devizes to
find one. It must, however, have been comparatively
early in the present century when a Bank was opened
in Swindon, by, it would appear, a firm consisting of
members of several families, and known by the name
of Messrs. Strange, Garrett, Strange, and Cook, afterwards changed to James and Richard Strange and
Co.; James Strange carrying on, in addition, the business of a draper on the premises now occupied by Mr.
Horder, in High-street, and Richard that of a grocer,
on the premises now occupied by Messrs. P. H. Mason
and Co. After this, again, the firm was changed to
that of Messrs. Thomas and Richard Strange, both of
whom have died very recently, and at great ages:

Richard, who died at Mannington, June 23rd, 1883, aged 83 years, and Thomas, who died at Springfield Villa, Swindon, August 29th, 1883, aged 89 years. The Messrs. Strange also carried on business as coal merchants at the Wharf, from the time when the canal was first opened for traffic down to after when the Great Western Railway became the principal carriers of coal, as well as of general merchandise.

Neither of the Stranges, I believe, interfered to any extent with the management of the bank, leaving that principally to their manager, Mr. Mountford, who was quite a leading character in Swindon in my younger days, and about whom there used to be a great deal of scandal, after the business of the bank had been transferred to Messrs. Stranges' successors, principally to the effect that he used a sanctimonious appearance and religious profession as a cloak for practices which were not altogether on the square. He was the principal stay and support of one of the Nonconformist bodies in the town and neighbourhood. His appearance was almost unique. Slightly above the middle height, he was stout and heavy looking. His head was round and somewhat bullet-shaped, with closely-cut straight hair; his face was clean-shaved, and sufficiently flabby to make his eyes, nose, and chin appear somewhat small; his eyes, which were what is known as "baggy," took furtive glances rather than a good look at you in conversation, and his voice was so meek and gentle as to appear somewhat minikin, and issued from a mouth to which the proverbial illustration that "butter would not melt in it," might unhesitatingly be applied. His body, which had all the appearance of being well taken care of, was always scrupulously clothed in rigid quaker-like attire. Around his neck he wore a white kerchief, the ends of which were tied in a neat little bow under his chin, and on his head he wore a

rather wide and flat-brimmed, heavy-looking, beaver
hat. But his walk was his most remarkable feature.
He was somewhat round-shouldered, and, as his eyes
were generally on the ground, he looked as though he
was in a meditative mood when going to and fro from
his house—the old Wesleyan Chapel house—and the
bank in the High-street. His steps were short and
somewhat quick, the foot never being raised higher
than an inch or so. As he rose his feet he seemed to
give his body a jerk, which served to set his shoulders
in motion, gently impelling his person forward in a
slight and scarcely perceptible springy jump. Taken
all in all, he was just one of those staid-looking,
respectable old gentlemen who, on the one condition
that they might be warranted perfectly sound and
free from every kind of vice, as men warrant horses,
would well sustain the character of an angel ; but
who, if on the contrary, was only just a little bit
screwy, was nothing short of being viciously dangerous. It was, I believe, more than once understood
that the old bank was *in extremis*, but the partners,
who could rely on the assistance of some wealthy
friends, always managed to pull through, and no one,
so far as I have heard, was ever a penny the worse for
the bank, although it was among the first of the
private banks to succumb to the operations of the
Joint Stock Banks when they received their wonderful impetus in the year 1836. Joint Stock Banks had
been legalised by Act of Parliament as far back as
1826, but for the first ten years the principle on
which they were established made but little progress
in men's estimation, and it was not until 1836, in
which year no less than forty-two new establishments
were started, that their operations were conducted on
a very extended scale. The North Wilts Banking
Company, with its head offices at Melksham, was
established this year, and very shortly afterwards

they opened a branch at Swindon, with Mr. Adams as manager. I recollect Mr. Adams having interviews with my father about taking a room in our house for the purposes of a bank. My father then lived in a low straw-thatched house in Wood Street, which stood on the site of Mr. Deacon's two shops, the rent of which, I recollect, was £16 a year. [The rent of the two houses which now occupy the same site would probably be £116 a year.] The bank, however, was never opened in my father's house, but in the next adjoining it—in what is now Mr. Tarrant's shop. As I have watched new bank after new bank arise in Swindon, each one apparently striving to be more grand and imposing than the last, I have thought of the old room in my father's old house, in which it was first proposed to open a branch of the North Wilts Company.

The opening of the North Wilts Bank no doubt hastened the necessity for doing something with the private bank of the Messrs. Strange, and accordingly, in 1842, it was taken over by the County of Gloucester Banking Company, with the Messrs. Strange as its nominal managers, and Mr. W. B. Wearing as cashier. In due course the bank was removed from its old position, adjoining the drapery shop of Mr. Thomas Strange, to new premises which had been specially erected on the site of an old house which had been in the occupation of Mr. Joseph Gay, Surgeon, and about which I have already had something to say. Mr. E. A. Moore was then appointed manager, and subsequent to him, Mr. W. B. Wearing, who continued to occupy the position until 1881, when he was succeeded by Mr. L. Etty, the present manager.

At about the same time (1835-6) as the establishment of the North Wilts Bank, the Wilts and Dorset Banking Company, whose head offices were at Salisbury, and who were then establishing branches in

different parts of the country, cast their official eye
on Swindon, but the view taken, it would seem, was
not very promising, for besides Swindon there was
the older and more important borough and market
town of Wootton Bassett, where they were also desirous of forming a branch.   What best to do in such
circumstances the directors were at a loss to know.
At length, however, they hit on the happy expedient
of proving the pudding in the eating.   They opened
branches at both Swindon and Wootton Bassett,
taking a room in a house in the High Street, belonging to Mr. Scotford, tailor, &c., and now in the
occupation of Mrs. Daniel Smith, saddler, &c., for
the purposes of their Swindon branch.   After a few
months' practical experience, the directors considered
themselves in a position to decide which branch
should be kept going, and which shut up—Wootton
Bassett or Swindon—and after duly considering "all
things," past experiences as well as future prospects,
they unanimously decided upon keeping on the Wootton Bassett branch, leaving Swindon, and such prospects as other men might think it had, a fair and
open field for others of greater faith.   No further
attempt appears to have been made by the company
to do business in Swindon until the year 1876, when
they took premises in Wood Street for the purposes of
a bank, their manager being Mr. F. Harding.   Unlike
their former Swindon venture, this latter one would
seem to have been most successful, for, having acquired by purchase the old premises which had been
for generations in the occupation of the Blackford's,
the noted backsword players, they razed it to the
ground, and on the site erected the handsome and
imposing bank premises which now face the High
Street, at the corner of Cricklade and Wood Streets.
This building, which was commenced early in 1884,
was opened for business on Thursday, February 5th,

1885, Mr. G. S. Stock, who had succeeded Mr. Harding, being the manager.

There is just one other circumstance I would mention in connection with the establishment of Joint Stock Banks. And it is this : One of the first things the Reformed Parliament had to deal with in 1832 was the currency laws, and the special privileges enjoyed by the Bank of England through their charter. In renewing the charter to the Bank of England, the Government sought to make it conditional, among other things, that they (the Government) should have the right, when it was thought fit, to grant royal charters for the establishment of Joint Stock Banks within a certain distance of London. But in this they were opposed, and certain banking privileges were retained to the Bank of England for a circuit of sixty miles around London, as the North Wilts Banking Company afterwards found to their cost. Among other towns selected by this company for opening branches was that of Hungerford, and all the necessary preliminaries and expenses were duly made and incurred for that purpose, when the Bank of England interposed, and, setting up their special privileges, caused the scheme to be abandoned, it being proved after careful and special measurement, that the proposed bank buildings at Hungerford were just half-a-mile within the prescribed area. Of course no such objection could be raised to the Swindon branch, which was duly opened, and still exists, although it has since been merged in that of the Capital and Counties Bank.

Before leaving the subject of the old bank, I may mention that the Messrs. Strange followed the custom commonly adopted by bankers of making their notes payable to some particular person well known and esteemed for his position in the neighbourhood or radius of circulation, as well as to "bearer." For instance, they made them payable to David Archer, Esq., Kingsdown, or bearer ; Thomas Tuckey, Esq., Compton, or bearer; to William Farmer, Esq., Swindon, or bearer; the object being to increase the reputed stability of the bank by connecting it with the names of persons whose financial position was above suspicion, although in this no doubt they were sometimes mistaken. For instance, I have heard it said of Mr. Farmer that he always carried a roll of bank notes in his pocket, to be produced when occasion required to show what a rich man he was, yet he, when he died, was found to be over head and ears in debt.

This last circumstance reminds me of a tradition to the effect that our forefathers not only claimed, but exercised, a right to deal with persons who paid their debt to nature before paying those due to their creditors, by seizing the corpse and withholding from it the rights of christian burial until terms had been made for liquidating the liabilities by the " mourning" friends and relations. I think I have heard some such a tale as this told about Mr. Farmer. But I can give no particulars. Nor can I in another case about which I have heard, where, on a person, who shall be nameless, giving up the ghost, two coffins were prepared, one with all the show and ostentation of the undertaker's art, the other in secrecy. In due course both coffins were taken to the great house where the great man had died, steeped up to the hilt in debt. The body was quietly placed in the plain coffin, and at once secretly removed, and ultimately deposited in the family vault, in a church not far from Swindon, whilst in the elaborately decorated one was placed a quantity of large stones, which the creditors in due course pounced down upon and kept until the stipulated number of days which a corpse could be kept had something more than expired, when they proceeded

to make a closer examination of the contents of the
coffin, with the result of finding that they had been
"sold." There is one other anecdote I must notice,
as it not only had to do with Mr. Mountford, but
serves to show up something of his character. It
happened at the time when there was an "opposition"
coach running to London, that Mr. Richard Strange
was noticed to be a somewhat frequent traveller, and
that he invariably selected the old or regular coach to
travel by. This occasioned some little surprise, until a
friend spoke to him on the matter, and expressed astonishment that he did not travel by his own coach.
"Travel by my own coach—travel by my own coach,"
exclaimed Mr. Strange, in astonishment. "Pray what
do you mean ?" "Why, I mean that the 'opposition'
coach is your coach," replied his interrogator. "That
is, it is generally understood in the town to be yours,"
he added. "Dear me, dear me" said Mr. Strange,
indulging in an imaginary wash of his hands, "I
really don't know, but I will go and enquire." Mr.
Strange accordingly made off for the Bank, where he
was somewhat alarmed to find that if the "opposition" coach did not belong to him it had been heavily
subsidized and kept running by the bank funds. It
afterwards appeared that Mr. Mountford had taken
offence at something said or done in connection with
the running of the regular old coach, and that he had
put the new or opposition coach on the road by way
of retaliation.

I recollect that I once had a little account to
settle with the driver of the London coach—it may
possibly have been the identical one that raised the
ire of Mr. Mountford to "opposition" coach pitch. I,
however, had no bank fund to fall back upon for the
purpose of shewing how much I had been offended.
The cause of the offence was this : It was my work to
await the arrival of the coach by which the monthly

parcel of periodicals, &c., was to arrive, and to hasten off with it just as fast as my legs would carry me to my father's shop, where Corney Reynolds, who was the secretary, and others, who were members, of a reading society which had been started in the town, would be waiting to receive it. The coachman was a little man, with the asthma and a very cross-grained temper. He drove into the town that afternoon in a worse temper than usual. On asking him for the parcel he cursed me and the parcel too, and declared that he had not brought it. I felt, however, that the parcel was in the "boot" all the time, and there sure enough it was found an hour or two afterwards. Now, a habit of mine, when a child—of course I have not thought of doing such a thing since—was that of taking stock of and "understanding" any queer character with whom I was brought in contact. And in this way I had got to thoroughly know the old coachman, and to be able to at once touch him on his weakest point, which was his aversion to a fourpenny piece. The fourpenny piece had not long been introduced into the British coinage at this time, and by coachmen, hostlers, and stable-boys it was regarded with the utmost aversion. The effect of holding a red cloth up before a mad bull was as nothing compared with that produced sometimes by the sight of a fourpenny piece on one of the horsey fraternity, who used to declare they had been invented only to do them out of their rights, and to put them off with a fourpenny instead of a sixpenny piece. My time came with the old coachman when on the following morning I had to see him and pay him his bill for the carriage of parcels. The amount altogether was between six and seven shillings. And this is how I proceeded to settle that little bill: I went to the shops in the town until I had managed to change my sixpences and shillings into fourpenny pieces, which I very carefully wrapped up in paper and laid down in front of the old man on the table in the " Bell," where he was making up his way bill.   I waited in the immediate neighbourhood of the table only long enough to see Mr. Coachman begin to open the paper, when I made for the doorway, but before I could well pass out there was an explosion which might have been heard all over the house---

My friend :
He coughed and swore :
Then rushed for the door :
Then cussed and swore all the more
At the little urchin who had gone before
He could lay his hands on him :
And who was all " a-galore"
At the fun he was having
With the little old man who
Was ready to snivel and cry bo'hoo,
And who fell " whop" on the floor,
When he could swear and cuss no more,
As though he'd given up breathing.

⌐Old✳Town✳Characters⌐

KNOW not how it is with others, but
my own experience decidedly is that there
are not now half the old people there were
fifty years ago, that is, so far as I can see.
Indeed, I have more than once within
recent years pulled up sharp, and asked myself what
had become of all the old, and especially the dirty old
snuff-taking and mud-soiled men and women of my
childhood's days: why there were so few old people and
so many pretty children now compared with the time
when I first began to take notice of men and things ?
Did this same thing ever strike you, my reader ?   If
it has, just tell me what you think about it.   If it has
not, just give five minutes to the thought, and then
tell me that if in this matter things have not been
entirely changed about. No doubt different minds and
different experiences would supply very different explanations for this, whilst in some cases, possibly, the
conclusion at which I have arrived would be disputed
altogether.   But if there be those who would do this
latter thing, I at once tell them I pity, and do not

envy, them. Fifty years ago we were in the full
enjoyment of the rich ripe fruit of the preceding fifty
years of glorious war on the European continent, in
which we had been so busily engaged. In those wars
my father had played his part, and in the course of
them had lost a limb. But what was his loss, I
should like to know, to the glorious privileges his
children enjoyed through those wars; privileges which
we enjoyed both sleeping and waking, morning, noon,
and night? The bread we ate, and the tea and coffee
we drank, and the sugar we sweetened it with, were all
taxed ; the light of heaven was taxed if it only came
to us through the window of a house : the glass in the
window was taxed—I had to pay over £4 window
duty yearly on the second house I rented for occupation—our candles, with which we got our light by
night, were taxed ; and the soap with which we used
to wash ourselves was taxed. I must not, however, be
led into an attempt to give a list of the things that
were taxed at this time, for if I ventured upon it I
should exhaust my readers' patience before I had done,
and should have no room left for other matters. I,
however, may get over the difficulty by saying it is not
only difficult, but almost impossible, to recollect a
single thing that was in common use fifty or even forty
years ago that was not taxed. I have only mentioned
a few of the "taxed" causes, which I think must have
had much to do with the making of those nasty, dirty,
old men and women of fifty years ago, to whom I have
referred—old men who never washed either themselves
or their clothes, and the old women who took snuff.
But how many other old people I can recollect of my
childhood's days who were not remarkable because of
the dirt in which they lived, or for their filthy habits—
men and women who were simply old and wrinkled,
and doubled up, and who hobbled about, and who
looked as though if they stepped out, as the generality

of men and women did, they would be in danger of
stepping over some precipice into their graves, and be
lost for ever.   Our population has gone on doubling
and trebling since then, and, as our actuaries inform
us, the value of human life is some years greater now
than it was fifty years ago, so that there must be both
a larger number, and a larger proportion to the
number, of old people now to what there was formerly,
and yet there seems to be hardly any corresponding
class existing now to those to whom I have been referring as so common when I was a child.   And then,
what is still more remarkable is this : the number of
pretty looking and interesting children have increased
in every place and in every direction.   How is this to
be accounted for ?   I can give but one answer to my
question, and it is this :   As we advance in years our
view of things becomes toned down ; rough edges and
angular points lose their sharpness, hard lines become
graceful curves, and rough places become smooth. As
we settle down to our own rest, things around us seem
more restful than they ever were before, and age is
mellowed rather than crabbed.   And this is why we
do not see so many old people as formerly, although
in number, and to the world, they have never been so
plentiful.   And then as to the children !   It would
seem by the ordering of an all-wise and ever-bountiful
Providence that as we journey on toward that bourne
from whence no traveller returns we are brought into
greater sympathy and touch with the innocence and
happiness—with the graces—of the child life, and there
win a foretaste of an existence into which we are im-
perceptibly to glide as in a dream, where there will be
a mingling together of all that is pure and innocent
with the very highest and best both in thought and
deed we have ever reached through the labours of our
lives ; where the noblest and best we have ever
yearned after in our humam sympathy will be the

T

germs out of which there will spring fruits of richness
and of beauty which human eyes could not bear, nor
mortal thought imagine.

It would be nothing short of a curse for either a
man or a woman to have with them through their
lives creatures of that Ghoul class whose representative in my childhood days was old Nanny
Kernel. Where this old woman came from, or who
she belonged to, I never heard. All I ever knew was
that she lived somewhere in the Workhouse yard,
where she had a large number of cats, which, it was
understood, were her only companions, and through
whom she maintained communication with those evil
spirits which were popularly believed to "live down
below." Children used instinctively to keep a respectful distance from her, and to quietly steal out of
her way when they saw her approaching. She had a
small weazen face, small features, and small and very
dark eyes. Her skin was like very dirty parchment,
and hung on her face, neck, arms, and hands in rolls,
not unlike the skin on an alligator's neck or belly. I
have no conception of what her real height was, but
as I recollect her she appeared to be under middle
height ; but that was probably due to her being bent
nearly double. She seemed to be kept from falling
forwards, when walking, by a stick on which she
leaned. I never saw her in but one dress, which was
of the period of George III., and which had the effect
of making her look as broad as she was high. In
fact, she was not unlike the half of a round ball, with
a head projecting in front, gliding along. Her dress,
before it had "seen its best days," must have been
an elaborate, as well as an expensive, piece of work.
The front of the petticoat, which was of some dark
material, was decorated with much needlework from
the waist to the bottom, as was also the stomacher or
top part or body, from the neck to the waist. The

dress itself was of quite another material and colour :
it was a kind of half-dress, cut away from the front
down the sides towards the bottom part of the back,
like a bantam cock's wings, leaving the petticoat
and stomacher quite uncovered in front ; the whole
dress being inflated to its utmost capacity by a stout
crinoline.   On the top of the dress she wore a scarlet
coloured cloak.   I have seen pictures of this same
dress many times in books, worn by Mother Shipton,
for instance, as she is riding through the air on a
besom, and by Old Mother Hubbard ; but I never
saw it in actual use except on the person of Old
Nanny Kernel.   I once saw, and never but once, a
male dress of the same period.   It was worn by an
old gentleman in the streets of Cirencester.   He was
quite an old swell of the first water, and carried a
gold headed cane in one hand and a snuff box in the
other ; low pump slippers, black silk stockings, knee
breeches, with ribbon bows, an elaborately frilled shirt
front, a long cut-away coat, the back of which was
simply filthy with hair powder, which shook, as he
walked, out of the long queue or pig tail which hung
from the bottom of his powdered wig down his back,
constituted the remainder of his attire.

But there was another character whose aversion
to children was as great as was that of Nanny
Kernel's, and whom the children held in quite as
much dread.   He was the ghoul of the old mill, in
Mill Lane.   He was rather above the middle height,
and rather stout and heavy built.   He used to wear
just about the same articles of dress as other people,
but he wore them different from most people.   For
instance, he wore heavy hob-nailed boots, which were
never laced up, and the tongues of which were always
lopping about on the fronts ; he wore thick worsted
stockings, but they were always down about his
ankles ; he wore breeches without braces, open at the

knees, and which were saved from dropping down by a regular and persistent "hitching up." His coat and waistcoat were never buttoned up, while his shirt was always unfastened and open, leaving in full view his hair-covered breast, which appeared to be a continuation of his grizzly beard, which was surmounted by such a shaggy head of hair as was but seldom to be seen. His favourite position and occupation was, after he had set his mill going, to rest his elbows on the bottom half of the mill door at the point where he could command a view of the lane, and of any children who might venture to enter it from the road end. With his elbows resting on the door, and his chin resting on his clenched fist, he would be content to wait for hours, like a cat watching for a mouse, in the hope of meeting with some children on whom he might scowl, and frighten out of their lives.

Old Tom Marcham was another character, whose great ambition it was to be regarded as the Parish Beadle for Swindon, and the custodian of the peace and order of the town. It was generally conceded that Tom had been somewhere abroad in his younger days, although there were those who contended that he had never got farther than Portsmouth, where it was said he went with the Militia, or some other "reserve" fighting party. Tom himself was always ready to contend that he had been through the whole of the Peninsula campaign, and that he had not only fought, but had actually shed his blood,. for the honour and glory of his native land ; and nothing ever appeared to give him greater satisfaction than when he was giving proof of this by a limping walk in some public thoroughfare, with the ladies and gents of the place looking on. Old Tom was quite a study on such occasions. He always carried a stout walking stick in his right hand : his left hand he would plant flat out

on his left hip. Having taken a peg forward with his
stick, he would screw his mouth together, which was
his favourite sign that he was concentrating the whole
force of both body and mind on some special labour
or thing, and would then hoist his stern forward with
his left hand as it rested on his hip, and having
repeated this operation a few times in quick succession,
he would make a sudden pause as though quite
exhausted, but, as the wicked boys of the period
would say, for the purpose of looking round for half-
pence and sympathy, and otherwise to see what effect
he had managed to produce. No doubt Old Tom was
a crafty and cunning old dog ; but do what he would
he could never succeed in getting himself regarded as
an authority on his wounds or his exploits abroad.
They used to chaff him, and say that if he had a
wound it was in his stern, and must therefore have
been received when his back was towards the enemy,
and possibly when his legs were frantically engaged
in making the breach between him and them as great
as possible ; the most popular belief, however, with
the boys was that Tom being discovered in the act
of pilfering when out with the soldiers was there and
then punished for the same, not at the hands, but
rather by the toes, of his comrades.

Old Tom waited long before actually holding any
office in the parish, although, as I have said, he
appeared to spend the whole of his days in assuming
the office of beadle and general preserver and custodian
of the peace. A favourite position of his was at
Blackford's corner, where he could command a view
of Wood Street, Cricklade Street, and High Street;
and also in front of the Masons' Arms, where he could
command Newport Street, Lower Town, and High
Street. At these two places he would spend most of
his time, professing all the while to have "his eyes on
the rascally boys of the town." His posing at these

two points used to afford me a considerable amount
of amusement : his right arm stretched out in front of
him, with his hand resting on his stick, and his left
hand resting on his left hip, which seemed to be projected out just as far as it would go, for the purpose of
affording a more convenient place for the hand to rest
on, he presented such a broadside for fun and ridicule
as was simply irresistible.   It is an old saying that all
things come to those who wait.   And office at last
came to poor old Tom Marcham.   At a Court Leet
held for the Manor of Swindon he was appointed ale
taster.   In a certain sense this was the very office
above all others for him, for he had an undoubted
weakness for ale tasting, especially when it cost
nothing but the trouble of drinking.   But Tom had
a soul above ale tasting.   The dignity and position of
parish beadle was far more to him than even ale tasting, and the first use he made of the office he had obtained was to use it to strengthen his claims to the one
to which he so earnestly and so persistently aspired.
And with this view, while his ale-tasting honours were
yet newly on him, he went off to the lord of the
manor, whose duly appointed officer he now was, once
more to urge his oft-repeated request for "a uniform,"
which, he maintained, had been repeatedly promised
him.   Mr. Goddard, who had had some military
experience, caused an old wardrobe to be overhauled
for something for Old Tom, and a military cloak and
cocked hat having been found, he was duly installed
therein, and having begged or borrowed one of the
long sticks or wands, painted blue, with a gilt top,
which the officers of the local tontine club carried in
their processions in the Whitsun week, he in due
course made his appearance in the public street in all
his new fledged dignity and importance.   He wore his
honors, however, for a brief time only.   The cause of
it I never learned, but he had no sooner attained to

that which had seemed to be his life's ambition than he began to draw away from the public gaze, and after a comparatively short time he was seen no more. Whether it was the ale tasting, or the heavy military cloak, or the cocked hat, or one or more causes of which the public knew little or nothing, that hastened on the end, I know not, but I recollect that one day when it was asked how it was that old Tom was not to be seen in the streets as usual, the answer was: " He's been dead and buried a long time."

Jenny Simmonds and 'Ria (Maria) Ladd were two other characters of my childhood days. They must, however, be mentioned together only for the purpose of drawing a contrast between them. Jenny Simmonds was a dirty, flabby, squab of a woman. Unlike Nanny Kernel, the only style in her dress was rags; anything was good enough for her to tie round her waist or throw over her shoulders. She was rather a fat old woman, with a large round face, a round chin, round cheeks, a round tip to her nose, and a round forehead. She used to bow her head forward on her breast, thrust her hands up the sleeves of her dress, so that her arms seemed to be always crossed in front of her, and would wander about the roads, streets, and gutters of the town, picking up such scraps as she could lay her hands on, like one without sense or feeling—a living scare-crow.

'Ria Ladd did not belong to Swindon, although she was daily to be seen in its streets. Her home was at Haydon Wick. I think I am correct in saying she was considerably over ninety years old at her death. When young she must have been an unusually tall woman, but in her old age she was somewhat bowed. She was also remarkably thin—she was literally a " bag of bones." Her physical strength, however, was something prodigious. In early life 'Ria had been the victim of a gay deceiver, and this would

seem to have made her, in a sense, a recluse from the
world. For her daughter, I had reason to know, she
had a somewhat passionate love, and for her neighbours she had a proper regard, but she had little or
nothing to do with them as companions. She seemed
to devote the whole of her existence to the work of
tramping, morning, noon, and night, between Moredon, Rodbourne, Haydon, and Swindon, and carrying
to and fro such loads of parcels, goods, merchandise,
and "all manner of things" as people chose to pile on
her back. For many years, day after day, the year
through, with the exception of one fortnight in the
year, the old woman used to make the to and fro
journey day after day, and sometimes twice, and even
thrice in the day. The aggregate weight of the goods
this poor old woman would bring into and take out of
Swindon in the course of a year must have amounted
to many tons, for she often had not only baskets and
bundles on each of her arms until there was no room
left for any more, but would then have in addition
baskets, parcels, and bundles fastened on her back.
She worked literally like a horse or beast of burden.
Toward the latter end of her time her appearance as
she struggled along under her load was very painful;
her thin, haggard-looking face, with its rolls of dirty-
looking skin, gave her a very weird look, whilst the
working of her large mouth, which was entirely
destitute of teeth, and her constant habit of licking
her lips with her huge tongue, gave one the feeling
that she wished to say something she could not find
words to express. My impression is that she never
made any fixed charge for carrying parcels, but was
always very thankful for any trifle that might be given
her, and especially so for little presents of tea, sugar,
and snuff. She was never, however, allowed to want,
or to go unrewarded, for she was regarded as being
indispensable at that time, and especially for taking

medicine to the poor from the surgery at Swindon. I
have referred to her affection for her daughter, and to
there being a lapse of a fortnight in the year when
she did not visit Swindon.   Her daughter on her
marriage removed into Gloucestershire, and year after
year the old woman devoted a fortnight to visiting
her.   The distance she had to travel was close upon
thirty miles, but she always managed to perform the
journey on foot in course of the twenty-four hours.
For some months before starting on her journey 'Ria
would commence saving up her pence, so that she
might take a few shillings to her daughter, and she
used to make my mother her banker for this purpose.
Once or twice in course of the year also my mother
would write a letter for her, describing the arrangements and fixing the time for the long journey into
Gloucestershire, the replies always being brought to
our house to be opened and read.   I have some faint
recollection of having written one of Old 'Ria's letters
to her daughter, my mother being, from some cause I
cannot explain, unable to do so.   If I am correct in
this recollection, this was probably the first letter
proper I ever wrote.   A remarkable feature in connection with old 'Ria was her utterly forlorn and
friendless condition.   She had absolutely no known
relatives or friends.   There was only her and her
" dater."   When questioned on the matter, she would
persistently maintain that she never had any friends
or relatives, and more especially that she never had a
father.   She was, she said, picked up in a flag-basket,
near a stile, in a field between Haydon Wick and
Swindon, but how she got there no one could ever
tell. 'Ria's account of how she was "found" was, I
believe, generally supported by the tradition of the
neighbourhood.

Billy Noad and Bobby Wood were characters of
quite another sort.   Their distinguishing character-

istics were romancing and practical joking. They
were both the sons of what are called "religious
parents;" Wood, it was understood, being the son
of a somewhat distinguished Wesleyan Minister.
Whether, in consequence of this, in their childhood
days, they were restrained from letting off that which
they undoubtedly possessed, a superabundance of
"animal spirits," and were driven to bottle them up for
future use, I am not in a position to say. But it is
certain that they devoted what may be called the
prime of their lives to romancing and the perpetration
of practical jokes. Two such companions in mischief
were but seldom met with, exercising their abilities on
a small town community. I recollect on one occasion
the shop in the High-street, where Wood was employed as a Grocer's Assistant, being stormed by a
number of irate mothers, who were all wanting to
know what Wood had been doing to their Jack's and
Tom's, and Harry's, and vowing vengeance against
him when they could lay their hands on him. This
was in consequence of an exhibition which Wood had
recently been indulging in of his "latest novelty," which
on this occasion was the model of a wind-mill affixed
to the end of a long tin whistle. Children who had
been sent to the shop for some trifling article which,
probably, "mother was waiting for" to complete
some arrangement in which she was engaged, were
induced, under the promise of some reward, to have a
blow at the whistle to see if they could turn the mill,
but only to find their nostrils, and sometimes their
eyes, full of snuff. Pranks of this kind, which were
regarded as fine fun, were of constant occurrence, and
not unfrequently led to many comical scenes. But
the chief exploits of the pair were reserved for the
time intervening between Saturday night and Monday
morning, which was generally spent by them in visiting the neighbouring villages, where, under one

excuse or another, they would not unfrequently perform mock religious services, which they would mix
up with the relation of the most extraordinary and
extravagant tales and romances, at which they were
great adepts, the relation of their (alleged) personal
experiences being generally the most outrageous.
Some time before this there had been produced
throughout the country quite a consternation through
the alleged doings of body-snatchers, and resurrection-
men, whose object, it was said, was to secure "subjects" for the hospital dissecting-room. I can recollect quite well when it was, by not a few, deemed
positively dangerous for persons to be out after night-
fall in the neighbourhood of Swindon, lest they might
have a "pitch-plaster" placed over their mouths, and
they themselves carried off by those who were making
a splendid thing out of supplying bodies for the sur-
geons' dissecting-table. It was one of the delights of
Billy Noad to tell of the resurrection exploits in which
he said he had been engaged, and he never had any
hesitation in accounting for a somewhat long absence.
from Swindon by declaring that he had spent it in the
body-snatching, pitch-plaster, and resurrection business. And with tales founded on the carrying out of
this alleged business he used to "make people's hair
stand on end." He was as peculiar in his dress as he
was in his talk. He invariably wore a large slouching
hat ; and over all his body-garments he wore a huge
smock-frock, which was usually stretched to its utmost
capacity by the bulged-out pockets of the coat underneath, and in which he appeared to carry the bulk of
his worldly goods and chattels. In his right hand he
carried a long staff, which he used *a la* pilgrim. In
course of time Wood returned to Bristol, where he died
in great poverty. Noad, when the County Courts came
in, got an occasional job as a "man in possession,"
and thus closed up his career.

—My*Schools*and*Schoolmasters—

THERE is nothing within my recollection in which there has been so complete a change as there has been in Schools and Schoolmasters. There is but one circumstance by which I can fix the date, and that only dimly, when I was sent to what was known as a Dame's School in Swindon. On the morning of November 23rd, 1830, the town and neighbourhood of Swindon was in a tremendous state of excitement. In my paper on the Yeomanry Cavalry I have given some particulars of the gallant deeds done on that day, and have told how a non-commissioned officer in the Swindon Troop fleshed his maiden sword in the stern of an unfortunate fellow at Liddington as he was attempting to crawl up a bank and through a hedge. This was only one of the remarkable events of this ever memorable day. Everybody and everything in and around the town must have been mad with frenzy and excitement on that day. As I had not yet reached the end of my fourth year, I think I could hardly have been sent to school at this time with a view of acquiring any school learning, but possibly rather with that of my being put out of the way at home and in a place of safety, where it would be the special duty of some particular person to look after me, with others. This was, no doubt, the first and leading object of Dame Schools, although I have no hesitation in saying, from circumstances which have come under my own observation, that many a lesson learnt in a Dame School has not only never been forgotten, but has stood both men and women in good stead in after life, when they have had to battle against the world and to meet the exigencies of their existence. The first school to which I was sent was kept by a Miss Noad, at a small house in Lower Town, adjoining the Bell and Shoulder of Mutton Inn, the door of which was approached by a flight of stone steps. On the outer wall of the Bell and Shoulder of Mutton, next the road, there was a staple and ring, to which horsemen visiting the house were in the habit of fastening their horses. I think that on the morning of this day I must have stolen away from our house in the Square and made off for the school in Lower Town quite unattended, for from what I have been told of the matter it would seem that I was attempting to get up the steps to which I have referred as being in front of the school, when I received a kick in the back of the head from the heels of a donkey that had been fastened to the ring in the wall of the Bell and Shoulder of Mutton. As I have said, every body and thing was mad with frenzy and excitement on this morning, when the rick-burners and rioters were said to be out, and the yeomanry after them. Even the poor old donkey, whose master had doubtlessly gone inside to discuss the situation with the landlord or his customers over some beer, became affected by what was going on, and, not satisfied with giving vent to its feelings in the "hee-haw" of its race, let fly with its heels, possibly as a further earnest of the depth of its appreciation of the surrounding circumstances, and succeeded in landing a terrific blow on the back part of my head. It was some days after this, I believe, before I regained consciousness. I have a distinct recollection of awaking as though from a long and by no means unpleasant sleep, to hear whispering voices near me. As I opened my eyes I found I was lying in a strange bed in a strange room. It was a large four-post bedstead, with heavy chintz furniture and curtains which were drawn close at the foot and side towards the window. Outside the bed the room seemed to be full of light, although inside all was dark. After listening for some time to the whispering, I heard footsteps stealthily approach the foot of the bed, and then the curtains were gently opened, and there appeared the anxious but happy smiling faces of my mother and of my schoolmistress. They seemed to come and go like a flash of lightning across my eyes, and were then lost to me for a time, although I have seen them many scores of times since as they then stood with bated breath before me. It must have been some time after this that I found my head enveloped in bandages, which were kept constantly moistened, and even still later on that the bed curtains were opened wider and wider day after day until I could bear the whole light as it entered the room by the window. And as this was done, and I could take a look around, there was but one object which met my eyes, and which impressed itself so thoroughly on my infant mind, that now, after a lapse of more than fifty years, I can oftentimes see it as plainly as I did then: It was a small black plaster figure of Shakespeare—a well-known model of the poet, where he is standing against a pedestal, on the top of which the elbow of the left arm is resting, the hand and arm being raised to the head —which stood on the mantleshelf over the fire-place.

I have oftentimes thought that children who are endowed with thinking, reasoning, and appreciative
faculties, who have been nursed by some kind and
thoughtful nurse through some severe illness, from the
effects of which they have subsequently entirely recovered, are among the most favoured of God's
creatures, for they, above all others, even in times of
trial, trouble, and difficulty, must be able to look back
and see angels' faces looking down upon and surrounding them as they lay the central figure in some
great and anxious sorrow.   I have also thought that
the home, however humble, adorned with a few
pictures or a plaster bust or two, where the means of
the occupants would not admit of anything better,
must always have a very different effect on the after
lives of those who have to spend their childhood days
in it than would the home which was altogether bare
of any effort to give it, I will not say an artistic, but
simply a more lively or pleasing character : and that
many a man and woman in their after lives have
enjoyed many a glorious day dream, and have looked
on life, its duties and its surroundings, from the best
and brightest aspects through the one little incentive
that was given to some happier thought by the bright
little picture or the artistically modelled bit of plaster.
Beyond the incident I have referred to, and which was
by far the most deeply impressed on my memory, my
only other recollections simply carry me back to my
sitting on a long low bench with a number of other
children, and holding a book in my hand.   How
long I remained at this school I am unable to say,
but possibly long enough to learn my letters and to
draw strokes and make pot-hooks and hangers.

My next school, in proper order, ought, no doubt,
to have been the one in Newport Street, of which
a Mr. Turvey was then master.   I, however, never
attended this school, but was sent for a time to

another kept by a Mr. Smith. As both Mr. Turvey and Mr. Smith were admirable types of country town and village school-masters of fifty years ago, I must describe both of them in turn, but not until I have given some particulars of the Newport Street School, which was one of the institutions of the town. I learn from the report of the Commissioners for inquiring concerning charities in the county of Wilts, that some time prior to the year 1764 a spurt was made to turn what educational property the town had to some practical purposes, and a fund was raised by voluntary contributions for the purpose of founding a free school at Swindon, to be managed by trustees; the following rules being agreed upon for the establishment and government of the school :—

1. That a school should be founded in the parish of Swindon, for instructing from time to time 20 of the children of the industrious poor living within the said parish, in the principles of the Christian religion, as by law established, in the Church of England, and in reading and writing the English tongue, and in common arithmetic, under the direction of the trustees for the time being, and that the said school should at all times be continued for the same purposes, and not for the teaching of any other language or science.

2. That there should be seven trustees chosen, and that the lord of the manor of Swindon, and the vicar of the parish for the time being, should be always trustees without the form of election, and that Thomas Goddard, Esq., and the other persons therein named should be the present trustees

3. That the trustees or the major part of them should have power to manage the revenues for the support and maintenance of the school, to elect the master and remove him at pleasure ; to appoint his salary, and to nominate and present such children as were to be taught gratis, and to make such rules and regulations for the good government of the school, as they should from time to time think necessary or proper.

4. That upon the death of any one of the trustees the survivors should, within six months, upon one month's previous notice in writing, meet at the school-house or some other convenient place, and appoint some other fit person in the room of the deceased trustee, so that the number of trustees might always be kept up.

5. That there should be annually chosen by the trustees out of their own body, a treasurer, to receive the rents and endowments and to pay the master his salary, and all charges and expenses incident to

the school, and which treasurer should yearly account to the rest of the trustees, and pay over the balance to the succeeding treasurer.

6. That the master of the school should be a layman of the church of England, of good character, and of sober and discreet conversation.

7. That the Bishop of Sarum, for the time being, should be visitor of the school.

In addition to this, Thomas Goddard, by deed bearing date January 1st, 1746, granted unto the trustees of the Free School a clear yearly rent charge of £5 on certain lands belonging to him, and William Nash, by deed bearing date February 20th of the same year, granted another annuity or rent charge of £5 a year to the same school. This latter charge, however, was afterwards commuted for £200 in three per cent. consols. Money was also left by Mrs. Mary Horne and Mrs. Elizabeth Cooper for the education of girls, the aggregate yearly income from property left for educational purposes being returned by the Commissioners at £57 11s. 1d. In 1765 the trustees, with £90, part of the fund raised by voluntary contributions, purchased for the residue of a term of 999 years, from Lady-Day, 1764, a dwelling-house, situate in Newport Street, with out-houses and garden, to be used as a school-house, and Mr. Thomas Barrett, grandfather of the present Mr. Thomas Barrett, builder, Newport Street, was appointed the first master, at a salary of £34, with an allowance of £3 3s. a year for coals, and for which he was required to instruct 38 boys in reading, writing, and arithmetic. Mr. Barrett was succeeded as master by Mr. Gosling, who in turn was succeeded by Mr. Turvey, to whom I have already referred.

I have said that Mr. Turvey was a characteristic schoolmaster of the period of my childhood. His son, who is still living, and approaching his eightieth year, tells me that he had no training whatever as a schoolmaster. He was a native of Swindon, born in

U

the year 1755, and died May 27th, 1850, at the great
age of 95 years, having given up the school in 1838.
When a young man he went into service with Mr.
John Harding Sheppard, who carried on the business
of a wool-stapler. Getting tired of his occupation, he
went to London to seek his fortune, and after a time
opened a school, which, however, did not prove successful, and he then joined the Commissariat Department in the Army in Egypt. In this position he had
considerable experience of the world. He was in
Egypt twice, and on both occasions the plague raged
with fearful virulence. On one occasion it carried off
every servant under him, his own life, he used to say,
being saved through a bottle of rum which he managed to husband, and from the contents of which he
took a small daily allowance. He also visited Spain,
and was at the first storming of St. Sebastian; was
with Sir Ralph Abercrombie when he received his
mortal wound, and was also at the battle of Waterloo,
and ultimately returned to Swindon in 1816. Through
either neglect or oversight, he failed to make application for a pension until it was too late to be entertained,
and he was in consequence once more thrown on his
own resources. His necessities no doubt brought to
mind his former experiences as a schoolmaster, and
there being a vacancy in the mastership of the Swindon
School, he was appointed to it, through the influence
of Mr. Goddard and Mr. J. Harding Sheppard. I am
told by those who remember him far better than I do
myself that he was a remarkably genteel looking
person, of fine presence, and with a remarkably fine
head of white hair. The present Mr. A. L. Goddard
and his brother John were Mr. Turvey's pupils up to
the time when they were sufficiently advanced to be
sent away to school, although the range of his teaching capacity could not have been very great, for Mr.
Thomas Barrett, who was also one of his pupils, tells

me he had learnt all Mr. Turvey could teach him by the time he was eleven years of age.   Some little time before Mr. Turvey's death, his son tells me, he went to the Lawn, and was very much gratified on his old pupil, Mr. John Goddard, consenting to accept from him as a present his sword.   The old school premises of 1765 remained until 1835, when they were pulled down and more suitable ones built on their site, Mr. Harding and Mr. Jenkins being successively masters.   In 1871 the old schools in Newport Street were entirely superseded by the new schools in King William Street, with Mr. Stote as master.

Mr. Smith, my schoolmaster, was also a man of the world, but his experience had been gained in the Excise, in which he had held the position of supervisor, but which office he lost.   Thrown on the world with very little or no means whatever, he sought to eke out what was but a poor existence by getting a few children together and teaching them to read, write, and sum.   His school was in a small and very poor thatched cottage at the top of Newport Street, where Mr. Clack's shoemaker's shop is now.   I recollect Mr. Smith as a thin, respectable-looking old man, whose back was bent by age, and I recollect the school-room through the holes in the mud floor, on which it was always difficult to make the one desk and two stools, which constituted the school furniture, stand steady. I do not think Mr. Smith ever regarded himself as an author, but he had nevertheless published a very remarkable card, and of which a second edition was printed.   It consisted of a mass of facts and figures concerning the Old and New Testaments, the number of chapters, the number of verses, the number of words and of letters ; the number of times certain words— such as God, Christ, the, and, by, but, and many others—were used ; how many times each letter in the alphabet appeared, and other information of a similar character, all of which Mr. Smith claimed to have ascertained for himself by actual counting.

There was one other school in our town, and one only. According to a sign over the door, it was a "Classical and Commercial School for Young Gentlemen, by Mr. George Nourse." In due course I was sent to this school for the purpose of being "finished off." I think I could not have remained at this school for more than twelve or eighteen months, and what I learnt during this period was but very little. I was, no doubt, somewhat improved in reading and writing, and as regards arithmetic, I had managed to get through the "Rule of Three," when I was finally taken away from school and my school days ended. At this time I could not have been more than nine or ten years, but, young as I was, I had already laid myself out for work, and had taught myself to bind books in a plain and simple way, in which I was greatly assisted by Mr. Axford, one of the medical men of the town, who used to let me have the whole range of his books to read or to bind, as I thought fit, and it was through his kindness that before I had passed my fifteenth year I had managed to bind several hundred volumes of books, many of which I had read, and all of which I had "looked" through. But to return to my schoolmasters proper, and to Mr. Nourse in particular. He was a nice, kind, old gentleman, scrupulously exact as to appearances, but altogether lacking firmness and ability to teach. Like Mr. Smith and Mr. Turvey, the necessity of doing something for a living had made him a schoolmaster, and he had adopted the art of teaching simply because it was more genteel, and was about the only thing he was supposed to have any qualification for, which consisted of his own ability to read, write, and do sums. He invariably dressed in black clothes, and wore a large white linen collar, which was kept in position by means of a somewhat large and elaborate white neckerchief. When taking his walks abroad, he would bend his head and neck forward, would either throw his arms loosely down by his side, or would carry them in front of him, his hands being clasped and so drawn up into the sleeves of his coat as to give him the appearance of nursing them, and, taking very long and deliberate steps, would jerk himself along, apparently oblivious of all that was going on around, and looking as though he was engaged in some deep study or meditation. The poor old gentleman soon found himself simply nowhere amid that more active life and quickened thought which came into the town with the railway ; his pupils began to leave him, until he had none left, and he ultimately died, it is to be feared, in great privation, if not in actual want of common necessaries. His father, who pre-deceased him some thirty-five or forty years, lived, for a short time, in the house adjoining the school. He had held some office in either the Army or the Navy, and eked out his old age with the assistance of a small pension, which, unfortunately, his son, after many years of incessant toil, did not, like him, possess.

—Markets and Fairs—

✦MARKETS✦

 N a paper read before the members of the Wilts Archæological Society at Swindon, September 16th, 1873, there occurs the following passage :—"The first mention of Swindon after Domesday is an order from King John to the Sheriff of Wilts, in A.D. 1205, in these words :—'Know ye that we have quit claimed to Hugh de Cature £7 18s., claimed from him for stock on the manor of Swindon, and therefore we command that you hold him discharged. Witness our order at Benton, 8th July.' In the reign of Henry III., the manor of Swindon was given to William de Valence, Earl of Pembroke. The Hundred Rolls, under Blackgrove Hundred, contain some interesting entries, showing the state of Swindon at this period :—*Hundred of Blackgrove.*—The Jury say that William de Valence holds one knight's fee of the King, in chief, in Swindon. And it is of the Honour of Pontlarge. The Abbot of Malmesbyrie holds half a knight's fee in Nether Swindon of the King in chief, and Robert Stine holds the other

half of the Abbot.   But how it was alienated, and
how it is held they know not.   William de Valence has right of gallows, assize, and bread and
beer in High Swindon, by grant from the Crown :
and has set up a new market in the said vill, but
by what warrant they know not.   They say that
William de Valence has warren in High Swindon.
Borough of Marlborough.—The Jury say that William
de Valence set up a market in the vill of Swindon
which is of much injury to the King, and to the
Burgesses of Marlborough, to the amount of 40s. a
year.   This he hath done for fifteen years past of his
own authority, and they know not by what warrant."
Mr. Waylen, in his " History of Marlborough," refers
to the same circumstance, and gives what appears to
have been a record by a jury empanelled to survey
and report on the state in which they found certain
manors and hundreds, towards the close of the reign
of Henry III. (1272), as follows, their testimony being
evidently given in the form of answers to questions
set forth for their guidance :—" The King holds the
Castle (Marlborough) with the borough in his hands,
as an antient demesne of the Crown ; and the Queen-
mother at present holds them by way of dowry.   The
Queen has the return of writs of the said borough, the
jurisdiction of trying felons, and the assize of bread
and beer.   William de Valence has for the last fifteen
years set up a market at Swindon, to the damage of
the King's Borough of Marlborough, but by what
warrant they know not.   The Bishop of Salisbury
has done the like [probably at Ramsbury, as that was
his seat.]   Also Philip Basset the like at Uphaven,
now in the hands of the Countess of Warwick.
William Heved has made an encroachment on the
King's highway in the town, 8 feet wide and 60 feet
long, and has held it fifteen years without payment.
William Gramery the like, 10 feet long, 2 wide.

Arnold le Fader has given a burgage and a half burgage in the town to the Priory of Bradenstock, by which 20s. a year are lost to the King and borough. Several other instances follow of alienations to religious houses in this town, in Reading, Stanley, and Bradley. Roger of the Oak, Constable of the Castle, is charged with corrupt dealing in the matter of an imprisoned homicide, whereby Geoffry Hernost [a burgess] loses 40s. Roger of the Oak has received £16 to pay the King's expenses in the Borough, but retains £11 0s. 6d.; yet credits himself with the treasury for the whole. The burgesses having been amerced before the Justices in Eyre in 25s., Richard of Kingston, sub-constable of the Castle, levied the amount, but gave no acquittance, whereby it is again demanded. The said Richard received of Nicholas Barbefleet, a burgess, 20s. as his tribute for green wax, but gave no acquittance. The sum is again demanded. The jury have heard that the King used to allow forty marks per annum in time of peace for the custody of the Castle, but do not know how much is absolutely necessary for that service. The following parties have refused payment of toll in the market: the men of the honour of Wallingford, the Bishop and Canons of Sarum and their tenants, the ecclesiastics of Winchester, the prior of St. Swithin's, the Bishop of B., the Abbot of Glastonbury, the Abbot of Bek and his tenants [this was in favour of the priory of Okebourn St. George], the prior of Sempringham and his tenants [this benefitted Saint Margaret's in the town], and the Earl of Leicester and his tenants."

From this it would appear that the King's rights as Lord of Marlborough were being very much interfered with, not only by the establishment of a market at Swindon, but in a variety of other ways and places. We are not told the effect of this enquiry

directly, although there is pretty good secondary
evidence that a very great change was shortly afterwards effected in the condition of some of the neighbouring Hundreds and Manors, for in the following
reign, that of Edward I. (1272-1307), there was a
complaint lodged against the Sheriff of Wilts that he
had upon his own authority held one Court for three
Hundreds conjointly — Kingsbridge, Thornhill, and
Blackgrove. As Swindon was included in one of the
Hundreds (Blackgrove) which could be thus treated in
so inconsequential a manner by such a high authority,
it is to be presumed that it had fallen into comparative
insignificance, and that its market, which had been
reported upon as an infringement on the King's
rights, had been discontinued. Be this, however, as it
may, we may take it for granted that a market was
held in Swindon as far back as six hundred and fifty
years, or more.

The next reference to the Swindon Market is to
be found in the Charter granted in 1627 by Charles I.
to Thomas Goddard, and by which the right to hold
both Markets and Fairs was duly authorised and
established. What immediate use was made of the
rights and privileges granted by this Charter does not
appear. The presumption is, a large market was not
at once established, for John Aubrey, writing of
Swindon in 1672, says :—" Here is on Munday every
weeke a gallant markett for cattle, which encreased to
its now greatnesse upon the plague at Highworth,
about 20 years since." What became of this gallant
market in course of the next hundred and fifty years
it is impossible for me to say, although there are some
grounds for supposing that, to a considerable extent
at least, it went back to Highworth after the plague
had gone away. At this time Highworth, which was
both a Hundred and a Borough, was by far the most
important town, and had enjoyed the privilege,

among others, of sending its own members to parliament, a privilege which it appears to have lost
simply through disuse or neglect to take the trouble
of making the returns required by the forms of the
House.

We have not to go far back to reach the origin of
the present corn market. I can well recollect the
printing of some prospectuses in favour of establishing a "pitched" market for corn. The late Mr.
Goddard, I recollect, offered to forego all claims to
toll for a certain number of years if farmers and
dealers would bring their sample sacks of wheat and
other grain and "pitch" them in the Square, with the
view of establishing a Corn Market for Swindon. In
consequence of this a couple of rows of moveable
posts and railings were designed and duly erected
every Monday morning in the Square, and against
these posts and rails farmers and dealers continued to
pitch their corn for some years, until, in fact, the
present Corn Exchange was erected, and opened in
the year 1866. Previous to the pitched market there
had been held what was known as a gin-and-water
market. Farmers used to come into the town on a
Monday, bringing with them in their coat pockets
small sample bags of such corn as they had to sell,
and, putting up at some inn or public-house, would
wait there over a glass and pipe until some dealer
should make his appearance after driving in from
Cirencester or some other market, which was of
course accepted by the landlord or his servant as a
signal for an order for another glass, which being
supplied, the pair would proceed to lay their heads
together with the view of making a deal. Sometimes,
of course this was effected right off, but at other times
it was otherwise. When a dealer did not happen to
turn up within the reasonable time allowed for a pipe
and a glass, a second and even a third pipe and glass

were had in, or an adjournment was effected to
another house, where it was hoped purchasers, would
be more plentiful.   And then again, on some occasions three or more publics would have to be visited
before a sale or satisfactory conclusion could be
arrived at, each adjournment, of course, meaning another pipe and glass, with always just one more
to bind the bargain when a sale had finally been
made.   There were both farmers and dealers who
had their regular house for business, and would use
no other.   On entering the town they would proceed at once to the smoke or public room, and
there wait patiently over their glass and their pipe
of tobacco until something or another should turn
up.   Against this system, which had many draw-
backs, there continued to be a great deal of railing,
and it was in consequence at last resolved to have
a "pitched" market.   But as this was necessarily
held in the open square, with no other covering overhead than the heavens, the alteration proved to be no
great improvement, and it not unfrequently happened,
especially in the winter season, that it was simply impossible for the farmers to open their sacks and
expose their samples, in consequence of rain or snow
falling, or some other impediment.   And then there
arose another complaint, and another demand for
a change, which resulted in the formation of the
Market Company, and the erection of the present
Corn Exchange.

     But the erection of the Exchange was not the first
attempt made to give character and importance to
the Swindon Corn Market.   The next important step
after providing the posts and rails for stacking the
sacks in the square, was the formation of the Swindon
Market Company, which had for its object the pulling
down of the old stables and warehouse in the Square
and erecting on the site the Market House, now

known as the Town Hall, and which was built by
Mr. Major, from designs by Mr. Sampson Sage, architect. This company was formed in the year 1852,
and the buildings were sufficiently advanced for the
directors to hold their first meeting therein for the
transaction of their business on August 23rd, 1853,
their meeting place up to that date having been
the Goddard Arms. The new building, however, was
never strictly used as a Market House. At a very
early date the cellars under the building were let
to Messrs. Brown and Nephew for wine stores, a
small room on the ground floor being retained for the
purposes of a sack office, which was let to Mr. Newton, who also had charge of the posts and rails. The
large room or hall having been duly opened by the
customary public dinner, was at once appropriated for
public meetings and other purposes, the first tenant
being the treasurer of the County Courts of Wiltshire, to whom it was agreed to let it on lease,
commencing October 1st, 1853, previous to which
date the County Courts had been held in the
Assembly Room at the Goddard Arms. The small
room reserved as a sack office proved to be more than
was absolutely required, for at a meeting of the directors, held March 20th, 1872, Mr. Offer, Mr. Newton's
successor, applied to convert the office into "a place
to put his cart in," which application was indignantly
refused. Mr. Offer, however, appears to have dis-
regarded this refusal, for at a subsequent meeting of
the directors, February 11th, 1873, the following resolution was ordered to be entered on the minutes :—
"Mr. D. A. Offer, tenant of the sack office, having,
contrary to the expressed wishes of the directors,
used the said office as a cart-house, it was, &c., that
Mr. Offer be given notice to quit and deliver up the
said premises." Very shortly after this the whole of
the ground-floor of the building went into the posses-

sion of Messrs. Brown and Nephew, now Brown and
Plummer, who are still the tenants.   In addition to
County Court purposes, the hall was used by the
Swindon Bench of Magistrates from 27th October,
1853, to 2nd October, 1873, when they removed to
the county buildings erected specially for their accommodation in connection with a police station and
lock-up.

    This reference to the old market company is inter-
esting as showing how completely it failed in its object
through not aiming high enough.   It provided only for
storing away a few bundles of sacks, or some posts
and rails when not in use, whereas what was really
required was a proper place for the exhibition of corn
under the most favourable circumstances, and where
the comfort and convenience of farmers and dealers
would be respected and cared for.   When this fact
had been fully realised, another Market Company was
formed, and the present Corn Exchange erected, the
builder being Mr. John Phillips, and the architects
Messrs. Wilson and Wilcox, of Bath.   This new
building was opened with great ceremony, and by, of
course, a public dinner, on April 9th, 1866.   In Dec.,
1873, the directors of the new company, registered as
the "Swindon Central Market Company (Limited),"
entered into negotiations with the directors of the old
Market Company for the purchase of their property,
and the same was ultimately agreed to, the last meeting of the directors of the old company being held
on October 20th, 1874.   Since April, 1866, the Swindon Corn Market has been held under the roof of the
new buildings, and has attained to sufficient importance to be selected by the Government as one of the .
very few in the country whose transactions are taken
for striking the average price of wheat for certain
public purposes.   I notice these Market Companies,
and the work they had to do, principally for the pur-

pose of recording a few dates which may hereafter
become useful for reference, and having done that I
return to the more congenial subject of things as they
once were, and of other days.

John Aubrey, the antiquary, it will be recollected,
referred to the gallant market for cattle being held
every week. This probably was through the "greatnesse" which had been thrust upon it by the plague at
Highworth, after which it no doubt fell down to the
monthly market as it existed at the beginning of the
century, and down to within the past twenty or thirty
years, when it existed as a "candle and lantern market." The market appears to have been always held
in the High-street, the practice being to form the cattle
in two rows down the street. Always, of course, providing the cattle themselves had no objection, their
fore feet were placed in the gutters on either side, with
their heads toward the footways and houses, and just
sufficiently close together to allow of their being
handled by the dealers Sometimes, on special occasions, the cattle thus placed would reach into Wood
Street and Cricklade Street, for the neighbourhood
always enjoyed great repute both for its young stock
as well as for its fat beef. I have never been able to
obtain any satisfactory explanation of the origin of
the custom, but the Cattle Markets, as I first recollect
them, were carried on by the aid of a candle and
lantern throughout the winter months. The market,
in fact, was practically carried on while the inhabitants were in bed and asleep. On the Sunday evening,
butchers and dealers would arrive, oftentimes in considerable numbers, at the various inns, many of them
coming long distances—twenty, thirty, and even forty
miles. As early as three or four o'clock on the Monday morning those having cattle to sell would drive
them in from their farms, or from some field in the
neighbourhood where they had been put for the Sun-

day, and place them, as I have described, in the streets
ready for inspection by the butchers and dealers, those
engaged in the work almost invariably carrying a
lantern and candle.   Whilst this was being done the
intending purchasers would be making their arrangements by taking such refreshments as suited their
appetites at their respective places of entertainment ;
after which, having got on their huge coats and mufflers,
and carrying their candle and lantern in one hand and
a stout ashen stick in the other, they would sally forth
to inspect the cattle and make their purchases, which
being done, the cattle would be at once sent off on
the road towards their destination in charge of trusty
drovers or cattle men, who always attended the market on the chance of getting a job, and who had
gained repute for trustworthiness.   As a rule, by the
time the morning broke and daylight began to appear,
the market would be practically over, and the
surveyor's men would be already engaged in scaveng-
ing the streets and preparing them for the ordinary
business of a small town, so that by the breakfast
hour there would be but very few signs remaining of
that active and often bellowing life so full of grim
characteristics which had so recently existed, and the
leading features of which were: a feast of lanterns as
described in an Eastern fable, and an English farm-
yard with its attendant muck and mire.   There is but
one reason I can give for this peculiar and, so far as I
am aware, unique, practice, and that is the great distance
dealers came to the market.   By starting back so
early in the morning they were enabled to get their
purchases home the same day, the journey then
always being made by road, and it would also give
them greater security against foot-pads.   As their
purchases would be for cash, they would necessarily
carry large sums of money with them, and this they
could do with greater confidence when no night

journey had to be taken. In course of time the
practice changed, and men seemed to be content to
get through the market any time before dinner
instead of before breakfast. The effect of this was so
ruinous that effort after effort had to be made to stop
the market from going altogether, which it probably
would have done had it not been for the enterprise
and energy of the late Mr. William Dore and the
establishment of his cattle sales, which have been
continued with such remarkable success by his successors, Messrs. Dore, Smith and Radway. Through
the establishment of these sales, private enterprise
has been able to do a great deal more than public
spirit ever attempted or thought of doing. At the
periodical cattle sales there is now a far larger trade
done than there was in the open market in the streets.
As a rule, purchasers, who come from all parts of the
country—Birmingham, Bath, Bristol and other large
centres, prefer the present system of doing business,
while sellers prefer it also through its relieving them
of all risk and responsibility in consideration of a
small fixed charge being paid. In illustration of the
amount of business done at these sales, I have it on
good authority that a total of 40,796 head of cattle,
sheep, calves, and pigs were actually sold under the
hammer between August 1st, 1877, and August 1st,
1882, the gross amount realised being £166,243 16s.,
or an annual average of 8,159 head, and £33,248 15s.
2d. value.

⁓Markets✴and✴Fairs⁓

✦FAIRS✦

⁓⁓⁓⬦◦⬦⁓⁓⁓

ONCERNING the Fairs : but little can be said about two of them. But that little may be made to go more directly to the point than much of that which may be said about the other two. For instance, the first fair in the year, held on the Monday before April 5th, was celebrated the country over as a fair for the purchase and sale of in-calf heifers, and dairymen and others would come in large numbers, and from long distances, to purchase young stock for their dairies. It was of the utmost importance to the dairyman that the cattle should be in the condition represented. This, however, from various causes, could not always be secured. Notwithstanding every desire to avoid deceit or misrepresentation " barreners" were frequently bought for " in-calvers" at the first fair on the Monday before April 5th, and a second fair was in consequence appointed for the second Monday after May 11th, specially for the sale of in-calf heifers, so as to enable dairymen who had missed obtaining their required stock at the first fair to get it at the second

W

one, a month afterwards. Here, then, we have the origin and object of what is known as Swindon May fair. The last fair in the year is held on the second Monday in December, and there can be no doubt as to the object for which it was established. It was specially intended for the sale of fat cattle or Christmas beef, and as such it always enjoyed great repute.

I now come to the two remaining fairs of the year, and for both of these I may, I think, claim quite a different origin. The Charter of 1627 did not create these fairs : it simply confirmed the authority for holding fairs already in existence, and which probably had been held for centuries, that on the Monday before April 5th since, probably, the reign of Henry III. (1216-1272), in celebration of the Feast of Saint Mary, and that on the second Monday after September 11th since, probably, the reign of Edward I. (1272-1307), in celebration of the Feast of the Holy Rood. It is generally admitted that many of the most celebrated fairs—or wakes, as they are called in some parts of the country—are not only of great antiquity, but that they are relics of even Pagan observances, which were continued by the early Christians. At Marlborough, two of the annual fairs are held on the anniversary of the Saints to whom the two churches are dedicated. Ramsbury fair is held on the Saint's-day to whom the church is dedicated ; the celebrated fair of St. Ann's Hill, or Tan Hill, is held on St. Ann's Day, and many other instances might be given in the immediate neighbourhood of Swindon. And then again, these wakes or fairs were generally held in the churchyard, so as to enable the people to attend to their devotions, their business, and their amusements in rapid succession and at the least possible trouble. The practice of using churchyards for the purposes of the fair was continued down to the reign of Henry VI., when it was forbidden ; but it

was not till the time of Charles I. that the holding
of fairs on Sundays was rendered illegal. That it had
been of common occurrence in the days of Queen
Elizabeth is evidenced by the command in her Book
of Common Prayer, "That upon all fairs and common markets falling upon a Sunday, there should
be no showing of any wares before the service of the
church was done." In the churchwardens' account
for the parish of St. Lawrence, Reading, for the year
1499, is this entry : "It. Rec. at the Fayer for a
standing in the church-porch, iiijd."

Strutt, in his "Sports and Pastimes of the people
of England," says :—"The wakes or fairs when first
instituted in this country were established upon
religious principles, and greatly resembled the agapæ,
or love feasts of the early Christians. It seems, however, clear that they derived their origin from some
more ancient rites practised in the times of paganism.
Hence Pope Gregory, in his letter to Melitus, a
British abbot, says, 'whereas the people were accustomed to sacrifice many oxen in honour of dæmons,
let them celebrate a religious and solemn festival, and
not slay the animals, diabolo, to the devil, but to be
eaten by themselves, ad laudem Dei, to the praise of
God.' These festivals were primitively held upon the
day of the dedication of the church in each district,
or the birth-day of the saint whose relics were therein
deposited, or to whose honour it was consecrated ;
for which purpose the people were directed to make
booths and tents with the boughs of trees adjoining
to the churches, circa easdem ecclesias, and in them to
celebrate the feast with thanksgiving and prayer.
In process of time the people assembled on the vigil,
or evening preceding, the saint's-day, and came, says
an old author, 'to churche with candellys burnyng,
and would wake, and come toward night to the
church in their devocion,' agreeable to the requisition

contained in one of the canons established by King Edgar, whereby those who came to the wake were ordered to pray devoutly, and not to betake themselves to drunkenness and debauchery. The necessity for this restriction plainly indicates that abuses of this religious institution began to make their appearance as early as the tenth century. The author above cited goes on, 'and afterwards the pepull fell to letcherie, and songs, and daunses, with harping and piping, and also to glotony and sinne ; and so tourned the holyness to cursydness ; wherefore holy faders ordeyned the pepull to leve that waking and to fast the evyn, but it is called vigilia, that is waking in English, and eveyn, for of eveyn they were wont to come to churche.' In proportion as these festivals deviated from the original design of their institution, they became more popular, the conviviality was extended, and not only the inhabitants of the parish to which the church belonged were present at them, but they were joined by others from the neighbouring towns and parishes, who flocked together upon these occasions, and the greater the reputation of the tutelar saint, the greater generally was the promiscuous assembly. The pedlars and hawkers attended to sell their wares, and so by degrees the religious wake was converted into a secular fair. The riots and debaucheries which eventually took place at these nocturnal meetings became so offensive to religious persons that they were suppressed, and regular fairs established, to be held on the saint's-day, or upon some other day near to it as might be most convenient ; and if the place did not admit of any traffic of consequence, the time was spent in festive mirth and vulgar amusements."

A leading feature of the two fairs held in March and September was the practice of hiring servants, which caused them to be known as hiring fairs, at which both male and female servants were hired by the year. The practice was for those in search of places to assemble in the streets of the town early in the morning, generally between the hours 9 to 12, and placing themselves where they were most likely to be seen, would stand there until they were accosted by those who wanted a servant. Men and boys desiring to be hired as carters would have a piece of whip-cord in their hats, cow-men and foggers a lock of cow hair in their hats, and the dairymaids would generally have a bunch of ribbons pinned on their breasts, by means of which they were to be distinguished from those who attended the fair for other purposes. As a sign that they had been hired, and were therefore no longer in search of a master, both men, boys, and girls, would pin long ribbon streamers to their hats or breasts. The practice originally was for these hirings, and their terms and conditions, to be by "word of mouth," the employer giving to the person engaged a shilling as "earnest" money, or to "bind the bargain." It was generally understood that servants had a prescriptive right to leave their service, even though their master and mistress should object, to attend one of these "Hiring Fairs" for the purpose of being hired to a new master, the hiring being invariably for the term of one year. Within more recent times, however, and principally in consequence of the frequent disputes which arose between master and servants as to the precise terms of the verbal agreement, printed hiring forms, to be filled in by the respective parties, have been generally adopted.

It has been sought by antiquaries to show that this practice of hiring servants is of very great antiquity, Plott going the length of quoting the passage in the twentieth chapter of St. Matthew ("And he went out about the third hour and saw others standing idle in the market place") in support of the antiquity of the practice. The practice here referred to, however, was not confined to servants in husbandry, for according to Eden's "State of the Poor," published in 1797, bricklayers and other house labourers were in the habit of carrying their respective implements to the places where they stood for hire, even in London ; Cheapside and Charing Cross being crowded with them every morning between five and six o'clock. In old Rome particular spots were assigned to servants applying for hire, and within the last few years I have myself seen large numbers of men and women assembled very early in the morning in the market place of some Irish town, each one carrying a scythe, rake, or a prong, both for use and for indicating the particular employment wanted, waiting to be engaged.

It was, however, always a very sad and sorry sight at our hiring fairs, and was regrettable for many reasons. On some occasions the foot-ways in the High Street would be literally impassable through the number of servants seeking situations blocking them up, a large proportion not unfrequently being young men and women, or rather boys and girls, who were making their first contact with the world which lay outside their own homes. The character of neither master or servant was very particularly enquired into; the law held any contract, which the master was prepared to swear he had made with the servant, binding for the term specified, and during which the servant became absolutely as much the property of another as though he had been of African blood and sold under the auctioneer's hammer. Under the practice servants with all kinds of characters were admitted as part and parcel of households where they could but be a source of constant trouble, while decent and respectable young people were tied down to and forced to spend their time in homes where

they could learn no good, and which were hot-beds
for the propogation of those vices which young girls
in particular first became acquainted with at the
hiring fair, for it was notorious that after the hiring
was over the remainder of the day would be devoted
to the enjoyment of the rude and rough amusements
of the fair, and especially to the attractions of the
bush houses, beer-shops, and public-houses, where the
beer "on tap" would usually be some concocted stuff
prepared specially for the occasion. From time to
time efforts have been made to supersede these hiring
fairs by some better plan, but only with indifferent
success. So long as the people were kept in ignorance they were the more readily attracted by that
which was often debasing and vicious. It is sincerely
to be hoped that as our Education Laws are working
out their beneficial results the hiring fair will gradually
become a thing of the past.

There is one other feature in connexion with the
Lady Day and Michaelmas Fairs which I must notice.
In addition to the Cattle Fairs in the High Street,
there was also the Horse Fair in what is now known
as Devizes Road, but which was formerly known as
the Horse Fair. Formerly the number of horses
brought into the town on the occasion of these two
fairs was very great. Like the cow cattle, they were
arranged along in rows on both sides the road, and I
have known them to reach from where Bath Buildings
now stand to where the railway passes under the
Wroughton Road. Gradually, however, the Horse
Fairs, like the Cattle Fairs, dwindled away, until they
were entirely superseded by the horse sales at the
Repository, established in 1871 by Messrs. Deacon
and Liddiard, and which, like the cattle sales of
Messrs. Dore, Smith and Radway, have become celebrated over the whole country. For several years past
these horse sales have been held fortnightly, with

occasional special sales for cart horses, and are always
very largely attended by noblemen, gentlemen, dealers,
and others from all parts of the kingdom, the sales
just before the commencement and at the close of
the hunting season being particularly well attended,
when generally some very valuable and well-known
horses are disposed of, from one to two hundred, and
even more, guineas being frequently realised. On
the great horse sale days the Repository is especially
attractive and interesting to the student of character,
and not unfrequently affords an amount of amusement
which I have often thoroughly enjoyed. The Repository has become a leading place for the sale of Irish
horses, and it frequently happens that when these are
accompanied by some excitable owner, and a party of
rale Irish stable boys, the fun enjoyed at the showing
of the horses is both exciting and amusing. Men
who know "something about a horse" are always
there, and would form material for many an interesting sketch. I can, however, only notice one of them,
and he only briefly. He was a blind man, who had to
be led about by a companion. Two or three years
ago he was a constant attendant, and was regarded as
one of the best judges of a horse, being guided entirely by his sense of touch and ear. By passing his
hands over the animal, and having it "trotted out on
the hard," he was enabled to discover the slightest
imperfection. As to the amount of business done at
the Repository it is simply enormous : for some years
past the average number of horses sent in for sale has
been 1,560 annually, the average sales effected being
1,300, the annual sum realised for the same ranging
from £40,000 to £50,000.

Having now stated the returns of money changing hands annually at the Cattle Yards and at the
Horse Repository, I may add that through the
courtesy of the officer of Excise, to whom the corn

returns are made, I am enabled to state that the value of the wheat, barley, and oats reported to have been sold in the Corn Exchange for the year ending December 31st last amounted to £40,181 0s. 6d., which, it is hardly necessary to add, is considerably under the average, and which, it is generally understood, through the imperfect way in which the returns are made, does not represent the actual trade done.

At the present time we can form but little or no conception of the importance of fairs in ancient times, or of the amount of business transacted at them. Weyhill and Tanhill Fairs probably give us the best idea of the general character of the fairs of ancient times. As is well known, these fairs not only extend over several days, but they are attended by persons travelling very long distances. As hops and other special articles are now bought at these fairs, no doubt general merchandise and even food was bought at the fairs in the olden times. An illustration of this is supplied by Brand, who tells us that the household accounts of the fifth Earl of Northumberland (1512) disclose that the annual supplies for his lordship's house at Wresille were obtained at fairs ; and similarly we gather from the accounts of the Priories of Maxtoke in Warwickshire, and of Bicester in Oxfordshire, in the time of Henry VI., that the monks used annually to lay in stores of various, yet common, necessaries at the fair held in Sturbridge in Cambridgeshire, which lay at least a hundred miles away from either monastery. It may seem surprising that Oxford and Coventry did not provide for the ordinary wants of the monks, not to speak of the extra expense of carriage of supplies from the fair ; but it was a rubric in some of the monastic rules regarding attendance at fairs. The fact that wine, wax, wheat, and malt were among the articles obtained by the Earl of Northumberland, moreover, is proof that fairs still continued to be the main marts for the purchase of necessaries in large quantities ; and the mention of " beiffes" and " muttons"—otherwise salted oxen and sheep—betrays evidence of the small progress then made in the science of cattle-breeding.

There is yet one other old custom appertaining to fairs which I must mention, and which comprised a whole system of " summary jurisdiction," the like to which nothing now exists : Courts of pie-powder (from *poudre des piez*, so called because justice was done to an injured man before the dust of the fair was off his feet) were granted to these fair gatherings for the repression of all offences and disorders thereat. How these Courts were constituted, or how their authority was exercised, I cannot here explain, but I recollect, when a child, a case in which justice was done in a very rough-and-ready and summary manner, and apparently without any other authority beyond that attributed to Judge Lynch. An unfortunate pick-pocket, who so bungled in his work as to be caught in the act, was instantly seized by the surrounding crowd and literally dragged by them down the Planks, across the paddock by the church well, in which was the fish-pond, and then across the little park, to the bank of the small pond which lies at the head or top of the first park pond, and which took the water directly after it had left the old mill. During the journey to the pond the poor wretch bellowed for mercy, but the more he prayed the more his persecutors seemed resolved to exact every possible bit of fun he could afford them. In due course a long waggon rope was procured, and this having been tied round his waist at about mid-way between the two ends, he was thrown bodily into the middle of the pond, which, by the way, seemed to be deeper in mud than it was in water. One end of the rope having been thrown to the opposite side of the pond it was seized by a number of men, and then with men at either end they dragged the culprit from one bank to the other, after the most approved manner of the most expert of tormentors. Again and again he would be allowed to grasp the bank and begin to climb up, when a good tug, and a tug altogether, would bring him back "whack" into the middle of the pond, amid the boisterous shouting of an excited crowd of spectators. What the consequences of the punishment were to the poor wretch I never learnt, but it was really a mercy that he escaped with his life, or was not torn in pieces, for on more than one occasion, while the upper part of his body appeared to have had all the life knocked out of it, and floated about on the water, his lower half was so firmly stuck in the mud that it required quite a succession of tugs to extricate it.

—The*Troublous*Times*of*1830—

I HAVE made more than one incidental reference to the troublous times of 1830. I am glad to think I can add little or nothing more concerning these times which is directly connected with the town of Swindon—that is, I am not aware of any actual rioting or serious disturbance taking place either in or around Swindon, or of any Swindon men being engaged in rioting elsewhere, although Sir Charles Wetherell, one of the most arbitrary tyrants of the age, and whose conduct in attempting to suppress the voice of the people in their cries of distress undoubtedly led to the dreadful riots and slaughter at Bristol, must have been well-known in name, if not in person, at Swindon, through his connection with Sevenhampton. The times were indeed troublous. There was one seething mass of trouble and discontent throughout the length and breadth of the land, until at length the flame of open rebellion burst forth in riots at Bristol, riots at Bath, riots at Worcester, riots at Coventry, riots at Warwick, and in

many other towns. Swindon, however, as I have
said, was spared from any of that open rebellion or
outburst of passion which brought so much trouble
upon this country. To understand aright the action
of the people at this time, it is necessary to know
something of the way in which they existed : and
where parish records have been preserved as scrupulously as they ought, we may obtain much valuable
information from them on this point. Accounts of
the parish officers, and more particularly those of the
Overseers of the Poor, are full of valuable information. I have been able, fortunately, to obtain a
few of these accounts for Swindon, which are not
only very significant in themselves, but they belong
to the time to which I have been referring, and which
I am desirous of illustrating. They disclose a system
of poverty, pauperism, and profligacy which is simply
appalling. As a rule, the poor people could neither
read nor write ; books were almost unknown amongst
them, and there were practically no newspapers
through which their troubles and condition could
be made known. To understand aright the facts
and figures I am about to quote, it is of the first
importance that we should remember that in the
year 1831 the population of Swindon was 1,742, and
the ratable value of the whole parish slightly under
£3,920.

From an account of the "Regular Pays to Swindon Poor," from Lady Day, 1824, to Lady Day, 1825,
by Messrs. C. Cripps, S. Bristow, and J. Gosling,
Overseers, I find there were during the year no less
than one hundred and forty-seven paupers in receipt
of relief; and, as many of these received relief for
their families as well as for themselves, the total number of paupers could not have been less than two
hundred, or one pauper out of (say) every nine of the
inhabitants. No less than ninety-two out of the

hundred and forty-seven were in receipt of relief for the whole of the 52 weeks, and were therefore regarded as permanent paupers, the remainder having received relief for a lesser period. The total amount of the weekly pays for the year was £1026 14s. 11d. In addition to this there were other expenses which the overseers had to meet during the year, amounting to £669 16s. 1d., making a total expenditure of £1696 11s., which was principally met by Poor Rates amounting to 7s. 6d. in the £ as follows :—

							£	s.	d.
1824—Received on account of rent, &c.			...	...		...	57	17	0
,,	from the putative fathers of Bastard Children maintained by the Overseers ...		...	...	...	...	89	7	6
April	,,	by a rate at 6d. in the £	..		...	...	134	9	5
May	,,	,,	,,	,,	...	...	134	12	6
July	,,	,,	,,	,,	...	...	134	16	10
Sept.	,,	,,	1s.	,,	..	...	192	2	6
Nov.	,,	,,	,,	,,	...	...	193	0	8
Dec.	,,	,,	,,	,,	...	...	192	17	3
1825									
Jan.	,,	,,	,,	,,	...	...	194	4	6
March	,,	,,	2s.	,,	...	...	387	6	0
		Amount of Receipts	...	...			£1710	14	2

In the year ending Lady Day, 1827, the Overseers received from the putative fathers of bastard children, whom the parish had to maintain, the sum of £132 5s. 6d. I give the particulars of these receipts, suppressing only the surnames of the parties:

Received of Thomas B . . . . . the sum of £22, as per agreement, to exonerate and discharge him from the future weekly payments, as specified in two orders of bastardy, first for a female child born the 13th March, 1815; second, for a male child born 28th March, 1820, and dated 10th August, 1820, for the respective maintenance of Mary T . . . . . 's said two children, being parishioners of Swindon. 22 0 0

The receipt on stamp was signed by Messrs. Wm. Farmer and Charles Cripps, Churchwardens; John H. Sheppard and Richard Strange, jun., Overseers.

Received of John D . . . . . the sum of £22, as per

	£	s.	d.

agreement, to exonerate and discharge him from the future weekly payments, as specified in an order of bastardy, dated the 26th day of April, 1821, for the maintenance of Harriet H . . . . 's boy, born the 19th January, 1821, in the parish of Swindon. 22 0 0

The receipt on stamp was signed by Messrs. Wm. Farmer and Charles Cripps, Churchwardens ; John H. Sheppard and Richard Strange, jun., Overseers.

Received of Henry F . . . . . ., Naunton, Gloucester, as deposit on account of Mary C . . . . 's child.   ...   5 0 0

Received of William H . . . . ., as per order of bastardy   2 5 0

Received of Moses K . . . . as deposit on account of Martha J . . . . . . 's pregnancy. 2 0 0

Received of Richard K . . . . . . order of bastardy for Sarah D . . . s' child. 2 2 6

Received of James A . . . ., amount of bastardy, at 1s 6d per week, Lady Day, 1827   3 18 0

Received of Thomas C . . . . amount of bastardy, at 2s per week, due Christmas, 1826   ...   .   5 4 0

Received of Uriah D . . . amount of bastardy, at 2s. 6d. per week, due 26th Nov., 1825.   ...   .   6 0 0

Received of James G . . . . amount of bastardy pay, at 2s. per week, due Lady Day, 1827. ...   .   5 4 0

Received of Robert H . . . . . amount of bastardy pay, at 2s. per week, due Lady Day, 1827. ...   .   5 4 0

Received of Thomas H . . . . do., 2s. do., 1827.... ...   5 4 0

Received of John K . . ., jun , do., 1s. 6d., do. 1827. ...   3 18 3

Received of Wm. L . . . . do., 2s., do., 1827 ...   ...   6 10 0

Received of James M . . . . . do., 2s., do., 1826.   ...   2 12 0

Received of John N . . do., 1s 6d., do., Michaelmas, 1826.   ...   .   1 19 0

Received of William N . . . ., do., 1s 6d., do , Christmas, 1826. ...   .   3 18 0

Received of Samuel S . . . . do., 2s. 6d., do., Lady Day, 1827.   ...   .   6 10 0

Received of Do., do., 2s., do., do., ...   5 4 0

Received of Caleb W . . . . do., 1s. 6d., do., do.,   3 18 0

Received of William N . . ., child, do., 1s. 6d., do., Christmas, 1826. ...   .   2 18 6

Received of Richard K . . . . . , 16 weeks' pay for child at 1s. 6d., per week, due Lady Day, 1827.   ...   ...   1 4 6

Received of John M . . the sum of £5, as per agreement, to exonerate and discharge him from the weekly payments as specified in an order of bastardy, dated 27th October, 1814, for the maintenance of Anne S . . . .'s boy, born the 7th August, 1814, in the parish of Swindon 5 0 0

The receipt on stamp was signed by Messrs. William

Farmer and Charles Cripps. Churchwardens ; Richard
Strange, jun., and John Gosling, Overseers.

In this year there were six shilling and a sixpenny
rate made for the relief of the poor.

In the year ending Lady Day, 1829, there appears
to have been a charge made upon the Overseers for
the maintenance of "Unemployed Labourers," for
under this head there is recorded an expenditure of
£73 13s. 5d., in amounts ranging from 7s. 6d. to
£4 5s. 4d., payments being made altogether to forty-
two persons. A similar charge appears to have arisen
in the Christmas quarter of 1835, when the amount of
£56 13s. 11d. was charged to the parish as having
been paid to "Surplus Labourers" (forty-five persons).
In this year the expenditure on account of bastards
increased to £50 18s., their number being *thirty-two.*

*Thirty-two illegitimate or bastard children kept by
the parish out of a population of say* 1,800 *inhabitants
fifty years ago!* If the people spoke out at all, is it
to be wondered at that the tone of their voice should
grate hardly on official ears? With neither money
nor work, nor bread to eat, is it surprising that the
people should think there was something very wrong
somewhere, or that they should give vent to their
feelings in acts of violence? The marvel is, not that
there were rioters and rioting, but rather that the
great mass of the poor did not rise as one man and
defy all law and all order in one terrible struggle to free
themselves from those trammels by which they were
bound down, and which seemed to deny them those
rights to existence which were enjoyed by dumb
animals and the beast of the fields. And yet there is
a reason I can assign for the fact that neither in or
around Swindon did the people rise in open rebellion,
and it is this : they were not tried so sorely as others
were even in other parts of Wiltshire. The Stone
Quarries, no doubt, always helped to find a certain

amount of employment. But at Bradford, Trow-
bridge, and some other places the Overseers had to
raise double, and even treble, the amount of that
raised in Swindon. At Wootton Bassett the Poor
Rate was 9s. 9d. in the £, or about 11s. per acre on
the land in the parish, the wages of the agricultural
labourer at the same time being 6s. per week. In
some other of the neighbouring parishes the poor rate
on several occasions reached 15s. in the £ for the
year. And yet every inducement was held out to
these unfortunate creatures to marry and surround
themselves with a family of children by an engagement on the part of the parish officers to supplement
out of the rates the wages of every labourer who had
a family of four children. In addition to the Poor
Rate there was invariably the Highway Rate, and
occasionally a Church Rate, lower in amount than the
Poor Rate, but yet considerable, whereas, now, in
rural parishes a rate of from two shillings to two
shillings and sixpence in the £ for the year will meet
all the requirements for the poor, the Highways,
Sanitary Purposes, the School Board, and the many
other charges which have been thrown on the Poor
Rate within the last twenty or thirty years. I quote
by way of illustration the parish of Wroughton, where
there are four quarterly rates for the year, out of
which all the parish charges have to be met. The
demands made by the respective authorities for the
year ending March, 1885, on the Overseers were as
follows :—

				£
For the purposes of the Poor, Police, County, and other charges	...	...	...	795
For purposes of the Highways	...	...	.	368
,, ,, ,, the School Board		...	...	240
By the Sanitary Authority	...	...	...	31

To meet which the Overseers made four rates,
amounting in the aggregate to 2s. 4d. in the £.

From these facts it will be at once seen that although at the present time there is an altogether new charge for Police, School Board, and Sanitary Purposes in particular, in addition to what were the ordinary charges of fifty years ago, the total amount now required in the shape of rates range from a fourth to one-half of what was required formerly, the lesser sum being now ample, solely in consequence of the improved condition of the industrial classes, and to their reduced requirements of assistance in the shape of Poor Law relief. In towns like Swindon, where there are heavy charges for gas lighting, water supply, and elaborate sanitary arrangements and appliances, the rates are no doubt higher, but even here they do not probably exceed in the yearly aggregate more than two-thirds the amount required fifty years ago for the maintenance of the poor and the subsidizing of the wages of the labouring classes, and for supporting them with those absolute necessities which their wages would not provide.

Having now given all the available local facts I am acquainted with bearing on the condition of the poor fifty years ago, I purpose supplementing these with extracts from the pages of history and the columns of the county newspapers, to show what it led up to. Molesworth, in his History of England, says:—" All interests in all parts of the kingdom seemed to suffer. Trade, manufactures, agriculture, all stagnated. Many parishes were reduced to such a state of pauperism that the whole property within their limits was insufficient for the maintenance of their poor; and assistance had to be sought from neighbouring parishes already over-burdened with the expense of supporting their own paupers. Landlords could not obtain their rents; farmers were impoverished ; the agricultural labourer, whose wages were often eked out from the poor rates, received just enough to enable him to procure for his family and himself the barest necessaries of life. The manufacturing operatives of Lancashire and Yorkshire were, in many instances, receiving only threepence and fourpence a day for more than twelve hours' labour. O'Connell stated in the House of Commons that in Ireland 7,000 persons were subsisting on three-half-pence a day ; and though this statement was perhaps exaggerated, there can be no doubt that great distress prevailed in that unhappy country, and that the peasantry were reduced to the smallest allowance of the lowest kind of food. . . . . Agricultural labourers were found starved to death, having tried in vain to support existence. Nay, we find that in the division of Stourbridge, in the county of Dorset, the magistrates published the following scale, according to which relief was to be given :—

	s. d.	s. d.	s. d.	s. d.	s. d.	s. d.
When the standard quartern wheaten loaf is sold at	1 0	0 11	0 10	0 9	0 8	0 7
The weekly allowance, including earnings, is to be made up to—						
For a labouring man ...	3 1	2 10	2 7	2 4	2 1	1 10
For a woman, boy, or girl, above 14 years old	2 4	2 2	2 0	1 10	1 8	1 6
For a boy or girl of 14, 13, or 12	1 11	1 9	1 7	1 5	1 3	1 1
,, ,, of 11, 10, or 9	1 7	1 6	1 4	1 3	1 2	1 0
,, ,, under 9 ,,	1 5	1 5	1 3	1 2	1 1	1 0

At the time to which we refer, the quartern loaf cost 10d. Let us suppose a family consisting of a man, his wife, one boy or girl of fourteen, one boy or girl of eleven, and one little child. For these five persons there are eight shillings and ninepence altogether ; that is to say, there are ten and a half quartern loaves, or forty-three pounds of bread to divide among the five, which gives a little more than eight pounds of bread for each to live on for a week, or rather more than a pound of bread per day for each to live and work on, and that without allowing anything at all for rent, fuel, drink, clothing, or washing. And to this condition the agricultural labourer was rapidly sinking

everywhere ; for if in some counties the allowance was
on a somewhat more liberal scale, in others it was
even lower than in Dorsetshire. It was clear that
such a state of things could not be allowed to continue.
Something must be done, and that speedily. Political
economists might demonstrate that it was unavoidable ;
but flesh and blood will rebel. It was not therefore
very surprising, though it puzzled legislators and justices of the peace a good deal, the agricultural labourers
who were thus provided for took the matter into their
own hands ; that they assembled in an altogether
unlawful manner, nay compelled others, though not
very much against their own will, to join them, and
go about tumultuously demanding increased wages ;
and when this demand was refused, that they began
to break thrashing and other agricultural machinery,
which they believed to be the chief cause of their distress. The farmers, thoroughly frightened, referred
their labourers to the clergyman or landlord to ask
for a reduction of tithe or rent, and thus to enable
them to pay better wages. However, acts of violence,
as might be expected, produced little or no benefit,
and things were rapidly going from bad to worse.
The peasantry, finding no more machines to break, or
forcibly prevented from breaking them, began secretly
to set fire to stacks of corn or hay ; and soon through
twenty-six counties, night after night, the sky was
reddened with the blaze of the nation's food going up
in flame and smoke skyward. The peasantry who
beheld these sad scenes often stood with folded arms
grimly smiling at the work of destruction ; nay, they
sometimes cut the hose of the fire-engines brought to
extinguish the conflagration ; never had so deep a
sadness weighed on the minds of all classes of the
population as towards the close of this year 1830.
Terrible imaginations magnified tenfold the terrible
reality. The political atmosphere seemed to be charged

with electricity. Members of the government, members
of the legislature, well-to-do country gentlemen, substantial and unsubstantial farmers, were all sorely
distressed, puzzled, bewildered, and affrighted. All
sorts of reports were in circulation ; all sorts of explanations were given of the supposed causes of these
fires. There were stories of foreigners, of elegantly-
dressed gentlemen riding on horses or in post-chaises,
who had come down to instigate the peasants to fire
the ricks, or who fired them with their own hands.
Cobbett also, who often employed very unmeasured
language in his efforts to draw attention to the sufferings of the labouring classes and the causes of their
distress, and who, notwithstanding a great deal of
violence, and a great deal of crotchety nonsense about
bank paper, saw clearly and told plainly what required
to be done, was accused most unjustly of being the
instigator of the outrages committed by the labourers.
Then again, there was a mysterious " Swing," with
whose name many threatening letters were signed,
who was generally supposed to be at the bottom of
all the mischief. Old Lord Eldon assured the House
of Lords that he was informed that the gaols contained
great numbers of persons who were not natives of this
country ; and Lord Sidney, in a long and intemperate
letter, repeated the statement. But there was no
shadow of foundation for these assertions. The agricultural labourers had been driven to the verge of
starvation and despair. They were going mad with
misery ; and in their madness they did mischief by
which they themselves were certain to be the first and
greatest sufferers."

─The✳Troublous✳Times✳of✳1830─

✦ƬHE ƬURПIПG OF ƬHE ШORM✦

WHILST the country was in the state described in my last paper—the very poor lingering in abject poverty, with many of those above them steeped in profligacy and immorality — the proverbial "last straw," which is said to break the back, was laid upon the poor unfortunate agricultural labourer by the invention of the thrashing machine. Towards the end of the year 1829 it became known that a Mr. Rider, a small farmer, residing on the Wallop estates at Westbury, in Wiltshire, had invented a portable thrashing machine, the cost of which was advertised as "between £8 and £10." This announcement caused a great deal of comment amongst the labourers of Dorset, Hants, and Wilts. They regarded the machine as certain to produce starvation and want amongst them and their families. It was in their opinion "an infernal machine, and nothing more nor less." The man who invented such an article, the farmer who purchased or used one, and the man who took charge of it, were a trio of "rascals" who deserved no consideration at the hands of "honest men." So the labourers reasoned. The inventor got frightened, and, acting on the advice of his friends, gave up the making of the machines; but other persons took up the trade, and improved agricultural implements were sold in all parts of the country. And then, as I have said, the poor, starved, and demented labourers rose, and in their mad frenzy smashed machinery, destroyed property, and fired ricks in every direction. As winter set in the distress which had existed through the summer became intensified. The riots which for months past had been going on in Kent had now spread into Buckinghamshire, Hampshire, and Wilt-shire. Hay and corn stacks and farm buildings were almost nightly destroyed, and life and property in agricultural districts became unsafe. Some idea may be formed of the terrible state of the country when it is stated that upwards of 800 offenders were in the gaols awaiting trial for crimes of this sort. In Buck-inghamshire alone sentence of death was recorded against no less than 23 persons for destroying ma-chinery. The extreme penalty of the law, however, was only carried out on four of these men; the rest were transported.

The disturbances seemed to have reached a crisis in the southern counties about the middle of November, 1830. In Berkshire, early in November, the fires were very numerous and the riots general. During the week ending November 20, ten ringleaders amongst the disturbers of the peace were apprehended and lodged in prison. During the fortnight preceding this date, there were many riotous assemblies in Hampshire, and the greatest alarm prevailed in many parts of the county. Andover and the neighbourhood for many days was in a state of terrible excitement. The labourers in most of the parishes for miles round formed themselves into parties, and moved from place

to place, destroying in their progress all the machinery
they could find that trenched upon manual labour;
and nightly they fired ricks and homesteads. Immense
rewards were offered everywhere for the discovery
of the incendiaries, but generally with no effect.
Machinery had in the disturbed districts to be wholly
discontinued, and farmers found it prudent to arrange
fire beacons, so that in case of attack they might
speedily communicate with the adjacent villages.
Threatening letters signed "Swing" were continually
dropped about, causing great terror.   At this time
Hampshire, from Basingstoke and Andover to Ringwood and Christchurch, was in a state of fearful excitement.   On the 18th and 19th November, in the districts
of Emsworth and Havant, a mob of labourers went
from farm to farm destroying machinery.   This was
done openly and in defiance of all attempts to protect
the property.   As the mob passed from village to
village, they pressed other labourers to join them.
In some cases this was done most unwillingly, but too
often the poor fellows were led to believe the destruction of machinery was the only way open to them of
obtaining increased wages.   The magistrates in the
neighbourhood of Havant collected together a number
of persons who were willing to act as special constables,
and with them they dispersed the mob and took some
of the ringleaders into custody.   Many of the men,
however, went off threatening to return in greater
numbers the next day.   In consequence of this Captain
Leeke and Sir John Lee proceeded to swear in additional constables, and immediately made application
to the Commander-in-Chief at Portsmouth for military
assistance.   The magistrates having collected together
a large force proceeded to a beerhouse, in a village
near Havant, the head-quarters of the rioters where a
" skirmish " took place. The rioters, finding themselves
overpowered, locked themselves in, but the doors were

speedily broken open, and ten or eleven of the leaders apprehended, whilst others escaped. Five prisoners were sent to Gosport Bridewell, four to Chichester, whilst several who had been taken into custody got safely away. The same night this took place, the whole of the barns and ricks belonging to Sir H. Wilson, at Barton Stacy, near Andover, were burned to the ground, and the dwelling-house was with difficulty saved from destruction. The same week there were fires at Hamble, Droxford, and places in the neighbourhood of Portsmouth. At Andover, on Saturday, the 20th November, the town was in a state of great excitement. The mob consisted of about 300 labourers, who destroyed a thrashing machine, and one of the ringleaders was apprehended. Shortly afterwards the mob broke open the place where the prisoner was confined and carried him in triumph through the streets, demanding liquor and money of the respectable inhabitants. All the shops and public-houses were speedily closed, and the peaceable householders did all they could to protect themselves and their property. A man named Cooper was in the town, and the labourers wanted him to address them, but this he then refused to do. He said the Mayor and Corporation had caused the riot, and he would not assist in quelling it. This man was the ringleader and chief cause of many of the disturbances which took place at this time, and was executed at Winchester for the prominent part he took in fomenting the disturbances. Some of the labourers of their own accord went before the magistrates, then sitting in petty session, and stated their grievances. They urged that their wages were miserably low, not sufficient for them to maintain themselves and their families, and worse than that, work was scarce, owing, as they believed, to the introduction of machinery. Sir Lucius Curtis addressed the labourers in a feeling

manner, expressing the deep sympathy which he and
the other magistrates felt for them, but strongly
advised all of them to abstain from the destruction of
property, pointing out that by the burning of corn
ricks, and destroying machinery, they were injuring
themselves as well as others. Some of the men took
the advice thus given, and raised the cry of "God
Save the King." Others, however, only went to their
homes for a time, again to join the mob when they
had an opportunity. About 300 men afterwards went
to Abbot's Ann and destroyed the property of Mr.
Tasker, which, in the words of the local chronicler,
they left a "melancholy wreck." A couple of troops
of Lancers were sent for, and when they arrived the
mob quickly dispersed. At Southampton, precautionary measures were taken in case of riots being
attempted in that town, and 300 special constables
were sworn in, whilst most of the inhabitants resolved
to "watch and ward their own property." At Romsey
there was a considerable amount of machinery destroyed. The mob pulled down West Dean and
Tytherly turnpike gates, and set fire to many houses
after having turned the inmates out of doors. As
they demanded money, this was freely given them,
with the hope of purchasing immunity from outrage.
As much as £20 to £30 a night was thus, for several
nights, collected. The Romsey rioters declared their
intention "to do for the parsons, and the excisemen,
and destroy all the turnpike gates." Some 250 special
constables were quickly sworn in, who succeeded in
dispersing a mob which was assembled at the house
of Captain Heathcote, at St. Germans. A number of
the rioters then went on to a neighbouring farm, where
they forcibly took possession of a quantity of wine
and spirits. Whilst so engaged, they were surprised
by a large body of "specials," who took twelve of
the men, whom they bound with cords and sent to

Winchester. A meeting was held of landowners and farmers at which it was decided to increase the wages of the labourers to 12s. per week. At Basingstoke, on the 26th November, there was rioting, and 30 men were apprehended and sent to Winchester Gaol under an escort of the 9th Lancers. At Winchester, on the 26th November, upwards of 400 of the inhabitants enrolled themselves as special constables. These men, with the Mayor of the City, daily assembled in the open space in front of the gaol, ready for duty if required. There were also about 300 of the 3rd Dragoon Guards quartered in the city, ready to proceed to any place in the neighbourhood requiring their assistance, whilst the 47th and 99th regiments of infantry were in the barracks, and from these corps a strong guard was supplied both day and night for the county gaol and bridewell. On the 23rd November a large body of labourers assembled at North Stoneham, about five miles from Southampton. The mob went to the farm of Mr. John Tribe, for the purpose of destroying his machinery and compelling his men to join them. Farmer Tribe, however, was a very resolute man, and having heard of their intended visit, had collected a number of his friends, and gave the rioters a "warmer reception" than they anticipated. By his energy Mr. Tribe was not only able to hold his own, but succeeded in capturing no less than 19 of the assailants. A military guard was sent for, and the men were at once marched off to Winchester Gaol. During the following night there was a fire at Baker's saw mills, Southampton. The incendiaries were no doubt under the impression that the machinery employed at these mills curtailed to some extent manual labour. Every effort was made to prevent the fire from spreading, but in less than two hours the entire place was destroyed, together with its contents.

In Wiltshire matters were no better than in Hants. On November 25th the Hindon Troop of Yeomanry marched westward on the road from Dinton to Salisbury. Intelligence reached them that a large mob had assembled at Pyt House, the residence of Mr. Benett, one of the members for the County of Wilts. The Yeomanry, however, arrived too late at the Home Farm to save Mr. Benett's thrashing machine from destruction. When the Yeomanry reached Home Farm the mob had just quitted the place for Lindley Farm, where they succeeded in breaking another machine, also the property of Mr. Benett. The troop first caught sight of the rioters as they were quitting the place, and ascending the hill on the road to Tisbury. The Yeomanry then divided itself into two companies, near a plantation of fir trees, one going to the right, the other to the left. The road being narrow for the space of more than 100 yards, the mob, stationed among the trees, pelted them with stones as they were passing. At the end of the plantation, where the two companies met again, the mob commenced a furious attack upon them, being armed with bludgeons, crowbars, pickaxes, hatchets, sledge hammers, stones, and other weapons. The greatest amount of patience and forbearance was for some time shown by the Cavalry, but eventually a general charge was made, some pistol shots were fired, and sabre wounds inflicted. The result was that a man named Harding was killed, another severely wounded, and others wounded to a less extent. Twenty-five rioters were captured and taken in carts, under an escort of Cavalry, to Fisherton Gaol, where they were lodged before midnight. Several members of the Hindon troop were also wounded, but not severely. Previous to the rioters attacking Mr. Benett's farm, that gentleman and Mr. Legge, his bailiff, remonstrated with them, for which they were rewarded with a shower of stones. Whilst this was proceeding in the neighbourhood of the city of Salisbury, other parts of the county of Wilts were in a terrible state of commotion. At Marlborough, Pewsey, Rockley, Wootton Rivers, Aldbourne, Ramsbury, Shalborne, Burbage, Froxfield, and other places, "the mob" assembled in vast numbers, and in many places did considerable damage, but were in every case dispersed by the Yeomanry, aided by the farmers and tradesmen, who stood by each other throughout this trying time. At Salisbury intelligence was received on the 23rd November that a party of rioters who were destroying machinery at Bishopdown Farm were coming toward the city armed with bludgeons, iron bars, and pieces of machinery, for the purpose, it was stated, of destroying the iron foundry of Mr. Figgs. On hearing of this Mr. Figgs placed a considerable quantity of gunpowder behind the foundry gates, which would have been fired had the rioters made any serious attempt to enter his premises, and other measures were taken to meet the disturbers of the peace. Mr. Wyndham, of the College, who placed himself at the head of a few constables, supported by the Salisbury Troop of Yeomanry, met the mob at the entrance to the town, and after having earnestly but vainly remonstrated with them on their illegal proceedings, directed the Riot Act to be read. The few constables present being unable to arrest their progress, the mob was charged under a shower of stones, and driven to the higher ground adjoining. The Yeomanry then mounted the hill, and the rioters were speedily driven off. In the course of the afternoon and evening 22 of the men were taken into custody, and 17 of these were committed for trial. The Yeomanry, after clearing the principal streets, dismounted in the market place. The remainder, with their horses bridled and saddled, held themselves in readiness to mount at a moment's notice. The whole of the Salisbury troop were under arms during the night, and a strong guard mounted at the Council House, where the magistrates were assembled. Special constables, in considerable force, were under the command of Mr. Brodie, and assisted in preserving order. The Hindon troop arrived in Salisbury under the command of Captain Wyndham, of Dinton, and on the following day, under the command of the Earl of Radnor and Lieutenant Baker, proceeded to Alderbury and Whaddon, and enabled the constables to apprehend twelve rioters, who were bound and conveyed in a waggon to the county gaol. The Salisbury troop, under the command of Captain Lord Arundell, accompanied by Lieut. Baker, on Wednesday, the 24th, rode off to West Park, above five miles from Salisbury, the residence of Mr. Eyre Coote. This place had been previously visited by a large body of rioters. A detachment of the troop remained at the Park during the night, under the command of Lieutenant Peniston. The mob had threatened to make a renewed attack on the house, but they had too much prudence, in the presence of the Yeomanry, to put their threats into execution. The horses and men of the Salisbury troop then returned to the city ; the horses not having been unsaddled nor the men unbooted from eleven on Tuesday morning until nine o'clock on Thursday evening. On the 23rd November about 400 rioters, under the leadership of James Thomas Cooper, *alias* Hunt, went to Fordingbridge, and then to the manufactory of Mr. Thompson, at East Mill, and destroyed machinery to the value of £3,000, in consequence of which 100 persons were thrown out of employment. The mob also went to Mr. Sheppard's Machine Works, at Tuckton, where they also did great damage. It seems that the leading rioters some time previously intimated their

intention of visiting Fordingbridge. Consequently
their visit was a premeditated and determined one.
Mr. Thompson and others remonstrated with the
men on their conduct, but it was of no avail. Cooper,
who was on horseback, and appeared to be the leader,
took upon himself the management of the tumultuous
assembly. He was told that the destruction of the
property would throw a large number of men out
of employment, but this had no effect on him. He
declared that he had no care for consequences, and
that if £500 were offered him not to destroy the
machinery he would carry out his purpose. Cooper
seems to have had unlimited influence over the
labourers, and when any of them remonstrated with
him as to any of his acts, he plainly told them
that they had placed himself under his command and
he would not be interfered with. The mob were
armed with bludgeons, axes, saws, and sledge hammers. After completing the destruction of Mr.
Thompson's mill, and at Mr. Sheppard's works, they
went to the houses of many of the inhabitants and
demanded money. In the evening a detachment
of the 3rd Dragoon Guards marched into the town,
but the place was then quiet and tranquil. A
number of horsemen from Ringwood also made their
way to Fordingbridge, but were too late to render
any assistance. The rioters on leaving Fordingbridge
again made their way to West Park Mr. Eyre
Coote, with his accustomed liberality, and no doubt
out of pity for many of the poor fellows, gave them
refreshments, but on their demanding "the house
or money," a desperate fight ensued, which resulted
in the apprehension of a number of them. Twenty-
five of the rioters were committed for trial at
Winchester for the Fordingbridge disturbance.

The newspapers of the period are full of similar
accounts to those which I have given, and which

have been collated and published in an interesting work by the editor of the *Poole and Bournemouth Herald*, under the title of "Then and now, or fifty years ago," and to his labours I am indebted for many of the particulars concerning the rioting I have quoted, as well as for the reports of the trials of the rioters, with which I intend to close this most sad chapter in our local history. It is unnecessary to add that these reports are matters of record rather than of opinion, and as the subject is almost too painful for comment, I make no apology for keeping to the record as I have found it left by other writers. And I may therefore only add that after the rioting had run its course in Dorsetshire and Somersetshire, there came the terrible reckoning, and the Special Commissions for the trial of the many hundreds of prisoners who had been committed to the various county gaols.

⌐The⁕Troublous⁕Times⁕of⁕1830⌐
⊹RETRIBUTION⊹

SORELY as the agricultural labourers of
Wilts and the neighbouring counties had
been tried, and terrible as their sufferings
had been before they rose in open rebellion, there could have been no doubt from
the very first as to what the end of it would be.   The
county gaols were soon full to repletion, and then
there commenced a long and terrible series of trials
which are unique in history.   When it was decided to
appoint a Special Commission for trying the rioters in
the Hampshire, Wiltshire, and Berkshire gaols, it was
not intended to include the County of Dorset in that
commission.   Dorchester Gaol, however, at the time
was very full of prisoners who had been committed on
various charges arising out of the disturbances, and
the county magistrates therefore decided on making a
strong representation to the Government as to the
necessity of the Commission being so extended as to
embrace this county.   The majority of the prisoners
at Dorchester had been committed on charges of a
lighter character than those for trial in the neighbour-

ing counties, and this, probably, was the reason the
county was not included in the notice of the Special
Commission for Hants, Wilts, and Berks, which
appeared in the *London Gazette* of December 5th,
1830. The application made by the magistrates to
the Government to include Dorsetshire in the Commission was strongly supported by the Lord-Lieutenant and the county members, and consequently was at
once acceded to. The Special Commission was opened
at Winchester on Saturday, the 18th December, by
Mr. Baron Vaughan, who presided. Mr. Justice James
Parke sat on his right, and Mr. Justice Alderson on
his left. The Attorney-General, Mr. Serjeant Wilde,
and Mr. Follett, were the prosecuting counsel for the
Government ; Mr. Missing and Mr. Dampier appeared
on the part of the county. The prisoners were undefended. The Duke of Wellington, who was Lord-
Lieutenant of Hampshire, was also present, together
with a large number of the county magistrates. Mr.
Baron Vaughan, in his charge to the Grand Jury, explained the law as it bore upon the offences with which
the prisoners were charged. His Lordship concluded
his address in the following words: "I have thought it
right to give you very full extracts from the statute
books of the present state of the laws as applicable to
the various offences in your calendar, in order that
the less enlightened part of the community may know
that, if firmly and fearlessly executed, they have made
ample provison for their prevention and punishment.
I would willingly hope that the melancholy catalogue
has not been swollen by any want of the most prompt,
resolute, and uncompromising exertions of the
magistracy and gentlemen of property and influence
in every department of the county, to put down, and
with a strong hand, the first indications of riot and
tumult. Be assured there can be no compromise or
capitulation with crime. The first concession to num-

bers tumultuously assembled in breach of the law, serves only to excite a keener sense for plunder, and to increase a spirit of resistance to the constituted authorities of the land. It may produce a momentary suspension (cessation I cannot call it) of hostilities, with the almost certain and speedy return, with augmented numbers and increasing fury, to further acts of outrage and aggression at a more convenient season. I cannot conclude this address without expressing my belief that the country may safely rely at this momentous crisis on the vigilance and attention with which you will discharge the duty of examining with care and anxiety the different charges which will be brought before you. As the grand inquest of the county, you are, by our constitution of government, placed as it were in the centre between accusation and conviction, to hold the balance even, for the suppression of private malice on the one hand, and the promotion of public justice on the other ; and I am persuaded you will not allow your indignation at the outrages which have been committed to excite any prejudice in your minds, when weighing the evidence against each individual accused, and deciding upon his participation in the crime imputed to him."

Sir George H. Rose was foreman of the Grand Jury, who, about twelve o'clock, returned into Court with a true bill against James Thomas Cooper, and eleven others, "for riotously and tumultuously assembling on the 23rd November, at Fordingbridge, and destroying certain machinery at that place, the property of Messrs. Thompson and others." The names of the prisoners were: James Thomas Cooper, aged 33; George Clarke, 20; Joseph Goulding, 23; George Moody, 23; Joseph Fulford, 50; William Webb, 21; Samuel Quinton, 26; William Arney, 27; Henry Eldridge, 23; John Kimber, 35; Charles Read, 34; and Charles Hayter, 53. All the prisoners pleaded not guilty. The prisoner Cooper was stated, in a report of the trials published at the time, to have been a middle-aged man, of peculiarly heavy, sullen, and ferocious aspect. In some of the reports he was said to have been of gipsy descent, but others affirmed that he was the son of a tenant farmer. His dark complexion, however, favoured the idea of his gipsy parentage. One thing is very certain, viz., that he was not an agricultural labourer, and his dress and appearance generally seemed to point to his having been a mechanic of some kind. George Clarke, the next important prisoner, was a fine active young man, of about twenty years of age. His countenance showed great determination without any admixture of ferocity. When placed in the dock he was dressed as a carter, and although his attire was such as was then common amongst agricultural labourers, he shewed a degree of smartness that attracted attention. William Webb was dressed in a smart blue coat with gilt buttons, and was described as having the appearance of a gentleman's servant. The other prisoners were more or less meanly clothed as agricultural labourers. The prisoners all fully realised the perilous position in which they stood, although Cooper and one or two others were regardless of the consequences. John Fulford, whose age was given in the calendar as 50 years, appeared considerably older. Of all the twelve prisoners he appeared to take the keenest interest in the proceedings, and each time his name was mentioned he leaned forward over the rail of the dock, apparently with the desire of catching every word of the evidence, as well as the remarks of the counsel· The Attorney-General stated the case for the prosecution. He first pointed out the law under which the proceedings were taken, and then stated the nature of the offence with which the prisoners were charged, which, summarized, was to this effect: that the

prisoners had riotously assembled in great numbers
under the guidance of certain leaders, for the purpose
of accomplishing a common object, which, when accomplished, could not be beneficial to any one
amongst them ; and that they then proceeded with
force to destroy a quantity of machinery belonging to
a gentleman of the name of Thompson, residing at
Fordingbridge. That being the offence, he would
now state to the jury that it appeared from the
evidence which he should have to lay before them
that all these prisoners assembled together on the
23rd of November last, and came from a little
distance from the town of Fordingbridge into it ; that
they were under the guidance and direction of the
first prisoner named in the indictment, James Thomas
Cooper ; that they expressed their intention of coming into Fordingbridge sometime before they
executed it ; and that they executed it at last in the
manner which the jury would hear from the different
witnesses. The circumstances which he had already
detailed to them would prove that the plan of the
prisoners was deliberately formed. He would also
show the jury that Mr. Thompson had met with the
prisoners on the road to Fordingbridge, and had
remonstrated with them on the subject of their conduct, which they avowed themselves determined to
pursue. The first person on the indictment, James
Thomas Cooper, a person of whom he could
not give them any clear account, did not belong
to that neighbourhood, nor, indeed, to Hampshire.
Indeed, he would fairly own to them that he could
not give them any history of that prisoner. He
would, however, prove to them that that man, Cooper,
was at the head of this tumultuous assembly—that he
was on horseback ; that he took upon himself the
management of its proceedings, and that when re-
monstrances were made to him respecting his conduct,

he admitted himself to have power to control it.
Cooper was told, when the first attempt was made
to destroy the machinery belonging to Mr. Thompson, that the injury which he would inflict upon
property would be great—nay, more: that it would
throw no less than 100 persons out of employment.
He stated that he cared not for consequences ; and that
if £500 were offered him not to destroy that machinery, still destroy it he would.   The jury would
also find the prisoner Cooper, after the act of destruction was completed, sharing considerable sums of
money with the persons assembled around him ; and
though some of those persons might be affected with
less moral guilt than others, in the eye of the law
they were all, by being present, equally guilty.   He
would prove to the jury that the prisoners were
armed with bludgeons, axes, saws, and other instruments calculated to produce terror.   He would prove
that they told Cooper that he was not to be interfered
with, that they had placed themselves in his hands,
that they were convinced that he was a real gentleman, and that they had unlimited confidence in his
guidance.   The jury would likewise find that these
unfortunate men had committed acts of violence and
outrage—that when they were remiss, Cooper had
excited them to greater exertions—and that he had
employed the power which he wielded over them
to lead them to all kinds of devastation and mischief.
The Attorney-General then called witnesses in support of the prosecution   After a full, and it seems a
fair, trial, a verdict of guilty was returned against J.
T. Cooper, G. Clarke, J. Fulford, S. Quinton, H.
Eldridge, Charles Read, Charles Hayter, and J.
Arney, and not guilty in favour of W. Webb, J.
Goulding, W. Arney, J. Kimber, G. Moody, and W.
Newman.   It was half-past nine o'clock before the
jury returned in court with their verdict, and the

judges postponed sentencing the prisoners until a future day. On the following day both courts were opened, Mr. Justice James Parke presiding in the Nisi Prius. Six men were then tried for an attack on Mr. Eyre Coote's house, and also for demanding money. The prisoners were undefended. The trial lasted all day, and the evidence being of the most conclusive character, all the prisoners were found guilty and sent to transportation for life. In the other court, before Mr. Baron Vaughan, Cooper and several other prisoners were tried for destroying Mr. Sheppard's manufactory at Fordingbridge. A verdict of guilty was returned, but sentence in each case was deferred. In all, several hundred prisoners were tried at Winchester, and the Court continued its sitting from the 18th to 30th December, sitting daily, except on Sunday the 19th, Christmas Day the 25th, and Sunday the 26th December. On the last day the three judges went on the Bench in their scarlet robes. The Duke of Wellington, the Right Hon. Sturges Bourne, and Mr. Pullen, were also present as Commissioners. Twenty prisoners, in four rows of five each, were placed in the dock to receive sentence of death. By direction of the presiding judge all the prisoners, with the exception of Cooper, Eldridge, and Gilmore, were removed. The judges then put on their black caps and sentenced the three men to death, assuring them there could be for them no hope of mercy. Three other prisoners were then placed in the dock—Robert Holdaway, James Annalls, and Henry Cooke, and they were in like manner sentenced to death without hope of mercy. Then 51 other prisoners were placed in the dock and had the death sentence recorded against them, with an intimation from the judge that, although the extreme penalty of the law would not be carried out, yet they must expect to have to leave the country. The sentences on all these 51 men were afterwards commuted to transportation for longer or shorter terms. A number of prisoners were sentenced to seven years' transportation, and others to imprisonment for shorter terms. Some were liberated on their own recognizances, and in a few cases the proceedings against the prisoners were quashed. Altogether 347 persons were disposed of as follows :—Death recorded against, 95 ; transported for life, 5 ; for seven years, 31 ; imprisonment and hard labour, 62 ; fined, 3 ; discharged on their own recognizances, 48 ; to appear at the next assizes, 6 ; acquitted, 67 ; no bills, 5 ; evidence for the Crown, 2 ; discharged for want of prosecution, 17 ; total, 347. The sentencing of so many persons to death and to terms of long imprisonment caused the greatest consternation in all parts of the country. The day named for the execution of the six men "left for death" was the 15th January, and from the solemn way in which they had been sentenced "without hope of mercy," it was universally believed that the dread sentence of the law would most assuredly be carried out on all six of the wretched men. A few humane individuals prepared a petition, to which they obtained a large number of signatures, praying that the death sentence might be commuted to transportation. This petition, which was addressed to the King, was handed by a large deputation to Lord Melbourne eight or nine days before that fixed on for the end of the tragic scene. Lord Melbourne promised to give the prayer of the memorialists his full consideration, and that the memorial should at once be laid before the King. Whilst this was being done other humane persons were interesting themselves as to the fate of the large number of others who had been sentenced to long terms of transportation. For several weeks after the special commission had closed the scenes witnessed daily in and around the gaol were heartbreaking, wives and children, brothers and sisters, and, in some instances, aged fathers and mothers, beset the gaol gates daily, begging to be permitted to see, for the last time, the members of their family who had been sentenced to go " beyond the seas," and terrible as was the meeting of the friends and convicts, the parting was still more distressing. The number of labourers who were convicted was so great that there was scarcely any part of the country where the deepest anguish was not felt in many humble cottage homes on account of the terrible punishment which had overtaken the law-breakers. We should mention that the special commission cost the country no less than £8,000 ; but, large as this sum was, it formed the smallest portion of the bitter ingredients in the cup of suffering which the mistaken acts of the rioters had produced.

Whilst Mr. Baron Vaughan and the other judges were sitting at Winchester, Sir John Allen Parke, Sir William Bolland, and Sir John Patteson, with the lay commissioners, the Earl of Abingdon and Mr. Charles Dundas, were at Reading trying the Berkshire rioters. The calendar for that county contained the names of 130 prisoners, the majority of whom were charged with destroying thrashing machines. The terrible work of incendiarism was still going on throughout the whole of the southern counties, but only one case was tried at these Assizes, owing to the difficulty of finding sufficient evidence to commit suspected persons. Of the 130 prisoners for trial only 25 could read and write ; 37 could read a little, and the remaining 76 could neither read nor write. Only 18 of the prisoners were over 40 years of age; the ages of the rest ranged from 17 to 35 years.

⸺The⁕Troublous⁕Times⁕of⁕1830⸺
✢THE TRIALS OF THE WILTSHIRE PRISONERS.✢

ERRIBLE as the scenes at Reading and Winchester had been, they appear to have been still more terrible at Salisbury when the prisoners were put on their trial. The narrative, from which we have already quoted, continues : Monday, the 27th Dec., 1830, was the day appointed for the opening of the Special Commission at Salisbury for the trial of the Wiltshire rioters, but so heavy was the Hampshire calendar that on the day when the judges of Assize should have left Winchester for Salisbury, fully one-third of the charges on the calendar were still untried. The judges held a consultation on the matter, and it was decided that Mr. Serjeant Wilde, as one of the Commissioners named in the Commission, should proceed to Salisbury and open the same. This was accordingly done. The usual formalities were observed in the opening of the Court, which was then adjourned for a few days. On the day when the Commission was opened there were no less than 300 prisoners for trial in the county gaol, but large as was this number, it was augmented by many new arrests, which took place between the time of the formal opening and the arrival of the judges. About two o'clock on Friday afternoon, December 31st, the judges arrived in Salisbury, having completed their work at Winchester. At some distance from the city they were met by the High-Sheriff and upwards of 100 of the gentry and Yeomanry on horses, and many of the nobility of the county also went out in their carriages to meet the judges. At the entrance to the city, the Mayor and the Corporation in eight carriages waited the arrival of the procession. Thousands of persons lined the street, and the excitement was intense. For the preservation of the peace, 400 special constables had been sworn in, and the Yeomanry held themselves in readiness to be called out if required. According to custom, the judges at once proceeded to the Cathedral, where they were received by the Deans, Canons, and other dignitaries. On the following morning Mr. Baron Vaughan, Mr. Justice Parke, and Mr. Justice Alderson, the judges ; the Marquis of Lansdowne, as Lord-Lieutenant of the county ; the Earl of Radnor, and Mr. T. G. B. Estcourt took their seats in the Nisi Prius Court, and the grand jury were sworn.   Mr. Justice Parke then proceeded to deliver the charge, which in substance was the same as that previously delivered by Mr. Baron Vaughan at Winchester, and which he had consented to allow to be published in the form of a pamphlet. After an absence of some time, the grand jury returned into court with a true bill against the seven-teen men who had been indicted for breaking and destroying a thrashing machine, the property of John Benett, Esq., on the 25th November. The Attorney-General, who prosecuted, then stated the case, and called Mr. Benett, whose evidence was to the effect that on the day in question, in consequence of information he received, he rode about three miles from his home, between nine and ten o'clock in the morning. He saw about 400 persons in the road, at a lime-kiln, near Hindon. The men had bludgeons, hatchets, hammers, large sticks, and weapons of various descriptions. One man, who had absconded, wore a sash of party colours, and carried a large stick. Another man named Jerrard, one of those then at the bar, also wore a sash. He spoke in a firm tone of voice to this man, and told him he was sorry to see him heading the mob. He told him that he was placing himself in great danger, and he entreated him to pull off the sash and get into the rear, for an example would be sure to be made of some of them, and the sash would hang him. The prisoner said he did not care. He asked the mob generally what they complained of. They replied they were going to break all the thrashing machines in the county, and they would have two shillings a day wages. He told the mob that there was a reward of £50 for every person who was detected breaking a thrashing machine, and £500 for the detection of any one burning ricks or homesteads. He persuaded the men to go to their homes, and he would take care, if they remained quiet, they should get as much as others hoped to obtain by their bad conduct. The mob, however, would not listen to his advice. They then went on to another place, and he followed them until they stopped at Mr. Candy's farm, where they broke a machine. The mob then went to Lawn Farm, and broke a machine belonging to Mr. Lampard. He then returned to his own residence at Pyt House, where shortly after he found 500 men assembled ; the same mob with augmented numbers. He had a thrashing machine at Pyt House Farm, worked by six horses. The mob broke open the door where the machine was kept, and commenced breaking

it. He told the men that he had not power then
to stop them, but if they proceeded to extremes
he should afterwards be able to punish them. He
spoke in such a way as they could all hear, but it was
of no effect. He was seated at the time on his horse,
and whilst the destruction of the machine was being
proceeded with, he received a blow on his head which
for a minute deprived him of his senses. When consciousness was restored, he found that his horse had
been taken away, unknown to him, into a lane. Stones
were thrown at him from every direction. He was
with the mob about three hours, and during this
time he saw many machines broken. A man named
Blandford had a sledge hammer in his hand and was
very actively employed. Other witnesses were called,
who proved the breaking of machines and rioting, and
a fresh batch of prisoners were placed in the dock,
against whom similar indictments were preferred.
Nearly all the prisoners were found guilty, two only
on the first day being acquitted. On Monday morning,
January 3rd, the court again assembled, when a young
man named Ford, only 17 years of age, was placed at
the bar on a charge of destroying carding and other
machines at Quidhampton Woollen Manufactory on
the 24th November. A witness proved having seen
the prisoner break the windows of the manufactory
and several times strike a tucker machine. A witness
also saw the prisoner bring out of the manufactory
several pieces of machinery, and throw the same
into the mill stream. The prisoner was found
guilty and sentence of death was recorded against
him, but on account of his youth the sentence was
commuted to transportation. Nine men were charged
with destroying a mill, engines, and machinery at
Wilton, the property of Mr. John Brasher, on the
25th November. The extent of the damage was
estimated at £500. All the prisoners, with one

exception, were found guilty.   All through the week
ending January 8th, the judges were fully occupied in
both courts trying prisoners at Salisbury.   In very
few instances only were counsel engaged for the
defence, consequently the charges were quickly disposed of, but as 330 prisoners in all had to be tried,
the closest attention of every person connected with
the business of the court was necessary to speedily
get through the calendar.   Saturday, which was the
closing day of the Assizes, was one of great excitement.   The courts were densely crowded, and the
greatest interest was manifested in the proceedings.
Throughout the week many of the prisoners had been
sentenced by the judges as the trials proceeded, but
in other cases, the graver ones, where deliberation was
necessary, the passing of sentence had been deferred,
and on this day the men who had been found guilty
of the more serious charges were to be brought up to
have judgment recorded against them.   Mr. Baron
Vaughan, Mr. Justice Parke, Mr. Justice Alderson,
Lord Radnor, and Mr. T. G. B. Estcourt took their
seats on the Bench at nine o'clock.   The first business
was the sentencing of 26 prisoners to various terms of
imprisonment and transportation, and then twenty-
six others were placed in the dock, that judgment
of death might be recorded against them.

The three judges then putting on their black
caps, Mr. Baron Vaughan said : Prisoners at the bar,
—In obedience to the authority of that Commission,
which has so long engaged the attention of the Court,
and of the country, the time is now arrived, for I
hope the last time of our meeting, when we are called
upon, in the painful discharge of our duty, to award,
those punishments due to those crimes of which you
have been severally convicted.   I now address myself
to you, Peter Withers, and you, James Lush.   You,
Peter Withers, have been convicted on the clearest

testimony of having maliciously wounded Oliver
Calley Codrington, with intent to do him some bodily
harm, and to resist your lawful apprehension. You,
James Lush, have been convicted of robbing Bartlett
Pinniger. The learned judge then entered into a full
explanation of the nature of the offences committed
by the prisoners. His lordship then said : The judges
have been put under the most painful difficulty in
selecting the most fit prisoners for punishment. They
would have been justified in punishing with death
many others, but in the hope that one example may
have the effect of deterring many others from the
commission of these dreadful offences, and that the
public may know that the crimes are not to be
committed with impunity, they have selected you—
this has been done, because from the evidence it
appears you were in front of the mob, the foremost to
use wicked imprecations, and that when you came to
Pinniger's house you made a demand for money,
which you extorted under circumstances of great
aggravation. Under these circumstances it is my
unfortunate duty to be called upon to pass the
sentence of the law, and to tell you, Peter Withers,
and you, James Lush, to prepare for the awful change
which now shortly awaits you. His lordship then
in the usual form pronounced the sentence of death
on each of the two prisoners. Immediately upon the
sentence being concluded, Withers, who had been for
some time holding up his hands in a supplicating
attitude, sunk back absorbed in grief. For some time
his face had been continually changing colour, but at
last it assumed a death-like paleness, and from
narrowly watching him it was evident his sufferings
must have been dreadful. The other prisoner, James
Lush, from the first moment of his appearing at
the bar, was very much affected, and from the time
when the judges put on their caps until the con-

clusion of the sentence, he leaned entirely over the bar, in a state of anguish not to be described— his sobs were dreadful—and his exclamations of " Mercy !" " Oh God, have mercy on me," accompanied by his piercing groans, thrilled through the hearts of all.   He was removed from the bar in a stooping position, as if pain and agony prevented his standing upright.   The *Dorset County Chronicle*, in reporting the proceedings, says :—" A more awful and affecting scene was perhaps never witnessed than that which the court presented as the learned judge proceeded with the sentence.   His lordship's utterance was repeatedly checked by the conflict which was raging in his own bosom, a conflict arising from the appalling effect produced on the unfortunate men (about forty in number), who were standing at the bar, and the knowledge that his duty to the country, in the just administration of those laws which had been entrusted to the court, on this unhappy occasion, rendered it imperative on his lordship to carry that duty into execution.   There were, it may readily be supposed, no dry eyes in the crowded court.   The tears of pity, of compassion, and regret, at the necessity of such severity were to be seen flowing and chasing each other down the cheeks not merely of the spectators, but of those who had long been accustomed to hear the last dreadful sentence which a human being has the power of passing on a fellow-creature in this world.   Mr. Justice Parke and Mr. Justice Alderson were frequently obliged to rest their faces on their extended hands, and even then the large drops were to be seen falling in quick succession.   Lord Radnor and Mr. Estcourt also gave evidence, from the rapid and frequent changes of their features, of the depth of their feeling.   The effect on the prisoner Withers was most extraordinary.   He had taken his station at the bar with an apparent firmness of resolu-

tion, but as the address of the court proceeded, he
gradually became pale, and the perspiration in globular
particles was visible on his face and forehead, till at
length the subdued groan testified that he was about
to faint.   Noticing this, Lord Radnor handed a note
to one of the javelin men to procure some water for
the unhappy convict, which, having drank as though
labouring under the overpowering effects of a long-
continued thirst, he appeared for a moment to be
renovated.   It was, however, but a fitful fancy, an
imaginary revival, for he soon became more deeply
affected, and with uplifted and clasped hands sank
down on the bench which was immediately behind
him, apparently insensible to all earthly proceedings.
Mr. Justice Parke, who had his eyes rivetted on the
unhappy prisoner, interrupted his learned brother and
drew his attention to the wretched condition to which
the principal object of his address was reduced.   Lord
Radnor quickly sent for medical restoratives, which
were speedily procured, and administered with a successful result.   During the time which was thus
occupied, we looked round the court, but more particularly at the other prisoners, every one of whom was
in a state of dreadful agitation—some sobbing aloud
and others with a pallid cheek—and showing every
indication of severe internal suffering. This scene was
more affecting because it was not the hardened—the
often-tried—and the desperate and the reckless robber
who stood before the court, meeting his merited and
just reward—but it was a portion of the agricultural
labourers of the country, the majority of whom had
hitherto passed their days in the path of sobriety,
honesty, uprightness, and industry—who were there
to receive the punishment of the offended laws of their
country.   The learned judge at length continued, and
the prisoner Lush, who had for some time given token,
by his outward appearance, of the struggle within,

z

here leaned over the bar in the front of the dock and
cried and groaned aloud. In this position he repeatedly interrupted the learned baron by his exclamations, " It was never me! I am innocent! I am not
the man! 'Lord have mercy upon me! Pray have
mercy upon me! My lord, it was never me! My
lord, never in the world was it me! It was other
people ; they have done it! It was not me." Judgment of death was then recorded against the other
twenty-four prisoners standing in the dock.

The *Chronicle* reporter says :—" On leaving the
court we mixed among the crowd who were waiting
to see the prisoners retire. The scene was heartbreaking beyond everything. A mass of women was
standing bathed in tears, supported by men, who
looked as having hearts which nothing could daunt,
but which had given way to feelings of their better
nature, and in endeavouring to support the weaker
sex, they themselves could not conceal their grief, and
were actually shedding their tears of pity and affection. At length the cell door was opened, and the
unfortunate criminals appeared, chained together.
We thought that in the court, and before the door
was opened, we had seen distress in almost every
form. We had witnessed it in those who had given
way to it, and had let the bursting tear escape. We
had also watched those who, having more command
of themselves, had prevented the outward show of
grief, but in whose countenances what they felt in-
wardly could easily be discovered, yet we had a sight
to witness even more distressing than all this. As
the men came out their wives, their mothers, their
sisters, and their children clasped them in their arms
with an agonizing grasp—the convicts, whose hearts
had been hardened by having before been incarcer-
ated in a gaol, gave way, they wept like children,
they no longer attempted to stifle their feelings or

brave their doom, nature had begun to play with every force, and the heart was broken. It required every effort on the part of the attendants to get them into the car, and at last the door closed ; then we could hear the exclamations of regret and farewell, and many a female hand was forced through the bars to take a last grasp of him who was now about to leave those who were dear to him, and to whom he was dear, for ever. The car drove off, and nothing was now heard but the deepest lamentations on the one side, and the kindest words of sobbing men endeavouring to console their more afflicted friends. We left the scene with the hope that it would have the effect desired, accompanied with a prayer that we might be spared from again being witnesses of such dreadful distress.

Having finished their dreadful business at Salisbury, Mr. Baron Vaughan and Mr. Justice Alderson proceeded on Monday, January 10th, to Dorchester, to try the prisoners there in custody. Mr. Justice Parke, who had been present at Winchester and Salisbury, did not go to Dorchester. As we have previously stated, the charges of rioting, machine breaking, &c., in this county were of a less serious character, as well as less in number, than those in the counties of Hants and Wilts. About one o'clock, the High Sheriff, John Bond, Esq., set out, accompanied by the Under Sheriff and a numerous body of javelin men, to meet their lordships at some distance from the town. There were also present about two hundred special constables from the neighbourhoods of Dorchester, Blandford, Cerne, &c. The whole company rode horses, and besides the escort provided by the High Sheriff, there was a large body of yeomen, headed by James Frampton, Esq., who preceded the High Sheriff's carriage as it entered Dorchester. On the judges arriving in the town they proceeded

direct to the *Nisi Prius* Court, where the Commission
was opened in due form, and the Court adjourned
until noon on the following day.

On the assembling of the Court on Tuesday, the
11th, Mr. Baron Vaughan took the central chair, and
Mr. Justice Alderson sat on his lordship's right. The
Earl Digby, the Earl of Shaftesbury, and Mr. C. B.
Wollaston, the three lay Commissioners, also occupied
seats on the Bench. The Grand Jury having been
sworn, Mr. Justice Alderson gave the charge, which
in substance was similar to those delivered at Winchester and Salisbury. John Thomas Cooper, who
had been tried at Winchester and sentenced to be
executed for being the ringleader of the rioters who
destroyed Mr. Thompson's Mill, and Mr. Sheppard's
Iron Works, at Fordingbridge, had also been the chief
instigator of the riots in Dorset, and it was therefore
intended he should be indicted at these assizes ; consequently, soon after the Grand Jury had left the
Court, Mr. Rowe, addressing their lordships, said :—
" My Lords,—I am instructed, that in consequence of
a person named John Thomas Cooper, against whom
an indictment has been preferred in this county,
having been capitally convicted and sentenced in
another county, the prosecutor does not intend to
offer any evidence. I have, therefore, to move your
lordships that the recognizances may be remitted."
To this Mr. Baron Vaughan consented. Shortly after
the Grand Jury returned into court with a true bill
against James Wilkins, aged 22, for feloniously
robbing Henry Moyle of certain monies, in the parish
of Cranborne, on the 23rd November. It seems that
the prisoner, at the time when Mr. Thompson's manufactory was wrecked at Fordingbridge, was engaged
at that place, and took a very active part against the
rioters ; he used considerable exertions to prevent
the destruction of his property, and he also on

another occasion took an active part against the disturbers of the peace. His plea now was that he had
been pressed by the mob to go with them, and that
what he had done had been under the influence of
others. Whatever truth there was in this statement
it was clear that he had gone to a house demanding
money, and the charge being proved he was found
guilty. Another man, named John Read, was brought
up on a similar charge. The case against this person
was also proved, and he was found guilty. Sentence
of death was recorded against each of them. The
other cases tried were of trivial importance, the
special commission lasting only two days. The
calendar contained the names of 50 prisoners, but
there were as many as 63 indictments, some of the
prisoners being charged with two or more offences.
Seven of the prisoners were under 20 years of age ;
27 between 20 and 30 years of age ; and 16 only
above that age.

The efforts made for obtaining a commutation of
the sentence of death against the six convicts in Winchester gaol were successful in four instances. The
intelligence of a respite was received by the gaol
authorities on the 14th January. The prisoner Eldridge had quite resigned himself to his fate, and
seemed greatly affected by the intelligence. The rest
of the prisoners indulged hopes that a respite would
be granted, and when Cooper and Cooke found that
all their hopes were gone they gave way to great
grief. The chaplain of the gaol was unremitting in
his attentions to the convicts, and he was always with
them—except at short intervals—up to the time of
their execution. When their final time came both
Cooper and Cooke were greatly affected. Cooper on
the previous evening had signified his intention of
addressing the crowd, but when the time came he
found himself unable to carry out his intention.

When the procession moved from the condemned cell
to the scaffold Cooper cried bitterly, exclaiming,
"Lord, have mercy upon me!" "Oh that it should
have come to this." He staggered very much, and
betrayed the greatest mental agony. Cooke was
more firm, and it is said he died without a struggle.
According to the custom of the times, the prisoners in
the gaol were brought out into the yards to witness
the carrying into effect of the dread sentence, and a
special place was appointed for those prisoners against
whom sentence of death had been recorded. These
men were not ordinary criminals, and most of them,
before they had been long in gaol, bitterly repented
of having taken any part in the rioting and machine
breaking. The witnessing of the execution of Cooper
and Cooke is said to have greatly affected all of them,
and many were so overcome that they had to lean
against the wall for support, whilst the cries and sobs
of many others were most heart-rending.

The terrible scene which took place in the Court
at Salisbury when Lush and Withers were condemned
awakened the most intense interest in the breasts of
many persons in their behalf. It was felt by all that
they had broken the law and therefore deserved some
amount of punishment, but there was a very general
desire on the part of thousands of people, not only in
Wiltshire, but in Dorsetshire and Hampshire, that
their lives should be spared. A memorial was at
once prepared for presentation to His Majesty King
William IV., and this was signed in a few days by no
less than 2,000 of the most respectable citizens of
Salisbury, including the Mayor, many members of the
Corporation, the Cathedral dignitaries, and other
persons of position. The Rev. Mr. Greenby, a
clergyman of the Church of England, the Revs.
Messrs. Good and Saffery, Nonconformist ministers,
and Mr. James Whitmarsh, proceeded to London for

the purpose of waiting on the Home Office and handing in the memorial. The greatest attention was paid to the representations made by the deputation, and they were assured that the memorial should without delay be placed before the King. The day fixed for the execution of Lush and Withers was Tuesday, the 25th January, but on the previous day a respite was received at the gaol for both men. When the intelligence was communicated to the prisoners they felt devoutly thankful for the efforts which had been made in their behalf. Lush had quite prepared himself for the worst, and had given up all hope of a respite. He acknowledged that he had been a great sinner ; but, raising his hands to heaven, he prayed that the blessing of God might be with him, and that, trusting in the mercies of the Redeemer, and assisted by the consolations of the Holy Spirit, he might hereafter lead a life dedicated to the worship of that God who had so mercifully delivered him in his extremest need. Thus, it will be seen, he shewed himself not altogether unworthy of the great blessing he had received Withers, who had also prepared himself for the awful moment of his dissolution, returned thanks to God with uplifted hands, and uttered a fervent prayer to the Father of Mercies that his future life might be dedicated to His service as a token of his sincere gratitude.

The prisoners having been thus disposed of, it now only remains to be said that the machinery, or agricultural labourers', riots of 1830 were of short duration. When the special commission, which had been appointed for the trial of the rioters was over, the villages in many respects resumed their usual quietude. The wages of the agricultural labourers in many parts of Dorsetshire and Wiltshire did not exceed 8s. or 9s. a week, with something extra for harvest time. The demand which was made by many of the rioters was that they should be paid two shillings a day, a sum certainly moderate, as everyone will admit. The farmers, however, demurred to this demand, alleging that the high rents which they were compelled to pay for their farms would not admit of it being done, and a good deal was said and written on the subject. Many of the landowners took the matter into their consideration, and believing that the labourers were fully entitled to increased wages, and that the farms were too highly rented, lowered the rents, on the condition that the labourers' wages should be increased. Another question which came up for discussion was: "What shall be done with the prisoners who have been sentenced to long terms of imprisonment?" It was admitted on all sides that the labourers ought not to be classed with ordinary convicts, and that special provision ought to be made for keeping them apart from that class of criminals who, having often been imprisoned, were hardened in vice and immorality. As "transportation beyond the seas" was then the only mode of disposing of our criminal population doomed to long terms of imprisonment, there was no alternative but that very many of the poor fellows should be sent to the Antipodes. To some of them this was a great blessing, as in the new country they soon regained their liberty, and found openings in life far better than they could have hoped for in their English village homes.

The⁕G.W.R⁕Brought⁕Through ⁓Swindon.⁓

FORMERLY, as well as now, a town had to possess some special advantages over its neighbours before it could hope to enjoy a greater distinction than they—the advantage of population, or of situation, or of some particular industry. But Swindon enjoyed neither of these. The town stood on a hill—that was about the most that could be said of it. If it had ever possessed any feature of interest likely to attract visitors it had been removed. And that this was done a "Mem." by John Aubrey in his Wiltshire Notes helps me to show. Aubrey remarks: "At Brome, near Swindon, in a pasture ground, near the house, stands up a great stone, *(qr.* Sarsden), called Longstone, about 10 feet high, more or less; which I take to be the remayner of a Druidish Temple; in the ground below are many stones in a right line, thus o o o o o o o" Canon Jackson, in his notes on Aubrey, says: "Of the great stones mentioned by Aubrey none are now remaining." This entry by Aubrey, and remark by Canon Jackson, having been brought to my notice many years ago by the late Rev. G. Pillgrem in a letter to the *Advertiser*, I resolved on finding out, if possible, what had become of "the remayner of a Druidish Temple," and after some years I was rewarded for my trouble by making the discovery that the stones were actually sold to the Waywardens of Cricklade, and removed to that town, where they were broken up and used to make good the "pitching" in the streets; land of considerable value having been left by a benefactor of the town for the special purpose of making and maintaining good roads and footpaths. If this was the use the Swindonians of old were prepared to make of "the remayner of a Druidish Temple," the world at large may feel thankful that they had no control over Stonehenge and Avebury. Compared with the neighbouring towns and villages, as recently as fifty years ago, Swindon occupied but a very indifferent position. It had no population, no manufactories, no "good neighbourhood," to support a local trade. As for population—the following figures, taken from the census returns for 1831, will be interesting :—

Place	Population	Place	Population
Albourne	1418	Malmesbury	3579
Chippenham	4333	Marlborough	3426
Chiseldon	1148	Newbury	5967
Cirencester	5420	Purton	1714
Cricklade	1642	Ramsbury	2290
Devizes	4562	Shrivenham	779
Fairford	1574	Wanborough	1016
Faringdon	2156	Warminster	6115
Highworth	3127	Wantage	2507
Lambourne	2386	Wootton Bassett	1896
Lechlade	1244	Wroughton	1545
Lyneham	1030	Witney	3190

SWINDON, 1,742

t,1811 the population of Swindon was 1,341, and in 1697 it was 806.

b. Practically, then, Swindon, with its 25,000 tic·lation, is as much a Great Western Railway town to ugh it had been created on a spot where there

had been no pre-existing population. But to what
circumstance does Swindon, which was not on the
Great Western road, owe its position on the Great
Western Railway. There is but one answer: To the
crass perversity of human nature.. The Act of
Parliament incorporating the Great Western Railway
Company, with a capital of £2,500,000, was passed
on the 31st August, 1835. The project of making
this railway was first advocated in Bristol, and simply
contemplated a junction of Bristol with London,
and in course of the years 1832-3 frequent meetings
were held with the view of promoting the scheme.
The opposition it met with was, however, overpowering, so much so, indeed, that at the first meeting of
the proprietors after the passing of the Act, on the
29th of October, 1835, it was found that £88,710 10s.
11d. of the proposed capital of the company had been
spent in preliminary expenses. This sum, however,
was considered, under the circumstances, to be so
small that the Chairman congratulated the proprietors
on its very moderate amount. At this time railways
in England were only ten years old, the first one
opened for traffic being the Stockton and Darlington
Railway, on the 27th September, 1825, but which had
been constructed as a tram-road only, worked by
horse-power. The first railway opened for passenger
traffic was the Liverpool and Manchester, on the 14th
September, 1830, or five years only before the passing
of the Great Western Act. Even now, only fifty
years afterwards, it is impossible for us to realise the
intensity of the opposition shewn to the introduction
of railways into a neighbourhood. Landed proprietors
and country squires would not have them because
they cut up and disfigured their estates, and town
people would not have them because "they were
certain to take all their trade away and send it the
London and other large places." At this time the first

was but one interest in the country to be considered, and that was the landed interest, and its representatives were all powerful in the two Houses of Parliament, and could make or mar any Bill it was proposed to pass into law. Perhaps the feeling that then animated this all-supreme interest was best of all exemplified in recent times by Lord Bolingbroke, when he set up some sentimental personal grievance of his own against the convenience of some five or six thousand working men : when he objected to the use of a steam whistle for calling the thousands of workmen to their labours on the ground that its noise might possibly frighten and disturb a few of his pheasants sitting on their eggs a few miles off. The original intention of the promoters of the railway was to follow the Great Western road of the old coaching days, as well from Reading to Bristol as from London to Reading, and with this view the first survey was made and the first Bill framed. This, however, would have materially interfered with the Savernake estate, to which the then Marquis of Ailesbury strenuously objected. It was understood to have been principally through his influence that the first Great Western Railway Bill was wrecked in the House of Lords. As his lordship threatened to remain obdurate, and his influence was unimpaired, the promoters were driven to change their course on leaving Reading, and to take a much more northern route, and hence the detour which looks so remarkable on a Great Western Railway map. It is therefore a former Marquis of Ailesbury that Swindon has to thank more than any other man for having been placed on the Great Western Railway. But it was not all smooth sailing along this track, and opposition in every conceivable form had to be met, and more or less submitted to. As an illustration of this, it may be mentioned that it was proposed to bring the line south of the canal, and almost close under Swindon hill, with the station at the bottom of the Drove-road. But "The Lawn" objected, and the line was driven further north. It is also understood that very many years after this a mandate was issued from the same place requesting the railway authorities to paint some new goods sheds, which they had recently put up, with "invisible green paint," so that they might not be seen in the view from "The Lawn." What may be regarded as the indignities to which railway promoters had to submit in their plans of fifty years ago may be illustrated by five clauses in the original Great Western Railway Act. By these provisions, the Great Western Company and all other companies were bound not to make a railway or tramroad, or construct a station or siding within three miles of Eton College, without the consent of the provost and fellows, given under their common seal. The company were also required to erect and keep in perfect repair a good and sufficient fence, on both sides of the line, for a length of four miles nearest to the College, and they were bound to keep a sufficient number of persons to prevent the scholars having access to any part of the railway so fenced off. These men were to be paid by the company, but were to be under the entire control of the College authorities, and were to be at any time liable to be dismissed "upon their representation and demand." Having seen how the Great Western was brought to Swindon, I now propose only to add a few dates and particulars which may be of interest for reference. In the year following (1836) an Act sanctioning the construction of a line from Bristol to Exeter was passed, as well as another for a line from Swindon to Cheltenham. In 1837 a Bill authorising a line connecting the City of Oxford with the Great Western Railway at Didcot was thrown out, but on being re-introduced in the following year was allowed to become law. The first instalment of the Great Western Railway opened for traffic was from Paddington to Maidenhead, on the 4th June, 1838, the first service of trains being eight each way daily, but afterwards reduced to six in consequence of insufficiency of carriage stock. On the 5th July, 1839, the line was further opened to Twyford, the number of trains being augmented to ten each way daily. But it was not until September in this year that the company commenced to carry goods traffic, and on the 4th February, 1840, the company carried Her Majesty's mails for the first time over their line from Paddington to Twyford. On the 6th April, 1840, the line was opened to Reading, and on the first of the following June it was further opened to Steventon. On the 20th of the following month (July) it was further opened to Faringdon Road, and on the 31st August in the same year (1840) the twelve miles between Bath and Bristol were first used for public traffic. The next opening was to Hay Lane, mid-way between Swindon and Wootton Bassett, which took place on the 16th December, 1840, and on the 1st June, 1841, a further portion was opened to Chippenham. On the same day the first instalment of the Cheltenham and Great Western Union was opened, and on the next day an experimental trip was made by the Great Western Directors and their friends from Bath to Bridgwater over the Bristol and Exeter Railway, which was then rapidly approaching completion. The whole country side appears to have gone mad—or nearly so—on the occasion. A correspondent who accompanied the opening train to Chippenham, and also the experimental train to Bridgwater. writes :—" It seemed as if a whole people had turned out to give joyous and grateful welcome to some hero of a hundred fights, or other equally great national benefactor." It will be admitted that the result has more than justified the jubilation.

There can be no doubt but that during the construction of the railway considerable damage was done by the navvies and others trespassing on adjoining properties, and the claims for damages which were occasionally set up in consequence were most amusing. The following particulars of a claim which was actually enforced in a court of law, with the result of the jury awarding the plaintiff £49, is well worth preserving. I give particulars of claim *verbatim et literatim:*—

" The   Railway Company,
    18   " To

		£	s.	d.
May. A Bridge laid across River for parth over four Meddows of grass—the crops of grass very much traled abought with Men and Dogs—I have found five large dogs with as many men in the crops at a time—almost «frade of being put into the river by them		20	0	0
When the hay on the cock sadley puled about and spoiled—have had 3 men at a time laying in the hay cocks—the hay sadley damaged		10	0	0
A horse drove in to the river—cost—and so much drowned as never stood any more		15	0	0
4, 5 and 6 cows at a time milked, drove from ther lodging and sadley disturbed		52	0	0
Removing post and rail fence across the third meddow—carrying away and laying up		3	0	0
Loss of growing 4 cwt. cattle cabbage seed at 3s. lb. ...		84	0	0
Loss of 2 acers for parths for years		40	0	0
Profit of the two acers 4 years		16	0	0
Trafick of timber carriages, horses, carts, &c., over the 4 meddows, repearing gates, locks and fences the 4 years		4	4	0
Stopping up hedges to ceap cattle from straying the 4 years		8	4	0
Garden fence broken, robed and plundered, the 4 years		2	0	0
Menewer as amendment on the 2 acers, land in the Spring of 1838—40 load 10s.		20	0	0
		£269	8	0

The idea of running excursion trains appears to have originated with the Great Western authorities, and the following newspaper account of their *second* excursion train is worth preserving by way of contrast with those accounts of later days, when from ten

to fifteen thousand persons have been sent in the course of a single morning from Swindon Station :—
"On Thursday morning last (Sept. 29th, 1842), the 7 o'clock train from Bristol, drawn by two engines, and containing between 600 and 700 persons, arrived at the Paddington terminus at about a quarter to 12. The train, which was a curiosity, from its extreme length and freight of passengers, conveyed a highly respectable body of the inhabitants of Bristol and its vicinity, who had availed themselves of the opportunity held out by the directors before the close of the summer, of taking a trip to the Great Babylon, and of spending Michaelmas amongst their friends. Each person in the party was provided with a ticket for the fare, which was reduced on the occasion to one-half the ordinary price. They were thus enabled to travel the whole distance from Bristol to London and back again at the economical charge of 21s.; about half-an-hour's delay was occasioned in the arrival of the train, principally owing to the high wind which prevailed, and from the train stopping to to take up a fresh load of passengers as it passed the Bath, Chippenham, and Swindon Stations. The party were encumbered with little in the shape of luggage beyond a few Michaelmas geese.

⟶Pioneers✷of✷Nonconformity⟶

LTHOUGH I can find no direct evidence that either of the Wesleys or the Foxes, the Penns or the Whitfields, visited Swindon in course of their perambulations, it is certain that there existed in the town that strong religious element which first of all sympathised with the "scandalous" and ejected ministers, and subsequently developed into Nonconformity; the families of the Stranges, Lawrences, Reynolds', and others being among its best-known supporters. And it is also certain that one John Cennick, who subsequently became a leader among the Moravians, and has been described as the "Evangelist of North Wilts," visited Swindon at least on two occasions. Cennick, it appears, belonged to a Reading family, and he himself had been engaged as an assistant to a surveyor. In 1739, however, when only nineteen years of age, he took to preaching to the colliers at Kingswood, near Bristol, in connection with Wesley and Whitfield. Shortly after this, in 1740, Cennick appears to have turned his attention more particularly to

2 A

North Wilts, where he tells us there was a remarkable
revival of Christianity. Fortunately, Cennick kept a
journal, from which I purpose giving such extracts as
have any bearing upon Swindon and its immediate
neighbourhood. The following extract will best show
Cennick's position and the nature of his work as he
entered upon it when only twenty years of age :—
" The awakening, or first stirring, among the souls of
this county, began in Castlecombe, a town about eight
miles from Tytherton, and four from Marshfield.
William Orchard, a tailor, of Castlecombe, who had
heard me preach at the Cross, in the open street, to
many people at Sodbury, in Gloucestershire, was
passing through Kingswood, where I then lived, on
his way to Bristol fair ; and, meeting me on the road,
earnestly desired me to come to his town and preach,
to which I consented. This was in January, 1740. I
preached the first time in the street of Castlecombe,
to a vast concourse, on Wednesday, 16th July, 1740.
Several persons from Lyneham, and particularly
brother John Bryant, with others from Chippenham,
Avon, &c., invited me from thence to their towns and
villages, further into the county, till, by degrees, I
preached in most places thereabouts, especially at
Hullavington, Malmesbury, West Kynton, Littleton-
Drew, Foxham, Lyneham, Brinkworth, and Somerford.
In the time of harvest, 1740, at the invitation of some
persons from Chippenham, I preached to a prodigious
multitude on Langley Common, and returned the
same afternoon to Kingswood. On December 28th,
the Sunday after Christmas Day, after preaching at
the two former places several times, I preached at
Lyneham in the morning, and in the afternoon at
Foxham, to some thousands. On Monday, the 29th,
I preached at Little Somerford, and from this time had
open doors everywhere. I was about a year in Wiltshire, and had no help from any person. Often I

stayed only a few days, and at other times two or three weeks, in the county, and then returned to Kingswood, to take care of a little society there. This I did from the time of my disagreeing with Mr. Wesley, till I entirely mingled with Mr. Whitfield and his friends, and so came, as his preacher, into Wilts; though it was observed, from the beginning, that the Methodists did not much care for their Wiltshire brethren, because they were esteemed as tinctured with Antinomianism, and only a few of the Methodist preachers could be content to stay long in Wilts; and both Herbert Jenkins and Edward Godwin, and others, wrote to complain of them in London on this account." Under date of January 19th, 1741, or just about a year after he had commenced his itinerant ministry, there is this entry in his journal :—" I preached first at Brinkworth, in a field near to farmer Langley's, and in the evening I discoursed in his house ; and thus began the awakening on this side of the county." He does not appear to have proceeded further in the direction of Swindon until after the lapse of several months, when he did so under the circumstances and with the results which he states as follows :—" After brother Howell Harris, of Wales, had protested against the doctrines of free-will and sinless perfection, as the Messieurs Wesley held them, he came to see me in Wiltshire, and on Tuesday, the 23rd of June, with about twenty-four on horses, he accompanied me to Swindon, about ten miles from Brinkworth, and not far from the Vale of White Horse, where I had appointed to preach. We found a large company assembled in the Grove, with whom I sang and prayed, but was hindered from preaching by a great mob who made a noise and played in the midst of the people ; and then with guns they fired over our heads, holding the muzzles of their pieces so near our faces that we were both made

as black as tinkers with the powder. We were not
affrighted, but opened our breasts, telling them we
were ready to lay down our lives for our doctrines, and
had nothing to say against it even if their guns were
levelled at our hearts. They then got the dust out of
the highway, and covered us all over, and then played
an engine upon us, which they filled out of the stinking
ditches, till we were just like men in the pillory.
While they played upon brother Harris, I spoke to
the congregation ; and when they turned the engine
upon me, then he preached, and this continued till
they had spoiled the engine, and then they threw
whole buckets of water and mud over us. When we
had stood in this manner more than an hour, a
spectacle of the utmost shame, before many weeping
people, and before the whole mob, we were led up to
the town to the person's house who had invited us
thither, where we borrowed some old things to change
us, and came back to Brinkworth. This persecution
was carried on by Mr. Goddard, a leading gentleman
of that place, who lent the mob his guns, halbert, and
engine, and bade them use us as bad as they could,
only not to kill us ; and he himself sat on horseback
the whole time, laughing to see us so treated. After
we had left the town they dressed up two images, and
called one Cennick, and the other Harris, and then
burnt them. Also the next day after we had been
there, they rose about the house of Mr. Lawrence, who
had received us, and broke all his windows with stones,
cut and wounded four of his family, and knocked
down one of his daughters, and so left them for that
day ; but if they heard them singing hymns, or supposed a minister to be there, they continued to riot
about the house. Some few days afterwards the mob
again got together, resolving to pull down Mr. Lawrence's house to the ground ; but as soon as they
began, there fell such a violent shower of rain as

obliged them to desist and disperse.   It was also remarkable that about this time an uncommon clap of
thunder was heard over the town, which sadly terrified
the inhabitants.   In this storm an oak tree, which
stood in the field of Mr. Goddard, was split into the
finest splinters, and scattered all over the field.   This
seemed to portend something bad, and was generally
observed when people saw what followed.   I had appointed, some time after this, to preach at Stratton, a
place not more than three miles from Swindon, at
which time, as was supposed, because in my address
to the people I made frequent mention of the blood of
Christ, the chief persons concerned in the former riot
got a butcher to save all the blood he could, in order
(as he said) that they might play it out of the engine
upon us, and so give us blood enough.   But before I
went to Stratton, God struck with particular judgments
all the authors of this design at once.   John and
Thomas Vilett, Esquires, the parson of Stratton, and
Sylvester Kean, a bailiff, all bled at the nose, and
some at the mouth, without ceasing, till one of the
former fell into dead fits, and could not any more be
trusted alone.   Neither did the minister recover, for
it brought him also to his grave.   As for Sylvester
Kean, he continued to bleed at times at such an extravagant rate that it threw him into a deep decay, in
which he lingered ten days, without having any one
to visit him, because he stank alive ; and on the 31st
March following he died, cursing terribly."

Within three months of this time Cennick visited
Swindon a second time, although possibly he did not
come into the town, his object being to visit Stratton,
and his course no doubt lay by way of the old Fleet
Lane, now known as Westcott Place and Fleet Street,
which is one of the ancient highways of the neighbourhood.   Returning again to his journal, I find the
following entry :—" On Saturday, 6th September,

after I had preached at Brinkworth school or meeting, about fifty persons on horses and as many on foot went with me to Stratton, where we had appointed a meeting for that day. On the road I opened my New Testament on those words, 'We are persecuted, but not forsaken,' which served to hint to me what would happen. However, we had many people, and a lovely meeting. But before I said much there came the mob again from Swindon, with swords, staves, and poles. Without respect to age or sex, they knocked down all that stood in their way, so that some had the blood streaming down their faces, and others were taken up almost beaten and trampled to death. Many of our dear friends were cut and bruised sadly, and I got many severe blows myself. We got away into a Baptist meeting-house just by, where I spoke to the houseful in much affection, and took leave. When we were again mounted, we thanked God who had counted us worthy to suffer thus for His gospel's sake, and then made towards Lyneham, thinking that now our enemies had fully revenged themselves upon us. But we soon found to the contrary, for presently they overtook us and beat us barbarously. Our horses were so startled that it was a real mercy we had not been killed or did not kill others who were on foot, for we rode through the midst of the people, our persecutors whipping the horses with all their might, while the people on foot to save themselves rushed into the hedges and ditches and hid themselves where they could. At last we came into a part of our road where were many gates (across the track), where they posted themselves and beat inhumanly each of us as we rode by. This they did for about two miles, when a countryman showed us a narrow lane which led into another road, by which we escaped further hurt, our enemies (unaware of our change of route) riding before into a straight place,

expecting we should come that way. In this hurry
several had lost their hats, handkerchiefs, &c., and
some with difficulty saved their lives. After we had
left the first road and were a little still and collected,
we could hear behind us most dreadful crying, for our
friends on foot were being pursued and used equally
ill as ourselves. Several of them came home so
bruised and hurt as is not easily to be believed. One
James Cottle, of Staunton, who had been unmercifully
beaten, seeing one that had beat him fall down by
means of a thorn which ran deep into his foot,
stopped and meekly helped him to get it out, and this
act so moved the man that he left off beating and
turned back with the rest of his companions. As
soon as we came to Lyneham we were welcomed back
with many tears by some hundreds of people who
had heard we were killed, for those who had made
haste before reported that they had heard the mob
swear that they would butcher us. When I came to
brother Bryant's door, I kneeled down and thanked
the Lord with my company that he had saved us this
day. I preached, and took leave of them all, and the
next morning set out for London, though my
shoulders remained black with the blows for three
weeks afterwards. Now Mr. Goddard rejoiced that
he had given us enough ; but not many days passed
ere, as he was riding the same horse on which he had
sat laughing to see us abused at Swindon, a servant
of his was cleaning the guns which had been fouled
in firing at us, and letting one off just as his master
rode into the court, the horse started and threw him,
by which means Mr. Goddard received some inward
hurt either from his saddle or from the fall, which in
a little time caused his death. Some of Swindon
affirm that he received his first hurt while he looked
on to see us abused, and that the fall which he afterwards got from the horse merely hastened his end,

for he left the world about a fortnight afterwards, raving with pain, aged about fifty years. As he died without making a will, his relations did not know who should be his heir, and he was left unburied till the stench of his corpse was intolerable ; at last he was interred at night privately. Sylvester Kean, as was before said, bled to such an unnatural degree that all his bowels corrupted, and so he miserably ended his life, even cursing himself and those who encouraged him to meddle with us. This was on the last day of March. Charles Gay, a tailor, one of the chief of the mob, and who in particular threatened to butcher us, as well as Thomas Perry, a breeches maker, were together tried for their lives at the assizes for stealing ten guineas, and hardly escaped the gallows. Thomas Looker, a soap boiler, and Thomas Holliday, a labourer, were soon after publicly whipped at Devizes for stealing fowls. Francis Gay, a brandy-seller, Edward Golding, Edward Archer, a mason, Henry Hoddam, a shoemaker, and Thomas Humphreys, glazier, ran away, some for buying stolen goods, and some for debt. Another went beside himself, and left the town in the deepest melancholy. All this happening so soon after they had persecuted us stopped all further troubles of this kind, and made all men afraid to interrupt us any more in those parts."

But it was not from open enemies alone that Cennick experienced opposition. Another entry in his journal reads as follows :—" About autumn, during the same year, 1741, Satan found out another way to hinder the work of God if possible, and to cause it to be ridiculed and blasphemed, which was by this means : One Anne Lawrence, a young woman of Swindon, came with her sister to Foxham, and began to pray and sing among the awakened souls, and sometimes stayed up with them all night, and often till midnight ; and as she came like a prophetess, many had a greater esteem for her, and whenever she kept a meeting it so happened that one or other of those present fell into strange fits, in which they were surprisingly agitated. The girl looked upon herself as peculiarly inspired, and gave out that these agonies were the pangs of the New-birth, without which none could be saved. At this time I was in London ; and as no preacher was left in Wilts she went on with full career till no house could contain the people that flocked to hear her, so that sometimes she kept her meetings in orchards and fields. Several joined with her and supported the delusion, such as Nathaniel Cole, of Foxham, and Thomas Scott, a servant at Avon, and the wife of Thomas Sympkins, at West-end. The nature of these fits was to be seized with sudden risings in the throat as if they should be strangled. They sighed and wept bitterly ; and when they fell down they roared as if they were just going to hell, all the while trembling and sweating astonishingly, saying they felt the pangs of hell in their hearts. Sometimes they lay beating themselves on the ground, rolling and crying for hours, until by the girl's praying and singing they were recovered, when they declared that they were converted, and rejoiced ; or else wept that they had not attained it. One thing was very remarkable. If any strangers, or others who were present when people were in the fits, laughed or mocked, they were sure to be themselves seized in like manner ; and this circumstance protected the poor deceived maid and her followers from suffering from those who did not like it. In the very height of this work I came from London into Wiltshire, and laboured in vain to convince the souls that it was a delusion of Satan's, and not a work of God, till one night as I was praying at Lyneham before preaching, one Lily Wastfield, of Foxham, cried out ; upon which I stopped, and forbade her to speak a word, and immediately all ceased, and we heard no more of it at all." Unfortunately, Miss Lawrence does not appear to have kept a journal ; or, if she did so, it has not been made public. Had she, like Cennick, published her troubles to the world, it is quite possible we might have found her saying hard things about the Evangelist of North Wilts, and, it may be, have attributed his early death through not believing in the genuineness of her ".fits."

On the 25th March, 1743, Cennick preached again at Stratton St. Margaret, where he says, " All was still and quiet, and the tumult and opposition entirely ceased." And this would appear to have been his last visit to the neighbourhood of Swindon, for no further reference is made in his journal to either Swindon or Stratton. In the year 1747, Cennick was married to a Miss Jane Bryant, of Clack ; and on July 4th, 1755, he died, at the age of thirty-five years. His journal abounds in accounts of persecutions and the ill-treatment to which persons like him were subjected. It is remarkable, however, that he is enabled to record some fearful or untimely end which overtook most, if not all, of the more prominent persecutors. On one occasion some of Cennick's companions were apprehended by the parish constables and committed to gaol as disturbers of the peace, Cennick himself escaping apprehension by pleading that he was a " freeholder," a term which appeared to have a terrible significance in the estimation of his would-be captors. About this same time, in Ireland, in which country Cennick laboured for some years, a Cork grand jury made a presentment to the following effect, concerning one of the founders of the Wesleyan body :—" We find and present Charles Wesley to be a person of ill-fame, a vagabond, and a common disturber of His Majesty's peace, and we pray that he may be transported."

Having seen what Cennick has to say about the treatment he met with at Swindon, we naturally turn to what contemporary history we have to see if he is in any way corroborated ; and, if so, to what extent. My first reference in this direction must be to the parish registers of burials, and turning to these I find there were burials of members of the Goddard family, as follows :—

" RICHARD GODDARD, September 1, 1732."
" PLEYDELL GODDARD, August 27, 1741."
" PLEYDELL GODDARD, an infant, January 26, 1742."
" EDWARD GODDARD, March 16, 1743.

As Cennick's first visit to Swindon was on June 23, 1741, and when, according to his own statement, he was accompanied by "twenty-four persons on horses," it would seem from the date of these entries that Pleydell Goddard is the Mr. Goddard to whom Cennick refers as his assailant. On Cennick's second visit, when he went to Stratton, on September 6th, he was, according to his own account, accompanied by " about fifty persons on horses, and as many on foot." It was when he was at Stratton that he heard of Mr. Goddard's death, which circumstance would again point to Pleydell Goddard as the person referred to. No doubt reference to family documents and records would at once settle the point. But in the absence of these we must look to other sources for information, and accordingly turn from the parchment register of burials to the stone and marble registers of deaths, virtues, and Christian graces which men are in the habit of putting up to their departed friends and relatives ; and as this is done other evidence comes to light bearing on Cennick's statement. On the east wall of the old chancel there is affixed a marble monument, which bears the following inscription :—

IN THE MEMORY OF
RICHARD GODDARD, ESQ.,
WHO DEPARTED THIS LIFE
AUG. 20TH. 1732,
AGED 56.
ALSO OF
PLEYDELL GODDARD, ESQ.,
WHO DEPARTED THIS LIFE
AUG. 18. 1742,
AGED 61.
THIS MONUMENT WAS ERECTED AS A TRIBUTE OF GRATITUDE BY
ONE OF THEIR SUCCESSORS.
ANN. DOM., 1798

Why a monument or monuments was not erected to the memory of these members of the Goddard family in the ordinary course, or why this " tribute of gratitude" was delayed for 66 years in one case and 54 years in the other, we must leave to conjecture. It is more than probable, however, that the three deaths in the family in the short space of less than eighteen months had the effect of very much mixing up matters, and possibly causing complications which were not readily set right.

From an inscription on another monument, it would appear that the next successor to the Swindon estates was Edmund Goddard, who died in 1776, at the age of 67 years. From the fact that he is referred to as the eldest son of Edmund Goddard, the presumption is raised that he was the representative of another branch of the family from that to which Richard and Pleydell belonged—a supposition which is strengthened by Cennick's remark that " Mr. Goddard died without making a will," and " his relations did not know who should be his heir." It may be that the "successor" of 1798 regarded himself as lawful heir to Pleydell Goddard, and that he gave expression to his feelings of gratitude, in imperishable marble, on coming into " his rights."

As to the allegation that the body was left un-buried until it could no longer be delayed, and that it

was then performed in the night, there is nothing to
support it beyond the fact that the death took place
on August 18th, and the burial on August 27th, or
nine days afterwards, whereas Richard Goddard,
against whom no such allegation is made, ten years
previously, died on August 20th, and was not buried
until September 1st, or ten days afterwards. No doubt
Cennick, like the generality of men with strong religious feelings, at times of persecution, was a great
enthusiast, and readily concluded that the Lord was
with him in all he did, whilst the Devil was with those
who in any way opposed him. It is certain, however,
that he knew well how to defend himself. His own
admission that he was accompanied by twenty four
horsemen on his visit to Swindon, and by fifty horsemen, and as many on foot, on his visit to Stratton,
would seem to show that his processions assumed
formidable, and even defiant, proportions, and not
unfrequently excited opposition from those who dis-
agreed with him. It does not appear that he was
accompanied in any such manner when visiting other
places beside Swindon and Stratton, and therefore it
may be that he had no occasion to record assaults
made upon him and his party. Long before Cennick's
time—in that of John Aubrey—North Wilts appears
to have been notorious for its "sour theology," which
was indulged in by those "who were from their very
constitution prone to rebellion, and greatly disinclined
to the government of bishops," and which circumstance
Aubrey explains in this way : " The soil of North
Wilts is sour ; from this sour soil springs a sour vegetation, and the sour vegetation in its turn produces a
sour theology." Many of the country squires, no
doubt, were acquainted with this saying, and it may
have been that when their neighbourhoods were in-
vaded by scores of horsemen and as many on foot
preaching and praying, and no doubt most unmerci-

fully condemning the popular practices, religion, and customs of the day, they felt themselves justified in opposing and putting down what they regarded as fanatical zeal.

I have said that neither of the Wesleys appears to have visited Swindon. It is certain, however, from Jackson's "Life of Charles Wesley" that both the brothers visited Devizes, where their reception was equally violent and disgraceful to that accorded to Cennick at Swindon. In Charles Wesley's journal there is the following entry : —

"February 24th, 1748. Between 3 and 4 in the afternoon we came to Mr. Clark's at Devizes. I found his daughter there, our sister Taylor (who has won him to Christ without the word), and a sister from Bath. We soon perceived that our enemies had taken the alarm and were mustering their forces for the battle. They began with ringing the bells backwards, and running to and fro in the streets as lions roaring for their prey. From the time my brother told me in London that there was no such thing as raising a mob at the Devizes, I had a full expectation of what would follow, but saw my call, and walked with my brother Meriton and M. Naylor to a house where the Society used to meet.

"The Curate's mob had been in quest of me at several places, particularly at Mrs. Phillips', where I was expected to preach. They broke open and ransacked her house ; but, not finding me, marched away to our brother Rogers, where we were praying and exhorting one another to continue in the faith, and through much tribulation to enter the kingdom. The chief gentlemen of the town headed the mob, and the zealous Curate, Mr. Innes, stood with them in the street the whole time, dancing for joy. This is he who declared in the pulpit, as well as from house to house, that he himself heard me preach blasphemy before the University. . . . . . He had gone about several days, stirring up the people and canvassing the gentry for their vote and interest, but could not raise a mob while my brother was here. The hour of darkness was not then fully come. While his friends were assaulting us . . . . I heard my own name frequently repeated, with ' Bring him out, bring him out.' Their design was first to throw me into the horse pond. They continued raging and threatening the first hour, and pressed hard upon us to break the door. The windows they did break to pieces, and tore down the shutters of the shop. The little flock were less afraid than I expected, only one of our sisters fainted away. But beneath were the everlasting arms.

"Our besiegers had now blocked up the door with a waggon, and set up lights lest I should escape; yet a brother got out unobserved, and with much entreaty prevailed upon the Mayor to come down. He came with two constables (one a faithful brother, the other a persecutor), and threatened the rioters, but so softly that none regarded him. It was the Lord who for the present rebuked the madness of the people. They hurried away from us to the inn where our horses were, broke open the stable door and turned out the beasts, which were found some hours after in a pond up to their chins in water. We were at a loss meantime what to do ; when God put it into the heart of our next-door neighbour, a Baptist, to take us through a passage into his own house, offered us his bed, and engaged for our security. We accepted his kindness and slept in peace.

"25th February. A day never to be forgotten. At seven I walked quietly to Mrs. Phillips', began preaching a little before the time appointed ; and for three quarters of an hour invited a few listening sinners to Christ. Then the boys, with their bells, like the Devil's infantry, began ; and soon after, his whole army assaulted the house to bring us forth. We sat in a little ground room, and ordered all the doors to be thrown open.   They brought a hand engine and began to play into the house.   We kept our seats, and they rushed into the passage.   Just then, Mr. Burrough, the constable came, seized upon the spout of the engine and carried it off in spite of them all.   They swore that if he did not deliver it they would pull down the house.   At that time they might have taken us prisoners, for we were in their sight, close to them, and none to interpose ; but they hurried out to fetch the larger engine.   Meanwhile we were advised to send to Mr. Mayor, but Mr. Mayor was gone out of town in sight of the people.   This was great encouragement to those who were already wrought up to a proper pitch by the painstaking Curate and gentlemen of the town, particularly Mr. Sutton and Mr. Willey the two leading men.   Mr. Sutton lived next door, and frequently came out to the mob to keep up their spirits.   Mr. Innes was there too, and quite happy on the occasion.   Mr. Sutton sent word to Mrs. Phillips that if she did not turn that fellow out to the mob he would send them to drag him out.   Mr. Willey passed by again and again, assuring the rioters he would stand by them and secure them from the law, do what they would.

"They now began playing the larger engine, which broke the windows, flooded the rooms, and spoiled the goods.   We were withdrawn to a small upper room in the back part of the house, seeing no way to escape their violence.   They seemed under the full power of the old Murderer.   One brother who keeps the Society they laid hold of first, dragged him away and threw him into the horse pond ; and broke his back, as was reported.   But another of the Society ran in resolutely among them, and rescued

him out of their hands by little less than a miracle.
His wife fell into fits again. We gave ourselves unto
prayer, believing the Lord would deliver us ; how or
when we saw not, nor any possible way of escaping.
Therefore we stood still to see the salvation of God.
As soon as the mob had emptied the engine, they
ran to fill it again, keeping strict watch on all sides,
lest we should escape. One advised us to attempt it
through the garden of a persecutor, and I put on my
coat on purpose, but could not think it the Lord's way
of bringing us forth. I laid aside the design, and saw
a troop of our enemies coming up the very way we
should have gone. Every now and then, some or
other of our friends would venture to us, but rather
weakened our hands, so that we were forced to stop
our ears and look up. Amongst the rest, the Mayor's
maid came and told us her mistress was in tears about
me, and begged me to disguise myself in women's
clothes and try to make my escape. Her heart had
been turned towards us by the conversion of her son.
Just on the brink of ruin, God laid his hand upon the
poor prodigal, and instead of running away to sea, he
entered into the Society, to the great joy and surprise of his parents.

"The rioters without continued playing their
engine, which diverted them for some time. But
their number and fierceness still increased ; and the
gentlemen plied them with pitchers of ale, as much as
they would drink. Mr. Meriton hid his money and
watch, 'that they might do good to somebody,' he
said, 'for, as to the mob, they should have nothing
of him but his carcase.' They were now on the point
of breaking in, when Mr. Burroughs thought of reading the Proclamation. He did so at the hazard of his
life. In less than the hour [required in the Act for
dispersing] of above one thousand wild beasts, none
were left but the guard. They retreated, as we sup-

2 B

posed, by the advice of the old serpent who sat
observing us at an opposite house in the shape of a
lawyer. We had now stood siege for about three
hours, and none but the Invisible Hand could have
kept them one moment from tearing us in pieces.
Our constable had applied to Mr. Street, the only
justice in town, who would not act. We found there
was no help in man, which drove us closer to the
Lord; and we prayed by his Spirit with little inter-
mission the whole day.

"Our enemies, at their return, made their main
assault at the back door, swearing horribly they would
have me, if it cost them their lives. Many seeming
accidents concurred to delay their breaking in. The
man of the house came home ; and instead of turning
me out, as they expected, he took part with us, and
stemmed the tide for some time. Then they got a
notion that I had made my escape, and ran down to
the inn and played their engine there. They forced
the innkeeper to turn out our horses, which he immediately sent to Mr. Clark's. This drew the rabble
and their engine thither, but the resolute old man
charged and presented his gun till they retreated.
Upon their revisiting us, Mr. Meriton was for sur-
rendering ourselves before the night came on, which,
he said, would make them more audacious, and that
there might be witness of whatever they did by daylight. But I persuaded him to wait till the Lord
should point out the way. Now we stood in jeopardy
every moment. Such threatenings, curses, and blas-
phemies, I had never heard. They seemed kept out
by a constant miracle. I remembered the Roman
Senate sitting in the Forum when the Gauls broke
in upon them ; but thought there was a fitter posture
for Christians ; and told our companions, they should
take us off our knees. We were kept from all hurry
and discomposure of spirit by a divine power resting

upon us. We prayed and conversed as freely as if
we had been in the midst of our brethren, and had
great confidence that the Lord would either deliver
us from the danger, or in it. One of my companions,
M. N., cried out 'It must be so : God will deliver us :
if God is true, we are safe.' I told my friend Meriton
(et hæc olim meminisse juvabit) that our most distant
friends were praying for us, and our deliverance
would soon occasion many thanksgivings unto God.
In the height of the storm, when we were just falling
into the hands of the drunken enraged multitude, he
was so little disturbed that he fell fast asleep. They
were now close to us on every side, and over our
heads untiling the roof. I was diverted by a little
girl, who called to me through the door, ' Mr. Wesley,
Mr. Wesley, creep under the bed ; they will kill you ;
they are pulling down the house.' Our sister Taylor's
faith was just failing, when a ruffian called out, ' Here
they are behind the curtain.' At this time we fully
expected their appearance, and retired to the further-
most corner of the room ; and I said, ' This is the
crisis.' In that moment Jesus rebuked the wind and
seas, and there was a great calm. We heard not a
breath without, and wondered what was come to
them. The silence lasted three-quarters of an hour
before any one came near us ; and we continued in
mutual exhortation and prayer, looking for deliverance. If ever we felt faith, it was now. Our souls
hung upon that arm which divided the sea. I often
told my companions, ' Now, God is at work for us :
He is contriving our escape : He can turn these
leopards into lambs ; can command the Heathen to
bring his Children on their ·shoulders, and make our
fiercest enemies the instruments of our deliverance.'

" In about an hour after the last general assault,
the answer of faith came. . . . . . Soon after
three o'clock, Mr. Clark knocked at the door and

brought with him the persecuting constable. He said, 'Sir, if you will promise never to preach here again, the gentlemen and I will engage to bring you safe out of town.' My answer was,—'I shall promise no such thing.'—'But will you not tell me that you have no intention of returning hither?'—'Not till you are better disposed to receive me; for, in obedience to my master, if you persecute in one city I will flee to another. But, setting aside my office, I will not give up my birthright as an Englishman of visiting what part I please of his Majesty's dominions.'—'Sir, we expect no such promise that you will never come here again: only tell me that it is not your present intention, that I may tell the gentlemen, who will then secure your quiet departure.'—I answered, 'I cannot come now, because I must return to London a week hence; but observe, I make no promise of not preaching here when the door is opened; and don't you say that I do.'

"He went away with this answer, and we betook ourselves again to prayer and thanksgiving. We perceived it was the Lord's doing, and it was marvellous in our eyes. Our adversaries' hearts were turned. Even Mr. Sutton and Mr. Willey laboured to take off the mob and quench the fire themselves had kindled. Whether pity for us or fear for themselves wrought strongest, God knoweth. Probably the latter; for the mob were wrought up to such a pitch of fury that their masters dreaded the consequence, and therefore went about appeasing the multitude and charging them not to touch us in our departure. I knew full well it was not in their power to lay the devil they had raised, and that none but the Almighty could engage for our security. We had hoped to make our escape in the dead of the night, if the house were not pulled down first, and had therefore sent our horses towards Seend, intending to walk after them; but now we sent for them back, and recovered them before they were got out of the town.

"While the constable was gathering his posse, we got our things from Mr. Clark's, and prepared to go forth. The whole multitude were without, expecting us. Now, our constable's heart began to fail, and he told us he much doubted if the mob could be restrained ; for that thirty or more of the most desperate were gone down the street, and waited at the end of the town for our passing. He should therefore advise us to hide ourselves in some other house and get off by night. Mr. Meriton's counsel was to escape by the back door while the mob were waiting for us at the fore door. I asked council of the Lord, and met with that word, 'Jesus said unto her, said I not unto thee, if thou wouldest believe, thou shouldst see the glory of God.' After reading this, I went forth as Luther to the Council.

"We were saluted with a general shout. The man whom Mrs. Naylor had hired to ride before her, was, as we now perceived, one of the rioters. This hopeful guide was to conduct us out of the reach of his fellows. Mr. Meriton and I took horse in the face of our enemies, who began clamouring against us, and I answering them, when the constable begged me to forbear. The gentlemen were dispersed among the mob to bridle them. We rode a slow pace down the street, the whole multitude pouring along on both sides, and attending us with loud acclamations. Such fierceness and diabolical malice I have not seen in human faces. They ran up to our horses, as if they would swallow us up, but did not know which was Wesley. We felt great peace and acquiesence in the honour done us, while the whole town were spectators of our march. After riding two or three hundred yards, I looked back and saw Mr. Meriton on the ground, in the midst of the mob, and two bull-dogs upon him. One was first let loose, which leaped at his horse's nose, but the horse with his foot beat him down. The other fastened on his nose, and hung there till Mr. Meriton with the butt end of his whip felled him to the ground. Then the first dog recovering, flew at the horse's breast, and fastened there The beast reared up, and Mr. Meriton slid gently off. The dog kept his hold till the flesh tore off. Then some men took off the dogs ; others cried, ' Let them alone.' But neither beast nor man had any further commission to hurt. I stopped the horse and delivered him to my friend. He remounted with great composure, and we rode on leisurely as before, till out of sight.

"Then we mended our pace, and in an hour came to Seend, having ridden three miles about ; and by seven to Wrexhall. The news of our danger was got thither before us, but we brought the welcome tidings of our own deliverance. Now we saw the hand of Providence in suffering them to turn out our horses, that is, to send them to us against we wanted them. Again, how plainly were we overruled to send our horses down the town, which blinded the rioters without our designing it, and drew off their engines and them, leaving us a free passage at the other end of the town. We joined in hearty praises to our Deliverer, singing the hymn

Worship and thanks, and blessing, &c."

~Pioneers * of * Nonconformity~

+THE WESLEYANS.+

ANOTHER interesting chapter in the history of Nonconformity in the town and neighbourhood of Swindon is that written by the Wesleyans, who celebrated the Jubilee Anniversary of their local circuit at Hodson, on Monday, July 1st, 1867, and on which occasion I wrote as follows concerning it :—" An old saying has it that ' It is an ill wind that blows nobody any good.' It must have been a good stout nor'-wester that first blew Methodism and Methodist preachers into what is now known as the Swindon Circuit. And many there are, no doubt, who, without being hypercritical about the truth or falsehood of old sayings in general, will at once admit that it was by no means a bad sort of wind that first brought to them and their fathers that new light in religious thought which had brightened up many a dark corner in England, and which had made the name of Wesley famous. Wesley has had his biographers, and Methodism its historians. With Methodism, then, in its general character, and with its founder, as regards

his special labours, we have little or nothing to do in
our present sketch; we have rather to do with the
'*blowing*' of the spirit of Wesley, as shown in the
work and life of one of his early followers, into our
neighbourhood. It is simply noting well-known facts
in history to state that John Wesley was born in the
year 1703, educated at the Charter House (the chief
funds for supporting which excellent establishment
are derived principally from this neighbourhood);
that he afterwards entered Christ Church College,
Oxford, and was ordained in 1725 by Bishop Potter;
that he then went to America, in 1735; that in 1738,
having returned from America, he resolved upon commencing that course of itinerant services which led to
the formation of a distinct Christian body known as
the Wesleyans; or that the foundation stone of the
first Wesleyan chapel was laid at Bristol in May
1739, forty-eight years before Wesley's death, which
took place on the 2nd of March, 1791. These, we
say, are facts known to the Wesleyan body throughout the world; but we must have a word or two
about the laying of that foundation stone at Bristol,
and the work it started. John Wesley does not
appear to have visited Wiltshire as a preacher, the
district having been left to Charles and others of the
brethren to work, as we gather from the account
of the doings at Devizes. The population must
have been too sparse, and the field for labour
too limited, for one who could find many friends in a
city like Bristol, and who could assemble many thousands together in Cornwall. His work was rather to
form centres from which co-workers could radiate.
This division of labour was more essential in Wesley's
day than it is now. The journey of some hundreds
of miles now is simply a matter of so many hours;
the journey of some twenty or thirty miles was *then*
a serious matter. A Spurgeon in 1885 may preach

at four of the most extreme points in the United Kingdom on four successive days, but a Wesley in 1767 would not have ventured upon the doing of more than a few miles of country road in the same space of time. Until quite late in the first half of the present century the only *direct* communication between this neighbourhood and Bristol was by means of an old waggon that accomplished the to and fro journey between Wootton Bassett and Bristol once every week! But the men of those days were equal to the exigencies of the times and circumstances. We are always meeting with something grand and noble as we make ourselves acquainted with the manner in which they got over their difficulties. They were earnest and determined in their work; obstacles became incentives; and, therefore, what work they did, they did it thoroughly and well. We have seen, in some former notices, that to speak against iniquity, immorality, drunkenness, profanity, and all kindred vices, was to subject the speaker to contumely, insult, and degradation; we now see that to get from one place to another in country districts was not the least of the difficulties a man had to encounter. Wesley made many friends at Bristol, and secured the co-operation of many an earnest worker there. Among others, there was one George Pocock, who, in addition to being an earnest worker, must have been an ingenious mechanic. Before the old stage-coach and the old road-waggon had reached even their limit of perfection, before even steam had been recognised as a motive power, or a railway thought of, men had been labouring hard to settle the problem, 'How to fly through the air?' Whether or not Mr. Pocock ever tried to solve this matter we are not in a position to say, but certain it is he was by no means satisfied with the ordinary locomotion of his time. To be dissatisfied is everybody's work; to remove the cause of dissatisfaction is a power not possessed by every one. Mr. Pocock did possess that power in respect to his objection to the ordinary loco-motion of the day at least, for after he had made himself a large canvas tent he constructed a machine (capable of carrying himself and his tent from one part of the country to another) to be drawn along the roads by means of paper kites flying in the air ! With that faith, then, which has done so much, and that dependence on right, and truth, and honesty of purpose which has marked the career of many of our pioneers, this Mr. Pocock, having packed up his tent and prepared his machine, would fly his kites in the air, and thus leave his Bristol home for any town or village to which the winds of Heaven might carry him, there to unfold what to him and to many others was a scheme of the most vital importance—a new religion, having in it, in their eyes, life, and light, and warmth, when compared with the dull unreality that then so generally prevailed. They were nicknamed fanatics and Methodists, and were met with contumely and scorn ; but they were true to the light they had : and whilst men are that their efforts will prosper, and God's work upon earth will be done. On more than one occasion Mr. Pocock's paper kites have flown over Swindon, his machine has lumbered over the roads of our neighbourhood, and his tent has been pitched at the top of Newport-street, in a field now let out in allotments. And it was in this novel way that 'Methodism' was brought into our neighbourhood— brought by the fair-blowing wind in the heart of an earnest worker. No one can wonder that the work undertaken by such men should be abiding work. Mr. Pocock's visits were as uncertain as the wind ; he was never 'planned' to come or to go, and when he came there was no 'society' to meet him. His paper kites, as they flew in the air, were his heralds, his tent

pitched was his landmark, and the crier's bell and
tongue announced his programme. We have no data
at hand by which to fix the date of these visits, but
Mrs. Tarrant, of Lower Town, Swindon, who well
recollects seeing Mr. Pocock and hearing him preach,
believes the visits to have extended down to as late
as the year 1812. Mr. Pocock's kites took him to
Wanborough, as well as to Swindon, and although at
both places he met with that ribaldry, outrage, and
abuse so prevalent at that period, he succeeded in
making both friends and converts, and the cause he
advocated has lived from that day to this. But the
place to which his kites first took him appears to have
been the little hamlet of Hodson, in the parish of
Chiseldon, and here it was that the first Wesleyan
Chapel in this neighbourhood was built. It has been
described as a particularly rude erection, the material
used being what is popularly known as 'wattle and
daub,' *i.e.*, hurdles such as are used by shepherds for
their sheep pens, fastened to poles driven into the
ground, and covered with mud gathered from the
road, forming the walls, the whole being covered with
a thatch of straw. The first Methodist 'circuit'
formed in this part of the country appears to have
been at Newbury, but at what time we are not in a
position to say. This, however, is clear, that by the
year 1810 the cause had made sufficient progress to
admit of the circuit being divided, and the Hungerford circuit formed. Seven years after this, namely,
by the year 1817, the Hungerford circuit had grown
sufficiently large to admit of its being divided, and the
Swindon circuit formed out of it. But before we
arrive at the formation of the Swindon circuit, we find
many little matters claiming our notice. All the
early preachers of the Pocock school, whether belonging to the Wesleyan or any other body, had difficulties of a most trying and disheartening nature to con-

tend against. There was an earnestness about all their work which contrasted strongly with the supineness and inactivity of the ordinary ministers of religion—a supineness and inactivity that shewed sparks of vitality only when it felt itself in danger of being called to action instead of to a deeper lethargic sleep. There was a warmth about their whole proceedings which caused them to be looked upon and denounced as fanatics. There was a vigour and unreserve in their denunciation of the popular vices of the day which at once arrayed against them all the many vested interests of wrong and evil. By many of the clergy, especially by those who had been false to their own work, they were looked upon as interlopers ; by many of the upper classes they were looked upon as disturbers of the public peace. By the lower orders they were looked upon as marks to throw mud and filth at, and many, we are informed, were the scenes of outrage and profanity that were witnessed in Swindon and the neighbouring places in those early days of Methodism and itinerant preaching. But there were others who not only welcomed the visits of men like Mr. Pocock, but who openly and readily allied themselves to their cause. This was the case at Swindon, where Mr. Noad, of Lower Town, and Mr. Edwards, of Eastcott, at a very early period, identified themselves with the new cause, and for many years before the erection of a Wesleyan Chapel, services were held at the house of Mr. Noad—the house now occupied by his daughter, Mrs. Tarrant, at Lower Town. And it was in this way that Methodism was first enabled to establish itself. At Hodson, a Mr. Thomas Wheeler allowed his house to be used for preaching purposes. Mr. Wheeler appears to have been a most earnest worker in the cause of Methodism. Having married his wife from Newbury, he had thereby become directly acquainted with the

Wesleyans belonging to that circuit, many of whom, at his invitation, occasionally visited Hodson for preaching purposes. But the annoyance consequent upon holding religious services at a private house, through the ill-conduct of the idlers of the village, was so great that it was determined to erect a public place for worship, and the Hodson chapel, the oldest Wesleyan chapel in the neighbourhood, was erected in the year 1800. But before this a "society" had been formed at Wanborough, in which village preaching was carried on in a soap-boiling room, belonging to a Mr. Thomas Smith. We are not acquainted with the extent of Mr. Smith's business, but those who only know the village of Wanborough, as it now exists, would never dream that there was ever enough enterprise there to carry on even so trifling a branch of commercial industry as soap-boiling ; yet it was in this same village that we first saw a loom, and watched the working to and fro of a shuttle, and, rude and slow going as this old machine was, neither the cotton palaces of Manchester, nor the marvels of the mechanics' art, with which they are crowded, have ever driven it from our recollection. The rude, rough wits of the last century used to turn the fact of the meetings being held in the soap-boiling room to good account. Their standing joke was that before every meeting night the boards, tables, &c., used in the soap-boiling business, were made to form one long inclined plane ; that every new candidate for admission into the society was placed standing on the highest and most slippery spot of this plane ; a certain ceremony was then gone through, during which, if the candidate succeeded in keeping his or her perpendicular without slipping, assistance, or support, he or she was pronounced ' fit,' and at once admitted into the society. Should, however, the candidate be unfortunate enough to slip, he or she was pronounced

as not being fit, and was summarily discarded, or sent
on probation, according to the amount of discomfort
exhibited on the soapy boards.   This, we say, was
the standing joke, and whenever there were a few
assembled together within the building, there was
sure to be a large concourse assembled outside, with
eyes peering through cracks and crevices in the old
window shutters, or with ears all intent for some
thumping proof of backsliding, or unfitness, waiting
to put the truth of the joke to its proof.   But meeting in private houses for divine worship and prayer,
subjected those who thus dared to BREAK THE LAW
to something more than contumely and insult ;
it subjected them to penalties and persecution
of the most violent and objectionable character.   We
find a remarkable proof of this recorded in the
memoir of Mr. Thomas Bush, of Lambourne, a
gentleman, who, born on the 8th of October, 1768,
at Letcomb, near Wantage, became in after life one
of the warmest supporters of Methodism, and who
exercised an almost unlimited influence in the establishment of the Hungerford and Swindon circuits,
and over the various congregations formed therein.
Some time about the year 1806, Mr. Bush first attended a Methodist chapel, and soon after that event
he commenced his labours as a class reader, school
superintendent, and preacher.   Being a man of some
property, unmarried, and an only child, he appears to
have devoted the larger portion of his life and his
means to the spread of Methodism.   It is recorded of
him that about the year 1820, when standing on
White Horse Hill, with his eyes wandering over the
glorious vale below, he made a solemn vow to devote
his time and his wealth to the spread of Methodism
in the district known as the Vale.   The occurrence is
thus recorded by Mr. Bush in his diary, with the
intent, no doubt, that it should act as a reminder

to him of the work he had undertaken, should he ever be tempted to forsake it in after years :—

On White Horse Hill I solemnly and unalienably made an entire surrender of body, soul, substance, time, influence, and talent of every kind, to Thee, as my Triune God, Father, Son, and Spirit ; and I took that whole district as my special vineyard.

In another part of the diary we find the following :—

I will lay out my yearly income faithfully for Thee—if not in the same year, yet uprightfully and faithfully. And if Thou sparest me to pursue the great work in the Vale of White Horse, I will plant the Gospel, and erect Preaching Houses, and settle them on the conference plan without selfish reserves. I will not lend my *yearly income* on interest, but will honestly lay it up for the cause of God. O make me as a child of eternity while in time. O, in sovereign mercy, give me to go through the world under the influence of special power from Thee. May I be raised above the influence of all sensual desires and pursuits. O give me to feel that I am ordained, called, qualified, and redeemed by Thee, for special service both in the church and in the world. O give me to live in this holy atmosphere at all times, and in all places and companies, in all humility of mind, and gracious, soul-humbling, soul-transforming feeling, for Jesus Christ's sake, for Thy name's sake, and for Thy own glory. O restore my voice again—Lord heal me, I beseech Thee, for these great and holy ends ! O let nothing incapacitate me for Thy service.

My Chapels shall be settled so that the surplus income go to support the regular ministry in the circuit.

The chapels at Swindon, Wantage, Faringdon, and other places, show how this vow was kept. But we have now rather to do with times before any of these chapels were built : to the times when the meeting under the domestic roof of some friend was the most that could be looked for, and even this indulgence oftentimes cost them very dear, there being many instances recorded of people living in the neighbourhood of Wantage and Lambourne being summoned before the magistrates to answer charges for permitting and conducting Divine worship in unlicensed places. This persecution was carried on with more zeal than discretion, for we learn at page 38 of Mr. Bush's Memoirs that

In September, 1810. an uninhabited house, belonging to William Kent, of Childrey, forming part of the present Chapel, was licensed for worship. On Sunday, October 14th, John Bush, the con stable, was sent by the Clergyman to demand the license. William Kent desired him to inform the Clergyman that if he would call upon him the day following, he should then see the license. The Clergyman called and the license was shown.

Again we are told that

Another expedient was tried. The house was licensed,— perhaps the preacher licensed,—but were the people licensed to pray? Service was usually held on a Sunday afternoon, when a sermon was preached, and there was a public prayer meeting in the evening. On Sunday, October 21st, 1810, they were assembled for prayer as usual. Lawrence Belcher, Margaret Partridge, the Clergyman's servant, and John Bush, the constable, were present. They knelt not with the rest, but stood during the service. Several engaged in prayer : among others William Kent and William Franklyn. These were both, on the evidence of Lawrence Belcher and Margaret Partridge, indicted for " praying or teaching," under a persecuting act of Charles II.

This act was made in 1670, by an unprincipled monarch, persecuting bishops, and a venial Parliament ; to silence the best men, and best ministers in the kingdom, and in the world. Baxter thought that some of its enactments had special reference to himself. Two thousand of the excellent men had in August, 1663, to leave their livings in the Church of England, and expose themselves to poverty, scorn, and persecution, for conscience sake Among those were Baxter, Howe, Manton, and many others—men who lived in troublous times—who in some things made mistakes,—but men of giant minds, of high and holy principle, whose writings contain the richest theology of any age since the Apostles, and whose works will be read, and their names revered, as long as the English language is known, and God has a Church upon earth. The statute referred to, enacted that all who should 'preach or pray otherwise than according to the Liturgy of the Church of England' in any company exceeding five persons, should be fined twenty pounds, and that all who attended such a service should be fined five shillings. The statute had been modified by the Tolera- tion Act, passed in the reign of William III. with reference to all licensed *to preach*,·—but who thought it necessary to be licensed *to pray* in a prayer meeting? It was further modified in 1812.

This statute was now drawn forth from its well merited obscurity, to crush the infant church. On Tuesday, the 23rd October, information was laid before W. H. Price, Esq. On Saturday, the 27th, the case was heard, and William Kent and William Franklyn were fined in twenty pounds each, for *praying*. Kent refused to pay the fine. The act required that his goods should be seized.

The Preachers who visited Childrey generally came from a con- siderable distance. A horse belonging to William Kent was frequently sent to meet the preacher, and was in consequence called 'the Gospel horse.' This horse was taken. Kent could not bear to part with his horse. The horse was bought back for twenty-five pounds, out of which the fine and expenses were deducted. Long after did the Gospel horse continue to perform his work.

William Kent appealed to the sessions, held at Reading, but without success. It was urged that praying was not preaching or teaching, as intended by the law. Still the jury decided that praying was preaching or teaching, and for teaching the law required him to be fined twenty pounds. A further appeal was made to the Court of King's Bench, where the proceedings were quashed, and the money returned.

Thus ended an attempt on the part of a minister of religion to prevent a few simple people from praying.

Thus it was that they whom we follow, and the richness of whose lives and labours we enjoy, had to kick against the pricks at every step they took. Thus it was that that liberty which we sometimes see sold for less than even a mess of pottage—sold because of a craven, coward fear of giving displeasure or offence —was fought for and won.

Mr. Bush appears to have had a great liking, if not a weakness, for making vows. On the 11th of March every year he was in the habit of renewing his vow to evangelise the Vale, the details of each vow being duly reduced to writing, and formally signed and sealed. But he was also in the habit of being true to his vow. He had an unreserved belief in the power of Methodism to carry out the work he had at heart. He therefore worked fearlessly and unselfishly for its establishment and progress. The church in whose cause such a man laboured, with all his heart and soul, may possess not a single charm for us : we may fail to go with him on any point of doctrine ; but it is next to impossible for there to be an event in such a man's life that does not at once command our attention and respect.

By about the year 1813 those persons who had been in the habit of meeting for Divine worship at the house of Mr. Noad, ventured to build the old Wesleyan Chapel (recently removed for the erection of the present structure) ; but their hearts being

2 C

bigger than their pockets, they overstepped the constable, and for something like ten years had to encounter most serious financial difficulties. At length, in 1824, it was contemplated to give up the cause, and sell the property, but Mr. Bush came nobly to the rescue, and, in addition to paying off the debt on the chapel, built two cottages adjoining, one of which was intended as a minister's residence. The whole of the property was made over to trustees, and so securely was the property made part and parcel of Methodism that some few years since, when it was proposed to sell the chapel and cottages and appropriate the proceeds towards the building of a new chapel in a more eligible situation, it was found that no practical alienation of the property from the Wesleyan body could be effected.

In 1814 a preacher was, for the first time, appointed for Swindon by Conference; but both he and his successors, for a very long time, must have had a very poor time of it, as will appear from certain entries in the society's books. Take, for instance, the following extracts.

At the first quarterly meeting, held October, 1817, the following little bill was discussed :—

Mr. Redford's Quarterage and travelling expenses...						£5	0	0
Washing	...	...	...	...	...	...	0	17	0
Letters and stationery...		...	...	...	...	0	10	6
Board Money, from August 10 to September 28, at								
10s. 6d. per week	...	...	...	...	3	13	6
						£10	1	0

N.B —In order to meet the above expenses the members assembled in Quarterly meeting subscribed among themselves 18s. 6d.

In March, 1818, such was the financial condition of the Swindon Wesleyans, that, at the Quarterly meeting, the following resolutions were passed :—

First.—That the Conference be requested to take into consideration the distressing case of Swindon Chapel, and grant permission to beg through three or four opulent circuits for its relief.

Second.—That the Conference be requested to send a young unmarried preacher to this circuit next year, as there is no provision for the residence of a married man, and no means to raise his Board, in consequence of the extreme poverty of the people.

In order to keep up the spirit of the Itinerancy, a change was appointed every six weeks between the Swindon preacher and one of the ministers from Hungerford. This plan is still in operation in solitary or single minister circuits. When this intercommunication between two adjoining circuits was first proposed, the Circuit Stewards were alarmed lest it should add to their liabilities, and we therefore find recorded in their proceedings the following :—

Dec. 1828 —It hath been said that Mr. Dod's change with Mr. Ash is to accommodate Swindon Circuit. We do not know that it wou d be any accommodation, and have no money to spend in the change.

Isaac Archer,
Thos. Bedford,} Circuit Stewards.

The request that Conference would send only a single man to Swindon was observed for several succeeding years; but at length a married man was sent, and amongst the names of those early ministers occur those of several who afterwards attained to a high position in the Wesleyan connexion. The circuit continued with one regular minister only, until the year 1835, when Mr. Bush, having built a chapel at Faringdon, a single man was appointed by Conference to live at Faringdon, and assist the Superintendent at Swindon in the management of the circuit.

Mr. James Murray, of Hodson, the oldest local preacher in the circuit, writing in reply to some questions we addressed to him, says :—"When I joined the society in 1823 the circuit contained only six chapels and two preaching places. The persecution we encountered was limited only by the inability of parties to carry it farther.

"Both myself and others have known what it was to want for everything but bread and tea. Peltings from the people and threats from the rich and opulent was the common lot of us all. But nothing could move the people from their stedfastness, or stop their making progress. At that time the number of members at Hodson was seven ; we have now three times that number. There were only two Sunday schools in the circuit ; there are now eleven, with their hundreds of children ; and the six chapels have increased to eighteen. Then there was not a local preacher in the circuit, supplies being obtained by men walking from Lambourne, Ramsbury, Shefford Woodlands, and Marlborough ; now there are twenty-four local preachers, and four on trial, in addition to the three ministers appointed by Conference."

[These remarks, it must be remembered, were made in, and apply to, the year 1867. In 1884 there were 26 chapels and preaching places in the Swindon Circuit; 1073 church members ; and no less than 56 local preachers].

Relative to the persecuting spirit alluded to by Mr. Murray, Mrs. Tarrant says she has often heard her father say that the gentry of the town used to make very particular enquiries as to who attended these early religious services, and when it so happened that the name of a tradesman with whom the party dealt was given, a peremptory demand was made for "My little bill."

As a pleasing contrast to some of the extracts we have quoted from the circuit records, shewing the poverty of the people in the early days, we may briefly state that in 1862 the Swindon chapel, relieved from debt by Mr. Bush in 1824, was pulled down and rebuilt at a cost of something like £1,200, and that at the present time it is in contemplation to build a

second chapel at New Swindon, at a cost of something like £2,500, and capable of seating 1,600
persons on the ground floor ; there being in addition
to this accommodation a gallery capable of accom-
modating from two to three hundred more.   In this
chapel, as well as the one at Old Swindon, there is a
very fine organ.

Mr. Bush's name being so intimately connected
with the Methodism of the neighbourhood, we conclude our hasty sketch by noticing briefly how he
kept his chapel-building vow.   In 1824, he relieved
the Swindon chapel from debt, and a forced sale.
In 1830 he built a chapel at West Hendred.   In 1831
he bought a chapel at Childrey.   In 1835 he built a
chapel at Lambourne.   In 1837 he built a chapel at
Faringdon.   In 1842 he built chapels at Highworth
and Longcot, and in 1844 he rebuilt a chapel at
Wantage, at a cost of over £500.   His last public
appearance at the opening of a chapel, towards the
erection of which he contributed £60, was in his
native village, Letcomb Regis.   He is said to have
given away every year at least £500 out of an
income of £700.   He died on Tuesday, November
2nd, 1847, and by his will he left £100 to the Bible
Society, £100 to the Wesleyan Missionary Society,
and £300 to other Connexional funds.   Claims on
chapels, to a considerable amount, were cancelled.
Ten pounds per annum he left to the Day School.
Provision was made for his housekeeper and man,
with a small legacy to the maid-servant.   Various
other legacies were left, varying from £100 to
£1,000 each.

We may have much, little, or no sympathy with
the peculiar religious views of Mr. Bush, but we must
be dullards, indeed, if we do not see that there is something in the life of such a man higher and truer than
mere religious belief, or a bowing down to creeds.

There was an unselfish determination to show forth what light and truth he had. He was a determined worker against all he believed to be evil and wrong. He does not appear to have speculated upon the result of a thing before attempting to accomplish it. " If the thing be right, then accomplish it at any cost," appears to have been his motto. And to men so constituted England owes much of her greatness.

As we have already seen, the Swindon circuit was formed in the year 1817. The present year would, therefore, bring the circuit to its fiftieth anniversary, or jubilee. The Centenary year of Methodism was celebrated in 1839. As a body, the Wesleyans are proverbial for their making much of anniversaries. A " little" debt on a chapel is no eyesore to them ; it furnishes them with fuel for a good warming up at an anniversary. The Centenary year was a Godsend to them. They collected something like £250,000 (two hundred and fifty thousand pounds) that year. This money was spent in the building of chapels, colleges, schools, &c. A pretty little corner-stone was laid that year on which to built the Methodism of the ensuing century. In the first century a somewhat noble structure had been built. In 1839 they commenced to add a wing to that building. That wing may be a dwarf by the side of a giant, or it may overtop the old structure just in proportion as Wesleyans are true to the spirit of Wesley—just in proportion as Methodists are strictly methodical in their determination to support truth, honesty, and integrity of purpose under all circumstances and at all times.

Can we be surprised to learn that anniversary-loving Wesleyans should determine not to lose the chance of celebrating a jubilee? The fifty years were about up on Saturday last, but long before that day preparations were made for celebrating the jubilee. We append the programme :—

On Sunday, June 30th, 1867, sermons will be preached as follows :
Swindon—Morning, Rev. J. B. Blanch ; evening, Rev. Henry Powis

Swindon New Town—Morning, Rev. Henry Powis ; evening, Rev. Joseph B. Blanch.

Hodson (in a marquee)—Afternoon, at half-past two, Rev. Joseph B. Blanch ; evening. Rev. C. Hillard.

Faringdon—Morning and evening, Rev. J. Peet.

Wootton Bassett—Messrs. S. Brown and W. Ellis. And all other places in the circuit, according to the plan.

On Monday, July 1st, the following services will be held, by kind permission, in a field at Hodson, under a spacious marquee :—At half-past two, a sermon by Rev. H Powis ; a tea meeting at half-past four, after which a public meeting will be held ; chair to be taken by W. Mewburn, Esq., of Wykham Park. The meeting will be addressed by the Revs. Henry Powis, J. B. Blanch, the ministers of the circuit, and other gentlemen.

We need hardly say more than that the programme was strictly observed and carried out. The principal attraction, however, was the public meeting at Hodson on the Monday. The tent was pitched on a spot surrounded by some of the most lovely scenery to be found in the neighbourhood. But we have no room for even an attempt to describe it. Next to the pleasure of spending an hour on such a spot is that of having to describe it. After some 750 persons had taken tea in a somewhat original and novel manner, the company dispersed—some to form singing parties, others to drink in the beautiful natural scenes (for there was a regular panorama of them) before them. At half-past six, there being a thousand present in the tent, the Rev. C. Hillard, in moving that the chair be taken by Mr. Mewburn, gave an interesting account of the present state of Methodism in the Swindon circuit." Like the Israelites of old, his (Mr. Hillard's) hearers could remember times of judgment as well as of mercy, times of sorrow as well as of joy, times of persecution and division as well as of peace, unity, and prosperity. God had done wonderful things for His chosen people, and Christians of these days could sympathise spiritually in all her vicissitudes. As of

old, He had sent His servants amongst them. He had
sent into this circuit some of the best and holiest of
men. To say nothing of the living—as, for instance,
the Ven. and Right Rev. Henry Powis (who was
present), and John Geden (who was absent), this circuit had been favoured with such men as Thomas
Eckersley, John Radford, Joseph Pratton, Daniel
Osborne, Elias Thomas, James Hopewell, James
Burley, James Ray, J. M. Joll, and Zepheniah Job—
all of whom had passed away to their reward. In
looking upon the past, they could say, with God's
ancient people, 'The Lord hath done great things for
us.' The history of the circuit might be divided into
two periods—the first period consisting of the first
twenty-five years, the second of the other half of the
fifty now ended. During the first twenty-five years of
the existence of this circuit, Swindon and its neighbourhood appeared to have been a poor and unproduc-
tive soil for the propagation of Wesleyanism. At the
close of the first period there were about 150 members
of the society, and eight preaching places—the increase being sixty members and one preaching place
in twenty-five years. From the commencement of the
second period, however, the circuit steadily advanced
in membership, in preaching places, and in finance.
They had now nineteen preaching places on the plan.
There were two causes apart from the blessing of God
that might be assigned for this. About the time
referred to the late Thomas Bush, Esq., of Lambourne,
began to take a warm interest in the spiritual welfare
of the people in this neighbourhood.

"He built Faringdon chapel, and gave it to the
connexion, so that a chapel existed there before a
methodist sermon was preached or a member admitted. For many years afterwards he regularly
and materially assisted this circuit financially; and,
humanly speaking, things could hardly have been as

they are now had it not been for that excellent man. Another apparent cause of progress had been the establishment at Swindon of the works of the Great Western Railway—by which scores of acres of mere pasture land had been taken into the busy hive of human industry. New Swindon had risen in a few years as if by magic. He (the speaker) was not a very old man, and when he passed the place first there was scarcely a house to be seen. Old Swindon, from a quiet village, had developed into a respectable town ; and the neighbourhood, once purely agricultural, and very sparsely inhabited, had been occupied by a mechanical population. So that the circuit, as he had said before, had steadily advanced in membership. People had been directed towards this new centre of industry from all parts of the kingdom, many of them being already members. Many more, through the preaching of the gospel, had become members : and the number, instead of being 150, was now 550—notwithstanding the numerous losses by death, removal, and backsliding. From these causes the circuit had lost, during the past year, 65 members. During the past twenty-five years, hundreds, if not thousands of souls, had been converted in this circuit, many of whom had gone to heaven ; and, if but one soul had been saved, it would have been worth all the effort that had been put forth. At the present time the circuit was in a very encouraging state. The great want was a more copious out-pouring of the Holy Spirit—they wanted a repetition of Pentecost. In reference to chapels in the circuit, they were in almost every part straitened for chapel accommodation ; and everywhere chapels were inconveniently crowded. The small chapels erected at Broad Town and Purton were crammed every Sunday, and he had some difficulty in preventing the friends in such places from extending their borders. He invariably told them to get money first, and then he should not have the slightest objection. And there was the great mammoth efforts for New Swindon, which, by the way, was keeping all other causes in *statu quo*. So the sooner the New Swindon chapel was open the better would it be for New Swindon and the circuit at large. He was glad to be there on such an occasion as the present. He would rejoice to see this jubilee celebration turned, to spiritual account. The old Mosaic law prescribed liberty to the bondsmen and the debtor, and he would rejoice at this jubilee, to see the bondsmen of sin and satan brought into the glorious liberty wherewith Christ makes his people free. He thought it would be a good thing, also, if all the chapel debts could be removed—thus relieving the trustees of their responsibilities in that respect."

The meeting was subsequently addressed by W. Mewburn, Esq., by the Rev. J. B. Blanch, by Mr. James Murray—who had to stand corrected, amid much laughter, on a matter of names and dates by *Mrs.* Murray, or rather, as Mr. Murray, by way of retort put it, " by that young woman there, on whose finger I put a hoop in the year 1823 "—by the Rev. H. Powis, who was stationed as a Wesleyan minister at Hungerford in 1825, by Mr. W. Ellis, of New Swindon, and by Mr. J. H. Mason, of Newbury. The customary votes of thanks having been passed, the meeting broke up, and the company, many of whom had come from long distances, began to disperse.

This, then, is another Chapter in the History of Nonconformity in Swindon, which I wrote and published on July 8th, 1867. I am not aware that any material addition or alteration can be made to it. Mr. James Murray is still alive, hale and hearty, at the great age of 85, and his name is still on the Wesleyan " Plan," occupying that honoured place where it has

been between fifty and sixty years : first on the list of
"Local" preachers.   The chapel built in 1862, at a
cost of £1,200, on the site of the old chapel of 1813,
has been altogether discarded by the Wesleyans.   A
way having been found out of the difficulties which
surrounded the sale of the property, it was for a time
converted into stables in connection with a horse
dealers' sale yard ; after which the tenancy passed
over to General Booth, whose army now occupy it.
In the meantime the Wesleyans removed to Bath
Road, in May, 1880, where they had erected a new
chapel at a cost of £6,000.   This chapel, which is a
particularly handsome structure, and both externally
and internally contains some of the best masonry and
carpenters' work to be met with in the district, was
built by Mr. Thomas Barrett, from designs by Messrs.
Bromilow and Cheers, of Liverpool.   Beneath the
chapel, which is capable of seating 800 persons, and
is furnished with a fine organ, there is a basement
floor, used as school and class rooms, and for public
meetings and other purposes.   At New Swindon also
great changes have taken place in the matter of
chapel accommodation.   The chapel, opened on May
26th, 1869, on the south-side of Fleet Street, was sold
and converted into business premises, and a large
block of buildings originally intended by the Great
Western Railway Company for a Model Workman's
dwelling, was converted into a chapel, from designs by
Mr. T. S. Lansdown, of Swindon, capable of accom-
modating 1,100 persons, and the hope of Mr. Hillard,
as expressed at the Hodson Jubilee Meeting, thereby
realised.   In addition to the chapel, there are extensive school and class-rooms in connection therewith.

—Pioneers*of*Nonconformity—

+THE+PRIMITIVE+METHODISTS.+

ANOTHER chapter in Nonconformity is supplied by the history of the Brinkworth Circuit of the Primitive Methodist body, which, at the present time, has chapels both in Old and New Swindon, as well as in all the neighbouring towns and villages. As in the case of the Wesleyan Methodists, so also in that of the Primitives, I am enabled to go back to reports of proceedings in which I have sketched the local history of these bodies, and which I prefer to reproduce, rather than re-write; for it is somewhat remarkable that, although, no doubt, both bodies have been carrying on a great and important work within recent years, the only really notable features in their histories, especially to outsiders, is connected with their early labours; when, in fact, they were opposed, tooth and nail, and when they had practically to fight for their liberty. In the *Swindon Advertiser* for May 29th, 1876, I wrote as follows in connection with the opening of the newly re-built chapel in Regent Street, there being at that time quite a crowd of political adventurers who were thrusting themselves before the inhabitants in the hope of being selected as candidates for representing the Borough and Hundreds in Parliament, and who were ready to lay a foundation stone, or even a brick, for a church or chapel, or preside at a public meeting or tea fight, or fetch or carry anything they were told, so that they might have a chance to ingratiate themselves into the good opinion of the people :—

"On the occasion of the laying of the foundation stone of a new Primitive Methodist Chapel, in Prospect, Old Swindon, in September, 1870, we gave a short sketch of the rise and progress of the Connexion in this neighbourhood, and, at the suggestion of friends whose opinions we respect, we re-publish what we then wrote. We then said :—

' " The history of the Brinkworth, as well as of many another district, of the Primitive Methodist connexion, has been a very chequered one. Although the founders of the society commenced their labours early in the present century, it was not until something about the year 1825 that their missionaries had succeeded in penetrating into this part of the country, and for many years after that date the scenes to be witnessed at many of their services were of the most disgraceful and disorderly character. The society had its birth-place in one of the Staffordshire colliery districts, and for a long time its ministers and leading supporters were found among the poorest and least educated classes. Men like these springing up and proclaiming their mission to evangelize their country, naturally excited the contempt of some, and the ridicule of others, whilst the class whom the society more particularly strove to bring within its fold met the attempt with blasphemy and riot rather than with simple indifference. Some of the early religious services of the body then, in our rural districts, were scenes of the wildest disorder, and there can be no doubt but that some of these scenes, if not instigated, were encouraged by those whose mission it was to do the work the strangers were professing to do, but who had been false to their mission. Whilst then it must be admitted that the preachers were men who could not either by their language or manners charm the fastidious with harmonious periods, and smoothly flowing diction, it was beyond question that some of the early leaders of the society in this district proved to be men whose characters would not bear strict investigation, and who by their conduct brought disgrace upon themselves, and retarded the work of others.

' " The first attempt to establish a mission in this part of the country appears to have been made at Cirencester, in the year 1824. But the opposition was so great that the attempt was abandoned. About this time the village feast was in its glory of riot, blackguardism and blasphemy, and the society's missionaries appear to have selected such occasions for inaugurating their work in a village. There was, no doubt, great moral courage displayed on such occasions, but little real good done. The Cirencester mission having been given up, in the following year Brinkworth was visited. It is said of this village that at this time it contained so many of the vilest characters that for years it had been deemed perilous for a stranger to ride through the village alone. The clergyman, who was a magistrate, offered the most determined opposition to the new comers. The missionaries, however, persevered in their labours, and it was not long before they succeeded in winning the support of the leading farmers and others of the village and neighbourhood. A society having been established in the village in the year 1826, five travelling ministers were appointed to it at the following conference—the circuit including the towns of Malmesbury, Chippenham, Wootton Bassett, Swindon, Cricklade, Cirencester, Calne, Devizes, and all the intermediate villages and country. The lives these missionaries had to lead may be gathered from the fact that at Cricklade, where they met with unusual success, they could seldom go out into the streets on their ordinary business without being pelted with stones. Generally, however, the mission was a success; so much so, that by March, 1828, the circuit numbered 500 members—forty of whom, we are told, were local preachers and exhorters. In a pecuniary sense, also, the mission was a success; the profits on the hymn books and magazines sold, not only paying the cost of four travelling preachers, but leaving a surplus for transmission to the central conference. The first chapel in the circuit appears to have been built at Seagry, the services in the circuit generally being conducted in some cottage, barn, or other place, placed at the disposal of the society by friends of the cause. Services in the public streets and thoroughfares were also frequently resorted to, and it was here that some of the most disorderly scenes were to be witnessed. The chapel at Seagry was followed by another at Broad Town, where some of the leading farmers had early become members of the society, including the Woodward's and the Miles'. A third chapel was built at Clack, and within two years of the time when the Brinkworth circuit was first established, a fourth chapel was built, this time at Brinkworth. Facts like these show the stuff the pioneers of the cause in this district were made of. At Wootton Bassett, which was afterwards to become the stronghold of the society in the district, the work of the missionaries was most trying. It appears that an unusual effort was made to establish the cause in this place on the occasion of holding the annual feast,

when the public street was disgraced by "backswording," and other barbarous sports common to the
neighbourhood at that time, and a fearful disturbance
was the result. The Missionary was taken before his
Worship, the Mayor, but on being released re-com-
menced his preaching. At this time, it appears, there
was no place of meeting except in the streets of the
town ; but shortly after this memorable occasion, a
long room, connected with one of the public houses
of the town, was taken for the purpose of public
worship ; and subsequently a regular chapel was built
As in many other places in the circuit, this chapel
has been more than once enlarged, until it has become one of the leading features of the town. At
several places,—at Wootton Bassett and Broad Town
in particular,—excellent schools have been established
in connexion with the cause, and there can be no
doubt but that by indomitable perseverance the
society has become a power in the district in which it
is located.

   ' "At Swindon, in these early days, the progress
of the cause was much less marked. For many years
the connexion had no regular place of meeting, the
cottages of some labouring men living at Eastcott
being the only available places, the services being
held at irregular intervals. Nor were these services
permitted to be conducted in peace or order. Thirty,
or five-and-thirty years ago, the small room in which
the service was about to be held was not unfrequently
filled by a crowd of disorderly lads, who availed themselves of every opportunity to worry the speakers and
disturb the proceedings. At this time, also, there can
be no doubt but that many of even the leading men
and women who took part in these services were
something more than untaught, and their illustrations
and quaint expressions, afforded ample room for the
ridicule and fun of the thoughtless and the idle. We

remember Hugh Bourne visiting Eastcott, and holding services in the house then occupied by Mr. Thomas Edwards. This visit of one of the leading men of the connexion to the place drew together a congregation from far and near, and a scene of the most indescribable confusion was the result. The small room in which the services were held was crowded to suffocation by persons standing, whilst outside the crowd was equally densely packed. The excitement was intense; the gesticulation of the speaker, the shouts and cries of the worshippers, the fainting of several women, and the rude remarks and horse-play of the mob made up a scene never to be forgotten. Some time after this Mr. Edwards became the owner of a field through which Regent Street now runs, and agreeably with a long-made promise, he gave up to the connexion a plot of his newly acquired possessions for the erection of a chapel. Funds being forthcoming, the building was erected and opened for the services of the connexion in the year 1848. The cause prospering, the chapel was enlarged in 1863, since which time there has been a further and steady increase in the number of society members. In addition to New Swindon, services for some years past have been held at Old Swindon, in a room having an entrance from Albert Street. But this room being small and inconvenient, a plot of ground was some years since secured in Prospect, on which the new chapel is now in course of erection.

"Since this period (1870) the cause of the society has gone on prospering, so that now, in 1876, the chapel at New Swindon has not only been found to be far too small, but a new and far more commodious building has been erected in its stead, and on Wednesday last was opened for Divine service with remarkable success. In fact, we think we are quite justified in congratulating the representatives of that

small and despised body of men and women who less
than fifty years ago met together in each other's
cottages, almost as fugitives and outcasts, to worship
God after their own fashion, with possessing, if not
the largest, certainly the neatest and best arranged
chapel in either Old or New Swindon, erected on the
ground originally given by Mr. Edwards, and every
inch of which is now covered by a building estimated
to cost £2,000.   [It will, of course, be recollected that
this was written before either the Wesleyan Chapel,
on the Bath Road, Old Swindon, or the Wesleyan
Chapel, on Faringdon Street, New Swindon, were
erected.]   In appearance the new chapel is neat
and effective, the chief drawback being its situation
immediately upon the road.   Externally, the building
is of brick, with Bath stone quoins and dressings,
with a somewhat massive pediment, which, however,
tallies well with the basement, where three flights of
stone steps lead to a central and two end platforms,
from which access to three entrance doors is obtained,
leading into the chapel ; the chapel proper being
situate over a basement floor, which is fitted up as a
schoolroom   At the back of the chapel there are
several smaller rooms, both up and down stairs, to be
used as a vestry, class rooms, &c., which, no doubt,
will be found very convenient and useful.   The chapel
itself is a singularly neat and well-designed building,
and appears fully to meet all the requirements for
which it was designed, and reflects much credit on
the architect, Mr. Baker, who has not only made the
most possible of all the space, but has in no instance
sacrificed ease and effect to mere convenience.   The
chapel is designed to accommodate 600 persons, there
being in addition to the ground floor a well pitched
and effectively arranged gallery along the two sides
and the end opposite the platform and desk, which
takes the place of the old tub or pulpit, in which the

minister formerly had to stand. The body of the room is lighted by three star-light pendants from the roof, other gas burners being distributed over the building. Unfortunately, the building was not sufficiently finished on the opening day to be seen at its best advantage, and we are therefore precluded from reference to it in the way in which we feel it to be entitled, and which, in a few weeks, when it is fully completed, will be made apparent. As it was seen on Wednesday, then, it promises to become, by the time the builders and decorators have done with it, one of the prettiest and best arranged public buildings we have in Swindon. The contractors were Messrs. G. Wiltshire and Son, who have carried out the work in a most substantial and satisfactory manner.

" The first service in connection with the opening ceremony, on Wednesday, was at three o'clock in the afternoon, when a sermon was preached by the Rev. J. Macpherson (connexional editor of the Primitive Methodist body) before a large congregation, which well filled the building, from the text, 'Whom not having seen, ye love ; in whom, though now ye see him not, yet believing, ye rejoice with joy unspeakable and full of glory.' From these words the rev. gentleman preached an eloquent and effective sermon on the manly character of Christ. There was an entire absence of any attempt at doctrinal illustrations, or mere theological teaching, Christ being held up and glorified as the most perfect man who ever lived on earth. There was, perhaps, one point only in his discourse which might be deemed controversial, and it was when he left Christ as a man and spoke of him as God, and his title to be spoken of in that character he proved in this wise : God is good, quoting Christ's words to show that there is no other entitled to that character. Christ also was good, and therefore he was God.

" At the close of the service a collection was made towards the building fund, when the sum of £10 was realised ; after which the company repaired to the school-room and the Peoples Hall, where tea was provided, after which the Rev. T. Pinnock, the pastor of the chapel, after eulogising the successful and in every respect satisfactory efforts of the architect and builder of the edifice in which they were assembled, —adding that the latter had promised them a beautiful font for baptismal services,—read the financial report, which showed that the original con-tract was £1,600, which, with extras, architect's fees, hire of other buildings, &c., was raised in round numbers, to £2,000. In hand there were £400 10s ; the afternoon collection of £10 14s ; profits of tea, about £20 ; third instalment promise, £13 ; and the estimated collection at that evening's service, £25, which, with promises of £200, would bring up the money balance to £1,000—or one half of the debt at the first anniversary of the building. This might not seem much to those who possessed plenty, but he assured them that the result had not been achieved without strenuous efforts and great sacrifices. Indeed, one of the local preachers of the chapel ate his bread and vegetables without meat, in order (by appropriat-ing his ' meat money ') to contribute his subscription to the chapel fund at the first anniversary ; while another had systematically—being a Methodist—put aside his 3s per week in order to fulfil his promise of a donation of £5. The members of the chapel, he confessed, were poor ; but they were hard-working and self-sacrificing, and so much deserved out-side help."

Since 1876 the Primitive Methodists have built two chapels in the Swindon district, one in Clifton Street and one at Even Swindon, and have acquired another at Wanborough. They have also built a new and handsome chapel at Lower Stratton in addition to the one previously existing there, and the Society may be said to be generally making progress both in Swindon and the neighbourhood. The number of members in the district may be put at about 2,000, with the Rev. J. Herridge as superintendent, and Rev. J. Sheppard second minister, and 66 local preachers.

The sacrifices made by individual members of the Primitive Methodist body have been undoubtedly always very great. Some one invented for them what I believe was called the "Golden System," by which enormous sums have been realised, first in promises, but afterwards in hard cash. The practice was, at some anniversary or other meeting, called for some special object, to invite and obtain every possible sum of money, and then to send slips of paper about among the audience inviting them to subscribe to a promise to pay a certain sum by—say that time twelve months ; to give, in short, a promissory note for a much larger sum than they could possibly give in cash. As a rule, I believe, these notes were always met at maturity ; the acceptor, in case the amount was larger than he or she could meet out of their own means, never hesitating to beg it from others. It was probably through this "Golden System" that the promises of £200 referred to at the opening of the Regent Street Chapel, and which were obtained, enabled the Society to clear off the handsome sum of £1,000, or one-half the total liabilities by the opening day.

The⁕Swindon⁕Troop⁕of⁕Yeomanry Cavalry.

T can hardly be necessary to point out that the paper on "Yeomanry Cavalry and Night Watchmen" had no claim or pretence to historical accuracy, or, indeed, to absolute literal fact. It was intended simply to revive and relate in an easy and informal manner what may be designated "Old Men's Tales" concerning times and circumstances of a stirring character, and in which the town and neighbourhood were deeply interested fifty years ago. I am glad to be enabled to deal with the Swindon Yeomanry Cavalry, and incidentally, the Wiltshire Regiment, in quite another manner, and to give its history for the first forty years of the present century, from which it will be observed that both the troop and the regiment has seen some real service, and on more than one occasion has earned the thanks of both Houses of Parliament, as well as the highest commendation from the military authorities.

The century appears to have opened with trouble in our villages, and work for our Yeomanry Cavalry

to do ; for the first circumstance I have to note within
the period indicated is a letter addressed by the Vicar
of Purton to the officer in charge of the troop at
Swindon, requesting assistance to quell a riot which
seemed imminent in that parish :—

To WILLIAM HARDING Esq., Swindon.

DEAR SIR,—The principal inhabitants of this place are now with
me, and request me to write to you, and inform you that there are
strong indications of a riotous disposition among their labourers.   They
have this morning refused setting about their work, and have collected
in large number, compelling all their fellows to join them ; towards the
afternoon or evening something serious is apprehended.   Nothing, perhaps, would more effectually restrain them than the appearance of the
Yeomanry Cavalry.   It is, therefore, particularly desired that you will
be so good as to attend here this afternoon with as many of the troop as
can be collected.   If they should disperse in the meantime, notice thereof
will be immediately sent to you

The bearer will explain matters further if necessary.

Yours very sincerely,

J. PROWER.

Purton, 26th May, 1800, Monday morning 11 o'clock.

Lieut. Harding appears to have acted with com-
mendable promptness, for he immediately issued the
following order for the assembling of the Troop :—

To Sergeant BURT.

Swindon, 26th May, 1800.

In consequence of the above letter you are requested to muster the
troop with all possible despatch, and parade at the Nine Elms, near
Purton, precisely at three o'clock, where I will certainly be to take the
command.

WM. HARDING.

N.B.—You will also bring with you some ball cartridges, in case
they should unfortunately be necessary.

Nothing serious appears to have come of this, and
I have been unable to learn that the Troop proceeded
beyond their meeting place at the "Nine Elms" on
their road to Purton. The condition of our poor, however, in the neighbourhood was terrible in the extreme
at this time. The dearness of food during this and
the following year put it practically outside the reach
of the poor, to whom it appears to have been doled
out as charity, in quantities just sufficient to sustain

life.   The years of 1800 and 1801 were years of great
scarcity to the consumer, and of prospertity to the
farmer.   Though the imperial average for wheat in
1800 is quoted at 127s., it fetched some weeks at
Warminster market 144s., and in the following year
the general prices in North Wilts 'were: Flour, 25s. a
bushel ; malt, 15s. a bushel ; hops, 5s. a lb. ; butcher's
meat, 9d. a lb. ; butter, 1s. 3d. a lb. ; cheese, four
guineas a cwt. ; potatoes, 16s. a sack ; onions, a
guinea a sack ; and pigs, 19s. 6d. a score.

The Devizes authorities recognised the seriousness
of the situation at this time by meeting together, and,
under the authority of the Mayor, issued the following series of resolutions :—

> That at this period it is the indispensable duty of every house-
> keeper who has the ability to provide meat and other articles of
> subsistence for his family, to be as economical as possible in the
> consumption of bread and wheat flour, in order that a greater pro-
> portion may be applied for the use of the poor, who have scarcely any
> other food to subsist upon.   And we do therefore agree that the
> consumption of bread shall not exceed the rate of one quartern loaf per
> week for each person in our respective families : and that we will
> abstain from pastry, and carefully restrict the use of flour in any other
> article than bread.
>
> That we will to the utmost of our power adopt and promote
> the use of substitutes for bread, as well as a strict economy in the con-
> sumption of every other article of subsistence.
>
> That we will as far as possible reduce the use of oats and other
> grain for horses, and confine the allowance in all cases to such a
> quantity only as is absolutely necessary for their subsistence.
>
> That these resolutions do continue in force until the first day of
> October, 1801.
>
> That the foregoing resolutions be fairly transcribed and signed
> by the persons now present, and handed to those inhabitants who are
> absent, requesting their signatures : and that the Resolution be also
> printed and circulated in the town and neighbourhood.

After their journey to the " Nine Elms," on May
26th, the troop does not appear to·have met again
until September 23rd, when it assembled for parade
for a field day, as it also did on October 3rd and
17th, at which latter parade there were some resigna-
tions and promotions, preparatory to an inspection, by

order of the commander-in-chief, of Yeomanry, Volunteers, and Associated Corps, at Marlborough, on the 29th and 30th October, by Lieutenant-General Stephens. On the 7th November there was another parade for a field-day, which, it was announced, would be the last for the winter.

From a Return Muster Roll, made the 1st January, 1801, the Swindon Troop at this time consisted of three officers and forty non-commissioned officers and men, as follows :—

Sergt. H. P. Burt, Swindon
  ,,   John Hughes, Broad Hinton
  ,,   William Brown, do.
Corpl. Robert Millington, Winterborne Bassett
  ,,   James Woles, Albourne
  ,,   John Sheppard, Swindon
Trumpeter Bryan Bewley, Liddington
John Tuckey, Winterborne Bassett
Edmund Maskelyne, Chilton
Jasper Maskelyne, Wootton Bassett
John Kent, Wanborough
Peter Dore, Liddiard Tregoze
Richard Watts Read, Purton
Francis King, Liddiard Tregoze
Richard Large, Cleeve Ansty
Richard Evans, Upper Stratton
Stephen Wells, Wanborough
George Lea,   ,,
John Carpenter,   ,,

Thomas Maysey, Swindon
Thomas Short, Wootton Bassett
Robert Smith, Broad Town
Henry Short, Wootton Bassett
William Horsell   ,,
Simon Crook, Flaxlands
John Smith, Wootton Bassett
William Mundey, Cotmarsh
William Packer, Purton
Thomas Butler, Wootton Bassett
Richard Leighfield,   ,,
Wm. Large, Liddiard Millicent
Peter Dore, Stratton St. Margaret
Richard Dore,   ,,
Edward Smith, Wanborough
Rich. Goddard, Esq., Cliffe Pypard
Robert Withers, Haydon
James Washbourn, Water Eaton
James Litton, Haydon
Thomas Prince, Wanborough
Robert Tuckey, Shaw

On the 24th of June following, another Return Muster Roll was prepared, showing the number of non-commissioned officers and men to be 39. And at this time a declaration of the object of the formation of the Troop was made, as follows :—

The above troop have engaged to serve for the suppression of any riot or tumult within the County of Wilts. And in case of actual invasion or the actual appearance of the enemy on an English coast to extend their service within any part of the south-west district.

(Signed)

T. GODDARD, Captain.

In a letter addressed by Lord Hobart to the Lord-Lieutenant of the County of Wilts, in July, 1801, there occurs the following :—

From circumstances which have come to the knowledge of Government, it is apprehended that persons have frequently entered into Volunteer Corps a short time previous to a ballot for the Militia, with a view to avail themselves of the benefit of the Acts of Parliament under which their enrolment in a Volunteer Corps is considered to exempt them from serving or providing a substitute in the Militia, and that as soon as the ballot has taken place, those persons have withdrawn themselves from the Volunteer Corps in which they had entered : Should the information that has been conveyed to Government on this subject be found to be correct, it will be proper that effectual measures should be taken to put a stop to such abuses. With this view, I think it right to suggest to your lordship the expediency of recommending both to the deputy-lieutenants and to the commanding officers of the different corps, to guard as far as may be in their power against this practice, and for this purpose to call their attention to the Act of the 39th year of His present Majesty, cap. 14, and to require a strict observance of the provisions thereof.

In consequence of this communication, and also of a letter received from head-quarters at Winchester, dated 24th July, the Swindon Troop was kept in constant readiness to be "called out," and certain members were appointed specially to summon and collect other members, whose names and addresses were supplied them, for instant duty, so that if there were any who went into the Yeomanry to escape the Militia they found it in the result very much like jumping out of the frying-pan into the fire, for the demand made on their time was somewhat serious, in consequence both of wars abroad and disturbances at home. Happily, however, there came a change. In course of 1802 the price of corn fell to just one half what it had been in 1801, consequent, no doubt, upon the conclusion of peace with France, which happy event was announced in a letter from the Right Hon. Lord Hobart, one of His Majesty's principal Secretaries of State, to the Right Hon. Lord Pembroke, Lord-Lieutenant of the County of Wilts, dated from

Downing Street, October 10th, 1801, and a copy of which was transmitted to the officers and men of the various Yeomanry corps and Volunteer forces raised in the county. The contents of this letter being read to the Swindon Troop on November 6th, the following reply was at once resolved on, and the several signatures, which we give, appended thereto :—

The Swindon Troop of Gentlemen and Yeomanry having heard read a letter from Lord Hobart to the Lord-Lieutenant of the County, and feeling a most lively sense of their Sovereign's most gracious approbation of their conduct, beg leave most humbly to offer a continuance of their services to His Majesty, until His Majesty in his wisdom shall no longer deem it necessary to call on them for their further exertions.

T. Goddard, Captain	Thos. Maysey
W. Harding, Lieut.	Thos. Short
A. Goddard, Cornet	Robt. Smith
H. P. Burt, Sergt.	Henry Short
John Hughes	John Smith
Wm. Brown	Willm. Mundee
Robert Millington	Wm. Packer
Jno. H. Sheppard	Thos. Butler
Bryan Bowley	Wm. Large
Jasper Maskelyne	Peter Dore
John Tuckey	E. Maskelyne
Jno. Kent	Wm. Horsell
Peter Dore	James Wells
R. W. Read	Richd. Dore
Francis King	Edward Smith
Robt. Tuckey	Robt. Withers
Richard Large	J. Litten
Richd. Evans	Thos. Prince
Stephen Wells	C. Bradford
John Carpenter	Richd. Hawkins
Geo. Lea	Henry Cooke

On the 17th November, the Commanding Officer issued an order stating that he would not require the Troop to assemble for any more field-days that year, and in consequence there was no further assembly of the Troop until March 29th, 1802.

On April 6th following, the thanks of the House of Lords, and also of the House of Commons, were again,—making the second occasion within the brief space of less than two years,—publicly awarded to the Wiltshire Regiment of Yeomanry Cavalry, as well as to the various Volunteers raised throughout the country, a circumstance which must have been highly gratifying to both officers and men.

Parades for Field-days were resumed early in 1803, commencing on April 1st, and continued fortnightly until June 23rd, on which day a meeting of the officers and men of the troop was held at the Bell Inn, Swindon, for the purpose of considering the application of certain persons to join the troop. At this meeting the following were proposed and duly admitted members of the Troop :—

Mr. John Henley, Vastern
,, Edmund Baden, Marston
,, Benjamin Stiles, Broad Town
,, John Langley, Cliffe
,, Christopher Tuck, Ham

Mr. Robert Hughes, Salthrop
,, Robert Donaldson, Wroughton
,, Cornelius Smith, Wanbro'
,, Wm. Cripps, Wootton Bassett

At this meeting a parade for a Field-day was appointed for July 29th, on which occasion " John Langley being considered by the Commanding Officer as an improper person to serve in the Troop was in consequence thereof discharged from further service ;" the following gentlemen being at the same time admitted :—

Mr. John Butler, Elcombe
,, James Bathe, do.
,. *Thomas Henly, Preston
,, *John Large, Freegrove
,, John Large, Tottenham Court
,, Jacob Large, Lyneham

Mr. Benjamin Bewley, Liddiard Millicent
,, Richard Millington, Bupton
,, Rich. Byrchall, Upper Stratton
,, Joseph Brind, Liddington
,, Richard Jefferies, Draycott

*These two gentlemen came in on the Old Establishment by Ballot.

The condition of membership at this time was as follows :—That each member should find and pay for such military equipments as the allowance of £9 by the Government should be found inadequate to procure.

On August 5th the following gentlemen were admitted members, making an addition of thirty-nine new members between June 23rd and August 5th :—

Mr.	John Bathe, Elcombe	Mr.	John Frampton, Hunt's Copse
,,	Jacob Pinniger, Tockenham		
,,	Adam Henly, Middle Hill	,,	William Frampton, do.
,,	Jacob Henly, Lyneham	,,	Wm. Pinegar, South Marston
,,	R. G. Bathe, Purton	,,	Richard Pinegar, do.
,,	Henry Crook, Corton	,,	George Brind, Liddington
,,	Thomas Jenner, Seven Bridges	,,	Thomas Jones, Southbrook
,,	J. O. Williams, Okus	,.	Thomas Brind, Wanborough
,,	John White, Cricklade	,,	John Edwards, Liddington
,,	Wm. Turvey, Wootton Bassett	,,	John Large, South Marston

Singularly enough, on the very day when these gentlemen joined the Troop a letter was addressed from London by Colonel Lord Bruce to Captain Goddard stating that in consequence of the very great offers received for raising Volunteer corps free of expense, the Government had come to the resolution of making no allowance whatever for the equipment of such persons as had entered their names since the 22nd of June, and offering to those who desired to do so the opportunity of withdrawing. In consequence of this communication a meeting was called for August 12th, when those more immediately concerned voluntarily determined to continue their offer of service, and unanimously agreed to provide themselves with all necessary clothes, arms, and accoutrements at their own private expense. At this same meeting

Mr. Daniel Jenner, Whotham	Mr. Charles Poulton, Chelworth
Mr. Charles Barnett, Swindon	

joined the troop and agreed to provide their own outfit.

On August 10th, 1803, the unanimous thanks of the House of Commons were again conveyed to the various Yeomanry and Volunteer forces for their valuable assistance, which appears to have been a prelude to an unusual amount of activity, especially among the Swindon troop, for between October 7th, 1803, and February 10th, 1804, there were no less than eighteen parades of the troop, for field-days, held either in Swindon or the immediate neighbourhood ; and following immediately after this, and throughout the months of April and May, the various Wiltshire Troops were assembled for permanent duty at Salisbury, Devizes, Calne, and other centres, which appears to have involved a larger sacrifice of time than some of the members had contemplated or were prepared to give, for on May 30th, 1804, the following entry was ordered to be made in the Orderly-book :—

The undermentioned privates of the Swindon Troop having refused (when called upon to volunteer their services by his Majesty) to come forward with the rest of the Troop, the Commanding Officer has thought proper to dismiss them as no longer worthy to belong to so respectable a corps.

The Quarter-Master will take care that they return their arms and accoutrements, and pay their fines :—

Richard Evans, Upper Stratton	Thomas Henly, Preston
George Lea, Wanbro'	Willm. Pinnegar, Marston
Cornelius Smith, Do	Richd. Pinnegar, Do.

On September 28th following, the troop had a parade at Beckhampton, on which day it was announced there would be no other parade until further orders ; and none were accordingly held until January 18th, 1805, the notice calling the same, issued on the 4th, reading as follows :—

The Troop will parade for a field day at Swindon on Friday, the 18th instant, precisely at eleven o'clock (in case the weather should then be open and without frost).

Parades were continued fortnightly from January 18th until March 1st, when they were discontinued until further orders. In May the troop went to Salisbury for inspection. In the year 1806 the Troop was out on six separate occasions for parade, and in the following year there were seven parades, that enthusiasm which had evidently previously existed beginning somewhat to cool down, which is made pretty evident by the fact that propositions made at meetings of the Troop both on May 25th, 1807, and on April 8th, 1808, that the Troop should again go to Salisbury for ten days' permanent duty, were lost, on the first occasion by a majority of 33 against 25, and on the second occasion by a majority of 31 against 10.

In 1809 the Troop again went to Salisbury, as well as having a number of parades at home. One of the notices issued for a parade during this year is worth notice. It ran as follows :—

23rd April, 1809. No meeting of the Troop having taken place on the 21st inst., owing to the heavy fall of snow : ordered that the Troop do parade for a Field-day at Swindon on Friday, the 28th instant, at Eleven o'clock.

From this time nothing of importance happened in connection with the Troop, beyond the ordinary parades, until June 6th, 1810, when the following letter was received from the Mayor of Devizes :—

Borough of Devizes,
4th June, 1810.

SIR,—

The Second Regiment of Wilts Local Militia, now quartered in and about this town, have manifested such a degree of insubordination and disposition to riot, particularly one company, that I consider it necessary to have the assistance of an armed force to preserve the peace of the town and neighbourhood. With this view I shall beg the favour of your attending with the Swindon Troop within this borough as early as possible in support of the civil power.

I have the honour to be, Sir.
Your most obedient servant,
WILLIAM HUGHES, Mayor.

Captain Goddard, Swindon Troop W.Y.C., or Officer Commanding Troop.

On receipt of this communication the following order was issued :—

" Having this instant received the above letter, in the absence of the Commissioned Officers of the Troop, I hereby Order the Troop to parade in full uniform, properly accoutred, at Beckhampton, with all possible dispatch." H. P. BURT, Q.M.

In consequence of the above order the Troop assembled at Beckhampton soon after two o'clock, and proceeded on their march to Devizes, where they arrived soon after three o'clock in the morning of the 8th of June, 1810, and immediately went into quarters. It would seem that June 9th, 1810, was an exceptionally wet day at Devizes, which circumstance had a depressing and restraining influence on the riotously disposed Militia. The Troop, however, remained on duty during the day, but they were finally dismissed to their homes at six o'clock in the evening.

The circumstances under which this call on the Yeomanry was made, is thus related by Mr. Waylen, in his " History of Devizes " :—" 1810. On the 7th of June a mutiny broke out among the 2nd Wilts Local Militia, stationed in this town, stimulated, as was asserted by unnecessary strictness of discipline. A sergeant having, in consequence, been committed to the guard-room at the Barracks in Back Street, a party of the regiment, after even parade, forced the guard-room and released the prisoner. The Mayor then summoned to his aid the Yeomanry Cavalry. On the arrival next morning of their Colonel, Lord Bruce, at the head of as many troops of the Yeomanry as could be mustered at so short a notice, the mutinous corps was disarmed ; and a ringleader, named Marmion, flogged on the Green."

In the course of the year 1811, parades for Field-days again became frequent, there being no less than fifteen in the course of the year. For the next sixteen or eighteen years, however, nothing appears to have been recorded in connection with the Troop which calls for notice, an annual parade, with an occasional visit to Salisbury, or some other place selected for an inspection, being the only duty performed.

On the 24th June, 1824, a Return Muster Roll of the Troop was made up as follows :—

R. Yate, Q.M., Swindon
William Mundee, Sergt.
Wm. Stalley, Trumpr., Purton
    Privates :—
William Parsons, Wootton Bassett
Abbott Large, South Marston
Richard Pinnegar,   do.
Thos. Sharpes, Highworth
William Jenner, Swindon
William Choules, Chiseldon
William Belcher, Swindon
William Gerring, Swindon
Henry Frampton, Wanbro'
Henry Freeman, Swindon

Joseph Reynolds, Swindon
Richard Litten, Haydon
Thomas Jenner, Swindon
Walter Stone, South Marston
James Martin, Swindon
Thomas Reynolds, Stanton
Robert Jenner, Highworth
John Green, Castle Eaton
Henry Coster, Swindon
Thomas Goodman, Stratton
William Hall, Stratton
Isaac Woodward, Liddiard
Richard Smith, Liddington
John Archer, Castle Eaton
Andrew Baden, Chiseldon

In October, 1830, the Swindon Troop, with the other Troops belonging to the Wiltshire Regiment, met for permanent duty and an inspection at Devizes, and were dismissed to their homes on the 6th of that month in highly complimentary terms by the Inspecting Officer, Lieutenant-Colonel Baker. Unhappily, however, their services were to be very shortly called for to assist in suppressing the most serious disturbances which have ever taken place in the South of England. The following entries, extracted from the orderly book of the Troop, will best explain the nature of these services :—

Devizes, 22nd Nov., 1830.

Dear Sir,—The High Sheriff requests that you will immediately assemble your Troop of Yeomanry Cavalry to assist the Civil Powers in quelling the present disturbance.

You had better assemble and join the Marlborough Troop. There will be four Troops here to-morrow, as being the centre of the county.

I am, dear Sir,

Your obedient humble servant,

W. E. TUGWELL.

To Captain Goddard, W.Y.C., Swindon.

Swindon, 23rd Nov. 1830.

Upon receiving the above letter from the Under-Sheriff (by express) the Troop assembled at Swindon in Marching Order, and at 4 o'clock marched against a mob at Wanborough, which they dispersed.

2 E

Swindon, Head Quarters, Nov. 24th, 1830.

The Troop paraded this morning at eight o'clock, and were ordered towards Aldbourn, counter ordered to the Parishes of Chiseldon, Burderop, Draycott, and Wroughton, where there was a great riot, and succeeded in taking eight prisoners. After being committed, they escorted them through Wroughton on their way to Devizes Gaol.

Swindon Head Quarters, 25th Nov., 1830.

The Troop paraded this morning at eight o'clock, and marched from Swindon to Stratton, Sevenhampton, and Highworth, where there were great disturbances, and succeeded in taking twelve of the rioters. The Troop remained under arms during the day.

Swindon, Head Quarters, 26th Nov., 1830.

The Troop was called out at seven o'clock this morning and marched to Cricklade, where they remained until the Civil Forces had taken several prisoners, and upon an express arriving from — Barker, Esq., of Fairford Park, Gloucestershire, they *innocently* marched to that place, and, after having succeeded in dispersing the rioters, returned to Head Quarters.

Swindon, Head Quarters, 27th Nov., 1830.

The Troop paraded this morning at ten o'clock, and remained under arms the whole day. All quiet.

Swindon, Head Quarters, 28th Nov., 1830.

The Troop remained under orders to be in readiness if called upon at a moment's notice.

Swindon, Head Quarters, 29th Nov., 1830.

The Troop paraded this morning at ten o'clock, and remained under arms during the day. All quiet.

Head Quarters, 6 p.m.

The services of the Troop for the present are dispensed with, but to hold themselves in readiness to be called upon at a moment's notice.

A. LARGE, Q.-M., 29th Nov., 1830.

Order having been restored, steps were taken to recognise the services rendered by the Yeomanry, the first to move in the matter being the Mayor and Corporation of Shaftesbury, as follows :—

At a Meeting of the Corporation of Shaftesbury, held on the 21st of December, 1830 :—It was proposed by Mr. Edward Buckland, seconded by the Worshipful the Mayor, and unanimously agreed to, that the thanks of the Corporation be presented to the Wiltshire Regiment of Yeomanry for their noble and spirited conduct in suppressing the late Riots, and particularly the officers, non-commissioned officers and privates, of the Hindon Troop, and the Mayor is respectfully requested to convey to the proper authorities the sense this Corporation entertain of their essential services.

(Signed)   JAMES COX, Mayor.

Following this there came a letter from the Secretary of State authorising the Regiment to use the prefix of " Royal," and which was communicated to the Swindon Troop in the following terms :—

Close, Salisbury, January 30th, 1831.

Sir,—

I am directed by Colonel the Marquis of Bath to forward a Copy of a letter from the Secretary of State.   I sincerely participate the pleasure its contents will convey to the ·Regiment of Royal Wiltshire Yeomanry Cavalry.

I am, Sir, with respect,

Your faithful and obedient servant,

J. PENISTON, Assist.-Adj.

Captain Goddard, Royal Wiltshire Y.C., Swindon.

Whitehall, 24th January, 1831.

My Lord,—

Having lost no time in submitting to His Majesty your Lordship's letter of the 16th instant, together with the Copy of the Resolution passed at a numerous meeting of the Magistrates of Salisbury, on the 31st of last December, I am commanded by His Majesty to acquaint your Lordship that His Majesty has received this report and testimonial with great satisfaction, and your Lordship is desired to express the same to Colonel Baker, and to the Corps under his command, and I am further commanded to signify to your Lordship that, as a mark of the sense which His Majesty entertains of the exemplary conduct, unwearied zeal, and admirable temper uniformly displayed by this Corps during the late unfortunate disturbances, it is His Majesty's pleasure that the Corps should be henceforth styled the " Royal" Wiltshire Regiment of Yeomanry Cavalry, which command your Lordship will be pleased to communicate.

I cannot omit this opportunity of adding from myself that estimating most highly the services recently rendered by the Wilts Yeomanry Cavalry, I have great satisfaction in conveying to them, through your Lordship, these testimonies of His Majesty's approbation.

I have the honour to be, my Lord,

Your Lordship's most obedient humble servant,

(Signed)   MELBOURNE.

The Marquis of Lansdowne.

The Troop appears to have remained in its normal condition—an annual parade, with an occasional inspection—until the latter end of 1834, when parades became very frequent. On September 21st the Troop met at Swindon in Field-day order, and continued so to meet daily for the next five days, when the members were dismissed until further orders. And from this time up to June 7th, 1838, on which date my present available records end, nothing more important happened than an occasional parade at Swindon or in the neighbourhood, and an inspection at Devizes with the other Troops of the regiment, when they appear always to have secured the warm approval of the Inspecting Officer.

The Troop having assembled at Swindon in Field-day Order, on June 15th, 1837, the following resolution was passed, and ordered to be entered in the Orderly Book :—

> The Troop assembled in Field-day Order, when Captain Calley informed them that he had received a letter from Lieut.-Col. Baker to request him to march his troop to Devizes on the 26th of July for eight days' permanent duty   The Troop unanimously agreed that they could not possibly leave their homes for so long a period at this season of the year ; but that they were ready when called on to march to Devizes for the purpose of being inspected, and to do the remainder of their duty at Swindon, or elsewhere, whenever Captain Calley shall think proper to call them out

In addition to the Yeomanry, the civil authorities occasionally drew up their forces to assist in quelling disturbances, or in meeting apprehended trouble. There were in particular the Night Watchmen, who, no doubt, were of great service, and possibly saved many a rick from burning. Unfortunately I can obtain no list of these men. Mr. C. A. Wheeler, however, informs me that he was one of the number. At Wootton Bassett a record was kept. I am indebted to Mr. Alderman Parsons for the following list of names of persons sworn as special constables on the 25th November, 1830, at the Town Hall of Wootton Bassett, on the occasion of the agricultural riots :—

John Smith, Liddiard Tregoze
James Strange, Do.
Charles Franklin, Do.
Thos. Besant, Do.
Charles Nipe, Do.
Thos. Freeman, Do.
Jas. Moulding, Do.
Wm. Besant, Do.
Thos. Little, Do.
James Theobalds, Do.
Wm. Turner, Do.
Edwd. Simmonds, Do.
George Herbert, Do.
James Theobalds, Do.
Wm. Beems, Do.
John Greenaway, Wootton Bassett
William Franklin, Liddiard, Tregoze
Isaac Iles, Do.
Ed. Walsh, Wootton Bassett
Geo. Franklin, Do.
William Cripps, Do.
Robt. Harding, Mayor, Do.
William Comley, Do.
John Matthews, Tockenham
John Lawrence, Wootton Bassett
John Pullen, Lyneham
Adam Henly, Middlehill, Lyneham
William Andrews, Wootton Bassett
Thos. Franklyn, Do.
Thos. Lawrence, Do.
Wm. Priddy, Do.
John Freegard, Bradenstoke
William Turk, Godshill
James Pratt, Wootton Bassett
Isaac White, Tockenham
John Little, Wootton Bassett
Charles Tibbalds, Liddiard
John Large, Lyneham
Joseph Short, Wootton Bassett
George Townsend, Lyneham
Thos. Thompson, Do.
Joseph Comley, Do.
John Gardner, Wootton Bassett
Elias Smaleham, Do.

Robert Blake, Wootton Bassett
William Short, Do.
Robert Stiles, Witcomb, Hillmarton
Thos. Kewth, Wootton Bassett
Charles Holton Do.
James Blake, Do.
Richard Parsons, Do.
Reuben Horsell, Do.
John Yorke, Do.
Thomas Kinchin, Liddiard Tregoze
Thomas Short, Wootton Bassett
Barth. Horsell, jun., Liddiard Tregoze
Charles Matthews, Brinkworth
George Blake, Wootton Bassett
Capt. Richard Goddard, R.N., Wootton Bassett
John Bryant, Wootton Bassett
Wm. Archer, Do.
Martin Scaplehorn, Do.
Richard Mills, Do.
Thos. Whitehead, Do.
Joseph Little, Do.
Bryan Rumboll, Lyneham
Jacob Large, Do.
John Hopkins, Do.
Wm. Pullen, Do.
T. Stanley, jun., Wootton Bassett
J. Henley, sen, Do.
J. Mills, sen., Do.
J. Jefferies, Do.
W. Smith, Do.
W. Hawkins, Do.
Danl. McIsaac, Do.
Jas. Archer, Do.
Jacob Woodward, Spittleboro', Liddiard
Robt. Smith, Wootton Bassett

For the Parish of Lyneham only :—

Edward Holloway
Robert Theobalds
John Turk
Jesse Ferris
William Norris

As far as is known, all these persons are "gone to that bourne from whence no traveller returns," with the exception of four—viz., Messrs. Richard Mills, William Archer, and William Short, of Wootton Bassett, and Mr. Robert Stiles, of Witcombe. The *agricultural* labourers of Wootton Bassett seem, as a rule, to have been conspicuous by their absence, having generally refused to be sworn. The first twelve names on the list were those of labourers in the employ of the late Mr. Cornelius Bradford, of Midghall. There appears to have been a mob at Clyffe Pypard on the following day (the 26th November), according to the official record of the duty done by the Marlborough Troop of Yeomanry, from which the following is an extract :—

Nov. 26th. The Troop attended Messrs. Baskerville and Goddard, Magistrates, to Clyffe, to disperse a mob of 200 persons, who had assembled to rescue some prisoners who had been taken to Devizes very early in the morning, and the mob being apprized of this, had dispersed before their arrival, and the Troop marched back through Wootton Bassett to Marlborough.

This was signed by "S. R. Ward, Lieutenant commanding Marlborough Troop W.Y.C." According to the same account the Troop was on duty from November 23rd to December 2nd, but the rioting was really quelled in about four days. Three hundred and sixty prisoners were tried at Salisbury by a Special Commission about the end of December, of whom 26 had sentence of death recorded against them, and two were sentenced to death, but reprieved, as related in the papers on "The Troublous Times of 1830."

~Parliamentary＊Elections·~

ITHIN the memory of the present generation of men there has been nothing
probably in which change has been so
marked as in the conduct of Parliamentary elections, and in the political
condition and thought of the people. My very
earliest recollections carry me back to what I may
call the fringe of the events and circumstances of the
ever-memorable year 1832. My father, who had
been through the Peninsular campaign, and had
taken part in several of the great battles, was naturally a somewhat keen politician, and his sympathies
being strongly with the popular, or reform, party,
young as I was at the time, I well remember the
anxiety there was for the arrival of the postman on
the morning when the weekly newspaper was due,
and of the practical suspension of all other duties in
the house until its contents had been well scanned,
and its leading remarks on the more stirring events
of the times read out aloud for all to hear. There
have been many stirring events, and much anxious

waiting for news and newspapers since then ; but for deep, heart-felt, interest and anxiety, there probably was never a time when it was equal to that which existed immediately preceding and following the period of 1832. There was that troubled .spirit of unrest abroad, not only in every county, but in every house and home, which made the boldest tremble, and the forebodings of the morrow appear more dreadful than the realities of the day. I refer, however, incidentally to these matters for the purpose of illustrating and giving effect to a scene which I can see as plainly now through the medium of my mind's eye as I did with my natural eye more than fifty years ago—a scene in which the principal figure was a little old woman standing in a doorway in Wood Street, with a large white linen cap, but no bonnet, on her head ; with a lighted candle in each hand ; with her eyes shut, her mouth open to its widest extent, and her voice shouting in its loudest and shrillest volume, " Reform for ever ! "

At the time to which I refer the handy-man of the town and parish was one James Page. In after years I knew Mr. Page in quite a variety of characters—as postman, as choir-leader, and violoncello player at the Wesleyan chapel, and various other occupations. But in the early days of the century he was what I have described as the handy-man of the parish ; and, among other things, occupied the position of parish constable, whose duty it would be to apprehend offenders, take them before the magistrates, and, after a commitment or conviction, to march them off to Devizes or Marlborough. He would also be employed by the Overseers and other parish officials to carry out their orders. On one occasion Page was sent off to Fairford with a lunatic, who was very securely tied up with cords in a covered van. This, no doubt, was done for the purpose of preventing the unfortunate person doing injury to himself or others on the journey. When, however, Page arrived with the van at the asylum, and every arrangement had been made for removing the lunatic, it was found that he was lying dead on the floor of the van, and for years after this the idlers of the town and neighbourhood never missed an oppor-tunity of reminding the unfortunate driver of the van of his misadventure, by calling out, "Who took the dead man to the mad-house?" To which the answer would be, "The man with the white hat." I mention this simply to show, that, although Page was a really respectable, harmless, and inoffensive person, his occupation brought him into disrepute with a certain section of the inhabitants, and no one, it would seem, was more conscious of this fact than Mrs. Page, who was one of those unfortunate married females who, not having the responsibilities of a parent, had time to seek and ferret out troubles in pastures new, and who could find time for much imagining, which was almost certain to be of a troublous character. In the eyes of Mrs. Page, Mr. Page was one of the most important personages of the town, and it was her firm conviction that, in the event of anything like a public rising against law and authority taking place, their hearth and home would be certain to be among the first to be sacked and desecrated. And, therefore, Mrs. Page deemed it to be a duty she owed to herself and to her husband to be very demonstrative on the occasion of the passing into law a measure about which the whole nation had been talking and praying for for many months, and she had evidently come to the conclusion that the only safe way of averting any threatened danger to her house and home was by siding with the popular cause, and showing the largest possible amount of jubilation over the passing of the Reform Bill. Now, the Page domicile happened to be a mean little cottage in Wood Street, on a spot now occupied by Mr. Bond's jewelry shop. The windows in front of the house were very small, but the one on the ground floor had many panes of glass in it— probably from twenty to thirty of the old lead lattice pattern. After the passing, and in commemoration of, the Reform Bill, a day was fixed on for a universal rejoicing and illumination, and it is the evening of this day that I so well remember. During the greater part of the day Mrs. Page had been engaged in arranging her windows for her illumination. She had designed a candle for each separate pane of glass, the candle being kept in position by a ball of soft clay. To arrange so many candles in so small a space, without causing the one to melt up the other, required all Mrs. P.'s engineering ability; but the feat was duly accomplished, and, as the evening set in, the worthy old lady had the satisfaction of seeing all her candles a-light, and burning fairly well under the circumstances. This, however, was not enough for Mrs. Page, who evidently thought that the moment was a most critical one, and there was no telling how soon a band of incendiaries from some of the neigh-bouring places might swoop down upon the town and envelop it in red ruin and destruction. To avert such a calamity, and from her own house in particular, Mrs. Page—after setting her window all ablaze—took up her position in the doorway with a lighted candle in each hand, which she held just about on a level with her head, and in this position she spent a con-siderable portion of the evening, shouting alternately, at the top of her voice, " Reform for ever!" and then, in an undertone, as though addressed to herself only, "We shall be all murdered in our beds, we shall!" the latter exclamation being made with the eyes screwed up as though to keep in check the burning and bitter tear of anguish and of dread.

From the circumstance I have related in connection with Mrs. Page, it may readily be understood
that the knowledge of political questions among the
poorer classes, in these days, was both limited and
peculiar, and that anything like popular excitement
was likely to run in very strange channels. At this
time political morality was not very strict in any part
of England, and possibly it had been more lax in
Wiltshire than in any other county. Previous to
1832 Wiltshire had had three of its boroughs disfranchised—Bradford (2), Highworth (1), Mere (1); and
by the Bill of 1832 it had seven other boroughs
totally disfranchised—Great Bedwin (2), Downton
(2), Heytesbury (2), Hindon (2), Ludgershall (2), Old
Sarum (2), and Wootton Bassett (2); and four other
boroughs—Calne, Malmesbury, Westbury, and Wilton, deprived of one member each; so that previous
to the Bill of 1884 the county had lost no less than
twenty-two members through the various Reform
Bills, or from other causes, but still leaving fifteen,
which number is now reduced to six, making a total
loss of thirty-one members of Parliament to the
county within—say, the last hundred years, a number
considerably in excess of the sum total of some of
the constituencies. In 1687, James II.—being
desirous of restoring the Roman Catholic faith
as the religion of the country—caused certain in-
quiries to be made through the Lord-Lieutenants of
counties throughout England as to the amount of
support he might look for from the various members
of Parliament, and the constituencies, in the event of
his taking steps towards that end, and at this time
Wiltshire was returned as having thirty-four Parliament men.

At an election for the borough of Cricklade, in
1774, the three candidates polled fifty-four, forty-
one, and six votes respectively, and with the two

former numbers two members were sent to Parliament as representatives of the borough. The defeated candidate on this occasion, not being satisfied with the result, presented a petition against one of his successful rivals ; but before the committee for trying the same was balloted for, the member (Mr. Dewar), we are told, thought proper to abandon his electors, and was supposed to have sold his seat in Parliament. Upon which some of the electors made their way to Lord Portchester—a man of considerable influence, a man of property, and of honour—and, at their request, he declared in the House of Commons that he would support their petition. He did so, and did it effectually ; for Mr. Peach (the other successful candidate, and against whom there does not appear to have been any previous petition) was turned out, and Mr. Dewar—against whom the defeated candidate, Mr. Petrie, had petitioned—was declared duly elected, and went and took his seat for the remainder of that Parliament. At the subsequent general election, in September, 1780, neither of the successful candidates in 1774 offered themselves ; but Mr. Petrie was again a candidate in opposition to Messrs. Benfield and Macpherson. But being again unsuccessful, as he alleged, through the systematic bribery of his opponents, he instituted what is known as the "Cricklade Case" for the recovery of penalties, in which he succeeded to the extent of obtaining no less than ten separate convictions, and verdicts for penalties amounting to £5,000, against one of the parties, and quite a number of verdicts, against other persons, the verdicts in eighty-three cases which the plaintiff obtained amounting to £41,500. The cases were tried principally at Salisbury, but they were carried, on appeal, through all the Courts at Westminster, and several special Acts of Parliament were passed in connection therewith, the whole proceed-

ings extending over a period of two years, and at a cost to the plaintiff of little short of £18,000. In commemoration of his victory, Mr. Petrie afterwards collected and published all the reports of the various trials and appeals in a large octavo volume of over 600 pages. In an address to the electors, dated June, 1788, Mr. Petrie says, "I have been plaintiff in one hundred and seventy-five actions, grounded upon the corruption in Cricklade in September, 1780. Of these, records of one hundred and twenty have been carried down to Salisbury for trial. Some of them were withdrawn, but I obtained eighty-seven verdicts." In 1784, Mr. Petrie was again a candidate, but after a canvass of the constituency he withdrew, and Messrs. Coxe and Adamson were returned, and in due course petitioned against; but after the merits of the petition had been duly inquired into by a Committee of the House of Commons they were declared duly elected. In 1790, Mr. Petrie was for the third time an unsuccessful candidate, the numbers being — Thomas Estcourt, 246 ; J. Walker Heneage, 194; Samuel Petrie, 111, numbers which look very insignificant by the side of those polled at the election in 1880, when they were—Professor Maskelyne, 4,350; Sir Daniel Gooch, Bart., 2,440; and Algernon Neeld, 1,748.

The popular practice at Cricklade appears to have been for the candidates to "lend " money to the electors, when seeking the honour of their vote and interest, which of course it was never intended to call in, being parted with without security of any kind. The amount required for a vote was indicated by the number of bars in a "gridiron" (usually ten), which the voters would chalk on their doors, and that number of sovereigns would be tendered as a loan. In one case, and one case only, was it known of the money so borrowed being repaid. The voter, after receiving the money, was so stricken with remorse that he went and drowned himself, upon which his widow insisted not only on repaying the amount received, but with it the legal rate of interest. At Wootton Bassett the mode of procedure appears to have been quite different. The qualification to vote in this borough was different from that in Cricklade down to 1832. At Wootton Bassett there was what was known as a " Scot and Lot qualification," which gave the right to vote to those who had a hearth over which they could swing a pot. On the eve of an election, and in anticipation of a visit from the candidate or his agents, the voter who required money for his vote would hang an empty pot over his fire-place, and in it he would usually find, after his visitors had left, the amount considered to be sufficient to secure his vote and interest at the pending election.

Wootton Bassett continued to enjoy its right to elect members of Parliament down to 1832, when the borough was disfranchised, and merged in the Cricklade Hundreds. Cricklade, however, had long before this to suffer for its open corruption. In 1782, a Bill was passed disfranchising Cricklade as an independent borough, and amalgamating therewith as an electoral district—afterwards known as the Borough and Hundreds of Cricklade—the Hundreds of Highworth, Staple, Kingsbridge, and Malmesbury. In this same year there was also passed the Act of Parliament known as " The 22nd of GEORGE the Third, Chapter 31st," and which it may be interesting to reproduce *in extenso*, as follows :—

An Act for the preventing of Bribery and Corruption in the Election of Members to serve in Parliament for the Borough of Cricklade, in the County of Wilts.

Whereas there was the most notorious bribery and corruption at the last election of burgesss to serve in parliament for the Borough of Cricklade, in the county of Wilts : And whereas such bribery and corruption is likely to continue and be practised in the said borough in future, unless some means are taken to prevent the same ; in order therefore to prevent such unlawful practices for the future, and that the said borough may from henceforth be duly represented in parliament ; be it enacted by the King's most Excellent Majesty, by and with the advice and consent of the Lords spiritual and temporal, and Commons, in this present parliament assembled, and by the authority of the same, That from henceforth it shall and may be lawful to and for every free-holder, being above the age of twenty-one years, who shall have within the hundreds or divisions of Highworth, Cricklade, Staple, Kingsbridge, and Malmesbury, or one or more of them, in the county of Wilts, a freehold of the clear yearly value of forty shillings, to give his vote at every election of a burgess or burgesses to serve in parliament for the said borough of Cricklade.

II. And be it further enacted by the authority aforesaid, That the right of election of a member or members to serve in parliament for the said borough of Cricklade shall be, and is hereby declared to be, in such freeholders as aforesaid, and in the persons who, by the custom and usage of the said borough, have, or shall hereafter have, a right to vote at such election ; and the proper officer for the time being, to whom the return of every writ or process does belong, is hereby required to return the person or persons to serve in parliament for the said borough, who shall have the major number of votes of such free-holders and other persons having a right to vote at such election ; any law or usage to the contrary notwithstanding.

III. Provided always, That such freeholders only shall be entitled to vote as shall be duly qualified to vote at elections for knights of the shire for the said county of Wilts, according to the laws now in being for regulating county elections.

IV. And be it further enacted, by the authority aforesaid, That every such freeholder, before he is admitted to poll at any election for the said borough, shall, if required by the candidates, or any of them, or any other person having a right to vote at the said election, first take the oath, or, being one of the people called Quakers, the solemn affir-mation following ; videlicet,

> I do swear, [or, being a Quaker, solemnly affirm], that I am a freeholder in the hundreds or divisions of Highworth, Cricklade, Staple, Malmesbury, and Kingsbridge, or any one or more of them, in the county of Wilts, and have a freehold estate, con-sisting of   [specifying the nature thereof ; and if it consists in messuages, lands, tenements, or tithes, in whose occupation the same are ; and if in rent, the names of the owners or possessors of the tene-ments out of which such rent is issuing, or of some of them], situate, lying, or being at   in the aforesaid hundreds or divisions, or in one or more of them, of the clear yearly value of forty shillings, over and above all rents and charges payable out of or in respect of the same ; and that I have been in the actual possession or receipt of the rents and profits thereof, for my own use, above twelve

calendar months [or, that the same came to me within the time aforesaid by descent, marriage settlement, devise, or promotion to a benefice in a church, or by promotion to an office] ; and that such freehold estate has not been granted or made to me fraudulently, on purpose to qualify me to give my vote ; and that the place of my abode is at   in   and that I am twenty-one years of age, as I believe, and that I have not been polled before at this election.

Which oath, or solemn affirmation, the proper officer, to whom the return of any writ or precept for such election shall belong, is hereby required to administer : and in case any freeholder or other person taking the said oath or affirmation hereby appointed, shall thereby commit wilful perjury, and be thereof convicted ; or if any person shall unlawfully and corruptly procure or suborn any freeholder or other person to take the said oath or affirmation, in order to be polled, whereby he shall commit such wilful perjury, and shall be thereof convicted, he and they, for every such offence respectively, shall incur such penalties as are inflicted on persons guilty of perjury, or subornation of perjury, in and by two Acts of Parliament, one made in the fifth year of the reign of Queen Elizabeth, intituled, An Act for punishing such Persons as shall procure or commit wilful Perjury, or suborn or procure any Person to commit any wilful or corrupt Perjury ; and the other, made in the second year of the reign of his late Majesty King George the Second, intituled An Act for the more effectual preventing and further Punishing of Forgery, Perjury, and Subornation of Perjury, and to make it Felony to steal Bonds, Notes, or other Securities for Payment of Money contrary to the said acts.

V. And be it further enacted, by the authority aforesaid, That such proper officer, to whom any writ or precept shall be directed for making any election for the said borough. shall, upon the receipt of such writ or precept, indorse upon the back thereof the day of his receipt thereof. in the presence of the party from whom he received such precept, and shall forthwith cause public notice to be given within the said borough of Cricklade, and the several towns of Highworth, Malmesbury, Swindon, and Wootton Bassett, by affixing up a notice thereof in writing on the market-houses, or on the doors of the churches of the said towns of the day of election ; and shall proceed to election thereupon within the space of twelve days, and not less than eight days, next after his receipt of the same precept.

VI. And be it further enacted, by the authority aforesaid, That this act shall be publickly read at every election for the said borough of Cricklade, immediately after the acts directed by any act of parliament to be read thereat, and before the persons present shall proceed to make such election.

The provisions of this Act do not appear to have been repealed by the Reform Bill of 1832, for down to within the last five or six years a separate list of voters was annually made of " Old

Right" Voters or Freeholders in the Borough and Hundreds — that is, of persons who retained the rights they possessed previous to 1832, and which would have entitled them to exercise their right to vote even though they had acquired no subsequent qualification. Mr. Robert Reynolds, who died in 1876, was, I believe, the last of the Swindon "Old Right" voters. Like most, if not all, others who held this right, he acquired a right under the Bill of 1832, but this in no way interfered with his rights under the Bill of 1782. His right to vote under both Bills was annually published on the church and chapel doors of the parish, and certified by the Revising Barrister, at his annual Court, up to the time of his death.

The first election in which I played a part must have been, I think, that of 1837, when Messrs. John Neeld and Ambrose Goddard were returned by 833 and 736 votes respectively, the Hon. Mr. Howard polling 719. I can, however, distinctly recollect the names of Robert Gordon and Tom Calley as candidates at a Cricklade election. At the election in 1837, there was what was known as "open house-keeping" by the candidates, each of whom had, or was supposed to have, his inn. All the inns and public houses in Swindon, however, were on this occasion taken up by Messrs. Neeld and Goddard, so that Mr. Howard's, or the "yellow," voters were in danger of being left "unrefreshed." This difficulty, however, was got over before the election day arrived, by a Highworth innkeeper taking a house in Prospect-place, which chanced to be vacant, and opening it as a "public" for the occasion. For the purpose of the election a large wooden building was erected in the Square, and here the voters for the division recorded their votes. On leaving this building the voters were handed tickets by the agents of those for

2 F

whom they had voted, which entitled them to dinner
for themselves and a friend at one of the inns. My
father having two tickets, took me with him to the
dinner at the Bell. Although I have taken a more or
less active interest in every election between that
time and the present, there is no scene I have witnessed in connection with election proceedings which
has more forcibly impressed itself on my memory
than that which presented itself as I entered the
room where the dinner was provided. It was somewhat late in the afternoon when my father "polled,"
and most of the voters had in consequence dined
before we reached the room. Most of those present
were either drunk, or well on the way ; food was
strewn all over the place; drink—beer, wine, and spirits,
was to be seen on the floor, as well as on the tables
and chairs, whilst bottles, cups, and jugs, were lying
about in every direction. What there may have been
earlier in the day I cannot say, but now there was no
order but disorder. Men who had been appointed to
act as waiters were either drunk or incapable, and
those therefore who wanted anything had to get it
themselves, and what they ate or drank was strongly
flavoured with the fumes of tobacco, and had to be
imbibed in an atmosphere reeking with filth.

But this feeding of the voters formed but a very
small item in the electioneering proceedings of half a
century ago, and which have now become things
of the past. There was "the nomination" on the
day preceding, and "the chairing" on the day after,
the voting, and at both of which ceremonies the non-
voters played a conspicuous part. For days, weeks,
or months, as the case happened to be, every one of
the forty odd parishes included in the Cricklade
Hundreds was kept in a perpetual state of excitement
in anticipation of the arrival of one of the candidates,
or some canvassing party, which would generally be

signalized by some one "setting the bells ringing;"
and in places where the candidate was in any way
popular the horses would be taken from his carriage
on the outskirts of the town or village he was about
to visit, and a band of men, waiting for the purpose,
would attach ropes to the carriage and draw it in
triumph, amidst shouting and yelling, to his principal inn or public house, where, of course, they would
be rewarded for their trouble by a copious supply of
beer.   The nomination, however, which always took
place at Cricklade, was the great event of the election,
and for which all parties reserved their forces.   In
the town itself "hustings" would be erected somewhere in the open, before which some five or ten
thousand persons might gather within sight and hearing of the candidates and their friends.   On the
hustings, the floor of which would be some four or
five feet above the level of the surrounding space,
there would be accommodation for from fifty to a
hundred persons.   Shortly before the reading of the
writ by the Returning Officer, the candidates, who
had previously secured for the occasion every available horse, carriage, coach, or other vehicle, would
assemble on the outskirts of the town with their
friends and supporters, and having been marshalled
into a procession, would proceed to move towards the
hustings, accompanied by bands playing, flags flying,
and all wearing the party colours.   There is a tradition that at one of the North Wiltshire elections one
of the candidates actually sold a field, comprising
fifty acres of good pasture land, to pay for ribbon
favours used by his supporters and friends at a
contest which was protracted beyond the regular
time, and which was very stubbornly fought out.
There is also extant a very remarkable and interesting copper-plate engraving representing a procession
in the High Street, Wootton Bassett, and which

gives a far better idea of what such a procession was like than any words, however ingeniously constructed, possibly could do. The engraving, which measures fifty inches long by seventeen deep, was undoubtedly a fine specimen of the engravers' art of the period, and bears the following inscription :—" A Representation of the procession at Wootton Bassett, on Wednesday, February 3rd, 1808, the morning after the election, on which occasion nearly the whole of the electors attended their Member, Mr. Walsh, from Wootton Bassett to Swindon on his return home. To the Worthy and Independent Electors ; This Print is inscribed in grateful recollection of so unexampled a mark of their Attachment and Zeal, by their faithful Representative and devoted Servant, B. Walsh." From this inscription it must be taken that the engraving was intended as a compliment to the inhabitants of Wootton Bassett, but Cruikshank himself never drew anything more grotesquely comical.

Arrived in front of the hustings, those who had formed the bulk of the processions would take up their respective positions, while the candidates, with their proposers and seconders, and a few friends, would take up theirs on the hustings. And this having been done, the business, the fun, and not unfrequently the fighting, would at once commence by the Returning Officer reading the writ calling upon the burgesses to elect their member or members. Each candidate would be then duly proposed and seconded in speeches in which their qualifications to deal with the leading public questions of the day would be most elaborately set forth, and not unfrequently amidst scenes of the wildest excitement, all references to party questions invariably exciting violent party demonstrations. The candidates themselves would then severally address the electors amidst still more frantic demonstrations, both of approval and disapproval, their supporters applauding, and their opponents laughing, hissing, and jeering at everything that was said. This part of the business over, the Returning Officer would proceed to call for a show of hands, to which the seething mass of excited humanity in front would respond by the exercise of every known means of approval or disapproval. On the result being announced, it would be, as a matter of course, challenged by the unsuccessful party, and a poll of the electors would be demanded, those voting by "show of hands" including non-voters as well as voters.

The day after the election would generally be appointed for the chairing of the member. For this purpose the member would attend at his principal inn with his friends, and the rank and file of the party having prepared a chair by lashing its legs with cords to two long poles, the member would take his seat therein, and the poles having been hoisted on to men's shoulders, he would be carried in triumph through the principal streets of the town, the newly-elected member being exhibited to the gaping multitude as an object of adoration, amazement, and awe. In celebration of the "chairing" it was a common occurrence for some enthusiastic brewer or other friend to roll a barrel or two of beer out into the Square at Swindon and distribute it amongst those who chose to drink it. In many respects an election brought an evil time to many a town and district, and involved it in drunkenness, riot, immorality in a variety of forms, and rank debauchery, the effects of which stuck to the people for years, and served to make them serfs, rather than help them to become free men.

A well authenticated anecdote, the central figure of the group about which it is told being a prominent Swindon man, will best illustrate another change

which I cannot resist noticing, and which will serve to
show what was expected of candidates for Parliamentary honours as recently as the beginning of the
present century. At the General Election of 1802
the nomination of members for Wiltshire took place,
as usual, at Devizes, and Mr. Ambrose Goddard and
Mr. Henry Penruddocke Wyndham, the old members,
having been duly proposed and seconded, the Sheriff
was about to put the election to the vote in the usual
manner, when Mr. Henry Hunt, who afterwards
became a well-known character, and was distinguished
as the great Radical agitator and orator, produced an
altogether unheard-of sensation by claiming the right
to put a question or two to the candidates. So
unheard of a proposal in Devizes, we are told, and
proceeding from a comparatively young man (Mr.
Hunt was then 29) took every one by surprise. A
general murmur arose among the old electioneering
stagers of the county, and Mr. Salmon, the Devizes
attorney, " King Salmon " as he was called, cried
" order, order," and suggested to the Sheriff to take
no notice of the intrusion, but to proceed to the
business of the day. Hunt thereupon told them that,
unless he were permitted to put his questions, he
should feel it his duty to propose some other candidate ; and the High Sheriff courteously recognizing
his right as a freeholder to do so, he renewed his in-
terrogatories, in spite of old Mr. Goddard's mournful
appeal that he had represented the county 30 years,
and had never before had a question put to him. The
two county members were then respectfully asked in
what manner they had voted on the recent measure
imposing two shillings a bushel on malt ; for, Wiltshire being a very considerable barley county, the bill
could not but seriously affect the interests of their
constituents. Mr. Goddard, in reply, stated that age
and ill-health had for the last two years incapacitated

him from fulfilling his Parliamentary duties, and he
feared he should never be able to attend again.   Mr.
Wyndham's reply was as follows : " Upon my honour,
Mr. Hunt, I cannot charge my memory as to whether
I was in the House or not on that occasion."   Upon
this, Mr. Hunt addressed the candidates at considerable length, showing how many acres of barley were
grown in the county, and that the large sum which
would be taken out of the pockets of their constituents by this tax was a charge affecting them even
more than the income tax, about which so much
complaint was raised ; and he instanced a brewer in
Devizes, who, in the form of additional duty on malt
and beer, would pay more than the entire population
of the town, consisting of six or seven thousand persons, would contribute to the income tax.   Finally,
he called the attention of the meeting to the stand
which the counties of Norfolk, Suffolk, and Hants,
had made against the measure   As might have been
expected, this mode of address had no influence in
impeding the election, and was merely resented as
an unwarrantable interference.   Of the independent
electors present, not one was found willing to second
Mr. Hunt's exertions, though some of them afterwards made him a present of their private thanks.
It would seem that the ordeal through which poor
Mr. Goddard was put on this occasion by Mr. Hunt
proved too much for his nerves, for he never faced
the electors again.   There was another election four
years afterwards, but Mr. Goddard, pleading old age
and thirty-four years' previous services, declined to
be again nominated, and Mr. Richard Long, of Rood
Ashton, was elected in his stead.

It may be open to controversy as to the precise
meaning of the term " Walloper," as applied to the
Wootton Bassett voters.   Etymologists give two
meanings to the term : to boil, and to strike, the latter

being, I think, the more general North Wilts meaning. In the pre-School Board days many a Wiltshire matron has been heard to exclaim, when, after struggling in vain, and her patience had been fairly exhausted, to get a comb through the tangled locks or the matted hair growing in all its native wildness on the head of some son or daughter, whom she had just seized by the shoulder and well shaken up: " I'll gie thee a good walloping, that I wool, if thee doesn't bide still a bit and kip thy yead steady, now." In this case the meaning was no doubt "to strike." And this, I think, must have been the meaning intended by the term " Pot Walloper": one who struck his pot as a signal that he had a vote for sale. The right to vote was undoubtedly given by the possession of a hearth and a pot, and the opportunity " to boil" the latter on the former. There is, however, a practice observed in North Wilts, and possibly in other parts also, on the swarming of a hive of bees, for those who desire to attract the honey carriers to a certain spot to raise a din by striking a pot or kettle with a piece of metal, and then, if virtue meets with its reward, the bees become captive, and the honey is secured. It may have been, and I think it very probable, that when the candidates and their agents were "out" those who held " scot and lot" would strike their pots as they hung over the hearth as a signal to attract them to the desired spot where they might be made captive and their honey secured. This, of course, is only conjecture, and I shall be both ready and willing to abandon it for something better.

I am indebted to Mr. Alderman Parsons, of Wootton Bassett, for the following bill and particulars of a Wootton Bassett election as recently as 1754. The election it will be seen was contested by four candidates for the two seats, viz., the Earl

of Drumlanrig, John Probyn, Esq., Thomas Estcourt Creswell, Esq., of Pinkney Park, and Robert Neate, Esq., of Corsham, Messrs. Probyn and Creswell, who were in opposition to the Clarendon, or local, interest, being returned. The bill is principally for expenses incurred by Messrs. Probyn and Creswell, at the various inns and public houses in the town, which were as follows :—

	£	s.	d.		£	s.	d.
Star	52	4	0	Brought forward	1027	16	1
King of Prussia ...	90	10	0	Cockades	77	13	0
Shoulder of Mutton	56	10	0	First canvass .	152	0	0
Horse and Jockey	107	4	0	Money paid for various expenses ...	11	11	0
Wm. Henley's ...	35	0	0	Total of votes then computed at 135,			
Waggon and Horses	78	11	0	30 guineas each .	4252	10	0
Oak ...	336	0	0	Money to men deserted or dead ...	441	1	1
Three Tuns ...	54	0	0				
Three Goats' Heads	47	4	0		5962	11	2
Cross Keys ...	90	0	0		*11	0	0
Hay and Corn ...	3	16	0				
King's Head ...	76	17	1				
	£1027	16	1		£5973	11	2

The Angel Inn, which was then in existence, under the same sign, does not figure in this list, and probably belonged to the other party, viz., Drumlanrig and Neate.

*No explanation is given of this charge.

At this (1774) election the price paid for a vote was 30 guineas—135 votes for 4050 guineas. This, I believe, was above the regular price, which, under ordinary circumstances did not rise above 20 guineas per vote. On some other occasions, however, it was considerably increased, and at the election of 1807, owing to the closeness of the contest, the price rose to 45 guineas per vote.

The neighbouring Borough of Malmesbury had a system of election peculiar to itself. The corporation, which consisted of thirteen members, had the return of two members. About a hundred years ago a local magnate got ten of the council into his pay at the rate of £30, afterwards increased to £50 per annum, on the condition that they would always vote for himself as high steward, and his nominees as members for the borough, under the penalty of £500, for which he took a bond from each of them. The annuities were surreptitiously conveyed to the recipients, being sometimes sent concealed under a cabbage, or at other times the annuitants were summoned to a banquet at the high steward's house, and, after the feast, the amount payable was found lying in some dish in the house which had been used by him, where it could only be found by those possessed of the key to the secret. The candidates never visited the borough, the high steward merely addressing his serfs, of whom sometimes only five were present, regarding the members *he* was about to support, and concluding by saying : " Gentlemen, you have been addressed on behalf of Messrs. A. and B., who are candidates to represent you in Parliament ;" and they were accordingly elected.

⏠The⁕Swindon⁕Justices⸱⏠

APPILY, so far as I am aware, neither the town or neighbourhood of Swindon has ever been identified with any great crime. In those times, when the agricultural labourers rose against that terrible bondage in which they had been held to the soil, and in their mad fury fired ricks and destroyed machinery, I believe I am correct in saying no very serious offence was committed in or around Swindon, although, of course, both town and neighbourhood were kept in a condition of perpetual alarm. There was, however, a circumstance to which I used very frequently to hear people refer, and which it may be interesting to relate, for it marks in a very striking manner the great change that has taken place in our criminal procedure and our treatment of criminals within the last fifty years. Almost one of my first recollections as a child is of hearing people talk about their going from Swindon to Purton to see a man hanged, just as I have heard them talk about going to an election at Cricklade, races at Burderop, backswording on White

Horse Hill, or some games or sports elsewhere. The criminal's name was Watkins. He was tried at the Assizes at Salisbury on a charge of attempting to murder a farmer returning from market, on the road between Purton and Cricklade, and, having been found guilty, he was ordered to be taken to the spot where the crime had been committed, and there hung. Early on the morning of the day before that appointed for his execution, Watkins left the gaol at Salisbury in a low-bodied, open cart, like those generally used by brewers, drawn by four horses, and accompanied by two sheriff's officers. The first day's journey was from Salisbury to Marlborough, where the party rested for the night, proceeding to Swindon on the following morning, where they were joined by the hangman—Jack Ketch, as he was popularly called—who had arrived the previous day in a yellow-painted post-chaise, one of the first conveyances of the kind, it is said, ever seen in the town ; and the Rev. T. H. Ripley, of Wootton Bassett, who was a county magistrate as well as a clergyman, who accompanied them to the scene of execution, at Purton Stoke, attended by an immense crowd of sightseers from the town and neighbourhood. As the procession started from the Goddard Arms, where the halt had been made, and during its progress through the town, the javelin men blew long brass horns to the notes of some dreadful and melancholy tune, which produced a feeling in strange contrast to the ribald noise created by the crowds of sight-seers who lined the streets and roads. So great, indeed, were the attractions of this day that I have heard it referred to as " Hang Fair Day." Before the execution had been got through—just, in fact, as the bolt was drawn after an unsuccessful previous attempt—a fearful storm, accompanied by thunder and lightning, broke over the neighbourhood, which, I have heard say, was never forgotten by those

who were out in it, and many an old person has told
me that they never recollect such a storm either before
or since. Both before and at the time of the execution
there was a very general impression that Watkins was
innocent of the crime for which he suffered, which was
afterwards very generally strengthened by the circumstances of the storm, which were rendered still more
tragic by a tradesman of Cricklade, who, either through
fright or over-exertion, dropped down dead as he was
running away from the scene of the execution and
attempting to get into a shed for shelter. After the
execution the body was spared the last indignity
of being gibbeted in chains, as was the common
practice not long previously, but after hanging the
usual time it was cut down and removed to a barn
not far from where Purton railway station now stands.
Men still living recollect the circumstances of this
execution—which took place about the year 1819—
quite well.

So far as I can learn, there are no means by
which it can be ascertained when Magistrates first
met in Petty Sessions at Swindon, with duly-appointed
clerk, and all the necessary paraphernalia for trying
and disposing of petty cases, and for hearing and
committing on charges of felony, &c. I believe I am
correct in saying that Mr. William Foote was the first
Magistrate's Clerk who kept a record of the proceedings and of the business transacted by the Magistrates
at their meetings at Swindon. There can, I think, be
but little or no doubt that their earliest meetings were
held at the hotel now known by the sign of the
Goddard Arms, but which was then called the Rose
and Crown ; and further, that the Justices were in the
habit of meeting an hour or so before the time
appointed for taking business, for the purpose of
taking lunch, which was always provided for their
accommodation, and over which, no doubt, they fully

discussed, and practically settled, any knotty point likely to arise in course of the subsequent proceedings. The lunch or dining room in due course became the Justices' room, and the Justices' table was not unfrequently graced with bottles and glasses, as well as with such law books as were deemed necessary to consult in the administration of the law.

The first business I can trace as having been done and transacted by the Swindon Magistrates is their verification of the sworn testimony of the Overseers of the Parish of Swindon that their accounts, as presented to the Vestry, were correct. The verification of the accounts for the year 1735 reads as follows :—

"17 May, 1736.   Seene and allowed by us, two of his Majesties Justices of ye peace for sd county.

"W. STANLEY,
"WM. VILETT."

The accounts do not appear to have been sworn to before Justices of the Peace again until 16th April, 1770, when the magistrates were John Jacobs and William Hardyman. But after this they appear to have been taken pretty regularly before magistrates for their signatures, the following names appearing as those of the magistrates who signed them at various times between 1735 and 1832, in addition to Messrs. Stanley and Vilett :—Fras. Askew, Thos. Vilett, Amb. Goddard, Barrington (Lord), T. B. Calley, T. G. Vilett, E. Goodenough, Robt. Wilsonn, T. R. Webb, Thomas Calley, Thomas Ripley, W. Jones, Wm. Harding, A. Goddard, R. Goddard, James Wyld, R. Montgomery, Fra. Warnford.

We are unfortunately left to our imaginations for an idea even of the way in which the Justices transacted their magisterial business at their inn, and occasionally over their walnuts and their wine. The late Mr. James Bradford, who for many years was their clerk and confidential adviser, was, I believe, full of anecdotes about their funny ways and doings, and could keep his friends amused for hours over them. One of his stock anecdotes, I am told, was to the following effect :—A remarkably pretty girl came one day before the Bench from down the other side of Cricklade to "swear a child" against a gay deceiver, who protested his entire and absolute innocence in the most vehement and even passionate manner. And then, as though to give extraordinary force to his asseveration, he exclaimed : " I wouldn't touch her with a three-grained prong, your worship ; no, that I wouldn't," upon which one of their worships, turning round to his companion, in an audible aside, remarked : " But I would, wouldn't you, Tom ? " It need hardly be added that an order was made in this case.

Then there were the "Officers of Justice," and especially the janitor or door-keeper, who occasionally afforded quite a fund of amusement. The parish constable was naturally a sharp man, and not unfrequently a "character" of the first water. There was one in particular—old Tom Tinson, about whom I have heard an amusing tale. As the Court-room at the Goddard Arms was very limited in size, and began to be inconveniently crowded with eight or ten people in it, it was Old Tom's duty on magistrates' meeting days to stand at the door and keep trespassers on the right side of it, any attempt to obtain admission being invariably met by an assurance from Tom that the room was quite full. To bribe Tom was never thought of by any one. He had a soul above bribery, but he had a very tender weakness for a glass of beer, and, as the "tap" was closely adjoining the justice-room, persons wishing to obtain admission to the latter invited Tom to visit the former, which he was always ready to do, even to the danger of neglecting his duties as janitor. The con-

sequence of this was, especially on busy days, that
before the business was over, Old Tom had managed
to get "both eyes wetted," and had got, I know not
how many sheets in the' wind.   And what was more,
on not a few occasions he managed to get gloriously
drunk at, and in virtue of, his post.   At this time the
Chairman of the Bench was a Dr. Vilett, who had a
happy knack in postponing noticing Tom's condition
until after all the business had been got through, and
there was nothing else left to do, when the *finale*
would be usually enacted in a colloquy, of which
the following may be taken as a sample, their
worships having got very wise over their wine, and
Old Tom somewhat audacious over his beer :—

The Chairman : Drunk again, Tom.

Tom : S-s-s-shober 's Judge, yer wor-shups.

The Chairman : We shall have to fine you for
being drunk in Court.

Tom : Shure, yer wor-shups, on my 'oner, quite
s-s-shober.   Only had just a glass with Mr. —— and
Mr. —— and Mr. —— and a few other gen'lmens
the whole sittin', yer wor-shups.

Tom would then be duly admonished, and
charged with the necessity of being more careful in
future, with the dead certainty of the whole thing
being then again repeated, and the proceedings
would be brought to a close.

I have said that the parish constables and their
men were generally "characters" in their way.   Old
Tom Tinson was no exception to the general rule.
The following anecdote has been related of him :
Seeing a man whom he considered had no right to
aspire to any means for travelling higher than that
afforded by " Shank's Pony" riding along the street
on horse-back, he paused and looked in apparently
the most profound astonishment.   He then "chucked
his chin in the air" and took a most palpable sniff at

nothing in particular, as was his wont when excited, and then gave vent to his feelings by exclaiming to a person standing by : " I'm going to have a hoss!"— " What in the world do you want a horse for?" replied the person addressed.—" To ride round the shop and tear the list off the cloth, to be sure," was Old Tom's prompt reply. Old Tom, I need hardly add, was by trade a tailor, which he carried on in conjunction with his duties as handy man to the parish constable.

If at this time the accommodation for the Magistrates was scant, the accommodation for the prisoners was such as would now be denounced as scandalous. The only place in which a prisoner could be locked up was the " Blind House," at the top of Newport Street, a dark and dingy hole, about eight feet square, without light or ventilation, except such as could be got through a small iron grating, about eight inches square, inserted in the door-way. There was a stone floor to this place, and there was a wooden bench fastened into the wall on which an inmate might sit or lie down ; but there was no other accommodation or convenience whatever. At the time when, and for some years after, the Great Western Railway was being made, this place was the only accommodation for the confinement of prisoners, and I well recollect one occasion, when a navvy was confined therein, some of his companions in the night time excavated a channel under the door and got him out. After this, when the police had a prisoner of any consequence, they made provision for him in an out-building connected with the superintendent's dwelling. It was not until November, 1852, that any serious proposition was entertained for making even decent accommodation for the detention of prisoners or of persons apprehended on suspicion of having committed some offence. From a movement then made the police station was built in Devizes Road, consisting of dwell-

2 G

ing-houses for the superintendent and sergeant, with three cells for the prisoners, the third cell being consented to only after considerable opposition by the chief constable, Captain Meredith, who contended that two cells would be amply sufficient for Swindon. In the following year, on October the 27th, 1853, the Magistrates held their first meeting in the Town Hall. In course of time the buildings in Devizes Road were found to be altogether inadequate, and the present extensive buildings in Eastcott Lane, consisting of residences for the superintendent, inspector, sergeant, and eight constables, with eight cells and public Court, were erected and substituted in their stead, the Magistrates using the new court-house for the first time on October 2nd, 1873. Since this, again, there has been constructed at New Swindon another police station, with residences for sergeant and three constables, and two cells.

It has only been within comparatively recent years that anything like decent provision was made for conveying prisoners from Swindon to the county gaol at Devizes. Previous to the introduction of the New Police in 1848, it fell to the lot of the parish constable who had charge of a case, to walk off with his prisoner, after he had been disposed of by the Magistrates at Swindon, a distance of over twenty miles to the gaol at Devizes, and for which he was allowed to charge one shilling per mile for his services, with an extra sixpence per mile for any additional prisoner.

It has been related to me as a veritable fact that on one occasion a man named Bye, who was employed in the Swindon Quarries, was committed to Devizes Gaol for a term of imprisonment for some offence of which he had been guilty, and he was handed over to the custody of the parish constable, who at the time happened to be the late Mr. Daniel Smith, butcher,

for the purpose of being " walked off " to durance vile.
In due course Mr. Smith started off on the road with
his prisoner duly handcuffed. They had not, however,
proceeded far before a number of Bye's companions
and fellow-workmen joined company, and exhibited
such signs as made it apparent that a rescue was intended when the opportunity offered. Seeing this, Mr
Smith, when they had got as far as Wroughton, determined on returning to Swindon, and succeeded in
inducing Bye to return with him, and thus upset the
little plot that had been planned. On reaching Swindon, however, there was no place to which Bye could
be taken for safe custody, and Mr Smith, in consequence, took him to his own house and chained him up
to the fire-grate in the kitchen, where he remained all
that day and night, Mr. Smith himself keeping guard
over him until the morning, when, having been duly
handcuffed together, they started off a second time for
Devizes before Bye's companions were about. Bye,
who was known as a very "slippery customer," resorted to quite a variety of expedients, which I need
not enumerate, on the road to get released, from his
companion, but Mr. Smith being a strong, powerful
man, Bye did not succeed, and was in due course
delivered at Devizes Gaol. Mr. Smith died in April,
1885. I need scarcely remark that it seems incredible
that one so recently deceased could have taken part in
the proceedings just described.

At the time of the Bye escapade, the Swindon
quarrymen were a desperate and well-known body of
men, who were no more ready for a row than they
were for a determination to settle any dispute or
argument into which they entered by a downright
good stand-up fight. They were a remarkably strong
and robust body of men, and invariably wore large
leather aprons which covered over the front of their
persons. For a quarryman to bow down his neck and

pull his leather apron over his head—the top of the apron fitting round the neck like a collar—was always accepted as a sign that he was prepared to "fight it out" to the bitter end. The effects of a blow from their fist was said to have been comparable to nothing so much as a blow from a sledge hammer. An inscription on a tombstone in the old churchyard recounts how one of these men was killed in one of the terrible encounters in which he and his companions so frequently indulged. There were some whose *forte* was talking and chaffing rather than fighting, and among the latter there was a man of the name of Atkins, who was the recognised orator of the Swindon Quarries. On one occasion there was a general turn out at the Quarryman's Arms to hear an address by Atkins in favour of one of the candidates at a then pending election, in the adjoining yard. As Atkins was a short man, there was some trouble for a time in finding a place where he could stand so as to be over the heads of his hearers. At length the difficulty was solved by placing a board over the top of a very tall water butt standing in the yard, and hoisting him on the top of it. For a time the plan acted admirably, and Atkins had got well on with his argument, when the board broke, and Atkins suddenly disappeared in the butt, which happened to be full of water. To get him out was more than Atkins' companions could manage, so they threw the butt over, and as Atkins and the water rushed out like a flood, several of the quarrymen's dogs made a rush at the unfortunate half-drowned orator and worried him terribly. Mr. Thos. Barrett tells me he was himself a spectator of this ludicrous scene.

When Sir Robert Peel's New Policeman was introduced to the town and neighbourhood, new and improved means were taken for conveying persons to Devizes, and arrangements were made with Mr. Wm.

Hopkins by which the use of his pony and trap were secured when required for the conveyance of prisoners to Devizes. In course of time prisoners were conveyed by rail to Chippenham, from which place they were "walked" to Devizes. Subsequently to this again, arrangements were made by which they were taken all the way by rail, and the practice now is to take prisoners from Swindon on a Thursday afternoon by ordinary train as far as Chippenham and then to send them on to Devizes by special train. The contrast between the parish constable sitting guard over his prisoner chained up to the kitchen grate all night, and then walking off with him in the early morning to Devizes, and the prisoners' special railway train appears to be as great as can well be conceived. And yet it is by no means the only contrast suggested by the circumstance. I have it from the lips of one of the actors in the scene himself, that some years after the execution of Watkins, a builder, living in Swindon, was sent for to go down to Haydon to see old Mr. Francomb about some alterations. The old farmer was generally regarded as a "very queer customer," and his likes and dislikes were so strong that he was very free with those whom he condescended to notice, whilst to others he did not deign a look, except of utter contempt. Now, the builder was one of the old man's favourites, and therefore on reaching the house was at once admitted to the old man's presence. Unfortunately, however, for him, instead of keeping to the business that had brought them together, he started off to relate some wonderful tale he had heard about men travelling by steam, of their going about in coaches without horses, and of their being able to get even farther than from Swindon to London in a day. Instead of the old man accepting this information with gladness, he at once took it very much to heart, as a most wicked and deliberate attempt on the part of an old friend to deceive and mislead him, and he refused there and then to hold any further intercourse with him, as one whose word was not to be relied on. He, the old farmer, had seen with his own eyes Jack Ketch's yellow post chaise, and that there was or ever would be anything more wonderful than that in the way of travelling about the country he could not, and what was more, he would not believe.

᚛Springs, ✲ Wells ✲ and ✲ Water ✲ Supply ᚛

HE heading I have given to this paper
would seem to be out of place in connection with either the Relics or the Reminiscences of an old town. And yet, in the
case of Swindon, it is not so. It may be
that the subject falls under the head of Natural History, rather than Archæology ; but, be this as it may, it
will be found, as we pursue it, that my sketches would
be imperfect without some reference to it ; and, further,
that the natural water supply to the town of Swindon
is very peculiar, and full of points for interesting
investigation. Fifty years ago the town of Swindon
was surrounded by a series of remarkable springs,
from the majority of which there were constantly
running streams of water of sparkling brilliancy, and
in no mean volume. Indeed, these streams became
running brooks, and ultimately joined such tributary
rivers as the Kay or Ray, the Lid, the Colne, and
several others. There were ten or twelve of these
springs which fairly overflowed, with quite a number
of others where the water simply rose to the surface

and created bogs or marshy places. In the valley
below, and for some distance around, the hill on which
the town stood, no spring water whatever was to be
obtained. What water there was was principally
runnings from the Swindon springs or from the more
distant ones which ran from the Greensand which
cropped out from below the chalk range on the south,
or from the coral rag on the north. Swindon Hill, in
short, was full to the brim with water. And yet the
visible water-shed for the supply of the hill was confined to the limited area of its own surface, which may
be put at less than one square mile, the "dip"
of such water-bearing strata as there is in the neighbourhood being away from the hill, the hill itself being
made up of a few insignificant layers of water-bearing
strata deposited, as it were, in a vast plain of Kimmeridge clay. In Swindon the best supply of water,
as regards both quantity and quality, was obtained
from the Portland rock which underlies the surface.
But how it reached this rock in such abundance has
always been a mystery to which there seemed but one
explanation—that there was a direct, but hidden, communication between the Portland beds at Swindon
and the narrow strip of Greensand which crops out
from under the chalk downs. This connection, if it
exists, must have commenced near the Coate Reservoir, to which point the Portland sands run out, and
then, taking a north-west direction, have joined the
Portland rock in Swindon Hill. If this suggestion be
correct, it is clear that an almost unlimited supply of
water might have been brought on to Swindon Hill
by its own gravitation, but at a somewhat low level—
that of the old Church Well, for instance. A channel
or break having occurred in the deep clay beds which
surround Swindon Hill, the water from the Greensand,
instead of breaking out into running streams, as at
Wroughton, Bishopstone, and some other places,

simply drained off into a subterranean reservoir amidst the Portland rocks at Swindon, which, having been filled to the brim, and with a considerable lateral pressure, was forced out at all the weaker points along the southern and western edges of the hill in the form of springs.

But this was not the only source of water supply to Swindon. There were several others, as I shall show, the water varying greatly both in quality and quantity, and being met with within an area of a few yards at most unequal depths. In addition to the Portland rock and sands there was another large reservoir, or rather sponge, for holding water, more particularly on the northern and north-western edge of the Swindon Hill, in the shape of a long, narrow, and somewhat deep band of Quicksand, lying between the Kimmeridge clay of the valley below and a super-incumbent bed of shale, which, although highly charged with decomposed marine shells, was, from its density, impervious to water, and formed an effectual barrier between the reservoir in the Portland beds and that in the Quicksand. Facing the band of Quicksand on the north there runs a long narrow band of coral-rag, from which there issues a number of constantly run-ning streams, there being a very strong one at Upper Stratton, which runs westward, and empties into the river Ray. In the valley between Swindon and Stratton there runs, apparently uninterruptedly, an un-broken bed of Kimmeridge clay of an hitherto un-ascertained depth, and which would seem to prevent the possibility of any connection between the bed of coral-rag at Stratton and the Swindon sands. Ex-perience, however, gained in the sinking of deep wells at New Swindon has proved that there are certain channels or courses through which water finds its way in the clay, and I would venture the speculation that it is through some such channel that the water with

which the Swindon Quicksand is so highly charged
finds its way from the coral reef lying in front, and
which runs for a considerable distance in a narrow
band east and west.

✠THE·SPRINGS✠

The principal spring was formerly known as
Church Well, being situate immediately in front of
the old church. Probably about 1750 the surroundings
to this spring underwent considerable alterations,
there being constructed around its mouth a large pond
or mill-dam. This pond was about thirty-five yards
wide by forty yards long, and from one to three feet
deep. Pipes from the bed of this pond connected with
the mill which stood at a much lower level, some sixty
or seventy yards south, in Mill-lane. By stopping
these outlet or supply pipes for the mill, for which
there was ample provision made, the water from the
spring would rise in the pond in the course of ten or
twelve hours to its highest level, *i.e.*, from two to three
feet, and at this point it would remain until it was
drawn off for the purposes of the mill, ten or twelve
hours' working of which would run the pond empty.
As a pond of the dimensions I have stated would contain, say, 125,000 gallons, it may be estimated that
this one spring was capable of supplying 375,000
gallons of water every twenty-four hours. The users
of two or three of the wells in Dammas-lane, as well
as one or two other wells in other parts of the town,
could always tell the height of the water in Church
Well by its height in their own wells.

The next considerable spring emptied on to the
Wroughton-road. Possibly the supply here was not
less than that at the Church well. The spring head
was in a dell in the field on the right-hand side of the
road when going towards Wroughton, and was brought
from thence in pipes to a large trough fixed in the

boundary wall, the supply being sufficient to fill a
three inch pipe the year through. The water from both
these springs was formerly held in the highest repute
by the inhabitants, who used it largely for both tea
and brewing purposes. Indeed, from these two sources
the inhabitants of Lower Town and Newport-street
formerly obtained their principal water supply for
drinking purposes, fetching the same in buckets morning and evening, which practice was continued long
after the establishment of the Swindon Water Company, more particularly from the spring on the
Wroughton-road. In course of time, however, both
these sources of supply were so effectually tampered
with that they became practically dried up through
the water being diverted into other channels. Before
this, however, had been finally accomplished, a good
business had been carried on by more than one person,
who hawked the water about the town with horse and
barrel, and retailed it at a halfpenny per bucket.

Another principal spring, or source of water
supply to the inhabitants, was known as Holy Well,
at the foot of Brock-hill, on the road leading out to
the Wharf. There was no running stream from this
spring, as in the case of Church Well and the
Wroughton-road spring. The water rose to a certain
level in a pit or dipping-place, from which it was
taken by the inhabitants of Cricklade-street and
Little London. This water also was formerly much
esteemed, and was very largely used for drinking and
for tea making. Subsequently, however, it became
so contaminated that it was condemned by the
local sanitary authority, and fell into disuse. I
regret that I can give no particulars as to the origin
of the name by which this particular spring was
known. As I shall show, Swindon was entirely
surrounded by springs, but this, so far as I know, was
the only one to which some distinctive name was ever

given beyond that of a mere local character. There
doubtless was some special reason why this one was
called Holy Well, but I have never heard of even the
faintest trace of a tradition as to what it was. The
name naturally implies that it was regarded with
veneration, and encourages a suspicion that its water
was celebrated for either remarkable purity or for
some medicinal property. There is one suggestion I
would venture to make with regard to the origin of
the name. And it is this : That the well was formerly
the resting or trysting place of Pilgrims or parties
journeying to and fro between religious houses or
monastic establishments. Formerly this well stood
by the side of one of the oldest roads in this part of
the country : a road which ran east through what we
now know as the tything of Walcott, Wanborough
Nythe, Marston, and on towards Reading ; and west
up Little London, across the Okus Down Field, by
Wroughton Wharf, and on past Bradenstoke Abbey,
and on into Somersetshire. To the general public in
recent times this road has been but little known, and
it, like the well, has been "absorbed" as private property. But old drovers used to tell of the road, and
of their driving cattle along it for scores of miles,
with the two advantages of being able to feed the
cattle they drove by the way, and of escaping the
payment of toll at the turnpike gates erected along
the nearer and more direct roads. Many of these old
greensward roads and lanes were known and used long
before the great bulk of the land over which they
passed was enclosed, and were, no doubt, used by the
general public who travelled, and especially by the
Monks and Friars, and Pilgrims, as well as by drovers
and cattle men. To such travellers a never-failing
spring of pure water at the foot of the hill, and
possibly surrounded, as now, by noble elm and shade
trees by the way-side, would be much esteemed and

so generally used as to become in time regarded even with veneration, and designated the Holy Well. I am inclined to think that the water in this well was from an altogether different source from that which supplied Church Well—from that which I have already indicated as belonging to the Quicksand.

Another spring, well-known and esteemed for its remarkable coldness and purity, is at Westlecott, where it breaks out on the side and nearly at the top of the hill at its south-west boundary. There is another spring at the north-west boundary of the hill at Okus, and which supplies Okus farm house with a never-failing supply of pure running water, in a similar manner to the spring at Westlecott which supplies the old manor house there. The source of these two springs is evidently from the Portland rock, as is also another on the south side of the town, which breaks out in the "Butts," and the water from which crosses the foot-path across the fields which lie between the Wroughton-road and the road to Coate.

Between Holy Well on the north by north-east and Okus on the north-west projections of Swindon Hill, there is quite a number of other springs, all of which are connected with the band of Quicksand. Most of these springs are simply dipping places, where the water "weeps" rather than runs out of the earth. Two of them, however, supply rather considerable streams, one of them breaking out in Eastcott, near Hay-lane cottages, and the other in a field just below the north-east corner of the cemetery. At the construction of the Wilts and Berks Canal provision was made for securing the water from this well and passing it along in its course by means of a brick-culvert built under the canal. When Cambria-place was built the first attempt ever made in Swindon for a direct water supply to a number of houses was made from this spring by Mr. Ellis, the builder, who connected its outlet with his houses by means of iron pipes.

There is one other source of water supply which remains to be noticed. It is derived from probably the smallest independent water shed in the country, and yet it is to be most distinctly traced by its remarkable effects. Formerly there was overlying what is now known as the Swindon quarries a small spot of Lower Greensand. Originally it extended something less than a quarter of a mile in length from east to west, and even less than the eighth of a mile in width from north to south. On its south and west boundaries this spot of Greensand has been entirely removed in the process of quarrying for the Portland rock which lies underneath. On the north and east boundaries, however, traces still remain immediately under the surface soil. There is but one circumstance in connection with this Greensand formation, and of the water which it supplies, calling for notice or remark, and it is this : It contains a large proportion of iron ore, and the water as it soaks through the Greensand becomes highly charged with iron. From the Greensand the water passes on down through the Portland sand and rock. Through the former it gets easily, but through the latter it can only get by finding out some weak place or crack. The Portland stone in the Swindon quarries is generally found in huge boulders, lying in, or surrounded by, sand. It is a rare occurrence, however, for one of these boulders to be found without some crack or seam in it, which the practiced eye of the quarryman easily discovers, although imperceptible to the ordinary observer, and by means of which he is enabled easily to break the rock up and remove it from its bed. The water also in its downward descent finds out these cracks, but the passage is so narrow that there is not room enough for it to carry the iron it took

from the Greensand along with it, and it is therefore
compelled to leave the iron behind, which it does
in black and brown patches of various degrees of
colour and thickness, and in forms which are not
unfrequently very grotesque. When I first became
a visitor to our quarries these patches of iron-stain,
for they are really nothing more, were a mystery
to me, as they no doubt have been to many others.

Returning once again to the band of Quicksand
running along the north side of Swindon Hill, and my
suggestion that it is in some way connected with the
coral rag and calcareous grit which faces it a few
miles off, I may say that its principal outcrop is on
the north-west-by-west point of the hill, just below
Okus Farm, and between it and the farm known as
West Leazes. The Swindon, Marlborough, and
Andover Railway was carried along on the Quicksand at this point for a considerable distance, and,
as a consequence, the difficulties encountered in
the construction of this part of the line were very
serious. The railway itself was constantly seized
with a "running fit," and, despite all the efforts
their ingenuity could suggest, the engineers, with
their gangs of navvies, could not make it "bide
still." It would run hither and thither, or sink down,
or rise up, or be guilty of any other provoking and
most outrageous freak ; but, as for standing still—
that seemed an impossibility. In course of time,
however, the difficulty was got over, the canal was
crossed, and after that again a very heavy embankment was carried on the top of the Kimmeridge
clay north of the Wootton Bassett road, and on to
Cricklade and Cirencester. But what I more particularly wish to point out is this : There have been
subsequent to the completion of the railway, at
points a long distance from the Swindon Quicksand,
and after the Kimmeridge clay had been well entered

upon, several serious subsidences of the embankment, which have not only sunk into the earth, but by its weight caused an upheval of the land in other places. As this has taken place at points nearly equidistant between the Swindon Quicksand and the coral rag and coralline grit lying northwards, I throw out the suggestion for what it is worth, that the line overlies a band of water-bearing strata lying as it were in a fault of the Kimmeridge clay, and which, acting as a conduit, supplies water to the Swindon quicksand from the water-bearing rocks which run in a narrow band from Wootton Bassett northwards to Pavenhill, Purton, and then north-east-by-east to Coxwell, in Berkshire.

✢THE•WELLS✢

I now come to the Wells of Swindon, and note their varying depths and the difference in the quality of their water. Although the top of Swindon Hill is not level, it is fairly so. The depth of the wells, however, vary from nine or ten feet to from ninety to a hundred feet. Along Prospect water is found at nine and ten feet. In Victoria Street the wells vary from ten to twenty feet. To the east of Devizes Road they run from ninety to a hundred feet deep, while in Newport Street they run from six feet to over ninety feet deep, the greatest variation being in wells only a few feet distant from each other. For instance : On the premises on the south side of the street nearest Lower Town, water is met with at twenty-three feet, but it is quite unfit for drinking purposes. On the adjoining premises next up the street, a plentiful supply of excellent water is found in a well *six* feet deep. On the next adjoining premises a well has been sunk to the depth of sixty feet without finding water ; and on the next adjoining premises to this the well is *ninety-six* feet deep. The distance from outside to outside of these four wells does not exceed one hundred feet. On the next adjoining premises the well is twenty-five feet, and this may be taken as the average depth of wells on the remaining premises on this side of the street, and as far as Springfield Villas on Quarry Lane. On the north side of Newport Street, the wells run from twenty to twenty-five feet deep. The water from many of the wells in Newport Street is quite unfit for drinking purposes, both in colour, taste, and smell, shewing it to be "weepings" from the clay. At a well at the North Wilts brewery, which is thirty-five feet deep, the supply of water is practically inexhaustible.

After the foregoing paper was in type, it occurred to me that the Rev. Ignatius Grant, M.A., S.J., of Bristol, out of his rich store of antiquarian lore, might be able to find me a shrine or two to and from which the Pilgrims using our Holy Well might travel, and I accordingly sent a *proof* on to him. I need hardly say how gratified I was on receiving by the next post the following :—

"Being, in company with the Hon. Walter Clifford, at luncheon with a learned clerical acquaintance who has made the Antiquities of Bradford-on-Avon his special study, conversation turned upon the route taken by pilgrims of old to the Shrine Well of *St.-Anne's-in-the-Wood, Brislington, Somerset.*

"You know that this was a famous place of resort for pilgrims before they left our port for Compostella, Rome, or the Holy Land. A long list of persons—royal and other—to St. Anne's can be compiled, ending with Edward IV. and his Queen, and Henry VII. and his Queen, the two last depositing the usual offering of a "mark"—6s. 8d.

"Now, we followed up the pilgrims' path from Bradford, and from the old church of St. Leonard's—

2 H

of perfect Saxon architecture—to a pilgrims' halting place by a well on the confines of the old Blackmore Forest ; thence through Pewsham Forest to *Chippenham*, and to *Studley*, near *Calne*. Thence to Pottern, Clyffe Pypard, to Bushton, Elcombe, and so to *Holy Cross, Swindon.* Further than that point I know nothing. But from Bradford-upon-Avon to Phillip's-Norton, and thence to Keynsham Abbey, Whitchurch, Brislington, the road could be traced. It, however, diverged somewhere from about Bedminster Down to Knowle, and so through Tablot Lane, and through Mrs. Poole King's garden, down Arno's Vale, and over Mr. Proctor-Baker's Park, to St. Anne's-in-the Wood.

   ·   "I am persuaded that 'Holy Wells,' all through the country, were halting places, rendezvous, and picnics, for pious-folk in the thirteenth, fourteenth, fifteenth, and sixteenth centuries.

   "'Health-springs' and their 'celebrity' came from the East, and so did the custom of visiting them. Without going back to Hagar's Well, Jacob's Well, or David's Well, in Bethlehem, or to the Health Spring of Bethesda, I mention one curious fact, viz., that at the present day, the 'Humhmums,' in Covent Garden, 'Hammans, in Jermyn Street, St. James', are Oriental baths, whose name, or rather the derivation of it, is from the same root as 'Emmaus,' the village 7½ miles from Jerusalem, where Christ, in the garb of a pilgrim, had his interview with the two disciples (Luke xxiv., 13) ; mentioned also by Josephus as the halting place of Vespasian's army.

   "There was another 'Emmaus,' near Tiberias, where were the hot baths which gave it the name 'The Hamman' (130 deg. Fahrenheit). At this and at Nain (N. Hamman) reports linger among Orientals that 'Our Lord washed His feet, and there left a healing virtue,' &c., &c.—Pious Legends.

"To return to Swindon. I cannot learn that there was any healing property, nor chalybeate, nor bituminous quality in it. It is nowhere mentioned as such, though the 'Encyclopædia Britannica' gives an accurate list of all such health resorts.

"My impression is that, like Lourdes, in France; like the Well at Montaigu, in Belgium; and that of Nôtre Dame de Liesse, in Soissons; as also the Wells in Bonchurch, Isle of Wight—*Puteum Sainte Boni-faici*—they came to be called Holy Wells because early missioners baptised their converts there, as St. Paulinus of York did in the River Swale, and at several Holy Wells in the North; and also because pilgrims recited prayers and litanies together, according to the injunctions of the Roman Ritual, at setting out, at halting, and on arriving—just as I saw them the year before last, at Montaigu, recite, at the bidding of the Chief du Pèlerinage."

Another esteemed correspondent, writing in reference to my suggestion, and the Reverend Father's *corroboration*, as well as in relation to the parish of Clyffe Pypard, says :—

"I can readily imagine pilgrims or travellers moving from Chippenham to Elcombe taking Bushton in their way, as there is a direct ancient road from Chippenham to Elcombe (partly a bridle road) through Bremhill, falling into the Calne road, Hilmarton, Bushton, Cotmarsh (bottom of Broad Town), to Hay Lane Bridge, and thence to Elcombe. This road was very much frequented in my early recollections, when farmers and others rode in to their business (there was only one gig at that time kept in all this neighbourhood); but Clyffe Pypard would have been quite a mile out of the above direct road, except the object was to visit a chalybeate spring there is at the top of the village, long and still known and used on account of the softness of its water for tea-making and sore

eyes. The water at the end of the village is not
chalybeate. The spring is known as the 'Patney
Spring.' I conclude as there is iron stone at Elcombe,
there was, and probably still is, chalybeate water
there. I should add that I never heard anything
about the 'Pilgrim's Path' through this place, which
must have been much out of the way from east to
west; but the direct road from north to south
(Malmesbury to Salisbury) was through this village."

Swindon*Hill*and*its*Lessons.

O many persons the peculiar geological formation of Swindon Hill is one of the most interesting features of the whole neighbourhood, and, in competent hands, the subject might be made attractive as well to the geologist as to the general reader. I, however, can only hope to treat it from a very mediocre standpoint, and after a somewhat haphazard fashion. I have often thought what an interesting book might be written under the title of "Just one turn round on my heel, and what I saw by the way, looking out from Swindon Hill." The title is a long one, but the subject would be found to be simply inexhaustible, and it would require a cool head, a calculating mind, a steady hand, and plenty of time to undertake such a work. I have a very vivid recollection of the leading circumstances of a day, many years ago, when the late Mr. Charles Moore, of Bath, was making free use of my shoulders, as a resting-place for his knees, for the purpose of enabling his hands to reach the Dirt bed, which lies between the

Purbeck and the Portland beds in the Swindon
Quarries, at the identical moment when his eyes
rested on the print or mould in a lump of clay of a
reptilian tooth, previously unknown to him, and which
seemed to be altogether out of place in this formation ;
and still more particularly do I recollect that, after
more delving and searching, and the expenditure
of much patience, the tooth itself was found and
carried off in triumph, to be afterwards exhibited and
lectured about.   If my shoulders could have spoken
and reasoned, they would most decidedly have said,
" Never trust to an enthusiast doing anything steady."
I also well recollect calling on the late Professor
Buckman, at his house in Cirencester, within an hour
or so after his return home with an exceedingly rare
botanical specimen which he had that day met with
when exploring at the foot of Silbury Hill, the result
being another reminder that it is difficult to know
how to deal with an enthusiast when he is " up in the
bows" with some new thing.   Indeed, I think I may
venture to assert that it is only those who have had
personal experience who know what it is to have a
lump of learning and a lump of enthusiasm "kneeling"
on their backs, or to attempt to get a reasonable word
or two on some mundane subject from one who is in
the ninth heaven of ecstacy over some new pet.   I am
afraid that the really competent man, from a learned
or scientific point of view, who should start off on
the work of describing all the Geological and Natural
History wonders which may be brought under the
eyes' ken by one turn on the heel on the top of
Swindon Hill would be very much disposed to go off
on a whirl from which he would never stop.   But, as
I have said, I can only approach the matter in fear
and trembling, and venture to make a note here and
there : all that I may venture to do is to brush up a
recollection or two of some wanderings in dreamland,

hammer in hand, searching after nuts to crack, or stones to break, and then in my own way attempt to tell what I have seen and heard, or, oftener still, fancied I had seen and heard.

Well, before now I have stood on Liddington Castle, one of those always interesting and very dear objects of interest with which North Wiltshire so liberally abounds, and, looking northwards, have had before me a scene of interest but seldom surpassed in any part of the country. Within the view, the eye, as it wanders off to the distant Cotswolds, passes over many of the index pages in the great tome of nature, as written in the many layers of the earth's crust, lying open, and with just their thin edges, as it were, exposed, but in such an admirable order as is but seldom met with. We are, indeed, enabled in this grand view to see the earth as nature, working through the ages of the world, has made it, and not, as we often find it, as left by some convulsion or act of violence. If we begin our explorations at, say, four or five and twenty miles distant—and on a favourable day we may very well take in that distance—and, working southward, we shall find we have in regular order the Liassic, Lower Oolitic, Middle Oolitic, Upper Oolitic, and the Cretacious series of rocks and earths, including Stonefield Slate, Fuller's Earth, Great Oolitic, Forest Marble, Cornbrash, Oxford Clay, Low Level Gravel, Coral-rag, Kimmeridge Clay, Lower Greensand, Gault, Upper Greensand, Lower Chalk, and Chalk Marl, and a spot of Plastic Clay, on which we are standing. All these various formations lie out before us, as I have said, like the edges of the leaves of a huge book, as we bring our eyes from direct north to the spot on which we are standing on Liddington Castle. If we turn and look south, and if we could cast our eyes over a similar distance, which we cannot, we should find little beside the chalk, with here and

there a pot-hole filled up to the level with fragments
belonging to the Tertiary series. If we look east, the
view is pretty much the same as when looking towards
the south, but if we look west the view is far more
varied, so far as it goes, which is not far, for as we
proceed towards the north-west boundary of Wiltshire,
we find a number of the most remote geological formations forced out of their natural order, and making
their appearance on the surface, having been "tilted
up" by a force sufficient to create a number of "faults"
or "breaks" in the regular layers of rock, and which
upheaval has had a two-fold result: that of bringing
the jagged edges of some of the lower rocks to be
exposed on the surface in a more or less vertical position, and of giving an inclination or dip to those layers
of rock which were less violently affected, and which
caused the whole of the rock-beds.of the south of England to drop or dip in a south-east direction.

But I now leave the more general outlook, and
concentrate my view on a spot not much more than a
square mile in area, which rises up boldly in the valley
below, right out of the Kimmeridge Clay, by which it
is surrounded.   This little spot lies two or three miles
to the left of the line direct north from Liddington
Castle; but it is directly on the line north from
Barbury Castle, and it is now known as Swindon—the
Swindon Hill about which at the starting I purposed
to have a few words.   I must, however, look at it
before it was known as Swindon—to countless ages
before there were men or women to inhabit it or give
it a name—to the time when the Kimmeridge Clay was
losing its muddy character and assuming something like
its present solidity. I wonder whether any of those who
may read these lines have ever watched a mass of
mud as it was getting hard and solid and being turned
into a compact mass ?   If they have, they will have
noticed how it will sometimes spit, and splutter, and

crack, and show other signs of internal disturbance as
the air, water, and various gasses are struggling to
get away from it.   More than once I have tried to
look down on the Kimmeridge Clay, and see it settling
down solid, as it were.   It was a rather considerable
bed of slush at one time, over which huge reptiles
crawled, wallowing in the mud.   This bed of mud
extended both to the right and to the left further than
the eye could reach—from Faringdon to Calne—but at
its widest part it was only a few miles across.   But
what has interested me most along the whole course
of this bed has been two " blow-holes," thrown up out
of its smooth surface, just as I have seen them thrown
up in the small mud heap of a few feet or yards
in diameter.   One of these " blow-holes" was at
Swindon and the other at Bourton, and, as the drying
process went on around, the jagged and irregular
edges of these blow-holes became firm and solid, and
presented appearances not altogether unlike that of
an extinct volcano.   After all this had been done,
and that huge saurian life which had been the characteristic of the period had sunk down and died in
the mud in which it had wallowed, the mighty waters
came again, carrying with them not only a variety of
living organisms, but those earths and minerals which
subsequently went to form and build up the Portland,
the Purbeck, the Greensand, and the Great Chalk
formations ; and some of each of these were in due
course, and in their natural order, deposited in and
over the two holes at Swindon and Bourton.   Now,
among the first of the deposits made in the Swindon
hole was a bed of oysters, cockles, clams, mussels,
and, in lesser quantity, a variety of other marine
shell fish.   This, however, was not the first deposit,
for everything was done in due and proper order,
and there was first of all a suitable bed for the fish
to lie on, and accordingly we find that immediately

above the clay there is a layer of hard and very dark coloured stone, which the quarrymen call the water rock. In appearance it is not unlike the Mendip rock. Above this there is a thin layer of limestone, and then upon this there comes the oyster, or, in the local parlance of the quarrymen, the cockle bed, which appears to have been pretty evenly spread over the whole floor of the hole to a depth of two feet. This bed of what was once a mass of living matter is now quarried chiefly for road making purposes, although it is sometimes used for lime-burning, but not often, for there is more sand than lime in it, and it does not in consequence burn well. The shells, which, with the exception of those of a very large and coarse oyster, are but rarely found, having been dissolved, that which is left consisting principally of sand washings which were gradually drifted inside the shell as the fish died and passed away.

Above the cockle-bed there is another thin layer of lime stone, and on this again a remarkable band of what appears at first sight to be very coarse sand of a light cream colour, but which, on being examined, is found to consist of crushed shells, breaking into still smaller fragments on being touched, and dissolving into powder on being pressed between the finger and thumb. Occasionally perfect shells of the *Trigonia* and of the *Cardium* are to be found in this bed, with their original colour and internal enamel fairly preserved, but they are so friable that exposure to the atmosphere will generally cause them to dissolve into dust. Above this there comes the well-known Portland stone, so much esteemed for building purposes, lying in beds and blocks, buried in beds of sand, which forms by far the most considerable, as it is also the most valuable, of the many beds which go to build up the Swindon Hill. The width of this bed from north to south is very limited—not more

than a quarter of a mile—its length from east to west
having originally been about half-a-mile, but with the
exception of a very small portion which now remains
eastward towards the town the whole of the Portland,
Purbeck, and Greensand formations have been removed
and utilized for building and other purposes.

Outside what I would call the edge of the " hole"
there are the Portland Sands—beds of sand generally
capped by a layer of lime stone, which, on being exposed, will break up into thin flakes or layers from
half an inch to an inch in thickness. Beneath
this, what stone is met with in the sands, which
lie on the Kimmeridge Clay, is nodular in form—a
huge conglomerate of shell, worked into a compact
and solid mass. This stone is never quarried for
building purposes, and it is not thought good enough
for road making, except as a foundation for other
stones. These masses of stone were evidently formed
as snow balls are formed on the hill side—by being
rolled about, some small and insignificant object,
possibly, forming the nucleus, by the action of water
on a clayey beach, and gathering up all the small
trifles in the shape of shells and other like things it
came in contact with.

I have purposely gone outside the quarries, where
the much esteemed building stone is found, and had a
look at the nodular masses which are lying about
there, so as to close up one great and distinct epoch
before entering upon another. Mr. C. Moore, in a
paper on the geology of Swindon, says :—" In passing
from the Portland to the Purbeck they, as it were,
passed from one world into another." But this
expression, comprehensive as it is, scarcely conveys
an idea of the vast space that lies between the two
periods. The total height from the surface soil
through the various formations in the Swindon Quarries, down to the Kimmeridge Clay beneath, is from

forty to fifty feet. I have already attempted to explain
how about three-fourths of the space has been filled
up. It was principally by means of a sedimentary
deposit from the waters of some great sea—water
highly charged with salt. How many ages or cycles
of ages it took to complete the Portland formation
men may speculate about for a life time without
getting any farther than a speculation as to whether
they had made any or no progress. This is all we
can know for certain : when this formation was going
on it was at the bottom of a salt-water sea. How
far the waters rose over and above Swindon Hill
no one can tell. But this we may know : That if
we could have taken our seat on a summer's evening
on some small island high and dry, and as far above
the level of Swindon as, say Liddington Castle,
we should have found that such vegetation as existed
was of a tropical character, and that the surface of the water was being rippled by the sailing
hither and thither of a whole. fleet of sailing ships,
manned by sailors who could perform greater feats
of sailing and of diving—of rising up to the surface,
and of sinking down to the bottom—than could any
other race of sailors either before or since. The sides
of these ships were of pearly whiteness, streaked
occasionally by bands of colours, representing all the
shades of the rainbow, and as they caught the rays
of the setting sun, they glistened like diamonds. In
construction they were simply marvellous : there was
one large outer compartment for the accommodation
of the captain and his crew, for the prow and the
helm, for the setting up and the storing away of
the sails, for the pumps and their proper working,
in short, for everybody and everything necessary for
the safety and the sailing of the ship. Following and
below this chamber there was the first of a long series
of air-chambers, each one smaller than its predecessor,

until the last one of all was reached in the centre of a
number of whorls or circles. The facility with which
the sailors put out and took in their sails was not
more wonderful than that with which they could make
their barque appear and disappear. By the simple
working of their pumps they could make the whole
ship ascend and descend through the water quite
as easily as they could make it sail along on its
surface. If in danger, and fearing an attack, the
captain could set his pumps to work on the com-
partments, and having exhausted them, would fill
them with water and cause the ship and all its
contents to sink to the bottom. And then again,
when danger was past, the captain by again setting
his pumps to work, could exhaust the air-chambers
of the water and thereby cause his ship to rise
to the surface, where he could again reef or
unreef his sails, and sail about on the bosom of
the mighty deep to his own content. In shape
these ships were, as I have said, circular, like a
serpent rolled up round and round from the point
of the tail ; and in size they varied from two to
three feet down to from two to three inches in
diameter. Within the past fifty years thousands of
casts from the inside of these little ships have been
carried away from the Swindon Quarries by collectors of fossils, and tens of thousands of others
have been broken up for road making and other
purposes, for it is of the Ammonite of the Geologist
and the rams'-horns of the Quarryman that I have
been writing. In specimens of the Ammonite from
the Kimmeridge Clay, the Lias, and some other formations, the wonderful pumping arrangements to
which I have referred are generally to be seen : they
are also to be seen in some of the Swindon specimens, but not so frequently, the coarseness of the
sand deposited in the air-chambers having entirely

destroyed the delicate machinery and the internal arrangements of these marvellously constructed little ships.

But when this scene had changed altogether, the waters had passed away, and dry land had once more appeared, there came another scene equally enchanting. I cannot say how long it was after the time when the Ammonite, the Nautilus, and the Bellamite were sailing about on the sea which flowed over Swindon—I cannot pretend to speak to its being ten or twenty thousand years more or less, afterwards : I can only say it was afterwards, and I think the climate must have been at least semi-tropical when dry land was clearly discernible all round Swindon. There was no Swindon Hill at this time. Indeed, I am inclined to think there was a fairly level country as far out south as Liddington Castle, and as far north as Blunsdon. To the east, out in the direction of the Vale of White Horse, the country must have slightly inclined downward, whilst in the west, out towards and past Wootton Bassett, it must have inclined upward. And for this reason : there was a good broad fresh-water river running right through Swindon. It ran along somewhere between Okus and Westlecott, at the back of Bath-buildings, along the south side of Wood-street, right across High-street, and then off towards Shrivenham and Wantage, where, or elsewhere, it emptied itself into some sea. This is also certain : the banks of this river were laden with such vegetable productions as we now see growing in England only under exceptional circumstances, including the palm, the cactus, and the gigantic tree and other ferns.

Now, one of the things this river did was to line its bottom with a bed of dirt, generally about eighteen inches thick, and which is now called the Portland Dirt bed. It was in this dirt bed that Mr. Moore found his wonderful tooth when kneeling on my shoulders.   As Mr. Moore, in one of his interesting papers, has had something to say about this dirt bed, I will venture to adopt his words in preference to my own in saying what I wish to say about it.   Referring to a similar bed at Swanage, in which he says he found twenty-three species of Purbeck mammalia, Mr. Moore says :—" I have examined a similar bed at Swindon, and found four of the mammals which occur at Swan·age.   These four were small insectivorous mammals —little kangaroos.   There were also six or seven reptiles, one possessing teeth of remarkable form."   I may add that other explorers beside Mr. Moore have been fortunate in their "finds" in the Dirt bed at Swindon.   I have been successful in obtaining a lower jaw of a small kangaroo, and I well recollect the satisfaction with which William Pike used to tell of some specimens of the *cycas*, and other fossils, which he had sent up to London, and which had been accepted by the authorities at the British Museum for exhibition. It will also be in the recollection of many of my readers that for many years there were standing in Mrs. Tarrant's yard in the Sands the fragments of a fossil tree which were found about the year 1856 by the quarrymen, lying in an horizontal position in this same dirt bed, about seventeen feet below the surface. This was, no doubt, the stem or trunk of a gigantic tree fern, one of many probably that were growing along the banks of the fresh-water river to which I have referred, but the like of which are now to be seen in England only under very exceptional circumstances, and where great trouble and cost is incurred in the cultivation, and the application of the necessary heat. I am glad to be able to give the following measurements of this very fine specimen : It was seventeen feet long, its circumference at the base was four feet six inches, and at the top, at the point where the leaves would commence to branch out, it was three feet, the decrease in bulk in the seventeen feet being one-third. Small pieces of fossil wood have been frequently found embedded in the same formation, but this is the only perfect trunk I have heard of as having been found at Swindon, although at Portland and in the neighbourhood of Weymouth quite a number of perfect trees are to be met with—that is, perfect as regards the trunk or stem.

Continuing his remarks, Mr. Moore said :— " Now he had shown them that ages ago Swindon was actually the home of a species of small kangaroo, they might ask him if there were any traces of the food of these creatures. There were. Evidences of the existence of the insects they fed on were plentiful. In the little slab, a couple of inches square, he had in his hand, there were the wing cases of thirty beetles. On another large slab, brought from a similar stratum in Germany, there was a complete impression of a dragon-fly, so perfect that it might seem to have been dropped in the stone but yesterday. There were also traces of the vegetation of the period. The bed was quite blackened in places with the traces of fossil vegetation : and now and then seeds were to be found. Some had the capsule attached   A specimen with the capsule which he found at Swindon was so perfect that a friend of his almost refused to believe it was a fossil at all. To settle all doubts as to its origin he went back to the quarry, and searched again, thinking that possibly some recent seeds might have lodged on the edge of the bed. But no, he found other specimens in positions they could not have reached except as part of the original deposit. Among other organisms of great interest were the minute bones of a species of batrachia, or frog ; the oldest of the true frog species. The very oldest true frog that ever walked the earth was an inhabitant of

Swindon. So that it would appear that these Purbeck beds were of considerable interest."

Unfortunately, however, they are well-nigh exhausted of all their treasures. There remains but very little stone suitable for the purposes for which it has hitherto been used, and the opportunities for carrying on further investigations or enquiries will be very limited, and can only occasionally occur. It is satisfactory, however, to know that possibly for many years to come there will be open to the view a portion of a cross section of the fresh-water river and bank about which I have been writing, in the north-east corner of the Quarry—the point nearest the town, and easily reached by the road from the Sands. There is also another section, showing the northern edge of the Portland formation, and overlaid by the Greensand. As these two sections are likely to remain undisturbed for many years to come, they alone, if there be nothing else, will make a visit to the Swindon Quarries, interesting and instructive to many persons.

Before the Greensand was deposited in the bed of the fresh-water river, it is clear from the result that what was to be its resting place was, for a time at least, both high and dry, and exposed to a considerable amount of heat, for the mud on the northern bank (there has been no opportunity for tracing it elsewhere in my time) was, through the evaporation of moisture and the contraction of the more solid parts, "cracked up" into the most fantastic forms. These "cracks" were not very wide, ranging probably from half-an-inch to an inch or two. They varied in depth from three or four to six or eight inches, and there were some hundreds of them in an area of a yard square. In course of time this cracked and hardened mud became covered with water, which, as it ran its course, left the Greensand with the iron which it carried, to sink into the cracks and there become solid stone around the hard clay cores, which, when it came to be quarried, had somewhat the appearance of honey-comb, but without its beautiful symmetry, the wax cell walls being represented by a dark-brown iron stone, and the contents, or honey, by lumps of a light-coloured hard clay. In 1883 I was fortunate enough to meet with a patch of this ancient. and dried-up river bed, several yards square, exposed by the quarrymen. Its appearance was very remarkable. Previous to this I had been able to meet with fragments only.

I can say but little more about the Dirt bed, except that the remarkable vitality noticed by Mr. Moore's friend in the appearance of the seed found therein has been noted by others. Indeed, there is a faint tradition that occasionally where the contents of this bed are strewn about and exposed to the sun strange plants will appear, and it is notorious that there are many botanical specimens to be met with distributed over the ballast or *débris* in the Quarries which are altogether unknown outside the Quarries. The botanical specimen which Professor Buckman was glorying over when I visited him was no doubt from a seed which had been locked up in the huge mound of earth known as Silbury Hill, and which, becoming dislodged and exposed to the light and air, had germinated into a plant, many centuries at least after the time it was dislodged from its parent stem.

The Dirt bed having been formed, principally, as we have seen, with material supplied from and around the banks of the river, the water still continued to flow on in its course, carrying with it innumerable shells, together with a vast mass of both organic and mineral matter, which in time silted up the river's course with those conglomerate masses of limestone in the form of fossil fish and shells which now constitute principally the Purbeck beds. To what height these deposits reached above the present level of Swindon, or to what extent they reached north, east, west, or south, or what other distinct formations of rock were formed on the top of the Purbeck and the Greensand, no one can tell, and the wisest can only conjecture.

But after this there came other great and marvellous changes, and icebergs floated about over the very spot where tropical plants had grown, and there was a great washing away instead of a building up period. Swindon Hill was washed down to the level at which it was found by its most ancient inhabitants, and the valleys around were washed out. As the icebergs sailed along on the northern side of the hill, one of them at least cut out a huge channel, which was afterwards filled in with sand of an altogether different kind to any of which the hill itself was composed, and as they sailed round to the south side many of them must have become land-logged, and in time have become dissolved, and in consequence dropped those huge masses of rock which they must have torn away like thieves from some distant rock-bound coast, and which were subsequently utilised by those who erected their altars out in the open for the purposes of their worship, whilst others, not good enough for this, were suffered to sink into the surface soil of the earth, as at Broome, and on the Local Board Farm, to become a trouble to the farmer and an impediment to the plough. And then there came the last great change of all before the final one, when the earth shall give up its dead: the waters receded, and there became dry lands on which man could dwell, pretty much as at the present time, except on some of our coast lines, where changes are still going on, and will continue to go on, until some terrible convulsion shall effect greater changes in a few moments than had been previously effected through many ages.

⸺Scraps.⸺

✦SELLING ✦ A ✦ WIFE✦

NFORTUNATELY, I have nothing by which I can fix the date, but it could not have been far either way from the middle of the present century, when a rumour ran through the town and neighbourhood that on the following Monday morning a sale of a very unusual character was to take place, and which aroused the expectations of the people to a remarkable pitch of excitement. The troubles of a young couple who "lived up in the Quarries" had long afforded material for gossip to their friends and neighbours. Indeed, they were but seldom heard of except through their domestic troubles, the cause of which, it was understood, arose through the lady having a lover who was not her lawful husband. Her hand she had given to a quarryman, but her heart she had given to a navvy. This, of course, was very awkward, and as neither of the lot were very highly trained in the art of dissembling their love, or in restraining their tongues, they occasionally broke out into what was then, and is still, known as a "row." The woman was a woman of

spirit, and stuck to the navvy ; the husband was a poor
weak-minded fellow, who hadn't pluck enough to stand
on his rights, but who yet didn't like it. At this time
there was no divorce court even for the rich who
wanted to put away their faithless husbands or wives.
However unfortunate the tying of the nuptial knot
may have been, there was no untying it except through
a special Act of Parliament passed to meet each particular case. Among the poor, however, in some parts
of the country at least, there existed a tradition that
a man might rid himself of a faithless spouse in an
equally legal but far less expensive manner—by putting a halter round her neck and leading her by it
from the home to the public market place, and there
publicly disposing of her by auction. The parties to
whom I have referred not only believed in this tradition, but they made all the necessary arrangements
for taking practical advantage of it. The halter was
bought, such notice as was considered necessary of
the intended sale was given, and the day and hour
fixed when the sale was to take place in the Swindon
Square or Market-place. It was, of course, also arranged that the young navvy was to be there and to
become the purchaser, for the sum, I believe, of sixpence and a pot of beer. At this time, no doubt,
there was a very general impression on the minds of
the ignorant and unlettered that such a sale of a wife
as that contemplated was legal, and that the liability
to maintain her was thereby transferred from the
vendor to the purchaser. For some reason, which I
never heard, the sale did not take place, although
there was a large gathering of persons in the Square
at the time appointed to witness it. Although at this
time the schoolmaster had not come in, the policeman
had, and I have always entertained a grave suspicion
that it was through his interference that so many
persons were deprived of the sight they went out to

see, and the town spared the disgrace of having a
woman led into the public square with a halter round
her neck for public sale.

+SUPERSTICIOUS · BELIEFS.+

I once had a donkey.

The other day I passed in the High-street, Swindon, a woman who once had a baby.

I always think of my donkey and her baby when
I see that woman.

It is not very many years ago when, one day, I
was called away from my books and papers to a woman
with a baby in her arms at my door. The poor child
was black in the face, and its body and limbs were
perfectly rigid as it lay in its mother's arms in the
throes of a fearful phlegmatic struggle.

"Oh, please, sir, I hope you won't be offended by
my asking, but would you let me pass my baby under
your donkey's belly? It has the whooping cough so
bad, and I am told that is the only way to cure it,"
piteously exclaimed the woman as I neared her.

"How many times has it to be done?" I asked
in reply, as it at once occurred to me that I had previously heard something of this remedy, with some
vague idea that the ceremony had to be performed
altogether nine times—three days in succession : then
an interval of three days : then another passing for
three days, and so on, until the child had been passed
nine times under the donkey's belly on nine separate
days, extending over a period of fifteen days, which,
it must be admitted, was long enough time to either
kill or cure the unfortunate patient.

"Only once, if you please, sir; but I must pass it under the belly three times. You won't mind my doing it, will you, sir?"

In this year of grace, eighteen eighty-five, the mother of that child is, probably, still under forty years of age. I often see her in our streets, but I have never had the heart to ask her what the effect of her passing her child three times under the belly of my donkey had.

✦OLD · SUPERSTICIONS.✦

An esteemed correspondent sends the following :—"There is an ash tree on this estate, about a quarter of a mile from the house, known as 'Doddells Ash' (Dodwell). The son of Dodwell, who occupied the farm on which the ash tree stands, was born with the affliction of hernia, and it was considered in such cases if the child was passed through a sapling ash split for the purpose, and afterwards bound together with a withe (of willow twigs), and as the sapling became again united and restored to its original state, so would the child's rupture. The tree still bears the mark in the bark made for passing the child through it. The circumstance must have occurred at the end of the last or quite at the beginning of the present century, as Dodwell lived to be over 80 years of age, and only died three or four years ago. This remedy for so serious an affliction was clearly intended as a comfort to the parents, and as an inducement to their friends and neighbours to believe that as the tree had grown together again so had the mischief to the poor boy, when he arrived at manhood.

"You have no doubt heard that the 'liver of a mad dog was a sure preventative of hydrophobia. To obtain this all the friends and neighbours of the bitten person were interested in hunting the animal to death, and so preventing further injury to others."

⌐Appendix.⌐

A CHARTER

GRANTED BY CHARLES IST TO THOMAS GODDARD ESQ., TO HOLD A
WEEKLY MARKET AND TWO FAIRS IN SWINDON.

CHARLES, by the Grace of God, of England, Scotland, France, and Ireland, King, defender of the faith, &c. To all to whom these present letters shall come. Greeting. Whereas by our writ of *ad quod domnum*, issuing out of our Chancery, to the Sheriff of Wiltshire directed. We commanded the same Sheriff that, by the oath of good and lawful men of his county, to whom the truth of the matter might be the better known, he should diligently enquire if it would be to the damage or prejudice of us or others or not if we should grant to Thomas Goddard, Esq., that he might have and hold within the town of Swindon one market on the Monday in every week, and two fairs there yearly, one of which upon Monday (to wit) the second Monday in the month of May yearly, and the other upon Monday (to wit) the second Monday in the month of December yearly; and if it would be to the damage and prejudice of us or others, or to the nuisance of neighbouring markets or fairs; then that he should enquire to what damage, and to what prejudice of us or others, or to what nuisance of the neighbouring markets or fairs and which of them, how, and in what manner, and the inquisition thereof distinctly and openly made; that he should send to us in our Chancery, under his seal and the seals of those by whom it should be made, without delay, and that writ. And whereas by a certain inquisition indented, taken at Swindon, in the county aforesaid, on the 24th day of March, in the first year of our reign, before Sir Francis Seymour, Knight, Sheriff of the county aforesaid, by virtue of our aforesaid writ to the same Sheriff, directed by the oath of good and lawful men of the county aforesaid, it was found that it would not be to the damage or prejudice of us or others, or to the nuisance of neighbouring markets or fairs, if we should grant to Thomas Goddard, Esquire, in the aforesaid writ named, that he might have and hold within the town of Swindon, in the county of Wilts aforesaid, one market in every week, and two fairs yearly, on the days in the said writ respectively mentioned, as by the writ and inquisition aforesaid, returned into our Chancery, and there remaining of record, is manifest and appear. Know ye that we, graciously regarding the public advantage and the emolument of the inhabitants of the aforesaid town of Swindon, in the county of Wilts aforesaid, of our special grace, and of our certain knowledge and meere motion, have given and granted, and, by these presents for us, our heirs, and successors, do give and grant to the aforesaid Thomas Goddard, Esquire, his heirs and assigns, full and absolute license, liberty, power, faculty, and authority, that he, the aforesaid Thomas Goddard, his heirs and assigns, have, hold, and keep, and may, and shall be able to have, hold and keep within the aforesaid town of Swindon, in the county of Wilts aforesaid, and the liberties and precincts thereof, one market on Monday in every week for ever ; and also two fairs or feasts yearly for ever, the first of the same fairs or feasts to be yearly held and kept on Monday (to wit) the second Monday in the month of May, and to continue and last throughout the whole of that day ; and the other of the same fairs or feasts to be yearly held and kept on Monday (to wit) the second Monday in the month of December, and to continue and last throughout the whole of that day, together with a court of pie powder there to be held during the time of the said market, and fairs, or feasts, and with all liberties and free customs, tolls, stallage, picage, fines, amerciaments, and all other profits, commodities, and emoluments whatsoever to such market, and fairs, or feasts, and court of pie powder, appertaining, arising, happening, contingent, or in any manner belonging. Wherefore we will, by these presents, for us, our heirs, and successors, firmly command and order that the aforesaid Thomas Goddard, his heirs and assigns, have, hold, and keep, and may, and shall, be able to have, hold, and keep, within the aforesaid town of Swindon, and the liberties or precincts thereof, the aforesaid market on Monday, in every week, for ever ; and also the aforesaid two fairs or feasts, the first thereof to be held and kept on the aforesaid Monday (to wit) the second Monday in the month of May yearly, and to continue and last throughout the whole of that day ; and the second of the said fairs or feasts to be held and kept on the aforesaid Monday (to wit) the second Monday in the month of December yearly, and to continue and last during the whole of that day, together with a court of pie powder, there to be held at the times of the said market, and fairs, or feasts, and with all liberties, and free customs, tolls, stallage, picage, fines, amerciaments, and all other profits, commodities, and emoluments whatsoever to such market, and fairs, or feasts, and court of pie powder appertaining, arising, happening, contingent, or in manner belonging. Provided, nevertheless, always, and our intent is, that all and singular, the inhabitants of the aforesaid town and parish of Swindon be, and shall be for ever, quit, acquitted, and discharged of, and from all stallage, picage, and tolls, whatsoever, by reason of the aforesaid market, and fairs, or feasts, due, or payable, anything in these presents, contained to the contrary, notwithstanding. Also, we will, and by these presents, for us, our heirs and successors, grant to the aforesaid Thomas Goddard, his heirs and assigns, that these, our letters patent, shall be good and firm in law, according to the true intent thereof. Although, express mention of the true yearly value or certainty of the premises, or either of them, or of other, the gifts, or grants, by us, or by any other, progenitors, or predecessors, heretofore made to the aforesaid Thomas Goddard, is now made in these presents or any statute act, ordinance, provision, proclamation, or restriction, heretofore had made, passed, ordained, or provided, or any other thing, cause, or matter, whatsoever to the contrary thereof, in anywise notwithstanding.

In testimony, &c.,

WOLSELEY,

By Writ of Privy Seal.

A DECREE

For the Enclosure of Eastcott, Dated 23rd September, 1657.

OLIVER, Lord Protector of the Commonwealth of England Scotland and Ireland and the Dominions and Territories thereunto belonging to William York, Gent., Thos. Vilett, John Vilett, Edmund Goddard, Richard Vilett, Gent., William Gallimore, Clerk, John Walklett, Roger Ewen, John Holloway, William Dyer, John Law, William Harris, William Fairthorne, Robert Morse, Thomas Stitchall, Elizabeth Fluce, Widow, Edward Thrush, William Stitchall, John Randolph, Gent., William Martin, Miles Farmer, Thomas Quarles, William Barnard, John Foster, Thomas Wild, Thomas Edney, Moses Bayley, Robert Tuckey, Charles York, Gent., John Fluce, William Avenell, John Ruddle, Richard Austin, and Katherine Heath, Widow, and to all other person and persons whom these presents do or may concern and to every of them greeting WHEREAS a certain Finall Judgment or Decree was lately made and passed before us in our High Court of Chancery and there remaineth on Record. The tenor whereof followeth in these words WHEREAS before this time (that is to say) In the Term of the Holy Trinity in the Year of our Lord 1656 Gabriel Martin of Westcott in the Parish of Swindon in the County of Wilts, Esquire exhibited his Bill of Complaint into this Honourable Court of Chancery against William York, Gent., Thos. Vilett, John Vilett, Edmund Goddard, Richard Vilett, Gent., Wm. Gallimore, Clerk, Vicar of the said Parish of Swindon, John Walklett, Roger Ewen, John Holloway, William Dyer, John Law, William Harris, William Fairthorne, Robert Morse, Thomas Stitchall, Elizabeth Fluce, Widow, Edward Thrush, William Stitchall, John Randolph, Gent., William Martyn, Miles Farmer, Thomas Quarles, William Barnard, John Foster, Thomas Wild, Thomas Edney, Moses Bayly, Robert Tuckey, Charles York, Gent., John Fluce, William Avenell, John Ruddle, Richard Austin, and Katherine Heath, Widow, Defts. DECLARING thereby that the said Complainant being for divers years last seized in his Demeasne as a Fee of and in the Manoure of Eastcott Westcott and in Netherscott with the rights members and appurtenances thereof lying and being within the parish of Swindon in the County aforesaid within which said Manour there were certain grounds parcel of the said Manour called the Downfield, the North Field, the East Field, the West Field, the Great Breach, the Little Breach, the North Breach, Benbroke, Eastcott Mead, Eastcott Marsh, and Lopers Hill In which the Complainant and the persons before named being Inhabitants Occupiers of Lands Freeholders and Copyholders of and within the said Manour had there several shares and proportions of land respectively according to their respective

Interest and Estates therein   And did jointly according to a certain rate and number of Cattle for every yard land and so proportionally Depasture and Feed together with their Cattle in the said Grounds and Premises at times fitt convenient and usually used for such purposes.   And having by long experience found that the said Grounds and Premises being part Tillable part Meadow and part pasture Ground had for a long time past remained much impoverished and Decayed by reason of the Unaptness of the Tillable grounds aforesaid for Corne and Grain which were more apt for grass and hay and by reason of the great Disorders which had a long time continued and been amongst them in Keeping Cattle in their Commons there whereby the said Commons were much oppressed both by themselves and strangers and by reason the said grounds and commonable places within the said Manour were very subject to infect Sheep with the Rott and Watercore which said Disorders and Inconveniences could not heretofore be reformed by the reason of the Disagreement and Wilfulness of some of the Inhabitants and Occupiers of land there and by reason of the diversities of Tenures and Estates and the said Grounds and Premises so lying open and dispersed the said Complainant and Defts were disabled without excessive Charge and trouble to improve or meliorate the same which might be done with much ease and less charges if every person's land should be laid together by itself inclosed kept in Severalty and freed from Intercommoning one with another   THEREUPON the said Complainant Sheweth that the said Complainant and the said other persons before named Did and had with their ull assent and consent agree to take in and Inclose the said Grounds called the Down field the North Field the East Field the West Field the Great Breach the little Breach the North Breach Benbrook Eastcott Mead Eastcott Marsh and Lopers hill and all other the Commonable places within the said Manour   And had caused a writing to be drawn and made accordingly   To which said writing as well the said Complainant as the said other persons before named had subscribed their several names or otherwise testified their severall assent thereunto   The which said writing imported and was to the Effect following (that is to say)   That the said Complainant and the said other persons before named were agreed and did consent That an Inclosure Severance and Division should be had of the Lands Commons and Commonable places within the said Manour   AND WHEREAS the said Thomas Vilett and John Vilett one of them being Seized of the Rectory and Parsonage of Swindon aforesaid and the Tythes and Tenths of the Lands Tenements and Hereditaments within the said Manour were then payable to the said Rector or Proprietor of the said Rectory and Parsonage of Swindon And to the End That the Occupiers of Tenements and Hereditaments in Eastcott Wescott and Netherscott aforesaid might be freed and acquitted from time to time and at all times from thenceforth for ever of and from the payment of all Tythes issuing out of the said Manour or Tything (Excepting and always reserving to the said Thomas Vilett and John Vilett their heirs and Assigns all such Tythes of all those Grounds called Kingshill Courtnapp New Close North Lanes lying within the said Manour which should be due or payable by the proprietors Occupiers and Tenants of the said Premises.   It was thereby assented and agreed unto That the said Thomas Vilett and John Vilett in Liew of the said Tenths and Tythes (Except such tenths and tythes as were before Excepted) should have the quantity of 46 acres of pasture ground at the South end of Eastcott Marsh aforesaid freed and discharged of all manner of Commons and Common of pasture whatsoever   AND ALSO that the said Thomas Vilett and John Vilett in Liew and Satisfaction of One Acre of Meadow Ground (where it more or less) lying in Eastcott Mead aforesaid belonging to the said Rectory or Parson-age of Swindon aforesaid should have allotted and sett forth to them so much ground proportionably according to the measure of the said acre likewise freed off and from all Commons and Common of pasture to be next adjoining to the said 46 acres being in the whole 47 acres which said 47 acres should be and Enure unto the said Thomas Vilett and John Vilett and to the Heirs and Assigns of them or one of them for ever in full Liew and Satisfaction of their tenths and tythes in Eastcott Westcott and Netherscott in the parish of Swindon aforesaid (Except as was before excepted) And that all and every the Inhabitants and Occupiers of Lands allowing each and every of them a true and just proportion according to the quantity and quality of their tythes formerly paid to the Rector or Parson of the parish of Swindon aforesaid should and would out of their several and respective Land and Tenements firmly and according to Law Settle and Assure the said 46 acres of land and one Acre more which was by way of Exchange in such place as was before mentioned discharged of all manner of Common To the Use of the said Thomas Vilett and John Vilett their Heirs and Assigns for ever in full Liew and Satisfaction of their Tythes as aforesaid And thereupon that the Complainant and all and every the Inhabitants and Occupiers of Lands within the said Manour or Tything should have their Just proportion of the said Lands and Grounds according to the true proportions quantities and qualities of each man's respective Lands and Tenements and Interest and Estate therein and for the better and Just performance thereof It was thereby further agreed and Assented unto that a Surveyor or Measurer should be had at the propor-tionable Costs and Charges of the said Complainant and persons before named for the Surveying and measuring of the said Lands and grounds in the said Manour and Tything and every particular Man's land so lying and being dispersedly within the said Manour and Commonable places thereof and for the Just and true dividing severing allotting and Setting forth unto each person his respective Estate to be had and accepted of upon the said Inclosure and for the deciding and final ending all differences that might happen to arise concerning the same it was thereby further agreed and assented unto that Indifferent men (that is to say) William Sadler Esqr. Alexander Cleve Gent. Giles Allsworth Gent. Thomas White Gent. Richard Morse Gent. Richard Butler Gent. and William Morse Yeoman or any Four of them should direct the said Inclosure and allott and set forth to each man his Estate upon the same in such places as should be most convenient and fitting and according to the quantity and quality of each persons respective Interest and Estate in the premises and should from time to time decide and end all differences about the same And it was thereby Further agreed and assented unto that the decree of this Court should be Obtained at the proportionable charges of all parties for the ratification and Corroboration of each persons Several Estate in the premises so to be Sett forth and appointed AND THAT every person should execute to each other respec-tively such other furthur Assurance or Assurances as by their Counsell learned in the Law indifferently chosen should be reasonably advised and required AND the Complainant Further Sheweth That before the said William Sadler Alexander Cleeve Giles Allsworth Thomas White Richard Morse Richard Butler and William Morse or any of them did Act to perfect the said Inclosure and Agreement One John Whiting being a Common Surveyor or Measurer of Land and one of honest Reputation and very well learned and knowing in the Art of Surveying was chosen and desired by the said Complainant and the other persons before named to measure and

Survey every particular Man's Land so lying and being dispersedly within the said Manour and in the open Commonable places thereof and to give a perfect discovery and exact Estimate of the certain and direct quantity proportion and number of Acres of every such particular person's land in writing unto the said William Sadler Alexander Cleve Giles Allsworth Thomas White Richard Morse Richard Butler and William Morse And that the said John Whiting having Surveyed and Meausred the said Manour Lands and Grounds accordingly had discovered and given up in writing the certain quantity and number of Acres thereof and of every the said particular person's land within the said Manour unto the same William Sadler Alexander Cleve Giles Allsworth Thomas White Richard Morse Richard Butler and William Morse or to such of them as acted in and concerning the premises And the Complainant further sheweth That the said William Sadler Giles Allsworth Alexander Cleve Richard Morse and Richard Butler (being Five of the persons chosen as aforesaid to direct and appoint the said Inclosure in pursuance of the said Agreement in performance of the trust in them reposed had thereupon Justly and Equally according to their best Judgements and Discretions appointed and directed the Inclosure of the said Lands Grounds Commons and Commonable places within the said Manour of Eastcott Westcott and Netherscott and had allotted unto each person therein concerned his Just equall and proportionable part thereof (that is to say) To the said Complainant and his Heirs One piece or parcel of Land as the same was then Mark'd out Lying and being in the Downfield aforesaid containing with Thomas Stitchall's proportion there Sixteen Acres One Rood and two Perches Also one other piece or parcell of Land as the same was then Mark'd out lying and being in Northfield and Longlands aforesaid containing with the said John Foster's proportion there 44 Acres two Roods and 24 Perches Also one piece or parcell of Meadow Ground as the same was then Mark'd out Lying and being in Eastcott Mead aforesaid containing with the said Vicar's and Thomas Farmer's proportion there 21 Acres 3 Roods and 3 Perches AND unto the said William York and his Heirs a certain Plot or parcell of Meadow Ground called Benbrook containing by Estimation 9 Acres one Rood and 26 Perches whereof he the said William York had heretofore the foreshare and was then by the said Agreement to have and Enjoy to him and his Heirs the After Feeding also freed and discharged off and from all manner of Tythes IN CONSIDERATION whereof he the said William according to the said Agreement had already paid and Secured to be paid to and amongst the said Impropriators the said Complainant and the rest of the said persons before named the Sum of £100 of Lawfull Money of England AND unto the said Thomas Vilett and his Heirs one piece or parcell of Land as the same was then Mark'd out lying and being in the Downfield aforesaid containing by Estimation Six Acres Three Roods and twelve Perches Also one other piece or parcell of Land as the same was then Mark'd out lying and being in the Great Breach aforesaid containing 22 Acres Two Roods and 20 Perches Also one other piece or parcell of Land as the same was then Mark'd out lying and being in Eastcott Marsh aforesaid containing 25 Acres One Rood and 30 Perches AND unto the said John Holloway and his Heirs one piece or parcell of Land as the same was then Mark'd out lying and being in the Downfield aforesaid containing 7 Acres 3 Roods and 11 Perches Also one other piece or parcell of Land as the same was then Mark'd out lying and being in the East Field aforesaid containing 14 Acres and 36 Perches And also one other peice or parcell of land as the same was then Mark'd out lying and being in the Great

Breach aforesaid containing 14 Acres two Roods and 15 Perches AND unto the said John Foster and his Heirs one piece or parcell of Land as the same was then Mark'd out lying and being in the Downfield aforesaid containing 6 Acres 3 Roods and 8 Perches And also one piece or parcell of Land as the same was then Mark'd out lying and being in the West Field aforesaid containing 16 Acres 3 Roods and 39 Perches Also one piece or parcell of Meadow Ground as the same was then Mark'd out lying and being in Eastcott Mead aforesaid containing 2 Acres one Rood and eight Perches AND unto the said Robert Tuckey and his Heirs one piece or parcell of Land as the same was then Mark'd out lying and being in the Downfield aforesaid containing 4 Acres and 13 Perches AND unto the said Roger Ewen and his Heirs One piece or parcell of Land as the same was then Mark'd out lying and being in the Downfield aforesaid containing (besides 18 Perches allowed for the said Thomas Edneys way) 5 Acres and 2 Roods Also one other piece or parcell of Land as the same was then Mark'd out lying and being in the East Field aforesaid containing 11 Acres 3 Roods and 23 Perches Also one other piece or parcell of Land as the same was then Mark'd out and being in Eastcott Marsh aforesaid containing 4 Acres and thirty-five Perches Also one other piece or parcell of Land as the same was then Mark'd out lying and being in the West Field aforesaid containing 29 Acres and 6 Perches (besides 40 perches allow'd for the said Katherine Heath's way and John Ruddle's way) Also one other piece or parcell of Meadow Ground as the same was then Mark'd out lying and being in Eastcott Mead aforesaid containing 3 Acres 3 Roods and ten Perches AND unto the said William Harris and his Heirs one piece or parcell of Land as the same was then Mark'd out lying and being in the Downfield aforesaid containing (besides for ways for the said William Dyer and John Holloway) 5 Acres and 34 Perches Also one other piece or parcell of Land as the Same was then Mark'd out lying and being in the West Field and North Field aforesaid containing (besides allowing for ways) 33 Acres 3 Roods and 14 Perches Also one piece or parcell of Meadow Ground as the same was then Mark'd out lying and being in Eastcott Mead aforesaid containing 4 Acres two Roods and 12 Perches AND unto the said William Avenell for the term of his life One piece or parcell of Land as the same was then Mark'd out lying and being in the Downfield aforesaid containing (besides two perches allowed for the Highway) one Acre two Roods and twenty perches And after the decease of the said William Avenell the same to remain and to come unto the said Miles Farmer and his Heirs for ever And also unto the said William Avenell for the term of his natural life One other piece or parcell of Land as the same was then Mark'd out lying and being in the West Field aforesaid containing (besides 55 Perches allowed for a way to Lopers Hill) Eight Acres one Rood and 39 Perches And after the decease of the said William Avenell the same to remain and come unto the said Miles Farmer and his Heirs for ever AND unto the said Miles Farmer and his Heirs one piece or parcell of Land as the same was then Mark'd out lying and being in the Downfield aforesaid containing besides twenty three perches allowed for a way for the said William Avenell 3 Acres 3 Roods and twenty eight perches Also one other piece or parcell of Land as the same was then Mark'd out lying and being in the East Field aforesaid containing 13 Acres One Rood and 27 Perches AND unto the said William Barnard and Mary Barnard Widow his Mother and unto the Heirs of the said William One piece or parcell of Land as the same was then Mark'd out lying and being in the Downfield aforesaid containing (besides 20 Perches for a way for the said John Holloway) 3 Acres 3

roods and 8 Perches Also unto the said William Barnard and Mary Barnard
and the Heirs of the said William One other piece or parcell of Land as the
same was then Mark'd out lying and being in the East Field aforesaid containing 9 Acres 3 Roods and 8 Perches AND unto the said John Randolph
and his Heirs one piece or parcell of Land as the same was then Mark'd out
lying and being in the Downfield aforesaid containing 4 Acres Also one
other piece or parcell of Land as the same was then Mark'd out lying and
being in the West Field aforesaid containing Nineteen Acres and twenty
four perches Also one other piece or parcel of Land as the same was
then Mark'd out lying and being in a ground or field called Lopers Hill
aforesaid containing (besides William Harris his way) Sixteen Acres One
Rood and thirty nine perches Also one other piece or parcell of Meadow
ground as the same was then Mark'd out lying and being in Eastcott Mead
aforesaid containing Three Acres one rood and twenty five Perches AND
unto the said Thomas Edney for the term of his natural life One piece or
parcell of land as the same was then Mark'd out lying and being in the
East Field aforesaid containing Six Acres One Rood and thirty two perches
and after the decease of the said Thomas Edney the same to remain and
come unto the said Robert Tuckey and his Heirs for ever AND unto the
said John Fluce and his Heirs one piece or parcell of Land as the same was
then Mark'd out lying and being in the Eastfield aforesaid containing Two
Acres and thirty perches AND unto the said Thomas Quarles one piece or
parcell of land as the same was then Mark'd out lying and being in the
East Field aforesaid containing Four Acres and twenty perches   To have
and to hold unto the said Thomas Quarles his Heirs and Assignes for the
term of three lives (that is to say) for and during the lives of —— And the life
of the longest liver of them The Remainder unto Thomas Goddard of
Swindon aforesaid Esquire and his Heirs for ever AND unto the said John
Law and his Heirs one piece or parcell of Land as the same was then
Mark'd out lying and being in the East Field aforesaid containing Twelve
Acres one Rood and fourteen perches AND unto the said John Vilett and
his Heirs one piece or parcell of Land as the same was then Mark'd out
lying and being XIII XIII XII XII XI XII XIII at the South end of Eastcott
Marsh aforesaid next adjoining to the East Field containing Forty seven
Acres and eight perches which was in Liew and Satisfaction of all such
tenths and tythes as were due and payable unto the said John Vilett or
unto the said Thomas Vilett his Father out of the said Manours of Eastcott
Westcott and Nethercote (Except such tenths and tythes as are before mentioned to be Excepted) and also in liew and satisfaction of one Acre of
Meadow ground belonging to the said Rectory or parsonage of Swindon
lying in Eastcott Mead aforesaid AND unto the said Richard Vilett for and
during the term of the life of Sandes Carter Wife of John Carter of Lam-
born in the County of Berks Yeoman One piece or parcell of land as the
same was then Mark'd out lying and being in Eastcott Marsh aforesaid
containing Eleven Acres one Rood and thirty perches And after the
decease of the said Sandes Carter the same to remain and come unto
William Stitchall aforesaid and his Heirs for ever Also unto the said
Richard Vilett for and during the life of the said Sandes Carter one other
piece or parcell of land as the same was then Mark'd out lying and being
in the ground or Field called the North Breach containing ten Acres two
Roods and four perches And after the decease of the said Sandes Carter
the same to remain and come unto the said William Stitchall and his Heirs
for ever Also to the said Richard Vilett for and during the life of the said
Sandes Carter One piece or parcell of meadow ground as the same was

then Mark'd out lying and being in Eastcott Mead aforesaid containing Four Acres one Rood and twenty four perches And after the decease of the said Sandes Carter the same to remain and come unto the said William Stitchall and his Heirs for ever AND unto the said William Martin and his Heirs one piece or parcell of land as the same was then Mark'd out lying and being in Eastcott Marsh aforesaid containing Three Acres and thirty eight perches AND to the said Complaint. and to John Goddard Arthur Vilett Gent. Roger Ewen the Younger Thomas Tuckey John Fluce the Younger Thomas Heath the Elder William Heath Clothworker Richard Holloway John Smith Thomas Holloway and the said Edmund Goddard John Vilett William Dyer William Harris Thomas Wild William Stitchall and Thomas Quarles and their Heirs in trust and for such uses as the lands late called parish lands (and late belonging to the said parish of Swindon) were And in lieu of the said lands One piece or parcell of land as the same was then Mark'd out lying and being in Eastcott Marsh aforesaid containing Seven Acres and one perch AND unto the said Edward Thrush one piece or parcell of land as the same was then Mark'd out lying and being in Westfield aforesaid containing Four Acres one Rood and thirteen perches To have and to hold unto the said Edward Thrush his Heirs and Assigns for the term of Three lives (that is to say) for and during the lives of John Thrush Henry Thrush and Edward Thrush Sons of the said Edward and the life of the longest liver of them The remainder to the said Complainant his Heirs and Assigns for ever and unto the said John Ruddle and his Heirs One piece or parcell of land as the same was then Mark'd out lying and being in the West field aforesaid containing Three Acres two Roods and thirty five perches AND unto the said Richard Austin and Dorothy his Wife for the term of their natural lives and the life of the longest liver of them one piece or parcell of Meadow ground as the same was then Mark'd out lying and being in Eastcott Mead aforesaid containing Three Roods and twenty four perches AND after their deceases the same to Remain and Come unto Robert Pleydell of Holy rood Ampney in the County of Gloucester Esqr. and his Heirs for ever AND unto the said Elizabeth Fluce for the term of her life One piece or parcel of Meadow ground as the same was then Mark'd out lying and being in Eastcott Mead aforesaid containing Four Acres three roods and five perches and after her decease the same to remain and come unto the said Complainant his Heirs and Assigns for ever AND unto the said Moses Bayly and his Heirs One piece or parcel of Land as the same was then Mark'd out lying and being in the Down field aforesaid containing Nine Acres two Roods and Sixteen perches AND unto the said Robert Morse and his Heirs one piece or parcell of land as the same was then Mark'd out lying and being in the Down field aforesaid containing five acres AND unto the said Thomas Edney and Sibill his wife and their Heirs one other piece or parcell of Land as the same was then Mark'd out lying and being in the Down field aforesaid containing Seven Acres three Roods and eighteen perches AND unto the said William Fairthorne and his Heirs One piece or parcel of Land as the same was then Mark'd out lying and being in East field aforesaid containing Fifteen Acres two roods and twenty one perches Also one other piece or parcel of Land as the same was then Mark'd out lying and being in Down field aforesaid containing Five Acres and six perches Also one other piece or parcell of Land as the same was then Mark'd out lying and being in Westfield aforesaid containing Five Acres and seven perches Also one piece or parcel of Meadow Ground as the same was then Mark'd out lying and being in Eastcott Mead aforesaid containing Two Acres three roods and sixteen perches Also One other piece or parcel of Land as the same was then Mark'd out lying and being in Lopershill aforesaid containing (besides thirty perches allowed for William Harris's way) Eighteen Acres and twenty perches AND unto the said John Walklet and his Heirs one piece or parcel of Land as the same was then Mark'd out lying and being in the Eastfield aforesaid containing Six Acres three roods and twenty eight perches Also one other piece or parcel of Land as the same was then Mark'd out lying and being in the Great Breach aforesaid containing Nine Acres three roods and twenty four perches Also one other piece or parcel of Land as the same was then Mark'd out lying and being in the Little Breach aforesaid containing Ten Acres two Roods and Twenty perches Also one other piece or parcel of Land as the same was then Mark'd out lying and being in Lopershill aforesaid containing Two acres and three roods AND unto the said William Dyer and his Heirs one piece or parcell of Land as the same was then Mark'd out lying and being in the Downfield aforesaid containing Six acres and thirty eight perches Also one piece or parcel of Land as the same was then Mark'd out lying and being in Westfield aforesaid containing Twenty four acres one rood and thirty perches Also one other piece or parcel of Meadow ground as the same was then Mark'd out lying and being in Eastcott Mead aforesaid containing Thirteen Acres three roods and thirty one perches AND unto the said Katharine Heath and her Heirs one piece or parcel of Land as the same was then Mark'd out lying and being in the Westfield aforesaid containing (besides allowance for the said Ruddles way) One Acre three roods and thirty two perches AND unto the said Thomas Wild and his Heirs One piece or parcel of Land as the same was then Mark'd out lying and being in the West field aforesaid containing Five Acres one rood and six perches AND the Complainant Sheweth that it was further appointed directed and allotted by the said William Sadler Giles Allsworth Alexander Cleeve Richard Morse and Richard Butler and assented and agreed unto by and between the said Complainant and the said persons aforenamed as followeth (viz) That the said William York should well and sufficiently mound from the South end of the said Mead called Eastcott Mead and so to Extend Northward to the said William Dyer's ground there and no further and that the said William York should have no way through William Dyer's said Ground THAT the Complainant should well and sufficiently ditch and mound his Plott or ground in the said Mead from Benbrook aforesaid unto a place there called the Mill Brook THAT the said Roger Ewen should well and sufficiently ditch and mound the North side of his Plott or ground in Eastcott Mead aforesaid THAT the said William Harris should well and sufficiently ditch and mound the North side of his Plott or Ground in Eas andtcott Mead aforesaid THAT the said William Fairthorne should well and sufficiently ditch and mound the South side and West end of his Plott or ground in Eastcott Mead aforesaid THAT the said John Randolph should well and sufficiently ditch and mound the South side and West end of his Plott of ground in Eastcott Mead aforesaid THAT the said William Dyer should well and sufficiently ditch and mound half the North Side of his Plott or ground in Eastcott Mead aforesaid and the South side from the Highway to the Millbrook and the West end of his said ground THAT the said William Stitchall should well and sufficiently ditch and mound one half of the North side of the said William Dyer's Plott or ground in Eastcott Mead aforesaid and the end next Benbrook aforesaid being the East part THAT the said Elizabeth Fluce should well and sufficiently ditch and mound the South side and the End next Benbrook of her Pott or ground in Eastcott Mead aforesaid THAT the said Edward Thrush should well and sufficiently ditch and mound the East end of his Plott or ground in the Westfield and the South side thereof against William Dyer's ground there THAT the Complainant should well and sufficiently ditch and mound the North side of his Plott or Ground in the North field aforesaid and the West end of Edward Thrush's Plott or ground in the West field and from the North East Corner of the said Thrush's Ground to the Corner of a ground or Close called the New Close THAT the said John Foster should well and sufficiently ditch and mound the East side and South end of his Plott or ground in the West field aforesaid THAT the said William Harris should well and sufficiently ditch and mound his Plott or ground in the North field aforesaid THAT the said William Avenell should well and sufficiently ditch and mound the South end next the Highway and the East side of his Plott or ground in the Westfield aforesaid THAT the said William Dyer should well and sufficiently ditch and mound the East side of his Plott or Ground in the West field and the North end from the said Edward Thrush's ground there THAT the said John Ruddle should well and sufficiently ditch and mound the East side and the North end of his Plott or ground in the West field aforesaid. THAT the said Roger Ewen should well and sufficiently ditch and mound that part of his Plott or ground in the West field next adjoining unto the said Katharine Heath's ground there and the North end of the said ground next a way called the Fleetway THAT the said William Fairthorne should well and sufficiently ditch and mound the East side and the North end next adjoining to the Highway of his Plott or ground in the West field aforesaid THAT the said William Harris should make a sufficient ditch and mound between the said Roger Ewen's ground in the West field and his own Plott or ground in the West and North field And also should make the mound next the Fleete way and the remainder of the mound about Thomas Wild's ground in the West field (Except Twenty Perches) and the said Thomas Wild is to make up the said twenty perches THAT the said John Randolph should well and sufficiently ditch and mound the West side to the Fleete way and the South side and East side of his Plott or ground in the Westfield aforesaid And also should well and sufficiently make repair and keep a sufficient gate in the said East side of his said Plott or ground And that the said John Randolph should well and sufficiently ditch and mound the North end of his said Plott or ground in Lopers Hill aforesaid and should also make half the mound between his said ground and the said William Fairthorne's ground there THAT the said William Fairthorne should well and sufficiently ditch and mound the North end of his Plott or ground in Lopers Hill aforesaid and should make half the mound between his said ground and the said John Randolph's ground there THAT the said John Walklet should make two third parts of the Fence and Mound which Severs and parts his Plott or ground in the Breach aforesaid from William Stitchall's ground there AND the said William Stitchall to make the other third part of the said Fence or Mound at the East end of the said ground THAT the said Thomas Vilett should well and sufficiently fence and mound the North side of his ground next John Holloway's said ground in the Breach aforesaid THAT the said John Holloway should well and sufficiently ditch and mound the North side of his Plott or ground in the Breach aforesaid THAT the said Thomas Vilett Should well and sufficiently ditch and mound round about his Plott or ground in Eastcott Marsh aforesaid (Excepting only the South and North sides of the said ground) THAT the said John Vilett should well and sufficiently ditch and mound the North side of his Plott or ground in Eastcott Marsh aforesaid THAT the said William Martin should well and sufficiently ditch and mound the North side of his Plott or ground in Eastcott Marsh aforesaid THAT the Plott or ground allotted unto the Complainant and the rest of the persons aforesaid in trust for the use of the said parish of Swindon as aforesaid in Eastcott Marsh aforesaid should be fenced and mounded on the North side by the Complainant and the said other persons Trustees aforesaid and their Heirs THAT the said Roger Ewen should well and sufficiently ditch and mound the North side of his Plott or ground in Eastcott Marsh aforesaid THAT the said William Fairthorne should make sufficient fence and mound from the Stake at his Barn in Eastcott aforesaid along the old ditch to the corner of his Close there and from thence to the east end of his piece and so round his plot or ground AND it was also appointed and agreed that the said John Law his Heirs and Assigns should have liberty at all times to fetch and carry water from a certain place called Colt close end and to water his and their cattle there and room for the Turning of his Cart or Carriage into the said William Fairthorne's ground in the East field aforesaid at the Entrance of the lane THAT the said Roger Ewen should well and sufficiently ditch and mound the South side of his Plott or ground in the East field aforesaid THAT the said John Walklet should well and sufficiently ditch and mound the South side and East end of his Plott or ground in the East field aforesaid THAT the said John Holloway should well and sufficiently ditch and mound round about his Plott or ground in the East field aforesaid THAT the said John Law should well and sufficiently ditch and mound the East end only of his Plott or ground in the East field aforesaid THAT the said Miles Farmer should well and sufficiently ditch and mound the south side of his Plott or ground in the East field aforesaid THAT the said William Barnard should well and sufficiently ditch and mound the South side of his Plott or ground in East field aforesaid THAT the said Thomas Quarles should well and sufficiently ditch and mound the South side of his Plott or ground in the East field aforesaid THAT the said John Fluce should well and sufficiently ditch and mound the South side of his Plott or ground in the East field aforesaid THAT the said Thomas Edney should well and sufficiently ditch and mound the South side of his Plott or ground in the East field aforesaid THAT the said Robert Morse shall well and sufficiently ditch and mound the South side of his Plott or ground in Down field aforesaid THAT the said Moses Bayly should make a sufficient Fence and mound on the North end of his South piece or plott of ground in the Down field aforesaid and should also make the mound between his said ground and Robert Tuckey's ground in the said Down field THAT the said William Barnard should well and sufficiently ditch and mound the North end of the East side of his Plott or ground in the Downfield aforesaid THAT the said Miles Farmer should well and sufficiently ditch and mound his plott or ground in the said Down field on the East side next adjoining unto the said William Barnard's ground and on the West side next unto William Avenell's ground THAT the said William Avenell should well and sufficiently ditch and mound the West side (next unto William Harris's ground) of his plott or ground in the Down field aforesaid THAT the said Robert Tuckey should well and sufficiently ditch and mound the North end of his Plott or ground in the Downfield aforesaid THAT the said Thomas Vilett should well and sufficiently ditch and mound the East end (next Robert Tuckey's said ground) and the North end of his Plott or ground in the Down field aforesaid THAT the said John Foster should well and sufficiently ditch and mound the East side of his plott or ground in the said Down field next unto

Mr. Vilett's said ground THAT the Complainant should well and sufficiently ditch and mound his plott or ground in the said Down field on the North and West side of John Foster's said ground and that part next John Holloway's Ground there. THAT the said Thomas Edney should well and sufficiently ditch and mound the South side of his plott or ground in the said Down field next unto the Complainant's said ground there THAT the said John Holloway should make a sufficient fence or mound on the North side of his Plott or ground in the said Down field next unto Thomas Edney's said ground there and on the South of Roger Ewen's ground there THAT the said Roger Ewen should make a sufficient fence or mound on the West side of his plott or ground in the said Down field next unto John Holloway's said ground and Thomas Edney's said ground there THAT the said William Harris should make a sufficient fence and mound on the West side of his plott or ground in the said Down field next unto John Holloway's said ground there and on the North side next unto the said Roger Ewen's said ground there THAT the said John Randolph should well and sufficiently ditch and mound that part of his plott or ground in the said Down field next adjoining unto the Highway and the South end of the same ground THAT the said William Dyer should make a sufficient fence and mound on the West side and South end of his plott or ground in the said Down field and should also make half the mound between his said ground and William Fairthorne's ground there being the North part THAT the said William Fairthorne should make a sufficient fence and mound on that side of his plott or ground in the said Downfield next adjoining unto Robert Morse's said ground there and should also make half the mound between his said plott or ground and the said William Dyer's said ground there being the south part thereof And it was further appointed allotted and agreed unto That each several person who upon the inclosure of the premises was to leave his old mounds should fairly cutt the said mounds according to Husbandry and not break the ground or Turfe ALSO THAT the Complainant and every the persons aforenamed should on or before Saint Thomas' day then last past ridd his and their Cattle of all sorts forth and out of the fields commons grounds and lands aforesaid ALSO that the Complainant and every the persons afore named should have time until the first day of March then last past for the cutting and carrying off the hedgerows late belonging to each person respectively and should have time until the twenty fifth day of March aforesaid for the cutting down and felling of Trees late belonging to them respectively and should have time to ridd and carry away the said Trees and Loppings from off the premises till the first day of May then following ALSO that the Complainant and every the said persons their Heirs and Assigns for his and their Necessary occasions should at all times thenafter have a foot path from his and their respective houses directly to and through the fields and grounds lately inclosed and to be inclosed and particularly for the parties concerned from the Village of Eastcott through Thomas Wild's ground John Randolph's ground and so directly to the end of the ground called the Breach ALSO that the Complainant and the persons aforenamed should have time until the fifteenth day of December then last past to consider whether each man had his due proportion of Land as the same was then Mark'd out and that there should be allowed for the way called Rodborne way two perches and an half in Bredth ALSO that there should be allowed unto William Harris for a way at the end (or side) of the said town of Swindon one perch and an half in breadth and that the said William Harris should well and sufficiently keep and repair and maintain the lower gate near his house And that the upper gate by the village of

Eastcott at the said Carter's house should be well and sufficently repaired
maintained and amended by such persons that use the same way and were
occupiers of Lands in Eastcott aforesaid ALSO that the said Edward Thrush
should hold and enjoy the ground lying from a ground called Kingshill unto
Rodborn way aforesaid paying for the same unto the said Complainant his
Heirs and As-igns according to the rate and value of the land next adjoining
unto the said ground ALSO That the said Thomas Edney his Heirs and Assigns should have liberty to dig a Trench in the Westfield side to the said Roger
Ewens Bank there to lett forth the water from his ground in the Down field and
also to scour the said trench at all times when there should be occasion and
when the said Thomas Edney should cutt or Lopp his hedge in the said West
field he should have liberty to through part of his Loppings on the Westfield
side and the same from thence to take and carry away at fitt and seasonable
times Also that each person aforenamed who had dung'd or manured his
land lying dispersedly in the Fields and Commonable places aforesaid with
the Sheepfold since the twenty-fifth day of March 1654 and had since that
time received no profit thereby either by Sowing the same with grain or
feeding or cutting the same That such person should have and receive
6s 8d an acre in respect thereof of such to whom the said land so dunged
and manured was allotted and appointed by the said Inclosure Also That
no person aforenamed when they drive or lead their cattle through any of the
ways sett out through any of the grounds aforesaid should suffer their said
Cattle to feed there unless the said ways were mounded and fenced out and
not lying open to the said grounds Also that every person in whose
respective grounds so sett forth and allotted as aforesaid there should be
any Springs or Watercourses arising or running through their said grounds
That such person should keep the passage for such water free and clear and
neither detain or divert the said water from his neighbours use or grounds
Also that there should not be allowed for any of the ways aforesaid above
one perch in Breadth (except for the way called Rodborn way the Fleete
way and the way on the East side of Eastcott Marsh aforesaid each of
which should be Forty foot in Breadth and the way from the great Elm unto
Eastcott aforesaid which should be two perches in Breadth and the way
from the gate near Oliver Carter's house in Eastcott aforesaid to the Fleece-
way which should be one perch and an half in Breadth AND THAT the
said Thomas Vilett should make a Sufficient mound or fence About his plott
or ground in the great Breach aforesaid next unto the said John Holloway's
ground there AND THAT the said John Holloway should well and sufficiently fence and mound his said plott or ground in Rushmore ALSO THAT
the said Charles York his Heirs and assigns should hold and enjoy all the
right of Feeding which the complainant and the said other persons before
named usually had and enjoyed in a certain ground called the Newclose next
adjoining unto a pasture ground called Courtnapp He the said Charles paying
in respect thereof unto the complainant and the said other persons the sum of
£26 13s 4d of lawful money AND THAT the said Charles York his Heirs
and assigns should occupy and Enjoy the said ground as the Complainant
and the persons aforenamed had formerly done AND THAT the said
Robert Morse should pay to and amongst the Complainant and the rest of
the persons before named in Liew of the Tythe payable for his said plott or
ground in the Down field and the afterfeeding there the sum of £6 of lawful
money ALSO THAT the said Edmund Goddard his Heirs and Assigns
should hold and enjoy his Close called Atkin-Mill-Close lying within the
said Manour freed and acquitted off and from all tythes issuing out of the
said Close and thentofore payable to the Rector of the Parsonage of Swindon

And that the same Edmund Goddard his Heirs and assigns should pay to and amongst the Complainant and the rest of the persons afore-named the sum of £2 10s of lawful money in Liew and Satisfaction for the tythes aforesaid ALSO THAT the said Moses Bayly his heirs and assigns should have and enjoy the after feeding also of his plott or ground in the Downfield freed and discharged off and from all manner of Tythes In Consideration whereof the said Moses Bayley should pay to and amongst the complainant and the rest of the said persons aforenamed the sum of £9 of lawful money And that the said Moses Bayly his Heirs and assigns should make keep and maintain a sufficient Cart gate at a place called the Old Sheard by the Highway leading to a place called Brockwell which gate should be for the use and benefit of the above named Miles Holloway William Barnard and William Avenell their Heirs and assigns Also That all other gates and stiles whatsoever which were or should be erected or made within the said Inclosed premises should be made kept and maintained by such persons their heirs and assigns who by the agreement aforesaid were to make and maintain their respective mounds through which such gates and stiles were or should be sett up and erected (excepting only one gate in Eastcott Mead between the grounds of the said William Dyer and Richard Vilett there which said gate should be made and erected and from time to time for ever then after maintained and kept in repair by the said Richard Vilett and his assigns during the term and Interest of him the said Richard Vilett in the said Ground and afterwards by the said William Stitchall his Heirs and assigns) Also that all trees whatsoever then standing upon the lands late called the parish lands should remain there untill occasion were to make use and imploy the same for the use of the said parish And then the said Trustees and their workmen to have free liberty to fell and carry them away And in the mean time the then owners of the said lands should have the benefit of Shrowding and Lopping the said trees and convert the same lopps and grounds to his and their own proper use And it was agreed and assented unto that the Complainant and the several persons aforenamed their several and respective Heirs and assigns should from time to time for ever keep and maintain the said several ditches mounds gates and stiles so severally and respectively directed appointed and agreed to be made by them as aforesaid AND it was further agreed and consented unto between the Complainant and all and every the persons aforenamed That the Complainant and the said several persons their several Heirs and assigns Should by good conveyance and assurance in the Law upon reasonable request in that behalf made lawfully convey and assure to each one and each one to the other the several pieces and parcels of land so severally and respectively appointed and allotted to them as aforesaid according to their several and respective rights interests and estates which they then respectively had or should have at the time of such Conveyance and Assurance so to be made as aforesaid and according to the true Intent and Meaning of all the parties to the said Agreement for the said Inclosure herein sett forth as aforesaid AND AS the said William Sadler Alexander Cleeve Richard Morse Giles Allsworth Richard Morse and Richard Butler had sett out and appointed To Hold and Enjoy the said several pieces and parcels of lands during their respective Estates discharged of all manner of Commons and common of pasture whatsoever AND the said Complainant further sheweth that as well he the said Complainant as the said other persons before named had severally accepted and approved of the said respective pieces and plotts and parcels of Land so by them the said William Sadler Giles Allsworth Alexander Cleeve Richard Morse and

Richard Butler appointed and directed and particularly allotted to them as aforesaid AND had also severally by themselves or their respective Tenants by their several assents and approbations entered into had or Enjoyed or might have enjoyed at all times since the Fifteenth day of December then last past the said pieces plotts and parcels of Ground and the rents issues and profits thereof to their own proper use and benefit in Severalty and not in Common AND that as well the said Complainant and all or most of the persons before named in Further Testimony of their said several agreements and satisfaction in and to the said several pieces and plotts of land so appointed and allotted to them as aforesaid had severally begun to ditch and mound and had ditched mounded and taken in the greatest part of their said several pieces plotts and parcels of land so respectively appointed and allotted unto them as aforesaid BUT the said Defendants and persons before named or some of them finding that the Complainant had disbursed and laid out much money about the Surveying ditching and mounding in his said several pieces and plotts of land and taking some frivelouse and causeless displeasure against the said intended Inclosure had lately pretended and given out in speeches that they did never assent or agree to Inclose or take in severally the said lands grounds commonable places and premises and seemed to deny to accept of their several pieces and plotts of land so severally directed appointed and allotted to and for them as aforesaid and to make and Execute such legal assurances and Conveyances in the Law as Reasonably should be required from them for the perfecting Establishing and lawful Settling the said lands and Inclosure and each Man's particular Allottments according to the Agreement aforesaid so as aforesaid generally by all the said persons Subscribed or otherwise assented unto IN CONSIDERATION whereof and for as much as the said Inclosure and laying out in Severalty of the said grounds and premises so as aforesaid was made Just and Equal and proportionably to every Persons Estate and Interest in the premises and by and according to the said several agreements of all and Singular the persons aforesaid and would be proportionably of as much advantage to the said other persons the said defts as to the said Complainant and not prejudiciall to any one of them whatsoever AND to the end the said Inclosure and Severalty made as aforesaid might be ratified and confirmed by the Decree of this Honourable Court and that the said Complainant his Heirs and Assigns might hold and enjoy the said several pieces and plotts of ground so directed divided appointed and allotted to him as aforesaid in Severalty and uncommonable against the said persons before named the Defts their Heirs and Assigns for ever AND to the end all the said particular agreements and each Man's particular Allotment as aforesaid might be accepted and confirmed by the Decree of this Court The said Complainant pray'd the Aid and assistance of this Honourable Court and that Process of Subpener might be awarded against the said Defts to appear and answer to the said Bill which being granted and the said Defts there with all served They appeared accordingly And all the said Defts (that is to say) William York, Thomas Vilett John Vilett, John Walklett Roger Ewen John Holloway William Dyer John Law William Harris William Fairthorne Robert Morse Thomas Stitchall Eliz'th Fluce Edward Thrush William Stitchall John Randolph, William Martyn Myles Farmer Thomas Quarles William Barnard John Foster Thomas Wild Thomas Edney Moses Bayly Robert Tuckey John Fluce Richard Vilett Edmund Goddard William Gallimore William Avenell Charles York John Ruddle Richard Austen and Katharine Heath by their answer did sett forth that the Complainant being seized of the said Manor of Eastcott Westcott and

Netherscott in the said Bill mentioned and they the Defts being Inhabitants Occupiers of Lands Copyholders and Freeholders of the said Manor had several shares and proportions of Lands respectively within the said Manor according to their several and respective Estates therein and that the said Complainant and the said Defts and their respective Tenants Did jointly according to a certain rate or number of cattle for each Yard land and so proportionably Feed and depasture together in the said lands and grounds and commonable places in the Bill mentioned with their cattle at times fit and convenient and observing the many inconveniences and hinderances to themselves and their Tenants in the usage plowing and depasturing the said lands and premises as in the said Bill of Complaint was sett forth That thereupon the said Complainant and the said Defts did as in the said Bill of Complaint was alleged) Mutually agreed to take in and Inclose the said Lands Commons and Commonable places lying within the said Manor of Eastcott Westcott and Netherscott in the said Bill mentioned in Severalty and that they did cause a Writings to be drawn and made according to that purpose whereunto the Complainant and the said Defts William York Thomas Vilett John Vilett John Walklett Roger Ewen John Holloway William Dyer John Law William Harris William Fairthorne Robert Morse Thomas Stitchall Eliz'th Fluce Edward Thrush William Stitchall, John Randolph William Martyn Miles Farmer Thomas Quarles William Barnard John Foster Thomas Wild Thomas Edney Moses Bayly Robert Tuckey and John Fluce Did Subscribe their several names or marks and that the other Defts namely Richard Vilett Edmund Goddard William Gallimore William Avenell Charles York John Ruddle Richard Austin and Katherine Heath who were not present and had not subscribed the same had since promised their Assents and did thereby give their assents thereunto which said writing the said Defts confessed was to the same effect and purpose as in the said Bill was sett forth and the said Defts Did all of them confess it to be true that John Whiteing in the Bill named a Common Surveyor and one of honest reputation and very well learned and knowing in the Art of Surveying (as they believe) was chosen and desired by consent of the Complainant and Defts to measure and allott every particular man's land so dispersedly lying and being in the said ground and fields and commonable places within the said Manor and to discover and give the certain size and number of Acres of every particular Man's lands in Writing unto the said William Sadler Giles Allsworth Alexander Cleeve Thomas White Richard Morse Richard Butler and William Morse in the Bill named being Indifferent persons by the said writing of agreement nominated and agreed upon for them or any four of them to direct and appoint the said Inclosure of the said lands and premises and the Divisions Exchanges and grants touching or concerning the same which the said John Whiteing had accordingly faithfully done and performed (as they believed) and the said Defts did all of them confess that the said William Sadler Giles Allsworth Alexander Cleeve Richard Morse and Richard Butler five of the persons aforesaid agreed upon for that purpose IN PURSUANCE of the trust in them reposed by the said Complainant and them the said Defts according to the said Agreement had according to the quantity proportion and Number of Acres of the Complainant and them the said Defts and of every owner of land within the said Manor or Tything Justly and equally appointed and directed the Inclosure of the said lands grounds and premises within the said Manor in the said Bill mentioned in such sort and manner and with such proportion and directions as the Complainant had in and by his said Bill of Complaint sett forth and declared AND the said

Defts did confess that the said Complainant and the said Defts by themselves
or their tenants by their assents and approbations had severally accepted of
the said pieces plotts and parcels of land so by them the said William
Sadler Giles Allsworth Alexander Cleeve Richard Morse and Richard Butler
appointed divided and directed particularly as aforesaid and had also
Severally by themselves or their Tenants by their assents and approbations
entered into and enjoyed the said pieces and plotts of ground ever since the
same were so divided and appointed and had received the rents issues and
profits thereof to their own proper use and behoof as pieces and plotts of
ground in severally and uncommonable AND that the said Complainant
and the said Defts in Further Testimony of their several agreement and
satisfaction of and to the said several pieces and plotts of land so
appointed and directed to them as aforesaid had severally already
begun to ditch and mound and take in all or the greatest part of their
said several pieces and plotts of land so appointed and sett out to
them in manner as aforesaid AND that they the said Defts were and
would be ready to make and execute such Legal Assurance and Conveyance for the perfecting Establishing and lawful Settling of the said lands
and Inclosure according to every Man's particular division and allotment as
should be reasonably required and as this Court should appoint and direct
and did submit and were well content THAT the said several agreements
and Inclosure in the said Bill of Complaint sett forth be ratifyed and confirmed by the Decree of this Court To the intent that the Complainant and
the said Defts and all and every the respective owners of any of the said
lands and premises might quietly and without disturbance enjoy their several
and respective shares and proportions in the said lands and premises according to their several and respective Estates Interest and Allotments they
conceive that the said Inclosure and laying out in Severalty of the said lands
grounds and commonable places within the said Manor to be made Just and
equal and proportionable to every ones particular Estate and Interest there
AND that the same would be advantagious to the Complainant and the
Defts and all others who had any Estate in the said lands and premises and
not prejudicial to any one of them whatsoever as in and by the said Bill and
answer of them remaining upon Record in this Honourable Court It doth
and may more fully appear IT IS THEREFORE this present term of Saint
Hilary (that is to say) on Thursday 12th day of February in the Year of our
Lord 1656 by the Right Honourable the Lords Commissioners for the
Custody of the Great Seal of England and by the Authority of the High
and Honourable Court of Chancery by and with the full and free consent of
all and every the said parties Plt and Defts Ordered Adjudged and Decreed
that the Division and Inclosure aforesaid of the said Manor grounds and
premises and all the particular appointments and agreements aforesaid in
the said Bill Sett forth be ratified and confirmed by the Decree of this Court
and that all and every of the said parties Plt. and Defts their Heirs and
Assigns respectively shall hold and enjoy each of them against the other of
the said several pieces plotts and parcels of land in Severalty uncommonable
so directed as aforesaid and according to the Allottments proportions
Interests and Estates mentioned and confessed to be Sett forth and allotted
by the said Bill and answer And that all and every of the said parties Plt
and Defendants shall upon reasonable request make and Execute each to
other respectively such lawful and reasonable Conveyance or Conveyances
Assurance or Assurances in the Law for Establishing and Confirming of the
said Inclosure of the respective parcels and proportions of Land of any of
the parties therein concerned as by Counsel learned shall be devised advised

or required WE DO THEREFORE command and firmly enjoin you the said William York Thomas Vilett John Vilett Edmund Goddard Richard Vilett William Gallimore John Walklett Roger Ewen John Holloway William Dyer John Law William Harris William Fairthorne Robert Morse Thomas Stitchall Eliz'th Fluce Edward Thrush William Stitchall John Randolph William Martyn Miles Farmer Thomas Quarles William Bernard John Foster Thomas Wild Thomas Edney Moess Bayly Robert Tuckey Charles York John Fluce William Avenell John Ruddle Richard Austin and Katharine Heath and you the said other person and persons above mentioned and every of you That all and singular the Matters and Things in the said Judgment or Decree contained for so much as concerns you or any or either of you You do observe fulfil and perform according to the Tenor true Intent and meaning thereof and hereof Fail not at your peril Witness ourself at Westm't. the three and twentieth day of September in the Year of our Lord 1657 ·|·

LENTHALL :·: N: MARTINE.

Ex'd 10th Nov'r 1813. }
 J.G. & W.B.   }

⸺The⁎Geology⁎of⁎Swindon·⸺

⸺◦◆◦⸺

The following description of the Geology of Swindon was compiled principally from "Memoirs of the Geological Survey of Great Britain," for the use of the members of the Geological Association, visiting Swindon on May 9th, 1865 :—

The Quarries, which are in the immediate vicinity of the town, abound in Ammonites, Trigoniæ, and other shells; and some layers are entirely composed of the casts of several species. The Ammonites are of two kinds, viz. :—A. biplex and A. triplicatus, and vary in size from a few inches to upwards of three feet in diameter; the specimens are casts only, no vestiges of the shell remaining. A large collection may be made in a few hours, and from some of the quarrymen the less common forms may probably be obtained.

In the large Quarries at Swindon the section in ascending order consists of Portland Sand, Portland Limestone, Purbeck Limestone, and a small thin outlier of Lower Greensand. The rocks are quarried partly for the Limestone, but chiefly for blocks and slabs of Calcareous Sandstone which is included in the softer sands in irregular lenticular bands. At the north-east part of the quarry, next to the town, the section, about 30 feet thick, described in ascending order, is as follows :—

1.—Portland Sand.—Soft yellowish brown sand, with irregular bands and ragged-edged masses of hard Calcareous Sandstone, containing vertical Annelide tubes, and casts and burrows of Lithodomi, together with a few remains of Trigonia incurva and an elongated variety of the same, all with the shell preserved.

2.—Bluish Grey Sand with Carbonaceous specks, and overlaid by vegetable fragments.

3.—Portland Limestone.—Yellow and cream-coloured, about 8 feet thick, including two thin bands of clay, and full of nodular masses rich in casts of shells.

3.—Purbeck Limestone, about 4 feet, of a pale yellow colour, shivered in angular pieces, containing fragments of shells.

On the north side of the Quarry, somewhat farther west, there is the following section described in ascending order :—

1.—Portland Sand, with hard Calcareous bands.

2.—Portland Limestone, consisting of large concretionary or nodular masses of Limestone, in a soft Calcareous matrix, with numerous casts of Trigonia gibbosa and Terebra portlandica, associated with Cytherea and Venus.

3.—Hard cream-coloured Limestone, from 1 to 6 feet thick, with Trigoniæ, &c.

4.—Band of dark Sandy Clay.

5.—Purbeck Limestone, consisting of hard pale cream-coloured Limestone, with an angular fracture and soft bluish marly Limestone. These sometimes alternate, and sometimes in the same beds pass suddenly into each other. They contain Cyprides (?), and the univalves Paludina and Bithynia.

6.—Lower Greensand, ferruginous.

In this Quarry the individual beds are so inconstant, that a few yards apart the details vary to a considerable extent. Thus, at the north west angle of the Quarry, above the sand, the Portland Limestone is represented by the nodular band, No. 2 of the preceding section, and all the remainder of the section, between the Portland Sand and the Greensand, is Purbeck Stone, consisting of white and cream-coloured Limestones variously inter-calated and mingled with soft bluish Marly and Sandy Lime, the whole being interstratified with thin irregular bands of Clay. On the west side of the Quarry the same kind of beds prevail, the Portland Stone being merely represented by very fossiliferous concretions; all the wedge-shaped hard and soft Limestones, Marly Bands, and thin Clay above, being undoubted Purbeck Beds, yielding, when well searched, casts of Paludinæ. At the south-west end of the Quarry the Greensand is absent.

. A section of the Strata from Swindon to the nearest point of the Chalk Hills would pass over in succession—1. Portland Oolite; 2, Lower Green-sand; 3, Galt; 4, Upper Greensand; 5, Chalk Marl; and 6, Chalk.

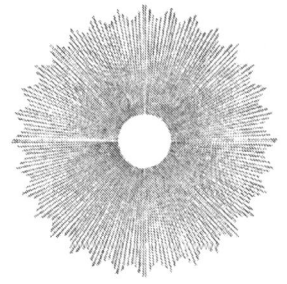

◉The✳Swindon✳Quarries◉

The diagrams (on opposite page), with the following explanatory notes, will still further serve to illustrate the Geology of the Swindon Quarries as well as the neighbourhood lying between Swindon and Liddington Castle :—

NOTES TO DIAGRAM No. 1.

a KIMMERIDGE CLAY.	*f* GAULT.
b PORTLAND SAND.	*g* UPPER GREENSAND.
c PORTLAND OOLITE.	*h* SOFT CHALK.
d PURBECK LIMESTONE.	*i* HARD CHALK.
e LOWER GREENSAND.	*k* OUTLIER OF PLASTIC CLAY.

NOTES TO DIAGRAM No. 2.

(a) "Portland Sand."—Soft yellowish brown sand with irregular bands and ragged-edged masses of hard calcareous sandstone containing vertical annelide tubes, and casts and burrows of "Lithodomi," together with a few remains of "Trigonia incurva" and an elongated variety of the same, all with the shell preserved.

(b) Bluish grey sand, with carbonaceous specks, and overlaid by vegetable fragments.

(c) "Portland Limestone."—Yellow and cream coloured, about 8 feet thick, including two thin bands of clay (marked with black lines below X) and full of nodular masses rich in casts of shells.

(d) "Purbeck Limestone," about 4 feet, of a pale yellow colour, shivered in angular pieces, containing fragments of shells.

NOTES TO DIAGRAM No. 3.

1. "Portland Sand," with hard calcareous bands.

2. "Portland Limestone," consisting of large concretionary or nodular masses of limestone, in a soft calcareous matrix, with numerous casts of "Trigonia gibbosa" and "Terebra Portlandica," associated with "Cytherea" and "Venus."

3. Hard cream coloured limestone from 1 to 6 feet thick, with "Trigonias," &c.

4. Band of sandy clay.

5. "Purbeck Limestone," consisting of hard pale cream coloured limestone, with an angular fracture and soft bluish marly limestone. These sometimes alternate, and sometimes in the same beds pass suddenly into each other. They contain "Cyprides," and the univalves "Paludina" and "Bithynia."

6. "Lower Greensand," ferruginous.

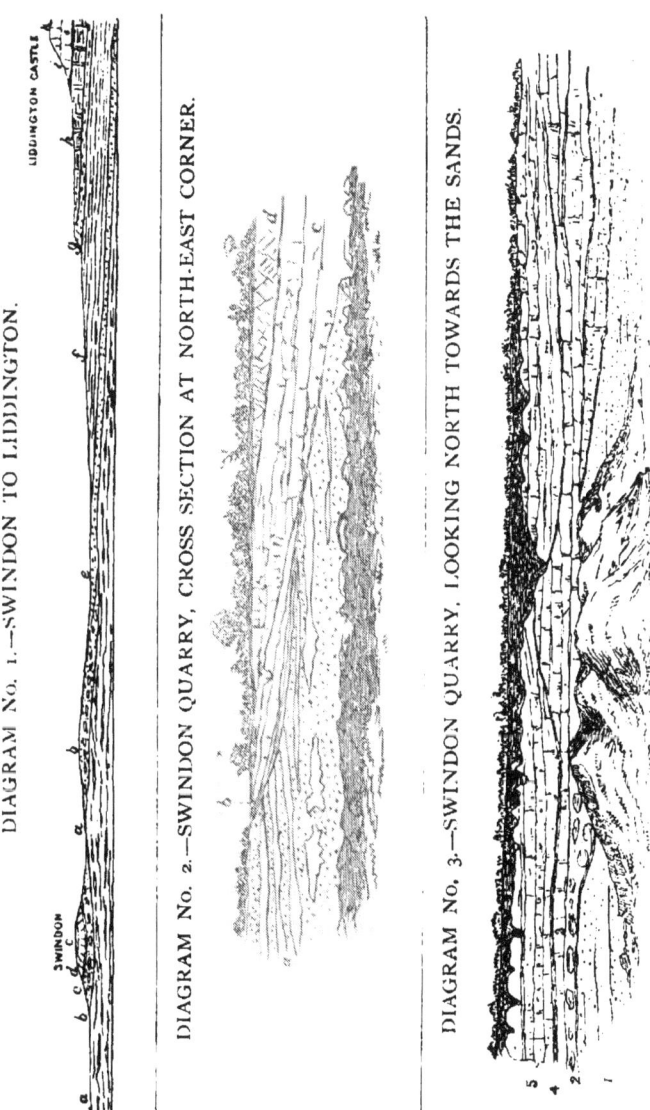

DIAGRAM No. 1.—SWINDON TO LIDDINGTON.

DIAGRAM No. 2.—SWINDON QUARRY, CROSS SECTION AT NORTH-EAST CORNER.

DIAGRAM No. 3.—SWINDON QUARRY, LOOKING NORTH TOWARDS THE SANDS.

www.ingramcontent.com/pod-product-compliance
Ingram Content Group UK Ltd.
Pitfield, Milton Keynes, MK11 3LW, UK
UKHW021159181125
9004UKWH00071B/87